The

DC CAPITAL KIDS

Family Guide
to Washington, D.C.

Featuring more than 50
Fun and Educational Scavenger Hunts

Chris Sylvester

Sarah Bixler

ISBN-10: 0983928207

EAN-13: 9780983928201

Acknowledgements

I would like to gratefully acknowledge the assistance I received in writing this guidebook. First, I want to thank Elizabeth Kelley for a wide variety of valuable help. I also want to thank the staff at the Smithsonian Institution, Destination DC, the National Park Service and the Library of Congress for their assistance in finding photographs, maps, and additional information used in the book. I would also like to thank the skilled museum guides and employees, docents, volunteers and National Park Service rangers for providing me and countless others with interesting information about the Washington, D.C., area's fascinating attractions.

*To Lizzie, Mom and Dad, and all my family and friends
who have inspired and supported my love for travel and history.*

Table of Contents

Introduction

Welcome to the capital city of the United States of America!

I have been a licensed tour guide in the Washington, D.C., area since 2006 and have enjoyed introducing many families and groups to the diverse wonders of the capital city of the United States. This book contains the unique insight I have gained from my experience guiding families and groups through this exciting area. My experience has enabled me to select and describe the most popular and interesting attractions in the area based on the reactions and feedback received from many visiting families and groups.

This book was primarily written for new visitors to Washington, D.C., but it will also work well for local families and groups looking to see known attractions in a new light and to discover new treasures.

Book Format

This book is a combination guidebook and interactive tool for families. The interactive heart of this book is the Scavenger Hunt section. The scavenger hunt is a tool adults and children can use together to learn interesting information about the main attractions in the Washington, D.C., area in an entertaining manner. My scavenger hunts include activities such as: finding and identifying features and items at the site, performing fun tasks and answering site-related questions. As a tour guide, a customized scavenger hunt has always been my favorite tool to get children (and adults!) more excited to learn about the sites we visit.

For those who don't want to utilize the tasks and questions in the Scavenger Hunt section, the book will still work well as a comprehensive family guide to the Washington, D.C., area.

Before the list of scavenger hunt questions, I have included a summary of practical information for each main attraction. This section gives adults a handy reference sheet with useful information on the site including: address and contact information, nearest Metrorail station, opening hours and ticketing details, as well as the closest bathrooms and refreshments available. I also provide an overview of the attraction highlights. I then list all the scavenger hunt activities along with a separate answer key containing information to help answer or complete the tasks.

In addition to the scavenger hunts and information concerning the main destinations in the area, I have included a wealth of information in the book about: additional attractions of interest, natural gardens and parks, amusement areas, theater and the performing arts, annual festivals, sports and recreational activities, and family oriented stores. I have also included planning tips, logistical information, maps, sample itineraries, recommendations on family friendly restaurants and accommodations in the area and suggested children's games.

At all the attractions and entries in the book I list the closest Metrorail station if it's within reasonable walking distance-within a maximum range of approximately 15 minutes.

Most of the information contained in this book comes from many visits to the attractions with families and groups as a licensed tour guide. I have also obtained useful facts, figures, and additional information from personal visits, extensive research using official websites and brochures, and from the skilled docents, guides, park rangers and volunteers who readily inform visitors at their respective locations. Please remember to utilize their expert knowledge and helpfulness when visiting these sites.

A Brief History of Washington, D.C.

Washington, D.C., is a unique city whose creation came about through the ratification of the U.S. Constitution in 1789. The selection of its location along the Potomac and Anacostia Rivers resulted from a compromise between northern states led by Alexander Hamilton and southern states led by Thomas Jefferson. Hamilton's northern group wanted the federal government to assume the states' Revolutionary War debts and Jefferson's southern group wanted the capital in a location friendly to their slave-holding agricultural interests. With the Compromise of 1790, the southern group got the capital location they wanted and the northern group, whose states had more burdensome debts from the war, received what they wanted: the assumption of the states' war debt by the federal government. George Washington chose the exact site of the city, close to his Mount Vernon, Virginia, home, and picked three commissioners to prepare for the arrival of the new federal government by 1800.

The original city was built within an independent district under control of the new federal government encompassing 100 square miles. This diamond shaped area was located between Maryland and Virginia incorporating Georgetown, MD, and parts of Arlington and Alexandria, VA. These towns were already prosperous centers of commerce and were included to provide a necessary economic structure and stability for the capital city.

The 100 square-mile district was originally named the "Territory of Columbia" after Christopher Columbus. The name also reflected the popular use of the term "Columbia" for America. People of the time referred to the capital city with federal buildings occupying this new district simply as Washington or the City of Washington. Thomas Jefferson called it the Federal Town and Washington himself simply called it the Federal City, a term that was also frequently used. The city and the territory were technically separate entities until Congress officially merged them in 1871 into the District of Columbia. Since that time, the term "Washington, D.C.," has been used to describe the area and to distinguish it from the State of Washington.

French-born architect Pierre L'Enfant, who served as an engineer in the Revolutionary War, designed the capital city's impressive layout. He envisioned broad boulevards, circles, and ceremonial spaces similar to Paris. Benjamin Banneker, a free African American who was a self-taught mathematical genius, worked with L'Enfant to survey and layout the city with careful precision. Andrew Ellicott revised the original plan of the city after L'Enfant was dismissed by Washington in 1792. Most of the city's infrastructure and the original federal government buildings were constructed by a labor force of slaves, indentured servants and free blacks.

Throughout its early history the capital was a remote and underdeveloped small city with a small federal workforce and unhappy foreign diplomats who would have preferred more cosmopolitan assignments. One interesting feature of the capital city during the first half of the 19th century was the large amount of boarding houses, primarily on Capitol Hill, where Congressmen, Supreme Court Justices and their staff members lived. Since Congress and the Supreme Court only met in the winter months, their members had no desire to rent or build houses of their own in the city. This community living produced some positive camaraderie and regional political unity as Congressmen tended to live with others from their region. However, this temporary boarding house living worked against national unity and reinforced the idea that the city was not a location where people wanted to permanently settle.

To make matters worse, much of the federal city was burned by the British on August 24, 1814, during the War of 1812. The British claimed they were retaliating for the American burning and looting of the capital city of York, Ontario, (now Toronto) in 1813. Fortunately a huge rainstorm and tornado hit Washington the day after the British attack, which extinguished the fires before they could do even more damage. After this tragic event, the federal city would be slowly reconstructed, but it remained a sleepy backwater until the start of the Civil War in 1861.

During the Civil War, the capital city became an armed, fortified camp in order to prevent the nearby Confederacy from attacking and occupying it. Numerous fortifications were built and thousands of Union soldiers encamped and drilled throughout the area. Many wounded soldiers also recuperated at hospitals in the city during the war. The famous poet Walt Whitman and American Red Cross founder, Clara Barton, tended to wounded soldiers at the many hospitals in the city during this difficult time.

President Abraham Lincoln insisted that the ongoing construction of the new Capitol Dome continue despite the war to send a clear message that the business of the country would continue. This inspiring symbol was finished near the end of the Civil War becoming the most impressive and distinctive sight in the capital city.

After the Civil War and into the first half of the 20th century, the city steadily grew and most of the now famous monuments and memorials were built. Washington's most important architect of the post Civil War period was German immigrant, Adolph Cluss, who constructed over 80 public and private buildings, including the Smithsonian Institution's grand Arts and Industries building. In the 1870s and 1880s the Washington City Canal was covered over and railroads became the most important transportation links in the area. Tracks from different railroad lines crisscrossed the city including through the area where the National Mall now lies.

The McMillan Commission, formed by the U.S. Senate, began fulfilling and enhancing L'Enfant's original city plan in 1902 with the creation of the tree-lined National Mall and other beautification efforts. The Smithsonian Institution constructed buildings on the National Mall and huge, neoclassical federal office buildings were steadily built throughout the city. This construction was especially intense during the Great Depression in the 1930s with the creation of the Works Progress Administration under President Franklin Roosevelt. The city grew rapidly during the two world wars as a vast supply of government workers and temporary and permanent structures were needed for administrative purposes.

In the 1960s Lady Bird Johnson, the first lady during President Lyndon Johnson's time in office, organized a capital beautification campaign with private and public funds that resulted in the planting of thousands of trees, plants and flowers throughout the city. Her efforts made the city more colorful and aesthetically pleasing and were heartily embraced by residents and visitors. Similar beautification projects have followed her lead through the present day, resulting in a city full of landscaped parks, trees, plants and blooming flowers.

Throughout its history, Washington, D.C., has always had a strong African American presence, which resulted in the development of distinct neighborhoods and many successful black-owned businesses. For example, the U Street Corridor in the Shaw neighborhood became known as the "Black Broadway" because of its many musical and theatrical venues in the early to mid-twentieth century. With the construction of suburban communities and the rise of the automobile after World War II, many white families left the city. In the Post World War II era, African Americans, already a large part of the capital city, developed an even more vibrant culture and influence throughout Washington, D.C.

The capital city was a rallying point for the Civil Rights movement, peaking with the March on Washington for Jobs and Freedom in 1963 featuring Dr. Martin Luther King, Jr.'s "I Have a Dream" Speech from the steps of the Lincoln Memorial. Tragically, the District was shaken by riots in 1968 after the assassination of Dr. King in Memphis. This terrible day in history was made worse by the subsequent burning and looting of parts of many U.S. cities including Washington, D.C. This unrest and destruction drove many whites and middle-class blacks permanently out of the city and into the growing suburbs.

Because Washington, D.C., is a federal district of the United States and not an independent state, there has always been debate on the voting rights of its residents and its representatives in Congress. Major changes occurred in the last half of the 20th century granting more autonomy to Washington, D.C., and its residents. In 1961, the District's residents finally won the right to vote in presidential elections with the passage of the 23rd Amendment. In 1971, the District elected a Delegate to the House of Representatives for the first time in almost a hundred years. This Delegate is a non-voting member allowed to serve in the House of Representatives, vote on committees and lobby on behalf of the District's residents. The Delegate, however, is not eligible to vote on matters coming to the House of Representatives floor. Since 1991, residents of the District have also been electing two Shadow Senators to lobby for their interests with the federal government. These Shadow Senators are not officially recognized by the U.S. Senate. Popular frustration with the District's powerlessness in Congress inspired the placement of the revolutionary slogan "Taxation without Representation" on Washington, D.C., license plates in 2000.

In 1973, the U.S. Congress passed legislation allowing the city to have home rule with a city council and mayor. The city has had mixed results since winning home rule. Successful developments include the construction and opening of the D.C. Metrorail system in 1976. On the negative side, corruption and mismanagement have plagued various city administrations. For example, the District was near insolvency in 1994 when the U.S. Congress was forced to create the District of Columbia Financial Board to oversee the city's finances.

Since 1998 the city has experienced a period of urban renewal and prosperity, regaining control of its finances in 2001. Although there are still economically depressed areas, many neighborhoods around the city have been revitalized with business investment and a steady stream of young residents. Examples of this rebirth include: the Penn Quarter/Gallery Place area near the Verizon Center, the H Street Corridor in NE and the Logan Circle area. The present city still retains its strong black culture and population, but the percentage of Hispanics, Caucasians, and Asians living in the District has increased over the last decade.

In the future, visitors from around the world will continue to come to Washington, D.C, to marvel at the city's impressive museums, monuments and memorials and be inspired by its powerful symbols of democracy.

Visitor Information Resources

There are many excellent sources of visitor information online and in print offering valuable information about the history of Washington, D.C., and its many attractions. For historical information and useful statistics about the District and the latest information on events and attractions in the city, go to the website of the city's convention and tourism organization, Destination DC, at http://washington.org.

The main local newspapers: the *Washington Post*, the *Washington Times*, and the weekly *City Paper* are also good sources for information on temporary exhibits and ongoing performances at museums, theaters and other venues. The *Washington Post's* "Weekend" section comes out every Friday and has a comprehensive list of weekend events. *Washington Parent* and *Washington Family Magazine* are monthly publications with useful articles for parents and calendars of family events. These magazines are available online at www.washingtonparent.com and www.washingtonfamily.com. For additional information about ongoing events pick up a free copy of the magazine "Now Washington D.C." found in many hotels and public locations. They have online information and apps available at www.nowguides.com.

Another excellent website for in-depth information on the culture and heritage of the District's various neighborhoods is www.culturaltourismdc.org. This site has downloadable brochures for walking tours of historic neighborhoods throughout the city and for African American Heritage Trails.

The National Park Service and the National Register of Historic Places have prepared a comprehensive online and downloadable guide to historic places and neighborhoods in Washington, D.C., at www.cr.nps.gov/nr/travel/wash. The National Park Service also has online information on the memorials, monuments and historic sites at www.nps.gov.

For more specific information about any of the sites and attractions in the book, please use the websites and contact numbers I have listed under each site's contact information.

Traveling to Washington, D.C.

Washington, D.C., is a major traveler destination and easily accessible by all forms of transportation. I have listed useful information below to assist you in formulating your travel plans.

Airports

Ronald Reagan Washington National Airport (DCA)
703-417-8000
www.metwashairports.com/reagan/reagan.htm

This airport is conveniently located in Arlington, VA, only a few miles from the center of Washington, D.C. This primarily domestic airport is the location that congressional members and federal workers most frequently use because of its proximity to the District. The airport has its own Metrorail stop on the Blue/Yellow Lines or is an inexpensive cab ride to or from the city. A shared van ride service is also available from Super Shuttle (800-Bluevan, www.supershuttle.com).

Washington Dulles International Airport (IAD)
703-572-2700
www.metwashairports.com/dulles/dulles.htm

Dulles is the largest airport in the area and serves domestic and international carriers. The airport is located about 25 miles from Washington, D.C., in Dulles, VA.

The Washington, D.C., Metrobus offers the express **5 A Line** which operates between L'Enfant Plaza Metrorail station and Dulles Airport with stops at Rosslyn Metro station, Tyson's Westpark Transit Station, and the Herndon, VA, Park and Ride. The trip takes about 45 minutes (allow extra time during rush hours) and the regular fare is $6 and $1.90 for seniors. Have exact change ready for the driver. Go to www.wmata.com/bus/timetables to view the timetable which varies on weekdays and weekends.

A taxicab ride to or from downtown Washington, D.C., will cost you at least $60. Super Shuttle (800-Bluevan, www.supershuttle.com) is a shuttle bus company offering shared van rides with a trip to or from downtown Washington, D.C.,-including multiple stops-costing about $22. The Washington Flyer provides coach transportation between Dulles Airport at Arrivals Level Door 4 from the main terminal and the West Falls Church Metrorail station for $10 one way and $18 roundtrip.

Baltimore Washington International Thurgood Marshall Airport (BWI)
410-859-7111
www.bwiairport.com

BWI Airport is located 33 miles north of Washington, D.C., heading toward Baltimore, MD. The airport is farther away than the other two Washington area airports, but has more economy airlines offering bargain fares. The Washington, D.C., Metrobus offers the express **B30** Line which provides service between the Greenbelt Metrorail Station and BWI Airport. The bus proceeds directly to two stops at the airport in about 30 minutes (allow extra time during rush hours) for a regular fare of $6 and $3 for seniors. Remember to have exact change ready for the driver. Go to www.wmata.com/bus/timetables to view the timetable which varies on weekdays and weekends.

The Super Shuttle (800-Bluevan, www.supershuttle.com) shared ride service operates at BWI with a trip to or from downtown Washington, DC,-including multiple stops-costing about $35.

Amtrak trains stop regularly every day at the BWI train station for a fare around $12 one way to and from Union Station in Washington, D.C. The **MARC** (Maryland Area Regional Commuter) train stops regularly on weekdays at the BWI train station with a normal fare of $6 one way to and from Union Station. BWI Airport provides a complimentary shuttle to and from the BWI train station marked Amtrak/MARC on the bus. Check www.amtrak.com and http://mta.maryland.gov/services/marc for fares and timetables. Remember to buy your train tickets from the ticket booth or automated ticket machines in the station to avoid extra fees on the trains.

Private Car Services

These private car service and limousine companies are available for trips to the airport and other transportation services.

United Limousine Service
http://uniteddclimo.com, 202-540-8043

ABC Limousine and Corporate Transportation
www.limowashington.com, 866-941-4900

Family First Transportation
571-235-6664

Parking Facilities at Airports

The three airports offer valet, short term, daily and long term parking facilities with complimentary shuttle buses to and from the terminal. There are also private parking facilities offering long term parking. These facilities generally offer slightly cheaper rates, but their distance from the airport may be farther.

Rental Cars

The major rental car companies have locations at or near the airports and provide complimentary shuttle buses to and from the terminals. Short-term rentals and car sharing are also available at Zipcar locations throughout the area-check www.zipcar.com for more information.

Rail

Union Station in Washington, D.C., is located near the U.S. Capitol Building and is a major railway destination for **Amtrak** routes operating up and down the east coast. From this major train station, you can travel to and from Washington, D.C., to anywhere in the country. One advantage of using Amtrak is that you will arrive in the middle of the District as opposed to arriving at an airport outside of the city. Go to www.amtrak.com for schedules, fares, and more information.

The **MARC** and **VRE** are regional/commuter rail systems operating in Maryland and Virginia, respectively. These lines run on weekdays and provide quick and inexpensive access to the District. For schedules, fares, and more information go to: http://mta.maryland.gov/marc-train and www.vre.org.

Bus

Washington, D.C., has a central bus station located behind the Union Station train station where the major lines **Greyhound/Peter Pan** and some charter bus companies operate. These lines offer bus transportation to destinations nationwide. The Greyhound Bus terminal address is:
1005 First St NE
Washington, D.C. 20002
202-289-5141

For routes, fares and more information go to www.greyhound.com, www.peterpanbus.com or call 1-800-231-2222 or 1-800-343-9999.

In addition to these major bus lines, there are also a host of budget bus companies offering discount travel between Washington, D.C., and major cities throughout the Northeast corridor. These buses leave from Union Station, Penn Quarter, Dupont Circle, Downtown and other locations throughout the city. Please check their websites as their arrival and departure locations change occasionally.

Popular budget bus companies are **Megabus, Boltbus, DC2NY, Washington Deluxe** and **Vamoose**. Check their websites for routes, timetables, pricing and online ticketing.

Planning Your Visit

Washington, D.C., with its impressive monuments, memorials, museums, federal sites and other attractions is a prime tourist destination attracting visitors from around the world. About 16 million visitors come to Washington, D.C., annually including more than one and a half million international visitors. Whenever you come to this exciting destination you will find a good number of fellow travelers. The amount of visitors, however, varies by season as explained in the next section.

When to Visit

One of the most frequent questions I receive as a guide when planning trips with clients is: **When is the best time to visit the Washington, D.C., area?** My answer is: it depends on what your main goals for coming to the area are. The traditional high tourist season is late March through August with the low season running from September to mid-March.

If you are coming to see as many museums and monuments as possible and want to navigate the city with the least amount of fellow visitors, I would recommend coming in the winter months of November-February. At this time of the year, your family or group will enjoy easy access to most of the area's attractions and will not have to endure the unpleasantness of crowds and long waits in lines. In addition, aside from during the holidays, travel and lodging costs will be less expensive. The disadvantages of visiting at this time are the chillier weather and reduced opening times with some attractions closed outright. Please double check the opening times for all of your must see attractions before deciding on visiting during the winter months.

If you prefer milder weather and don't mind moderate crowds, a good option would be visiting in mid-September, October or early to mid-March. The weather in the early fall and in March is normally temperate if a bit cooler at night and the crowds are much lighter than during the high season.

In the spring the weather becomes more pleasant, but you will be joined by large crowds of schoolchildren, families, and tour groups from around the world. The April school vacation weeks are particularly crowded. In the late spring and summer months the weather becomes hot and humid and all the attractions are at their most crowded-not a good combination.

In short, if you want to see the most attractions with the smallest crowds come in the winter. If you want more moderate weather and thinner crowds than the high season, come in the early fall or in the early spring after the National Cherry Blossom Festival (this normally takes place for 16 days at the end of March/beginning of April).

If you prefer warm to hot weather and are only interested in seeing a select few attractions and/or are not bothered by large crowds, then come in the late spring and summer. If you don't have as much interest in visiting museums or the White House and the U.S. Capitol, this last option may work fine for you. The advantages of visiting in the warmer weather include seeing blooming flowers and lush trees and the enjoyment of activities such as: cruises on the Potomac, watching a fireworks show on the 4th of July or a movie on the National Mall and admiring the views from rooftop terraces such as at the Kennedy Center. In addition, when the United States Congress is in recess in the summer, there are cheaper lodging options available.

Washington, D.C. Climate

The District has a temperate climate with pleasant springs and falls, hot and humid summers and mild winters that only average about 17 inches of snowfall. The climate chart below gives you an idea of what type of weather to expect during your visit. Please remember to check an extended forecast before you depart as temperatures can vary dramatically over a short time period.

Average Monthly Temperature and Precipitation for Washington, D.C.

	Average Low (Fahrenheit)	Average High (Fahrenheit)	Average Precipitation (Inches)
January	24	43	3.57
February	26	47	2.84
March	33	55	3.92
April	42	66	3.26
May	52	76	4.29
June	62	84	3.63
July	67	89	4.21
August	65	87	3.90
September	57	80	4.08
October	44	69	3.43
November	36	58	3.32
December	28	48	3.25

Climate Chart courtesy of Destination DC.

Trip Planning Tips

I recommend that you read/skim through this guide before your trip to get a better sense of the attractions you most want to visit. The first thing to keep in mind is that there is no possible way to see every site of interest in the area even if your group has planned an extended visit. Take some time before your trip to clearly identify the most important sites for your unique group, as family and group members will often have surprisingly different interests. After determining your must see/do list, formulate a rough plan that incorporates adequate time to enjoy them. If you have extra time after you have seen your must see sites, then you can move on to your secondary attractions.

In my experience, people usually dramatically underestimate the time needed to see and explore what they want at various locations, especially at museums. It is preferable to have more quality time at one location than to race through three attractions just to say you saw them. **Most importantly, your visit is meant to be enjoyable and not a test of endurance or speed.** Take the necessary time to experience an attraction to your satisfaction and make frequent rest and refreshment stops to keep your natural batteries charged.

Your group will be walking a lot indoors and outside during your visit, so be prepared with comfortable shoes, clothing, hats, sunscreen and bottled water. The heat and humidity of the District in the late spring and summer months make this preparation even more important. Layers of clothing are a good idea in the early spring and fall as the warm daily temperatures drop in the evening.

Timing your Visits to Attractions

The two most important things to remember about the timing of your visits to attractions are: plan ahead and arrive early. **If you are coming in the high season, plan ahead well in advance (60 to 120 days).** Make online reservations and/or contact your congressional representative's office to make reservations at the most popular attractions requiring **timed tickets** including: the **White House, U.S. Capitol, Bureau of Engraving and Printing, Washington Monument (the ascent to the top requires reservations), National Archives, and the U.S. Holocaust Memorial Museum.**

If possible, visit the memorials and monuments during the weekend or in the early evening and visit your target museums, federal sites and other attractions during the week when they are less crowded. Arrive at your main sites as early as possible-the Smithsonian museums normally open at 10 AM and the private museums and federal sites open earlier. One useful tip is to keep touring the museum locations through the main lunch time of 12 PM-1:30 PM, and then have your lunch afterwards in a less crowded museum restaurant.

If you weren't successful in getting online tickets to some of the attractions above, make plans to stand in line early for your preferred destination. The White House is the only site that does not offer possible same day tickets for early risers prepared to wait in line. The problem with this system is you will have little control over your ultimate entry time, which can cause problems with the rest of the day's plans.

One early morning destination popular for families with young children and early risers is the **National Zoo**, where the grounds (but not the buildings or concessions) open at 6 AM.

The memorials and monuments (aside from the ascent up the Washington Monument) are open around the clock with visitors coming and going so timing is not as much of an issue with them. I also highly recommend visiting the memorials and monuments at night when the crowds have thinned and the lighting of the monuments and buildings gives you a completely new perspective.

Sample Itineraries

I have prepared sample itineraries according to length of stay and the amount of intensity desired. These itineraries can all be carried out on foot and through use of the D.C. Metrorail system.

The average stay for families visiting the area is about three days so I have prepared a detailed itinerary for that time frame. The **Intensive 3-Day Itinerary** covers some of the most important attractions, including the memorials, monuments and the most popular Smithsonian Museums. This is an extremely full itinerary I use with tour groups prepared to stay on an aggressive and tight schedule. Below this I have included suggestions for more relaxed itineraries and itineraries for shorter and longer stays.

Each family or group must realistically assess the endurance and interest level of the participants when planning their itinerary. My main recommendation is to schedule fewer attractions in your itinerary, which will allow for regular breaks and more rewarding, less time-stressed visits at each site. In short, I recommend quality over quantity.

The attractions I include in my itineraries are the sites I recommend most highly for visiting families. However, all of the sites listed in this book have something interesting to offer, so substitute freely according to your group's specific interests.

In my experience, even older children can only handle two big Smithsonian museums in a full day, so try to mix in the memorials and other attractions as demonstrated below. **Use my scavenger hunts to guide you more effectively and efficiently as you will see more of the highlights of the big museums in less time.** Also, take plenty of rest breaks throughout the day to make your touring time more enjoyable and productive.

Read through the guidebook and get a feel for any additional attractions your family/group would want to experience and adjust your itinerary accordingly. If you have more time, trips to the attractions in nearby Old Town Alexandria, Mount Vernon, Arlington and Maryland are worthwhile. I have provided information on these locations with scavenger hunts at the main attractions.

Intensive Three-Day Itinerary

First Day

9:30 AM-11 AM	Visit Ford's Theatre & Museum and Petersen Boarding House (House Where President Lincoln Died)
11 AM	Walk to National Museum of Natural History
11:15 AM-1 PM	Visit National Museum of Natural History featuring: Mammals Hall, Oceans Hall, Insect Zoo, Butterfly Pavilion, Hall of Gems-Hope Diamond

1 PM-2 PM	Lunch at Atrium Café in National Museum of Natural History
2 PM	Walk to Washington Monument
2:15 PM-6 PM	Visit Washington D.C. Memorials/Monuments featuring: **National Mall:** Washington Monument, World War II Memorial, Reflecting Pool, Lincoln Memorial, Korean War Veterans Memorial, Vietnam Veterans Memorial **Tidal Basin:** Martin Luther King, Jr. Memorial, FDR Memorial and Jefferson Memorial **Make sure to take 1-2 rest breaks during this time. One alternative is to break this important area into two days-visiting the monuments/memorials on the National Mall one day and the Tidal Basin memorials on another day. Another alternative is to make a visit to some of the monuments and memorials in the evening.**

Second Day

10 AM-12 PM	Visit National Air and Space Museum featuring: Historic Aircraft and Spacecraft, Galleries such as "How Things Fly" and "Apollo to the Moon," Interactive Flight Simulators, and Einstein Planetarium Show "Journey to the Stars"
12 PM-1 PM	Lunch in Mitsitam Café of National Museum of American Indian (NMAI)
1 PM-3 PM	Visit National Museum of the American Indian (NMAI) featuring: Multimedia presentation "Who We Are" in Lelawi Theater, Exhibits on tribal customs, art and artifacts found in "Our Lives," "Our Peoples," and "Our Universes"
3 PM	Metrorail/walk to Newseum (Alternative museums include sites such as the National Geographic Museum and the International Spy Museum)
3:15 PM-5 PM	Visit Newseum or alternative private museum
5 PM	Metrorail to White House
5:15 PM-6:15 PM	Walk-by visit of White House and Lafayette Park

Third Day

9:30 AM-12 PM	Tour U.S. Capitol, Visit to House and/or Senate Galleries
12 PM-1 PM	Lunch at U.S. Capitol Visitor Center, Library of Congress or Union Station

1 PM	Metrorail to Arlington National Cemetery
1:15 PM-3 PM	Visit to Arlington National Cemetery featuring: Arlington House, JFK Eternal Flame, Tomb of Unknown Soldier (Changing of Guard Ceremony)
	Optional: Visit adjacent U.S. Marines Corps War Memorial (Iwo Jima) and Netherlands Carillon
3:15 PM	Metrorail to National Museum of American History
3:30 PM-5:15 PM	Visit to National Museum of American History featuring: Star Spangled Banner, National Treasures of Popular Culture (Kermit the Frog, Dorothy's Ruby Slippers), Gunboat *Philadelphia*, The American Presidency, Spark! Lab, Invention at Play, First Ladies, America on the Move
5:15 PM	Metrorail to Foggy Bottom and Shuttle Bus to Kennedy Center
6 PM-7 PM	Attend Daily Free Performance at Millennium Stage at the Kennedy Center

Relaxed Three-Day Itinerary

For a Relaxed Three-Day Itinerary I recommend the removal of one major site per day from the Intensive Itinerary above. This change will add two hours of time to your day to relax and spend more time at your other target destinations. For example, on the first day take your time at only one chosen destination-either Ford's Theatre or at the Museum of Natural History. In the afternoon, you also could eliminate one of the war memorials and/or save the Tidal Basin memorials for another day or future visit.

On the second day, visit either the Air and Space Museum or the Museum of the American Indian and then take more time at your chosen destination and the other sites during the day. One compromise would be to visit the Air and Space Museum and then have a relaxed lunch at the Mitsitam Café at the Museum of the American Indian, which will enable your family to get a feel for the marvelous architectural interior of this museum.

On the third day, spend more time visiting the U.S. Capitol area and choose to visit either Arlington National Cemetery or the Museum of Natural History instead of seeing both attractions.

Four or More-Days Itinerary

This is probably the best case scenario for seeing the major sites in the area with more quality time and less stress. In this case, you can see all of the sites in the Intensive Three-Day Itinerary and possibly include some additional main attractions such as the National Archives, the National Gallery of Art, the U.S. Holocaust Memorial Museum and the Bureau of Engraving and Printing.

Your family could also visit some of the additional attractions of interest listed in this book or experience some of the amusement or recreational activities. In addition, your family could take advantage of having more time to see Mount Vernon, Old Town Alexandria, Arlington, and other worthwhile attractions in nearby Virginia and Maryland.

Two-Day Itinerary

For an intensive tour follow the first day of the Intensive Three-Day Itinerary and include the Tidal Basin Memorials. For the second day, follow either the second or third day of the Intensive Three-Day Itinerary. For a Relaxed Two-Day Itinerary follow the first day of the Relaxed Three-Day Itinerary and either the second or third day of the Relaxed Three-Day Itinerary.

One Day or Less Itinerary

If you only have one day or less I recommend visiting the main memorials and monuments on the National Mall and one of the three most popular Smithsonian museums choosing from Air and Space, Natural History or American History. Alternatively, you could visit the U.S. Capitol or one of the main private museums in place of one of the Smithsonian museums. At the end of the day, walk by the White House and Lafayette Square.

Substitute/ Add in a Park, Amusement area or Recreational Activity

Depending on your family and their interest level in museums and sightseeing, consider substituting in one or more of the amusement/recreational activities during your visit. I would recommend doing this in the later afternoon when their interest level in sightseeing may have waned. Also, if you are spending more time in the area make sure to vary your routine this way.

Favorite Activities/Attractions by Age Group

The sites and attractions in this book generally have something to offer children of all ages. However, there are some sites and activities that are particularly popular with children of different age groups. Here is a list of some of the most popular attractions by age group:

Ages 5 and under:

-Touch Tank at National Aquarium
-"How Things Fly" Gallery at Air and Space Museum
-Insect Zoo and Discovery Room at Natural History Museum
-Carousel on the Mall
-"The Building Zone" hands-on exhibit at the National Building Museum
-Constitution Gardens
-Playgrounds
-Indoor play areas

Ages 6-9:

-National Zoo
- Bureau of Engraving and Printing
-"How Things Fly" Gallery at National Museum of Air and Space
-Insect Zoo and Discovery Room at Natural History Museum
-Spark!Lab, Lemelson Center, and "Invention at Play" Exhibit at National Museum of American History
-Storytelling Time and interactive kiosks at Museum of American Indian
- Concourse of National Gallery of Art with moving walkway
- Mount Vernon
- National Gallery of Art Sculpture Garden and Hirshhorn Museum Sculpture Garden
-The FDR Memorial and Lincoln Memorial

Tweens:

-The World War II Memorial, Washington Monument, Lincoln Memorial and FDR Memorial
- Smithsonian Museums: Air and Space, Natural History, American History, Postal Museum
- Changing of Guard Ceremony at Tomb of Unknowns, Arlington National Cemetery
- U.S. Capitol
-Ford's Theatre and Museum
-White House
- C & O Canal boat ride
-Old Post Office Tower

Teens:

-Private museums such as: the Newseum, International Spy Museum, Museum of Crime and Punishment, Madame Tussauds
-Simulator rides at Smithsonian Museums
-IMAX and Planetarium shows
- Smithsonian Museums: Air and Space, Natural History, American History
-U.S. Capitol
-White House
-Ford's Theatre and Museum
-U.S. Holocaust Memorial Museum
-Visit to shopping malls (e.g. Pentagon City, Tysons Corner, White Flint, and The Shops at Georgetown Park).

Organize a Scrapbook and Journal from your Visit for each Child

Bring folders with pockets and/or plastic zip lock bags that the kids can use to save their ticket stubs, brochures, postcards and other paper mementos and souvenirs from their visit. During your visit and upon returning home, each child can organize a scrapbook with these souvenirs, photos and other reminders of your visit.

Some children also enjoy keeping a daily journal of their visit where they record their thoughts on the day's activities. Buy a journal for each child before you go in preparation for the trip.

Making a personalized scrapbook and combining it with a journal will give each child an unforgettable and lasting souvenir from your visit to Washington, D.C.

Getting Around Washington, D.C.

T hese maps and the information in this section will help you get oriented before and during your visit to Washington, D.C. I recommend taking some time before you arrive to use these maps and the guide to get oriented to the areas where your hotel and planned destinations are located.

Map of Washington, D.C.

Courtesy of National Park Service.

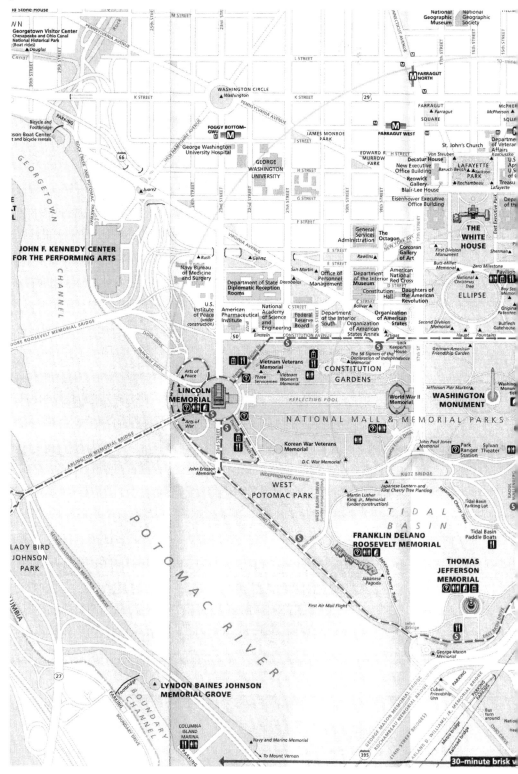

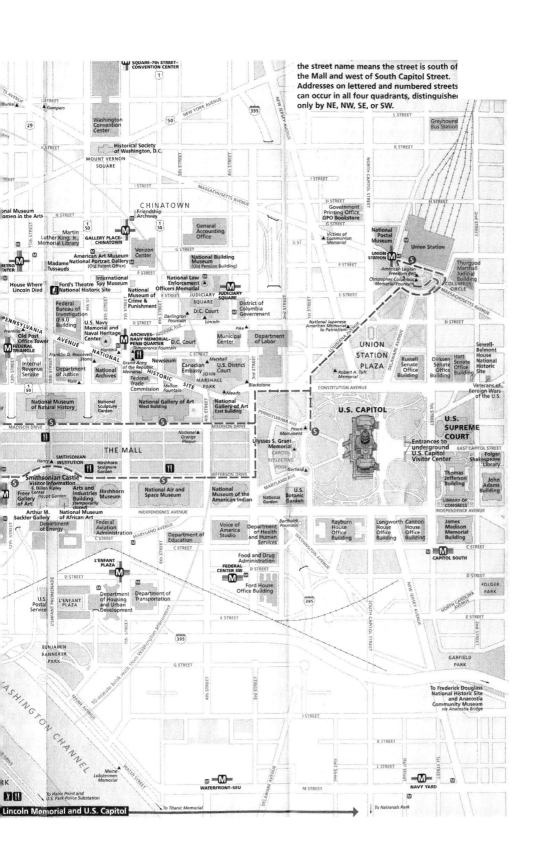

the street name means the street is south of
the Mall and west of South Capitol Street.
Addresses on lettered and numbered streets
can occur in all four quadrants, distinguished
only by NE, NW, SE, or SW.

Lincoln Memorial and U.S. Capitol

Map of Smithsonian Institution National Museums

Courtesy of Smithsonian Institution.

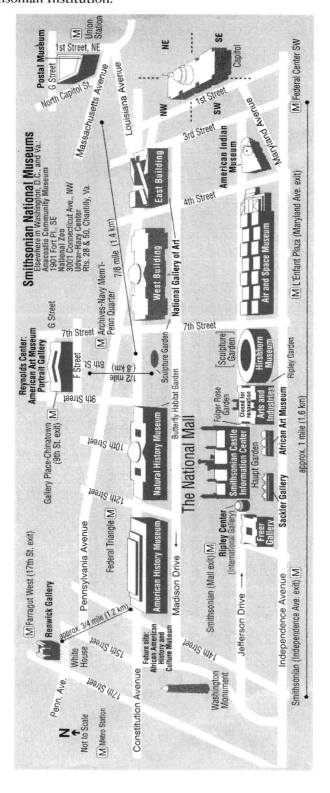

Getting Oriented in the District

Locals call this amazing city "the District," and you will be doing the same after a short time here. Washington, D.C., was originally created as a 100 square mile diamond with the top corner pointing north. This land area came from sections of Virginia and Maryland located around the Potomac and Anacostia Rivers. In 1849, Virginia took back part of this land, which extended into Arlington and Alexandria, so that the District now consists of about 68 square miles.

French-born architect/designer Pierre L'Enfant created the new capital city in the tradition of a European city with broad avenues, spaces and circles for memorials, monuments and fountains and an overriding symmetry using a grid system. The city is divided into four quadrants by direction: NW, NE, SW, and SE oriented around the U.S. Capitol Building in the center. NW or northwest is the largest quadrant, while SW or southwest is the smallest as much of it was reclaimed by Virginia. Generally streets running north-south are numbered streets, with one set ascending to the east of the Capitol Building and one parallel set ascending to the west. For example, there is a 5th Street, SE running parallel to 5th Street, SW. These streets change their designation to 5th Street, NE and 5th Street, NW when they pass the dividing line of the U.S. Capitol Building at East and West Capitol Streets.

Most of the District's main visitor attractions are located on or near the National Mall, on Capitol Hill and in the northwest or NW section of the city.

Streets running east-west generally have letter or place names that are alphabetical in relation to North Capitol Street and South Capitol Street, which run directly through the U.S. Capitol Building. These streets go from A to W, but there are no B, J, X, Y or Z Streets and I Street is often written as Eye Street. These streets then become two syllable names in alphabetical order followed by three syllable names the farther you get from the Capitol Building. These streets maintain their names but change their quadrant designation as they enter new quadrants. Street address numbers become higher the farther away you are from the U.S. Capitol Building.

For lettered streets, you can find the cross street by the first number in the address. For example, the National Building Museum is located at 401 F Street, NW, meaning it is found near the intersection of 4th and F Streets, NW. For numbered streets, you can count the blocks by the hundred in the address and use the first number as an indication of the lettered cross street. For example, the National Geographic Museum's address is 1145 17th Street, NW. This is in the 1100 block, so by counting up 11 letters alphabetically (remember to exclude B and J!) you will know that this address is near M and 17th Streets, NW.

There are also diagonal avenues running across the grid, named after every state in the Union. These avenues frequently connect some of the major circles in the District, such as Dupont Circle, Scott Circle and Logan Circle.

The most famous avenues are Pennsylvania Avenue connecting the U.S. Capitol with the White House, Massachusetts Avenue with many foreign embassies located on it, and Constitution and Independence Avenues, which lie on the north and south sides of the National Mall. Wisconsin Avenue runs from Georgetown up past the National Cathedral into Maryland. Connecticut Avenue starts in Downtown and runs past the National Zoo into Maryland. 16th Street, NW, starts in Downtown and runs into the ethnically diverse neighborhood of Columbia Heights and brings visitors to some of Rock Creek Park's main attractions.

One feature of the District you will immediately notice is that the buildings are not very tall. The U.S. Congress passed the Heights of Buildings Act in 1910 to keep the height of buildings limited to the width of the adjacent street plus 20 feet. This act has kept buildings at a maximum of 160 feet tall with a few exceptions, such as the Basilica of the National Shrine of the Immaculate Conception, which is 329 feet high. This act was passed to maintain the original design and character of the city and to allow clear views of the federal buildings, monuments and memorials.

Main Neighborhoods/Areas

Washington, D.C., is home to about 600,000 residents with more than five million people living in the greater metropolitan area. I have listed a brief description of the main neighborhoods/areas of interest to visitors below to help with orientation. Please note that my descriptions of boundaries are approximate as opinions differ on exact dividing lines for neighborhoods.

Capitol Hill
This neighborhood encompasses the area around the U.S. Capitol Building and Union Station and goes as far south as the Navy Yard. Main attractions include: the U.S. Capitol, Library of Congress, Supreme Court Building, National Postal Museum, Eastern Market and the Folger Shakespeare Library. This neighborhood also has many pleasant parks and is a lively residential area.

National Mall
This nearly two mile rectangular stretch of land begins at the west front of the U.S. Capitol Building and stretches to the Lincoln Memorial. This is the main area of interest to visitors as most of the Smithsonian Institution Museums, major monuments and memorials and the National Gallery of Art are located here.

Tidal Basin
Bordering the Southwest quadrant, the Tidal Basin is the man-made lake that was built to handle the overflow of water from the tidal Potomac River. Its banks are lined with cherry blossom trees, which make it the focal point of the annual Cherry Blossom Festival. Memorials in this area include: the Martin Luther King, Jr. Memorial, Franklin Delano Roosevelt Memorial, George Mason Memorial and the Thomas Jefferson Memorial.

Southwest Waterfront
Located in the smallest quadrant in D.C., the Southwest Waterfront area consists mainly of modern condominium and apartment buildings, townhomes and an active waterfront area along the Washington Channel. The waterfront features a marina, seafood restaurants, and the Maine Avenue Fish Market. Main attractions include: the boat cruise companies operating from the waterfront area, the Titanic Memorial, Arena Stage, and the nearby Nationals Park, home of the Washington Nationals baseball team. The area is expected to be a site of massive retail and commercial development in the next few years.

Anacostia
This Southeast neighborhood is a central point of black culture and community in the District. It lies east of the Anacostia River and south of Pennsylvania Avenue in the Southeast quadrant

of the city. The area's main attractions are: the Frederick Douglass National Historic Site (Cedar Hill) and the Smithsonian Institution's Anacostia Museum and Center for African American History and Culture.

Downtown

This largely commercial area is roughly defined as between 12th and 22nd streets NW, with Constitution Avenue to the south and M Street to the north. Many private office buildings are located in this area. Main attractions include: the White House and Lafayette Park, the Old Post Office Pavilion and Clock Tower, the National Aquarium, and the Corcoran Gallery.

Penn Quarter/Gallery Place

This revitalized Northwest neighborhood around the Verizon Center includes a small Chinatown area and many retail and eating venues. Main attractions include: the National Archives, National Portrait Gallery, Navy Memorial, National Building Museum, Ford's Theatre, International Spy Museum, the Newseum and the Museum of Crime and Punishment.

Dupont Circle

This Northwest neighborhood around the historic circle and fountain extends to 15th Street to the east, 22nd Street to the west, M Street to the south, and to Florida Avenue and the Adams Morgan neighborhood to the north. This trendy neighborhood has many attractive residential row houses, foreign embassies, private museums, art galleries and popular restaurants. Its main attractions include: the Woodrow Wilson House, the Phillips Collection, Anderson House, the Textile Museum, and the Christian Heurich House Museum.

Adams Morgan

This ethnically diverse Northwest neighborhood features a great range of international restaurants, cafes and shops. Its borders are Florida Avenue to the south, Connecticut Avenue and Rock Creek Park to the west, Calvert Street and Harvard Street to the north, with 16th Street to the east. This is a lively nightlife and culinary area of the District.

Shaw/ U Street Corridor

Shaw is a Northwest neighborhood with a celebrated history as a center of black cultural and intellectual life. Its rough borders are New Jersey Avenue to the east, 11th Street to the west, Massachusetts Avenue to the south and Florida Avenue to the north. The U Street Corridor is the business and entertainment center of the neighborhood and was known as the "Black Broadway" in the early to mid 20th century, where local resident Duke Ellington and other famous black artists performed. Howard University, a famous historically black college founded in 1867 is located in Shaw. The African American Civil War Memorial and Museum and the Lincoln Theatre are main attractions in this area.

Foggy Bottom

This Northwest neighborhood lies south of Dupont Circle, north of Constitution Avenue and to the east of Georgetown. Its unusual name came about as a result of the heavy mist that once rose off this swampy and industrialized area in the earlier days of the District. This area's attractions include: George Washington University, the U.S. State Department and the Kennedy Center.

Georgetown

This fashionable Northwest neighborhood was already a successful port town in Maryland when it was ceded to the new capital city. Its borders are the Potomac River to the south, Glover Park to the north, Rock Creek Park and Foggy Bottom to the east, and Georgetown University in the west. This hilly neighborhood is known for its trendy restaurants, chic retail venues and for its beautiful historic homes where much of the District's elite reside. It also features an attractive waterfront area with restaurants and hotels called Washington Harbour. Its main attractions include: the Old Stone House, Georgetown University, Dumbarton House, Tudor Place, Dumbarton Oaks, and the C & O Canal mule-drawn barge rides.

Upper Northwest

This large area in Northwest consists of the Cleveland Park, Woodley Park, Glover Park, Van Ness and Tenleytown neighborhoods and is primarily an upscale residential area with excellent dining and retail venues. The area also includes the wealthy Palisades neighborhood running along the Potomac River and C & O Canal, as well as the affluent Friendship Heights neighborhood, which is partially located in Maryland. Main attractions include: the Washington National Cathedral, the National Zoo, Kreeger Museum, Hillwood Estate Museum and Gardens, and American University.

Brookland

Located in the Northeast quadrant of D.C., this neighborhood's borders are Michigan Avenue to the north, Rhode Island Avenue to the south, South Dakota Avenue to the east and 9th Street to the west. The area is nicknamed "Little Rome" because of the many Catholic institutions concentrated in the area. Its main attractions are: Catholic University, the Basilica of the National Shrine of the Immaculate Conception, the Franciscan Monastery, and the Lincoln Cottage and Soldier's Home.

Public Transportation

Washington, D.C., Metrorail in action. Courtesy of Destination DC.

The Washington Metropolitan Area Transit Authority administers an efficient and inexpensive public transportation system that locals and visitors rely on to get around the Washington, D.C., area. The Metrorail system or "Metro" has 5 color coded train lines traveling throughout the area: Blue, Green, Orange, Red and Yellow. The train will identify itself with the color and final destination displayed on the front, side, and rear cars. Digital monitors on the platform will indicate when the next trains will arrive. I have listed the nearest Metrorail stations for each scavenger hunt attraction and at other sites and entries in the book for your reference. Use "**Metro's Trip Planner**" found on their website at www.wmata.com to easily plan any trip throughout the area.

The Metrorail fare depends on when and how far you travel. The highest fares are charged during "peak" rush hours on weekdays between opening-9:30 AM and 3 PM-7 PM, and on weekends from midnight to closing. Lower off-peak fares are charged at all other times. Fares are posted in all Metro stations. Up to two children 4 years old or younger ride free when accompanied by a paying passenger.

Visitors should also consider buying a **One Day Metrorail Pass** for $9, which is valid for one day of unlimited travel on weekdays after 9:30 AM and all day on Saturday, Sunday, and federal holidays. The pass expires at 4 AM on the day following first use.

Visitors staying more than 3 days should consider purchasing a 7-day **Rail Short Trip Pass** for $32.35. This pass is valid for seven consecutive days of Metrorail trips costing up to $3.25 during peak periods (weekdays 5 AM-9:30 AM and 3 PM-7 PM) or trips of any cost at all other times. This pass works perfectly for most visitors who are using the Metro for relatively short trips to see the main attractions. For visitors planning to travel on longer trips during peak times throughout the 7 days, then a 7-**Day Rail Fast Pass** is recommended. This pass costs $47 and is good for 7 days of consecutive unlimited travel. All farecards and passes can be bought online at www.wmata.com or at vending machines at Metrorail stations.

Avoid buying farecards and SmarTrip cards at Metrorail stations during peak riding times as vending machines will be crowded with impatient commuters. These vending machines can take a little time to master. Don't be afraid to ask a Metro employee, normally located at a station kiosk, for assistance.

The Metrorail operating hours are:

Monday-Thursday:	5 AM-12 Midnight
Friday:	5 AM-3 AM (Sat. morning)
Saturday:	7 AM-3 AM (Sun. morning)
Sunday:	7 AM-12 Midnight

The area's **Metrobus** service is also a reliable and inexpensive way to get around the city and complements the Metrorail system. The standard fare is $1.70 per ride and exact change (dollar bills are ok) is necessary. Bus stops are marked by red, white, and blue signs throughout the area. Check on routes and timetables online and use your phone to check on the next bus by calling the phone number on the bus stop sign.

Visitors who will be using the Metrorail and Metrobus extensively for longer stays should buy a **SmarTrip** permanent, rechargeable card that can hold up to $300 in fares and parking value. The card costs $5 and can be constantly recharged and used for Metrorail and bus fares as well as Metro station parking. With this card visitors can buy a 7-Day Regional Bus Pass for $15 or $7 for a senior/disabled passenger.

Riding Tips

The Washington, D.C., Metro system is well-maintained and clean with strict regulations to ensure it stays that way. Don't eat or drink while using the system or you may have to pay a substantial fine.

Make sure to keep a careful eye on children at all time. When using the escalators remember to stand on the right and pass on the left. Always stand back from the edge of the track platform behind the marked line for safety. When the train stops, stand to the side to let the people get out of the car first before entering. These rules are especially important to follow during the peak rush hour times when the ridership increases dramatically and the stations, platforms and trains are crowded.

For more information about the public transportation system visit: www.wmata.com.

Washington Area Metrorail System Map

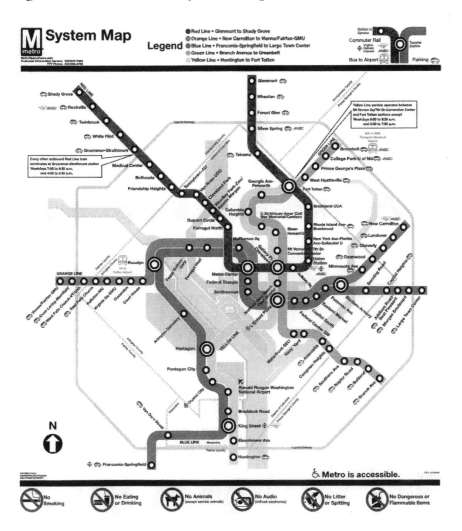

Map Courtesy of Washington Metropolitan Area Transit Authority

Additional Public Transportation Options

D.C. Circulator
The D.C. Circulator provides inexpensive, frequent bus service around the National Mall, between Union Station and Georgetown, and between the Convention Center and the National Mall.

Georgetown Metro Connection
The Georgetown Metro Connection stops at all Metrobus stops in Georgetown, and provides bus transportation between Georgetown and the following Metrorail stations: Foggy Bottom-GWU, Rosslyn and Dupont Circle stations. This service is especially useful as there is no Metrorail station in Georgetown.

MARC Train Service
MARC is a commuter train running along four routes to Union Station in Washington, D.C. The starting points are Baltimore, Frederick, and Perryville, MD, and Martinsburg, WV. The MARC train also has a stop at Baltimore Washington International Airport. MARC service operates weekdays only.

Virginia Railway Express (VRE)
VRE is a commuter train running from Fredericksburg, VA, and Broad Run Airport in Bristow, VA, to the L'Enfant Plaza and Union Station Metrorail Stations in Washington, D.C. It also has stops in Crystal City in Arlington and in Old Town Alexandria, VA, near the King Street Metrorail station. VRE service runs weekdays only.

DASH
The DASH bus system provides bus service within the City of Alexandria, and connects with Metrobus, Metrorail, and VRE.

ART-Arlington Transit
ART is a bus system serving Arlington County, Virginia. It provides access to the Crystal City Metrorail station and the VRE commuter train.

Fairfax Connector
The Fairfax Connector is the local bus system operating in Fairfax County, Virginia, which connects to Metrorail.

Ride On (Montgomery County)
The Ride On bus system provides bus transportation throughout Montgomery County in Maryland and connects to the Metrorail's Red Line.

The Bus (Prince George's County)
The Bus system provides bus transportation throughout Prince George's County in Maryland.

Taxicabs

Taxis in the district cost $3 for the first 1/6th of a mile and 25 cents for each additional 1/6th of a mile. There are also extra charges for additional passengers, handled luggage and sometimes a fuel surcharge. The maximum regular fare for travel within the city is $19. The same mileage rate applies to trips outside the district, but there is no maximum. Most cabs do not accept credit cards so be prepared to pay with cash. Tip anywhere between 10-20% depending upon service.

Taxis in Virginia and Maryland are slightly more expensive costing $2 a mile after the first mile with similar extra charges. Except for rides to and from the area airports, taxicabs from D.C. are forbidden from picking up new passengers in Virginia and Maryland and vice versa.

Driving in the D.C. Area

Driving your own car or a rental car in the D.C. area is not a recommended option for touring the sites. Parking in the district is difficult with limited meter parking, aggressive parking enforcement and relatively expensive parking garages. In addition, traffic is heavy throughout the day within and around the city and extremely heavy during rush hour times. The rush hour is heaviest between 7 AM-9:30 AM and 4 PM-6:30 PM and street parking is further restricted at these times.

Driving around the D.C. metro area is always a challenge, especially on the main I-495 beltway that surrounds the city. Some of the main routes are listed below. I-95 runs North and South from the beltway connecting Baltimore, MD, to Richmond, VA, around the outskirts of the District. The Baltimore-Washington Parkway connects these two major cities as well. The other main routes include I-66 running East-West from the District to Virginia, I-270 running North-South from the I-495 Beltway into Maryland and I-395 running North and South from Maryland through the District into Virginia. The George Washington Memorial Parkway runs from the I-495 beltway in Maryland along the Potomac River all the way to Mount Vernon in Virginia. The area is continually ranked as one of the most traffic-congested in the nation, so avoid driving at rush hour times whenever possible.

Bicycle

Washington, D.C., has a bicycle-sharing service called Capital Bikeshare. This service enables visitors to rent bikes at 110 stations throughout the District and Arlington, VA, at a cost of $5 per day or $15 for five days. Visitors pay by credit card at automatic kiosks and can return the bikes to any of the stations. Visitors will enjoy quiet residential streets but also should be prepared to deal with the challenge of bicycling in the downtown traffic of a major city. www. capitalbikeshare.com.

There are additional companies that rent bikes throughout the metro area including Bikestation near Union Station, Rollin' Cycles near Thomas Circle, Bike and Roll in Alexandria, VA and Big Wheel Bikes with locations in Georgetown, Bethesda, MD, and Arlington and Alexandria, VA.

The various parks I have mentioned in this guidebook have excellent biking trails for all abilities. Popular bike trails in the area include the **Mount Vernon Trail,** which follows the Potomac River starting from Roosevelt Island near Rosslyn, VA, through Alexandria, VA, to Mount Vernon, VA, and the **Capital Crescent Trail** connecting Georgetown to Bethesda and Silver Spring, MD.

General Information

Money and Costs in Washington, D.C.

As a prosperous and popular metropolitan area Washington, D.C., is an expensive place to live in and to visit. The main cost of your visit will be for lodging although there are some budget alternatives available as listed in the "Family Friendly Lodging" section. Restaurants also can be expensive although many offer lunch, happy hour and fixed menu specials to consider. Also, remember to take advantage of family discounts, online discounts and discounts from organizations for lodging and eating.

On the other hand, Washington, D.C., offers perhaps the finest amount of free attractions of any major tourist destination including: the Smithsonian Museums, the National Gallery of Art, all Federal Government sites, all National Park Historic Sites and all the memorials and monuments. There is also a huge variety of free concerts and other entertainment offered throughout the year.

Taxes in Washington, D.C.

The sales tax in the District is 5.75%, restaurant tax is 10% and hotel tax is 14.5%. In Maryland, the sales tax is 5% and the hotel tax varies by county between 5-8%. In Virginia, the sales tax is 5% and the hotel tax varies by county between 9-10%.

Tipping in Washington, D.C.

In restaurants, a minimum gratuity of 15% of the total bill is expected with 20% or more for good service. If you are in a large party (generally 6 or more) make sure to check your bill to see if a gratuity of 18-20% has already been added. Buffet servers should get between 10-15% for good service. Tip bartenders $1-$2 per drink or 15-20% of the total bill. Tip about $1-$2 per guest per day for maids and attendants in hotels. Tip taxi drivers anywhere between 10-15% depending upon service. Airport baggage handlers and valet staff at hotels expect about $1 per bag. Tip valet car service parkers $2-$5 when picking up the car. Hairdressers, barbers and spa workers expect around 20% for good service. Tip coat check staff about $1 per garment. Tip hotel concierges for good service about $5 per request. Tour guides appreciate a 10-20% tip.

Local Telephone Area Codes

The area code for Washington, D.C., is (202). The area codes for the Northern Virginia area are (703) and (571) and the area code for the Maryland suburbs is (301).

Electric Power

Electricity in Washington, D.C., and throughout North America is 110 volts alternating at 60 cycles per second. Devices that do not operate on this voltage will require a voltage converter.

Foreign Currency Exchange Locations

International travelers can exchange currency at convenient locations at area airports and at area banks, but the companies listed below normally have more favorable rates and smaller service fees.

<u>Currency Exchange International</u>
Fashion Centre at Pentagon City
First Floor Food Court Area
1100 South Hayes Street
Arlington, VA 22202
703-418-2344
www.washingtondccurrencyexchange.com
Open Monday-Saturday 10 AM-9:30 PM, Sunday 11 AM-6 PM.

<u>Peoples Foreign Exchange</u>
The Old Post Office Pavilion
1100 Pennsylvania Avenue, NW
Washington, D.C. 20004
202-589 0770
www.peoplesfx.com
Open Monday-Saturday 10:30 AM-5 PM.

Safety in Washington, D.C.

Washington, D.C., is a large city and has some of the negative aspects of being an urban environment. The areas most frequented by visitors including the National Mall, Downtown,

Georgetown, Foggy Bottom, Dupont Circle, Upper Northwest and the area immediately adjacent to the federal government buildings on Capitol Hill are generally safe at all times. However, it is always advisable to stay alert especially at night.

Visitors should be cautious about traveling in the more impoverished areas of the city such as Anacostia, much of Southeast, Northeast D.C. east of 15th Street and the Southeastern waterfront area close to the Navy Yard. Also, be careful when visiting Shaw and Adams Morgan east of Columbia Road and 16th Street, NW. When in doubt about visiting a location, ask your hotel's staff for advice.

General safety tips include: travel in groups when possible, stay on main streets, avoid parks at night, avoid using alleyways and shortcuts, avoid visiting dangerous areas especially at night, and take a cab to avoid long walks in questionable areas at all times of the day.

Always keep a close watch on your personal belongings and be aware of your surroundings. Thieves especially like to snatch iPods, iPhones and similar electronic devices in and around crowded Metrorail stations.

Remember to always keep a close eye on children in Metrorail stations and when crossing busy streets.

For general safety questions or concerns, petty crimes and minor incidents dial 311 or 202-737-4404. For police or medical emergencies dial 911. The Metro Transit Police number is 202-962-2121.

Health Care

As in most major cities in the United States, Washington, D.C., has a host of excellent, fully-equipped hospitals to care for any health emergency. Please remember to bring your health insurance cards to avoid any complications before or after treatment. Major Washington, D.C., area hospitals are listed below:

George Washington University Hospital
900 23rd Street, NW
Washington, D.C. 20037
202-715-4000
www.gwhospital.com
Metro: Foggy Bottom (Blue/Orange Lines)

Children's National Medical Center
111 Michigan Avenue, NW
Washington, D.C. 20010
202-476-5000
www.childrensnational.org

Georgetown University Hospital
3800 Reservoir Road, NW
Washington, D.C. 20007
202-444-2000
www.georgetownuniversityhospital.org

Sibley Memorial Hospital
5255 Loughboro Road, NW
Washington, D.C. 20016
202-537-4000
www.sibley.org

Washington Hospital Center
110 Irving Street, NW
Washington, D.C. 20010
202-877-7000
www.whcenter.org

Providence Hospital
1150 Varnum Street, NE
Washington, D.C. 20017
202-269-7000
www.provhosp.org
Metro: Brookland or Fort Totten (Red Line)-free shuttle bus

Howard University Hospital
2041 Georgia Avenue, NW
Washington, D.C. 20060
202-865-7677
www.huhealthcare.com
Metro: Shaw (Green/Yellow Lines)

Inova Alexandria Hospital
4320 Seminary Road
Alexandria, VA 22304
703-504-3000
www.inova.org

Virginia Hospital Center
1701 N. George Mason Drive
Arlington, VA 22205
703-558-5000
www.virginiahospitalcenter.com

Washington Adventist Hospital
7600 Carroll Avenue
Takoma Park, MD 20912
301-891-7600
www.washingtonadventisthospital.com

Suburban Hospital
8600 Old Georgetown Road
Bethesda, MD 20814
301-896-3100
www.suburbanhospital.org

Holy Cross Hospital
1500 Forest Glen Road
Silver Spring, MD 20910
301-754-7000
www.holycrosshealth.org

Tour Guide and Sightseeing Services

If your family/group would like to get an overview of the city's attractions before start-ing off on your own, there are some reputable vehicle tour companies you can use. Many of these services are available starting at Union Station. One popular vehicle tour company is **Old Town Trolley**, which features a narrated tour in trolley-like vehicles. Their website is www.trolleytours.com with the telephone number 888-910-8687. Another interesting over-view tour is offered by **D.C. Ducks**, which features a 90-minute tour through the city and on the Potomac River riding in an amphibious vehicle. Their website is www.dcducks.com with the telephone number 202-832-9800. Most of these vehicle tours have live narration by licensed guides and hop on and hop off possibilities at major sites. **Be forewarned, how-ever, that during the high season, these tour vehicles can get crowded and waiting for seats and for vehicles to arrive can occur. This is not a pleasant experience in the hot weather!** For best results, ride on these tour vehicles on weekdays as early as possible after the morning rush hour.

There are also various tour companies offering scooter, segway and bike tours. For **scooter rentals and tours** go to Scootaround's website at www.cityscootertours.com or call 888-441-7575. For **segway tours** there are a few options: Capital Segway Tours at www.capitalsegway.com, 202-682-1980, City Segway Tours at www.citysegwaytours.com , 202-626-0017, and Segs in the City at www.segsinthecity.com, 800-734-7393. For **bike tours** there are also a couple options: Bike and Roll at www.bikethesites.com, 202-842-2453, and Capital City Bike Tours at www.capitalbiketours.com, 202-626-0017.

If your family or group are interested in a private tour guide for a more personalized and in-depth look at the area's attractions, please contact my company **DC Capital Kids.** For more information go to our website at www.dc.capitalkids.com. You can contact us via email at info@dccapitalkids.com or by phone at 703-371-9927.

Tips for traveling with Small Children

As with visiting any major city, traveling with small children in Washington, D.C., is both a blessing and a challenge. When planning your itinerary contact your main attractions to make sure they allow strollers and other necessary equipment for young children. Equipment and bag restrictions at locations change occasionally, so I recommend a quick call or visit to a website. For example, most secure federal buildings such as the White House, Supreme Court, and the Bureau of Engraving and Printing (during tour) do not allow strollers or medium large backpacks, while the Smithsonian Institution Museums, National Archives and the National Gallery of Art do. Strollers are permitted in the U.S. Capitol Visitor Center and on the public tour, but not in the Senate and House galleries. Walking on the National Mall and visiting the memorial and monuments (except for the ascent up the Washington Monument) are well-suited for strollers. Private attractions have accessibility policies that vary as well.

The Metrorail and Metrobus systems allow strollers, but avoid using them during peak times as the crowds of commuters will make the experience unpleasant. Also, check their website at www.wmata.com to see where elevators and escalators are under repair to avoid having to carry strollers and other heavy equipment up a non-moving escalator. My main recommendations are to pack as lightly as possible with the most streamlined equipment and to check your destinations in advance for any restrictions.

For information about daycare and childcare options, go to the Washington Child Development Council's website at http://daycareindc.org or call 202-387-0002. They have a database of licensed childcare facilities in the District. They also can provide information to families with special needs children. *Washington Parent* and *Washington Family* magazines also have lists of various recommended childcare providers in the area at www.washingtonparent.com and www.washingtonfamily.com.

Resources for Physically Challenged Visitors

Washington, D.C.'s attractions, hotels, restaurants and public transportation systems are generally accessible to physically challenged visitors. The Smithsonian Institution provides information for special tours, interpreters and an accessibility guide at www.si.edu/opa/accessibility. The National Park Service, which oversees many of the monuments, memorials and historic sites in the area, has information for disabled visitors at www.nps.gov/pub_aff/access. The D.C. Metro system has reduced fares and information for the physically disabled and elderly available at www.wmata.com/accessibility.

One useful guide for disabled visitors for the District in general is available for purchase at www.disabilityguide.org. The Columbia Lighthouse for the Blind and Visually Impaired offers free helpful resources by calling 202-454-6400 or on their website at www.clb.org.

Family Friendly Lodging by Location

The Washington, D.C., area has well-known hotel chains and a wide variety of family friendly lodging options available. I have listed some of the most popular lodging choices for a variety of budgets. I created this list from my personal experience and from the recommendations of family, friends and clients.

I normally recommend staying within the city limits when possible so that you can get a better feel for everyday life in the District. There are, however, plenty of comfortable and reasonable lodging alternatives in the surrounding suburbs in Virginia and Maryland that are Metrorail accessible. With the exception of the National Harbor, MD, listings, the hotels in this section are all close to Metrorail stations.

The accommodation options I have listed range from budget to moderately and reasonably priced up to upscale and luxury. These descriptions are general terms roughly corresponding to the 1-5 star hotel rating system. These terms give you an idea of what to expect, as rates can fluctuate widely depending upon the season and availability. Sometimes special deals at luxury and upscale hotels can bring their rates down a couple categories, while the high season can occasionally push the price up on formerly budget and moderately priced hotels.

Most of the hotels listed will provide rollaway beds and cribs usually for an additional fee. When making a hotel reservation, inquire about the availability of this equipment, if all linens are provided and the cost.

Many hotels in Washington, D.C., offer significant weekend and off-season discounts, family discounts and online discounts, so inquire directly with the hotels you are considering. Remember to take advantage of discounts from AAA and AARP and other organizations where possible. Another option is to browse reliable online discount sites to compare rates and find lodging deals. In short, a little bit of research will go a long way in securing the ideal hotel room at the lowest price.

National Mall/ L'Enfant Plaza Area

Holiday Inn 6th street
550 C Street SW
Washington, D.C. 20024
202-479-4000
www.hicapitoldc.com
Metro: L'Enfant Plaza (Green/Yellow Lines and Blue/Orange Lines)

This reasonably priced and comfortable hotel is located near the National Air and Space Museum and the National Mall. The hotel offers guests a daily written calendar of family events in the D.C. area. This Holiday Inn also features a swimming pool and fitness center, free Wi-Fi, and a restaurant, gift shop and Starbucks in the lobby area.

Mandarin Oriental
1330 Maryland Avenue SW
Washington, D.C. 20024
202-554-8588
www.mandarinoriental.com/washington
Metro: Smithsonian (Blue/Orange Lines) and L'Enfant Plaza (Green/Yellow Lines and Blue/Orange Lines)

This luxury hotel is for the family or group looking to be pampered in a great location near the National Mall. The hotel gives kids a welcome package including: a stuffed animal, children's passport, treats, toys and a special children's menu. The hotel features a spa facility and fine dining restaurants, lounges, and a riverside terrace offering great views of the city.

L'Enfant Plaza Hotel
480 L'Enfant Plaza SW
Washington, D.C. 20024
202-484-1000
www.lenfantplazahotel.com
Metro: L'Enfant Plaza (Green/Yellow Lines and Blue/Orange Lines)

This reasonably priced hotel is in a great location near the National Mall and offers all the amenities for visitors including a rooftop pool. Kids get a gift bag at check-in and enjoy special children's menus. An underground shopping area and Metrorail station are in the same complex.

Downtown

J.W. Marriott
1331 Pennsylvania Avenue NW
Washington, D.C. 20004
202-393-2000
www.marriott.com/hotels/travel/wasjw-jw-marriott-washington-dc
Metro: Metro Center (Blue/Orange Lines and Red Line) and Federal Triangle (Blue/Orange Lines)

This luxury hotel is located near the White House and within easy reach of the National Mall and Smithsonian museums. Families enjoy the large indoor pool, whirlpool and fitness center.

Willard Intercontinental Hotel
1401 Pennsylvania Avenue NW
Washington, D.C. 20004
202-628-9100
http://washington.intercontinental.com
Metro: Metro Center (Blue/Orange Lines and Red Line) and Federal Triangle (Blue/Orange Lines)

This luxurious, legendary hotel is located around the corner from the White House and offers top of the line amenities in a charming setting. At this historic location Martin Luther King, Jr. wrote his famous "I Have a Dream" Speech, and Julia Ward Howe wrote the Union's Civil War anthem called "The Battle Hymn of the Republic."

Hilton Garden Inn Washington, D.C.
815 14th Street NW
Washington, D.C. 20005
202-783-7800
www.hiltongardeninn.com
Metro: Metro: McPherson Square (Blue/Orange Lines)

This moderately priced hotel is located near the White House and close to excellent restaurants and a Metrorail station. Guest rave about the comfortable, spacious rooms, free Wi-Fi, great staff, and complimentary fresh-baked cookies and fresh fruit.

The Hay Adams Hotel
800 16th Street NW
Washington, D.C. 20006
202-638-6600
www.hayadams.com
Metro: McPherson Square (Blue/Orange Lines)

This luxury hotel on picturesque Lafayette Square is about as close as a visitor can get to the White House without staying there. The hotel offers luxurious rooms and suites, some with views of the White House and Lafayette Square and first class amenities such as a fitness center, concierge service, fine dining and free Wi-Fi. The hotel gives young visitors a welcome gift package featuring a bathrobe, picture book, rubber duck or other toy and a children's room service menu.

Hamilton Crowne Plaza Hotel
14th and K Streets NW
Washington, D.C. 20005
800-914-8318
www.hamiltonhoteldc.com
Metro: McPherson Square (Blue/Orange Lines)

This upscale hotel is in a great location near the White House, the National Mall and the Penn Quarter and only one block from a Metrorail station. Regular guests like the attentive staff and extra comfortable beds and pillows. The hotel also features a fitness center and a restaurant and Starbucks located onsite.

Penn Quarter/Gallery Place

Hotel Monaco
700 F Street NW
Washington, D.C. 20004
202-628-7177
www.monaco-dc.com
Metro: Gallery Place-Chinatown (Green/Yellow Lines and Red Line)

This luxury Kimpton boutique hotel is housed in a neoclassical marble building built in 1839, which used to be the General Post Office Building. It's perfectly located near the Verizon Center and the National Portrait Gallery. Kids become Kimpton Kids when they check in receiving a packet at check-in that includes: a free gift, their own comment cards and a list of kid-friendly activities in the area. Kids can also use animal print bathrobes during their stay.

Red Roof Inn
500 H Street NW
Washington, D.C. 20001
202-289-5959
www.redroof.com
Metro: Gallery Place-Chinatown (Green/Yellow Lines and Red Line)

This moderately priced hotel is located in the heart of the Penn Quarter area near the Verizon Center. Visitors especially enjoy its central location with plenty of restaurants, shops, and entertainment in the area.

Courtyard by Marriott Washington Convention Center
900 F Street NW
Washington, D.C. 20004
800-393-3063
www.Marriott.com/Courtyard
Metro: Gallery Place-Chinatown (Green/Yellow Lines and Red Line)

This reasonably priced hotel is housed in a charming old bank building. It is located in the heart of the Penn Quarter/Gallery area near the Verizon Center, International Spy Museum, National Portrait Gallery and Ford's Theatre. The hotel offers a pool and fitness center, free Wi-Fi, concierge lounge and a central location with a variety of excellent restaurants, shops and entertainment in the area.

Morrison-Clark Historic Inn & Restaurant
1015 L Street NW
Washington D.C. 20001
202-898-1200
www.morrisonclark.com
Metro: Mount Vernon Square 7th Street- Convention Center (Green/Yellow Lines)

This comfortable inn, a combination of two restored 19th century Victorian townhomes, provides guests with old world ambiance and modern conveniences at reasonable rates. The rooms and suites are decorated with authentic period furniture. Guests also enjoy the highly regarded restaurant in the inn. This is a great location for any group or family attending events at the nearby Washington Convention Center. Inquire about their "kids stay free" options.

Dupont Circle/Logan Circle

Hilton Washington Embassy Row
2015 Massachusetts Avenue NW
Washington, D.C. 20008
202-265-1600
www.hilton.com
Metro: Dupont Circle (Red Line)

This reasonably priced hotel is ideally located near the Dupont Circle fountain within walking distance of many excellent restaurants and boutiques. The hotel also features a rooftop restaurant/ bar area and pool.

Embassy Circle Guest House
2224 R Street NW
Washington, D.C. 20008
202-265-1600
www.dcinns.com/embassy.html

This luxury bed and breakfast is located within an elegant former embassy building and is decorated with antiques and Persian carpets. It is located within easy walking distance of the vibrant Dupont Circle neighborhood and Metrorail station.

Hotel Helix
1430 Rhode Island Avenue NW
Washington, D.C. 20005
202-462-9001
www.hotelhelix.com

This Kimpton luxury boutique hotel is located in the trendy Logan Circle neighborhood and stresses both its eco-consciousness and kid-friendliness. Kids become Kimpton Kids when they check in receiving a packet at check-in that includes a free gift, their own comment cards and a list of kid-friendly activities in the area. Kids can also use animal print bathrobes during their stay. The rooms feature Nintendo game systems for the kids. For a small additional fee, they offer a family summer package including milk and cookies and a movie each night of your stay.

American Guest House Bed and Breakfast
2005 Columbia Road NW
Washington, D.C. 20009
202-588-1180
www.americanguesthouse.com
Metro: Dupont Circle (Red Line)

This elegant late 19th century mansion offers visitors a more intimate and interesting lodging experience in a great location. The guest house offers historic furnishings and woodwork, a delicious made-to-order breakfast, a Wi-Fi connection, and a library. The house is convenient to the attractive Adams Morgan and Kalorama neighborhoods and a short walk from the Dupont Circle Metrorail station.

Foggy Bottom/West End

Embassy Suites
1250 22nd Street NW
Washington, D.C. 20037
202-857-3388
www.embassysuites1.hilton.com
Metro: Foggy Bottom (Blue/Orange Lines) and Dupont Circle (Red Line)

This reasonably priced, family oriented hotel is located in the quiet West End area of D.C. between Foggy Bottom and Georgetown. It is only a 4 block walk to the Metro. Highlights include: spacious suites, a huge complimentary breakfast, a pool and game room, and regular feedings of the koi fish at their atrium pond.

The River Inn
924 25th Street NW
Washington, D.C. 20037
202-337-7600
www.theriverinn.com
Metro: Foggy Bottom (Blue/Orange Lines)

This luxury inn offers spacious suites equipped with kitchen furnishings in a residential area of Foggy Bottom. This quiet neighborhood location is close to the Kennedy Center, George Washington University, Foggy Bottom Metrorail station and Georgetown. Regular guests rave about the location, comfortable suites and helpful staff.

Doubletree Guest Suites
801 New Hampshire Avenue NW
Washington, D.C. 20037
202-785-2000
www.doubletree.com
Metro: Foggy Bottom (Blue/Orange Lines)

This reasonably priced hotel offers large suites equipped with kitchens in a location close to the Metrorail station, the Kennedy Center and Georgetown. Kids receive a backpack loaded with crayons and activity books at check-in. Families also like the nearby Safeway supermarket found in the Watergate complex.

Georgetown

Four Seasons
2800 Pennsylvania Avenue NW
Washington, D.C. 20007
202-342-0444
www.fourseasons.com/washington
Metro: Foggy Bottom (Blue/Orange Lines)

The friendly staff at this luxury hotel will anticipate your needs and pamper you throughout your stay. This hotel pays special attention to kids by offering them stuffed animals, children's books, bathrobes and special desserts. The hotel features a pool and spa area, fine dining and an ideal location to experience the shops and restaurants of Georgetown.

Hotel Monticello
1075 Thomas Jefferson Street NW
Washington, D.C. 20007
202-337-0900
www.monticellohotel.com
Metro: Foggy Bottom (Blue/Orange Lines)

This reasonably priced boutique hotel is located in the heart of Georgetown steps away from the shops and restaurants of M Street. Guests rave about the price, location and comfort of the hotel as well as the friendliness of the staff. They offer a complimentary continental breakfast and vouchers for the use of a nearby fitness center.

The Latham Hotel
3000 M Street NW
Washington, D.C. 20007
202-726-5000
www.thelatham.com
Metro: Foggy Bottom (Blue/Orange Lines)

This boutique hotel is located on M Street in the middle of lively Georgetown. The hotel features the neighborhood's only rooftop hotel pool, a fitness center, and the award-winning restaurant Citronelle.

Georgetown Suites
1111 30th Street NW
Washington, D.C. 20007
202-298-7800
www.georgetownsuites.com
Metro: Foggy Bottom (Blue/Orange Lines)

This moderately priced hotel is located conveniently in the middle of Georgetown. The hotel offers large suites equipped with full kitchens, a complimentary continental breakfast, free Wi-Fi, a fitness center, and discount tickets to the nearby movie theater.

Upper Northwest

Marriott Wardman Park
2660 Woodley Road NW
Washington, D.C. 20008
202-328-2000
www.marriott.com
Metro: Woodley Park-National Zoo/Adams Morgan (Red Line)

This upscale hotel is the largest hotel in the District with more than 1,300 rooms. It is conveniently located near the National Zoo Metrorail station and the internationally diverse Adams Morgan neighborhood. The hotel also has a friendly staff, a fitness center and sauna and an outdoor pool.

Omni Shoreham
2500 Calvert Street NW
Washington, D.C. 20008
202-234-0700
www.omnihotels.com
Metro: Woodley Park-National Zoo/Adams Morgan (Red Line)

This historic luxury hotel is located near the National Zoo Metrorail station and the Adams Morgan neighborhood. The Omni Shoreham boasts an old world style with a tasteful lobby and dining areas, tranquil gardens and excellent views of Rock Creek Park. The hotel also has a helpful staff, fitness center and pool.

Woodley Park Guest House
2647 Woodley Road NW
Washington, D.C. 20008
866-667-0218
www.dcinns.com/woodley.html
Metro: Woodley Park-National Zoo/Adams Morgan (Red Line)

This elegant but cozy bed and breakfast is located within steps of the Metrorail station and the many shopping and dining opportunities in the Woodley Park and Adams Morgan neighborhoods. Guests rave about the delicious breakfast, comfortable bedrooms and common space, friendly staff and the interesting visitors they meet from around the world.

Days Inn Connecticut Avenue
4400 Connecticut Avenue NW
Washington, D.C. 20008
877-78-hotel
http://washington-dayinnconnecticut.com
Metro: Van Ness/UDC (Red Line)

This moderately priced hotel is located one block from the Van Ness Metrorail station and near the Cleveland Park neighborhood. There is a restaurant and Avis rental car office onsite and many good dining and retail stores nearby.

Capitol Hill

Hotel George
15 E Street NW
Washington, D.C. 20001
202-347-4200
www.hotelgeorge.com
Metro: Union Station (Red Line)

Similar to its Kimpton brother locations, Hotel Monaco and Hotel Helix, this boutique hotel stresses both its eco-consciousness and kid-friendliness in the Capitol Hill/Union Station area. Kids become Kimpton Kids when they arrive receiving a packet at check-in that includes a free gift, their own comment cards and a list of kid-friendly activities in the area. Kids can also use animal print bathrobes during their stay and play Nintendo game systems in the rooms. For a small additional fee, the Hotel George offers a family summer package including milk and cookies and a movie on each night of your stay.

Washington Court Hotel
525 New Jersey Avenue NW
Washington, D.C. 20001
202-628-2100
www.washingtoncourthotel.com
Metro: Union Station (Red Line)

This reasonably priced hotel is in a convenient location near the Capitol Building, Union Station and the National Postal Museum. The hotel offers a billiards room, fitness center and fine dining at the Bistro 525 restaurant.

The Liaison Capitol Hill
415 New Jersey Avenue NW
Washington, D.C. 20001
202-638-1616
www.affinia.com
Metro: Union Station (Red Line)

This reasonably priced Affinia hotel has an art deco style and features a rooftop pool and modern artwork-including portraits of world leaders in its lobby. The hotel is conveniently located near the Capitol Building, Union Station and the National Postal Museum. The hotel offers a fitness center and a highly regarded soul food restaurant called Art and Soul.

Alexandria, VA

Hilton Alexandria-Old Town
1767 King Street
Alexandria, VA 22314
703-837-0440
www.hilton.com
Metro: King Street (Blue/Yellow Lines)

This reasonably priced hotel is located a stone's throw from the King Street Metrorail station at the beginning of Old Town. It is a perfect hotel for a family that wants to experience Old Town Alexandria and also have convenient access to Washington, D.C.

Hampton Inn-Old Town
1616 King Street
Alexandria, VA 22314
703-299-9900
www.hamptoninn1.hilton.com
Metro: King Street (Blue/Yellow Lines)

This moderately priced hotel is in a great location in Old Town surrounded by shops and restaurants and also near the King Street Metrorail station for easy access to Reagan National Airport and all area attractions.

Embassy Suites Hotel Alexandria-Old Town
1900 Diagonal Road
Alexandria, VA 22314
703-684-5900
www.embassysuites1.hilton.com
Metro: King Street (Blue/Yellow Lines)

This moderately priced hotel offers spacious suites and rooms. It is located across from the King Street Metrorail station providing easy access to Old Town, Reagan National Airport and the entire region.

Morrison House Hotel

116 Alfred Street
Alexandria, VA 22314
703-838-8000
www.morrisonhouse.com
Metro: King Street (Blue/Yellow Lines)

This luxury Kimpton boutique hotel pampers guests in the heart of Old Town. Guests enjoy the friendly staff, cozy interior, period furniture and exceptional dining at the Grille at Morrison House. Kids receive a packet at check-in that includes a free gift, their own comment cards and a list of kid-friendly activities in the area. Kids can also use animal print bathrobes during their stay. The hotel is also pet-friendly. The Morrison House Hotel is within easy walking distance of the King Street Metrorail station for quick access to Washington, D.C.

Arlington, VA

Embassy Suites
Crystal City
1300 Jefferson Davis Highway
Arlington, VA 22202
703-979-9799
www.embassysuites1.hilton.com
Metro: Crystal City (Blue/Yellow Lines), Pentagon City (Blue/Yellow Lines)

This reasonably priced hotel is located in Crystal City near Reagan National Airport and the Pentagon City and Crystal City malls. The hotel has free shuttle service to the airport and Metrorail stations. The hotel offers guests an information packet upon check-in, a pool and fitness center, and complimentary breakfast and happy hour buffets.

Marriott Crystal Gateway
Crystal City
1700 Jefferson Davis Highway
Arlington, VA 22202
703-413-6630
www.marriott.com/hotels/travel/waspt-residence-inn-arlington-pentagon-city
Metro: Crystal City (Blue/Yellow Lines)

This upscale hotel is located above a Metrorail station and the underground Crystal City Mall and is minutes from Reagan National Airport with a free shuttle service. They offer all the amenities including spacious rooms, excellent dining options, an indoor pool, a well-equipped fitness center, and a friendly and helpful staff.

Hampton Inn and Suites Reagan National Airport
Crystal City
2000 Jefferson Davis Highway
Arlington, VA 22202
703-413-6630
www.hamptoninncc.com
Metro: Crystal City (Blue/Yellow Lines)

This moderately priced hotel offers large suites for families at a great location near Reagan National Airport and a Metrorail station. Amenities include a pool and fitness center, free breakfast and a free shuttle to the airport and surrounding area.

Americana Hotel
Crystal City
1400 Jefferson Davis Highway
Arlington, VA 22202
703-979-3722
www.americanahotel.com
Metro: Crystal City (Blue/Yellow lines), Pentagon City (Blue/Yellow lines)

This budget hotel is no-frills but it's clean, comfortable and a great bargain for the area. It is located in Crystal City near Reagan National Airport and close to the Pentagon City and Crystal City malls. The hotel is near a Metrorail station and has free shuttle service to the airport. There is also a free continental breakfast, helpful staff, and free Wi-Fi in the lobby area. Their website offers a 15% discount for first-time guests.

Residence Inn
Pentagon City
550 Army Navy Drive
Arlington, VA 22202
703-413-6630
www.marriott.com/hotels/travel/waspt-residence-inn-arlington-pentagon-city
Pentagon City (Blue/Yellow Lines)

This reasonably priced hotel is located near the Pentagon City Mall with its huge selection of shops and restaurants. The nearby Metrorail station provides quick and easy access to Washington, D.C. Guests also rave about the breakfast buffet. The hotel also has free shuttle service to the airport and the nearby area.

The Ritz-Carlton Pentagon City
Pentagon City
1250 South Hayes Street
Arlington, VA 22202
703-413-6630
www.ritzcarlton.com/PentagonCity
Pentagon City (Blue/Yellow Lines)

This luxury hotel is located in the Pentagon City Mall complex offering many shopping and dining options. The Metrorail station is feet away and provides quick and easy access to Washington, D.C., attractions. The hotel features plush and comfortable rooms, a fine dining restaurant and a huge fitness and spa area including an indoor pool and sauna.

Hyatt Arlington
Rosslyn
1325 Wilson Boulevard
Arlington, VA 22209
703-525-1234
www.hyatt.com
Metro: Rosslyn (Blue/Orange Lines)

Guests enjoy comfortable large rooms and modern conveniences at a reasonable price at this Hyatt. The hotel is located conveniently next to the Metrorail station with restaurant options and a Starbucks in the lobby. The bustling Georgetown neighborhood is also within walking distance across the Key Bridge.

Clarion Collection Hotel Arlington Court Suites
Rosslyn
1200 North Courthouse Road
Arlington, VA 22201
703-524-4000
www.clarionhotel.com
Metro: Rosslyn (Blue/Orange Lines)

Located in a suburban area outside of the city, this moderately priced hotel offers families spacious apartment type rooms with kitchen facilities. The nearby Rosslyn Metrorail station, reachable on foot or via hotel shuttle, will quickly get you to the main attractions in the area. The hotel is pet friendly and offers a free breakfast buffet, a recreation room and a fitness center.

Highlander Motor Inn
Virginia Square/Ballston
3336 Wilson Blvd.
Arlington, VA 22201
703-524-4300
www.highlandermotel.com
Metro: Virginia Square (Orange Line)

This family owned small budget motel offers clean rooms, free Wi-Fi, and a complimentary continental breakfast. They are in an excellent location near restaurants and a shopping mall and a short walk from the Metrorail station.

Bethesda, MD

Residence Inn
7335 Wisconsin Avenue
Bethesda, MD 20814
301-718-0200
www.marriott.com
Metro: Bethesda (Red Line)

This reasonably priced hotel is conveniently located in the downtown area of Bethesda with many excellent restaurants and shops. The Metrorail station is located nearby for easy access to Washington, D.C. The hotel has an outdoor pool, fitness center and a complimentary breakfast buffet.

American Inn of Bethesda
8130 Wisconsin Avenue
Bethesda, MD 20814
301-656-9300
www.american-inn.com
Metro: Bethesda (Red Line)

This budget hotel is located near the National Institutes of Health, the National Naval Medical Center and the shopping and dining hub of downtown Bethesda. They offer a swimming pool, free Wi-Fi, free parking and a complimentary breakfast. The Metrorail station is also within walking distance and the hotel offers a free shuttle to it and the nearby area.

Rockville, MD

Bethesda North Marriott Hotel and Conference Center
5701 Marinelli Road
Rockville, MD 20852
301-822-9200
www.marriott.com
Metro: White Flint (Red Line)

This reasonably priced hotel is conveniently located near a Metrorail station and the boutique shops, restaurants, and entertainment venues of the White Flint Mall. The hotel offers a pool and fitness center. Guests particularly enjoy the Sunday brunch at the Meritage Restaurant in the hotel.

Silver Spring, MD

Courtyard by Marriott Silver Spring Downtown
8506 Fenton Street
Silver Spring, MD 20910
301-589-4899
www.marriott.com
Metro: Silver Spring (Red Line)

This is a comfortable and moderately priced hotel with an excellent location in downtown Silver Spring. Guests enjoy the retail and dining opportunities near the hotel and the convenient Metrorail access to Washington, D.C.

Crowne Plaza Hotel Washington, D.C.,-Silver Spring

8777 Georgia Avenue
Silver Spring, MD 20910
877-859-5095
www.crowneplaza.com
Metro: Silver Spring (Red Line)

This moderately priced hotel is conveniently located near shopping and dining venues in downtown Silver Spring. The hotel offers an indoor pool and fitness center. The Metrorail station is only three blocks away and the hotel offers a free shuttle service to the station and the nearby area.

National Harbor, MD

Gaylord National Hotel and Conference Center

201 Waterfront Street
National Harbor, MD 20745
301-965-2000
www.gaylordhotels.com/gaylord-national

This huge new luxury hotel on the banks of the Potomac River features an 18-story glass atrium with more than 2,000 rooms. Guests enjoy views of the river, Old Town Alexandria, and the landmarks of Washington, D.C., about 8 miles in the distance. There are many retail and dining opportunities in the complex and the National Harbor area. The hotel offers an indoor pool, giant spa and fitness center and a rooftop lounge. The resort also entertains guests with nightly water fountain shows, roving performers along a river boardwalk area and a Saturday night fireworks display. Guests can access Alexandria and Washington, D.C., via private water shuttles and shuttle buses to Metrorail stations.

Hampton Inn and Suites National Harbor

250 Waterfront Street
Oxon Hill, MD 20745
301-567-3531
http://hamptoninn.hilton.com

This moderately priced hotel has more than 150 rooms and suites and is located in the heart of the National Harbor area with all of its attractions. The hotel has an indoor pool and fitness center. Guests can access Alexandria and Washington, D.C., via private water shuttles and shuttle buses to Metrorail stations.

Hostel

Hostelling International
1009 11th Street NW
Washington, D.C. 20001
202-737-2333
www.hiwashingtondc.org
Metro: (Blue/Orange Lines and Red Line)

This budget alternative is primarily used by young international students, but people of all ages are welcome. This hostel is located conveniently close to Downtown and the Penn Quarter.

Campsites

Cherry Hill Park
9800 Cherry Hill Road
College Park, MD 20740
800-801-6449
www.cherryhillpark.com

The closest camping area to Washington, D.C., is the popular Cherry Hill Park in College Park, MD. This full service campsite offers spaces for RVs, campers, and tents, and provides cabins and rentals. Amenities include a restaurant, store, pool and onsite public transportation to the D.C. Metro system. The campsite is open year round, but they recommend making reservations well in advance during the high season.

Washington, D.C./Capitol KOA Kampground
768 Cecil Avenue
N. Millersville, MD 21108
800-562-0248
www.capitolkoa.com

This full service campsite offers spaces for RVs and tents and also provides rental cabins and lodges. Amenities include shuttle service to Washington, D.C., Baltimore, and Annapolis, free Wi-Fi, store, pool, outdoor playground and organized games.

Family Friendly Restaurants by Location

The Washington, D.C., area is filled with exceptional restaurants featuring cuisine from around the world. In this section, I have listed some of my favorite places for families to enjoy. Don't be shy about asking hospitality workers and other locals for their own favorites as there are many excellent restaurants in every price range throughout the D.C. metropolitan area.

It is also possible to take advantage of group and other ticket discounts for restaurants found on restaurant websites and on various online subscriber sites.

Most of the restaurants listed are suitable for children of all ages, although there are some locations that may be too formal or exotic for younger or less adventurous diners. Please read the descriptions and call or go online if you need more information about the restaurant.

The majority of these restaurants are inexpensive costing between $5-$15 per person for food, drink and tax and tip. There is an "IN" next to their name for inexpensive. The restaurants costing between $15-$30 per person are marked "M" for moderate. The restaurants costing between $30-$60 per person are marked "E" for expensive. Most of these restaurants have cheaper lunch menus as well as children's menus with reduced portions and prices.

I recommend eating outside the rush dining times of 12 PM-1:30 PM and 6 PM-8 PM to avoid crowds and maximize your time at attractions.

National Mall

Mitsitam Café (IN)
National Museum of the American Indian
4th Street and Independence Avenue SW
Washington, D.C. 20024
202-633-1000
www.nmao.si.edu
Metro: L'Enfant Plaza (Blue/Orange Lines and Green/Yellow Lines)

This unique café at the National Museum of the American Indian offers a variety of native foods at stands representing five regions in the Americas. Favorites include salmon, venison, pheasant, buffalo-sandwiches and chili, wild rice salad, squash dishes, tacos, tamales and fry bread. If you can't choose from the many selections order a Five Region Sampler Platter, which gives you the food highlights from every region. In the Great Plains area there is also a kid's menu featuring chicken tenders and fries. The setting of the restaurant is also unique as you can sit in front of huge windows and eat your food while watching a man-made creek slowly flowing around boulders. In the high season I recommend coming before or after the lunch crowd from 12 PM-1:30 PM.

Cascade Café (IN)
National Gallery of Art
4th and Constitution Avenue NW
East Building, Concourse Level
Washington, D.C. 20565
202-712-7454
www.nga.gov/ginfo/cafes.shtm
Metro: Archives (Green/Yellow Lines)

The Cascade Café offers entrees, sandwiches, salads, wood-fired pizza and desserts with a pleasant view of the cascade waterfall in the concourse level of the National Gallery. There is also an espresso and gelato bar next to the café offering homemade gelato, sandwiches and pastries.

United States Holocaust Memorial Museum Café (IN)
100 Raoul Wallenberg Place SW
Washington, D.C. 20024
202-488-6151
www.ushmm.org/visit/cafe
Metro: Smithsonian (Blue/Orange Lines)

This buffet-style café provides sandwiches, salads, pizza, knishes, and kosher entrees. Groups of five or more can pre-order their meals online or by phone and pick them up when they arrive.

Southwest Waterfront

Maine Avenue Fish Market (IN)
1100 Maine Avenue, SW
Washington, D.C. 20024
202-484-2722
Metro: L'Enfant Plaza (Blue/Orange Lines and Green/Yellow Lines)

This busy waterfront market area has a variety of vendors offering fresh seafood delicacies in a lively setting. Favorites include steamed crabs, crab cakes, oysters, clams and fish sandwiches, as well as hush puppies and desserts. There is limited outdoor seating here.

Captain White's Seafood City (IN)
1100 Maine Avenue, #3 SW
Washington, D.C. 20024
202-554-5520
www.captainwhiteseafood.com
Metro: L'Enfant Plaza (Blue/Orange Lines and Green/Yellow Lines)

This huge seafood vendor offers cooked crab cakes, oysters, shrimp and fish sandwiches, as well as sides and soups, which you can pre-order by phone.

Jenny's Asian Fusion (M)
100 Water Street SW
Washington, D.C. 20024
202-554-2202
www.jennysdc.com
Metro: L'Enfant Plaza (Blue/Orange Lines and Green/Yellow Lines)

This cozy restaurant offers an excellent variety of Asian favorites such as Orange Chicken, Drunken Noodles, and Pad Thai. Locals enjoy the tasty Asian food and the relaxing waterfront view.

Downtown

Old Ebbitt Grill (M)
675 15th Street NW
Washington, D.C. 20005
202-347-4800
www.ebbitt.com
Metro: McPherson Square (Blue/Orange Lines)

A favorite of locals and visitors alike, this always bustling restaurant near the White House features an excellent selection of entrees, appetizers and desserts to satisfy the whole family. Its seafood entrees and oyster bar are especially popular. Established in 1836, the original location served as the District's first saloon and was a favorite of politicians and famous visitors. After a few moves throughout the years, the restaurant settled at its present location in 1983. The interior features antique furnishings and fixtures, historic beer steins, wooden bears imported by Alexander Hamilton and animal heads reputedly bagged by Teddy Roosevelt. Its polished wood walls, mahogany bars and separate themed rooms combined with its prized location across from the Treasury Building make it extra special.

The Shops at National Place (IN)
529 14th Street NW
Washington, D.C. 20045
202-662-1250
Metro: McPherson Square (Blue/Orange Lines), Metro Center (Blue/Orange Lines and Red Line)

This location features an excellent food court with a wide selection of popular restaurants. There is something here to suit every taste with plenty of American favorites as well as delicious international cuisine. Try to avoid coming here at the peak lunch time of 12 PM-1:30 PM, especially in the summer, as it gets crowded with both local workers and visitors.

Maoz Vegetarian (IN)
1817 M Street NW
Washington, D.C. 20036
202-290-3117
www.maozusa.com
Metro: Farragut North (Red Line)

This international chain is popular for its delicious and inexpensive falafels and other vegetarian favorites.

Luigi's Restaurant (M)
1132 19th Street NW
Washington, D.C. 20036
202-331-7574
www.famousluigis.com
Metro: Farragut West (Blue/Orange Lines)

Since 1943, Luigi's has been serving up traditional Italian favorites in a relaxed Trattoria-type setting. Patrons enjoy the cozy atmosphere with checkered tablecloths and candles in Chianti bottles. Regulars particularly enjoy the pizza and homemade pasta dishes.

G Street Food (IN)
1706 G Street NW
Washington, D.C. 20006
202-408-7474
www.gstreetfood.com
Metro: Farragut West (Blue/Orange Lines)

G Street Food offers cuisine from around the world in a relaxed setting. The diverse selection includes breads and salads from the Middle East, Montreal-style bagels, Vietnamese Banh sandwiches and Chinese noodle pancakes with scallions.

Ronald Reagan Building and International Trade Center Food Court (IN)

1300 Pennsylvania Avenue NW
Washington, D.C. 20004
202-312-1647
www.itcdc.com/explore.php?p=13
Metro: Federal Triangle (Blue/Orange Lines)

The food court in this impressive modern federal government building offers selections from 18 different restaurants. Groups can pre-order prepared meals online or by calling in advance.

Penn Quarter/Gallery Place

Carmine's D.C. (M)

425 7th Street NW
Washington, D.C. 20004
202-737-7700
www.carminesnyc.com
Metro: Archives (Green/Yellow Lines), Gallery Place (Green/Yellow Lines and Red Line)

This New York City import offers classic family style Italian food. Customers love the tasty entrees such as spaghetti and meatballs and lasagna and their huge portions.

Hill Country (M)

410 7th Street NW
Washington, D.C. 20004
202-556-2050
www.hillcountrywdc.com
Metro: Archives (Green/Yellow Lines), Gallery Place (Green/Yellow Lines and Red Line)

This huge, bustling Texas hill country themed restaurant offers a great selection of barbecue entrees and sides such as corn pudding and mashed sweet potatoes. Regulars enjoy the brisket, ribs and chicken dishes.

Chinatown Express (IN)

746 6th Street NW
Washington, D.C. 20001
202-638-0424
Metro: Gallery Place (Green/Yellow Lines and Red Line)

This bustling, small no-frills restaurant is one of the few remaining authentic Chinese restaurants in the shrinking Chinatown area. Regulars love the homemade noodles and dumplings.

Wok and Roll (M)

604 H Street NW
Washington, D.C. 20001
202-347-4656
Metro: Gallery Place (Green/Yellow Lines and Red Line)

This modern restaurant serves a combination of Chinese and Japanese favorites. They also offer a sushi bar and karaoke singing nights. Because of its popularity, Wok and Roll has added a new location in Adams Morgan at 2400 18th Street, NW.

Matchbox Chinatown (M)

713 H Street NW
Washington, D.C. 20001
202-289-4441
Metro: Gallery Place (Green/Yellow Lines and Red Line)

This lively restaurant is popular for its delicious mini-burgers, brick oven pizza and its large variety of tasty and healthy salads. They also offer a weekend brunch menu and outdoor seating.

Hard Rock Café (M)

999 E Street NW
Washington, D.C. 20004
202-737-7625
www.hardrock.com
Metro: Gallery Place (Green/Yellow Lines and Red Line)

Located next door to Ford's Theatre, this is a great spot to go with kids especially if they are music fans. The interior is decorated with rock and roll memorabilia and loud music plays at all times. They offer a full menu of American favorites. The restaurant gets crowded at the normal lunch hour, so I recommend getting a reservation after 1 PM and putting your name in before you begin touring Ford's Theatre. You can also plan ahead and make an online reservation.

Ollie's Trolley (IN)

425 12th Street NW
Washington D.C. 20004
202-347-6119
Metro: Metro Center (Blue/Orange Lines and Red Line)

This small family owned restaurant has been serving up specialty cheesesteaks, burgers, and sandwiches for over 30 years. Locals especially love the retro atmosphere and their tasty French fries.

Dupont Circle

Zorba's Café (IN)
1612 20th St NW
Washington D.C. 20009
(202) 387-8555
Metro: Dupont Circle (Red Line)

Zorba's offers delicious Greek sandwiches, entrees, and dessert favorites in the trendy Dupont Circle area. They also have a nice patio for relaxing and people watching.

Pizzeria Paradiso (M)
2003 P Street NW
Washington, D.C. 20036
202-223-1245
www.eatyourpizza.com
Metro: Dupont Circle (Red Line)

If you are looking for authentic brick-oven pizza, you've come to the right place. Pizza lovers savor every bite at this location and in Georgetown and Old Town, Alexandria.

City Lights of China (M)
1731 Connecticut Avenue NW
Washington, D.C. 20009
202-265-6688
www.citylightsofchina.com
Metro: Dupont Circle (Red Line)

This basement level Chinese restaurant offers delicious Hunan and Szechuan specialties including Peking Duck and steamed and fried dumplings.

Five Guys Famous Burgers and Fries (IN)
1645 Connecticut Ave NW
Washington, D.C. 20009
202-328-3483
www.fiveguys.com
Metro: Dupont Circle (Red Line)

This rapidly expanding restaurant chain originated in the area and continues to excel at its many D.C. metro locations. Their recipe for success: their burgers are never frozen, they get regular shipments of fresh potatoes to make their boardwalk style French fries and you get to munch on all-you-can-eat peanuts while you wait.

Buca di Beppo's (M)
1825 Connecticut Avenue NW
Washington, D.C. 20009
202-232-8466
www.bucadibeppo.com
Metro: Dupont Circle (Red Line)

They serve classic and tasty Italian entrees in huge family style portions. The boisterous setting, memorabilia focused on Italian Americans and décor from the old country make it a fun family oriented dining experience.

Shake Shack (IN)
1216 18th Street NW
Washington, D.C. 20036
202-683-9922
www.shakeshack.com
Metro: Dupont Circle, Farragut North (Red Line)

This burger and shake spot has created a stir among locals for its delicious beef and mushroom burgers, hot dogs, and French fries. The frozen custard and shakes-especially the chocolate Washington Monu-Mint version-are also excellent.

Café Green (IN)
1513 17th Street NW
Washington, D.C. 20036
202-234-0505
www.javagreen.net
Metro: Dupont Circle (Red Line)

Java Green (IN)
1020 19th Street NW
Washington, D.C. 20036
202-775-8899
www.javagreen.net
Metro: Farragut North (Red Line)

These organic vegan restaurants offer diverse menus of locally grown produce for the ecologically minded diner. These restaurants excel at tofu and imitation meat dishes and also offer green tea frappes and other interesting beverages and desserts.

Foggy Bottom/West End

Bobby's Burger Palace (IN)
2121 K Street NW
Washington, D.C. 20037
202-974-6260
www.bobbysburgerpalace.com
Metro: Foggy Bottom (Blue/Orange Lines)

Celebrity chef Bobby Flay's entry into the gourmet burger craze has been well-received by locals and visitors. Customers rave about the quality and selection of burgers and the onion rings, sweet potato fries and shakes. Patrons can "crunchify" any order to get potato chips placed on top of the burger patty. The 1970s décor and atmosphere are also a hit.

Devon & Blakely (IN)
2200 Pennsylvania Avenue NW
Washington, D.C. 20052
202-659-9070
www.devonandblakely.com
Metro: Foggy Bottom (Blue/Orange Lines)

They offer a wide variety of sandwiches, salads, soups, side dishes, and desserts at various prepared food stations. Regulars enjoy the delicious food, fast service and friendly staff.

FoBoGro (IN)
2140 F Street NW
Washington, D.C. 20037
202-296-0125
www.fobogro.com
Metro: Foggy Bottom (Blue/Orange Lines)

This grocery store in the George Washington University area offers a great selection of tasty and healthy deli sandwiches, paninis, wraps and salads.

Georgetown

Filomena Ristorante (E)
1063 Wisconsin Avenue NW
Washington, D.C. 20007
202-338-8800
www.filomena.com

Patrons love dining on authentic Italian food while surrounded by furniture and décor from the old country. Filomena offers special group menus with advance notice.

Martin's Tavern (M)

1264 Wisconsin Avenue NW
Washington, D.C. 20007
202-333-7370
www.martins-tavern.com

This Georgetown institution has been serving up delicious American favorites and seafood specialties such as jumbo lump crab cakes and oyster stew in a friendly atmosphere since 1933. Every president from Harry Truman to George W. Bush has dined here. Former Georgetown resident John F. Kennedy used to frequently dine here at booth number 1 and reportedly proposed to Jacqueline Bouvier at booth number 3 on June 24, 1953.

Clyde's of Georgetown (M)

3236 M Street NW
Washington, D.C. 20007
202-333-9180
www.clydes.com

This Georgetown favorite since 1963 serves up a great selection of seafood and traditional American entrees. The long oak bar, wood flooring, and oil paintings create an old-fashioned saloon atmosphere. This restaurant was the inspiration for the 1976 hit song "Afternoon Delight."

Old Glory Barbecue (IN)

3139 M St NW
Washington, D.C. 20007
202-337-3496
www.oldglorybbq.com

Old Glory offers a wide selection of sandwiches, entrees, and sauces to satisfy any barbecue fan. They also offer salads and starters such as sweet potato fries, fried green tomatoes, and barbecue grilled oysters.

Upper Northwest

Comet Ping Pong (M)

5037 Connecticut Avenue NW
Washington, D.C. 20008
202-364-0404
www.cometpingpong.com

This family friendly restaurant makes delicious pizza and serves it to you while modern art metalwork hangs overhead. In the back room your family can listen to music from a jukebox and test your skills at ping pong and foosball.

Cactus Cantina (M)
3300 Wisconsin Avenue NW
Washington, D.C. 20016
202-686-7222
www.cactuscantina.com

This large and vibrant Tex-Mex restaurant is near the Washington National Cathedral and is known for its fajitas and margaritas. They offer an extensive kid's menu of Tex-Mex favorites.

2 Amys (M)
3715 Macomb Street NW
Washington, D.C. 20016
202-885-5700
www.2amyspizza.com

Patrons savor the Neapolitan style pizza with fresh mozzarella and a variety of toppings at this loud, popular restaurant. Regulars also rave about the appetizers such as bruschetta and suppli.

Nam-Viet (IN)
3419 Connecticut Avenue NW
Washington, D.C. 20008
202-237-1015
www.namviet1.com
Metro: Cleveland Park (Red Line)

Locals enjoy the pho dishes, grilled salmon and shrimp dishes and spring rolls at this cozy Cleveland Park Vietnamese restaurant. Regulars recommend the Pho Bo, which contains noodles and sliced beef in a tasty broth.

Byblos Deli (IN)
3414 Connecticut Avenue NW
Washington, D.C. 20008
202-364-6549
www.byblosdc.com
Metro: Cleveland Park (Red Line)

This neighborhood favorite features authentic Greek and Middle Eastern cuisine including gyros, kabobs, shawarmas, falafels and spinach pie. Regulars especially enjoy the flavorful hummus. They also serve up delicious cheeseburgers, chicken wings and hot dogs.

Hot N Juicy Crawfish (M)
2651 Connecticut Avenue NW
Washington, D.C. 20008
202-299-9448
www.hotandjuicycrawfish.com
Metro: Woodley Park-Zoo/Adams Morgan (Red Line)

This bustling seafood restaurant features delicious crawfish, shrimp, crabs, lobster, oysters and other delicacies with a wide variety of sauces and seasonings to suit every taste. Put on a bib and prepare to get your hands messy.

Open City (M)
2331 Calvert Street NW
Washington, D.C. 20008
202-332-2331
www.opencitydc.com
Metro: Woodley Park-Zoo/Adams Morgan (Red Line)

This Woodley Park neighborhood restaurant serves traditional American food and is popular for its extensive all day breakfast menu.

Capitol Hill

Library of Congress Madison Cafeteria (IN)
James Madison Building, 6th Floor
101 Independence Avenue SE
Washington, D.C. 20540
www.loc.gov/visit/shop.html
Metro: Capitol South (Blue/Orange Lines)

This unique cafeteria offers entrees, sandwiches, salad bar and desserts with a nice view of the city. Kids enjoy walking the underground hallways from the Jefferson Building to get to the Madison building. There is also a coffee shop at ground level offering food and beverages. The James Madison Building cafeteria is open 9 AM-3 PM but closed to the public 10:30 AM-12:30 PM.

Tortilla Coast (M)
400 First Street SE
Washington, D.C. 20003
202-546-6768
www.tortillacoast.com
Metro: Capitol South (Blue/Orange Lines)

This Tex-Mex favorite is located near the House of Representatives office buildings. They have been serving tasty fajitas, tacos, flautas and margaritas to politicians, staffers and visitors since 1988.

Good Stuff Eatery (IN)
303 Pennsylvania Avenue SE
Washington, D.C. 20003
202-543-8222
www.goodstuffeatery.com
Metro: Capitol South (Blue/Orange Lines)

This family owned restaurant has become popular with locals and visitors alike who enjoy their delicious freshly made food. Regulars enjoy their amazing burgers, hand-cut French fries, farm fresh salads, and handspun ice cream products-especially the toasted marshmallow shake. A visit from President Obama has also raised their profile.

Mr. Henry's (M)
601 Pennsylvania Avenue SE
Washington, D.C. 20003
202-546-8412
www.mrhenrysrestaurant.com
Metro: Eastern Market (Blue/Orange Lines)

Rub elbows with Capitol Hill staffers and residents at this popular neighborhood restaurant offering large servings of American food. Kids 8 and under eat free on Tuesday night and can watch a free movie upstairs.

Market Lunch (IN)
Eastern Market
225 7th Street SE
Washington, D.C. 20003
202-547-8444
http://www.easternmarket-dc.org/default.asp?contentID=46
Metro: Eastern Market (Blue/Orange Lines)

Locals and visitors alike line up at the counter of this Washington institution at Eastern Market. Regulars love the blueberry buckwheat pancakes for breakfast and the crab cakes, soft shell crabs, burgers and oyster sandwiches for lunch.

Taqueria Nacional (IN)
400 North Capitol Street NW
Washington, D.C. 20001
202-737-7070
http://www.taquerianational.com
Metro: Union Station (Red Line)

They serve delicious traditional soft corn tacos with meat and fish and a variety of toppings and salsas. Regulars also like the yucca fries and their agua fresca fruit drinks. This restaurant is primarily takeout, but there is some outdoor seating available.

Adams Morgan

Amsterdam Falafelshop (IN)
2425 18th Street NW
Washington, D.C. 20009
202-234-1969
www.falafelshop.com
Metro: Woodley Park-Zoo/Adams Morgan (Red Line)

This small shop cooks up your falafel (deep fried balls made of chickpeas) order in front of you. When the falafel is ready you choose a white or wheat pita and add toppings and sauces to it. They offer 21 different sauces and toppings including beetroot, garlic hummus, dutch mayo, green chile sauce and red pepper. Regulars rave about the delicious taste of the falafels and the hand-cut French fries.

Jyoti Indian Cuisine (M)
2433 18th Street NW
Washington, D.C. 20009
202-518-5892
www.jyotidc.com
Metro: Woodley Park-Zoo/Adams Morgan (Red Line)

This cozy restaurant serves traditional vegetarian and non vegetarian Indian specialties such as vegetable Thali and Tandoori shrimp, salmon and chicken. They also serve delicious Naan bread, spinach samosa and spicy soups.

Super Tacos and Bakery (IN)
1762 Columbia Road NW
Washington, D.C. 20009
202-232-7121
www.supertacosdc.com
Metro: Woodley Park-Zoo/Adams Morgan (Red Line)

This carry-out/delivery option offers delicious tacos, tortillas, enchiladas and burritos with a wide variety of meat, toppings, and sauces. They also offer a salsa bar, a great variety of vegetarian options and tasty baked goods.

Meskerem Ethiopian Restaurant (M)
2434 18th Street NW
Washington, D.C. 20009
202-462-4100
http://meskeremethiopianrestaurantdc.com
Metro: Woodley Park-Zoo/Adams Morgan (Red Line)

Meskerem serves authentic Ethiopian food in an authentic setting with high chairs and low tables and no utensils. Customers enjoy the injera bread, vegetarian and meat combination platters such as the Meskerem Messob, sambusas, and their honey wine.

U Street Corridor/Shaw

Ben's Chili Bowl (IN)
1213 U Street NW
Washington, D.C. 20009
202-667-0909
www.benschilibowl.com
Metro: U Street (Green/Yellow Lines)

This legendary Washington, D.C., restaurant's favorite customer is comedian Bill Cosby, who never pays for his meals here. President Obama is also a fan. Stop by for a delicious chili dog, chili half-smoke or a bowl of beef or veggie chili.

Dukem Ethiopian Restaurant (M)
1118 U Street NW
Washington, D.C. 20009
202-667-8735
www.dukemrestaurant.com
Metro: U Street (Green/Yellow Lines)

This casual restaurant offers traditional Ethiopian favorites. Regulars recommend the sambusas, Goden Tibbs (rack of lamb), vegetarian and meat combination platters and their delicious injera bread. Dukem features an Ethiopian Cultural Show with dancers and musicians on Thursdays starting at 6:30 PM.

Old Town Alexandria, VA

Stage Door Deli (IN)
1324 King Street
Alexandria, VA 22314
703-836-7885
Metro: King Street (Blue/Yellow Lines)

If you're longing for an authentic Reuben, corned beef, Italian or liverwurst sandwich, and some real pickles, come to this no frills New York style delicatessen.

Pines of Florence (M)
1300 King Street
Alexandria, VA 22314
www.pinesofflorencedc.com
703-549-1796
Metro: King Street (Blue/Yellow Lines)

This family restaurant offers a wide selection of delicious Italian appetizers, entrees and desserts in a relaxed setting.

Bittersweet Bakery and Café (IN)
823 King Street
Alexandria, VA 22314
703-549-2708
www.bittersweetcatering.com
Metro: King Street (Blue/Yellow Lines)

This is a local favorite for breakfast, lunch and brunch offering a buffet-style assortment of entrees and side dishes as well as made-to-order entrees, sandwiches, salads and desserts. Regulars enjoy the tuna melt and veggie sandwiches as well as their fresh baked cupcakes. They also offer outdoor patio seating.

Bugsy's Pizza Restaurant and Sports Bar (IN)
111 King Street
Alexandria, VA 22314
703-683-0313
www.bugsyspizza.com
Metro: King Street (Blue/Yellow Lines)

This restaurant is owned by a former NHL player and is full of sports memorabilia. The restaurant features an all you can eat lunch pizza buffet and salad bar. Fanatical sports fans love the upstairs bar.

Jack's Place (IN)
222 N. Lee Street
Alexandria, VA 22314
703-684-0372
Metro: King Street (Blue/Yellow Lines), take free King Street shuttle to King and Lee Streets and walk two blocks north.

This neighborhood favorite serves up inexpensive breakfast and brunch specials featuring delicious omelettes, pancakes, French toast, breakfast sandwiches and home fries. They also offer cheesesteaks, grilled cheese and a variety of classic deli sandwiches. This family owned restaurant is small with counter service and a few tables with the owner normally manning the grill. Jack's Place is cash only.

Pop's Old Fashioned Ice Cream Company (IN)
109 King Street
Alexandria, VA 22314
703-518-5374
Metro: King Street (Blue/Yellow Lines)

Take the time to savor homemade ice cream and sit in an old fashioned ice cream parlor.

Union Street Public House (M)
121 S. Union Street
Alexandria, VA 22314
703-548-1785
www.unionstreetpublichouse.com
Metro: King Street (Blue/Yellow Lines)

This renovated colonial warehouse offers an old-fashioned ambiance and great seafood, steak, and other American entrées. It is also a popular weekend brunch spot for families.

Chart House (E)
1 Cameron Street (Waterfront harbor area)
Alexandria, VA 22314
703-684-5080
www.chart-house.com
Metro: King Street (Blue/Yellow Lines)

This elegant and upscale restaurant is located next to a marina on the banks of the Potomac River with pleasant waterfront views. It has an outdoor deck dining area that is popular in the warmer months. The menu offers a great selection of seafood including a raw oyster bar and serves other classic American entrees. The Chart House is an excellent place to come for a special occasion. Regulars rave about their signature hot chocolate lava cake.

Royal Restaurant (IN)
734 N. Saint Asaph St
Alexandria, VA 22314
703-548-1616
www.theroyalrestaurant.com
Metro: Braddock Road (Blue/Yellow Lines)

This local favorite is hidden a bit away from the mass of restaurants on King Street. They offer an excellent variety of entrees, sandwiches, and desserts (especially for pie lovers!). The staff is efficient and genuinely welcoming, too.

Arlington, VA

Athena Pallas (M)
Crystal City
556 22nd Street South
Arlington, VA 22202
703-521-3870
www.athenapallas.com
Metro: Crystal City (Blue/Yellow Lines)

This family owned establishment serves up authentic Greek classics in a friendly atmosphere. Regulars enjoy the seafood, lamb, combination platters and desserts such as baklava and Greek tiramisu.

Johnny Rockets (IN)
Pentagon City
Pentagon City Mall
1100 S. Hayes Street, Suite M134
Arlington, VA 22202
703-415-3510
www.johnnyrockets.com
Metro: Pentagon City (Blue/Yellow Lines)

Johnny Rockets, located inside the Pentagon City Mall, has décor like a 1950s malt shop complete with counter service and jukeboxes. It serves up delicious burgers and chili cheese fries as well as milkshakes and sundaes. They also have locations in Dupont Circle, Georgetown, Union Station and Shirlington.

California Pizza Kitchen (M)
Pentagon City
1201 S. Hayes Street, Suite F
Arlington, VA 22202
703-412-4900
www.cpk.com
Metro: Pentagon City (Blue/Yellow Lines)

This restaurant is located in the Pentagon Centre shopping area next to the Metrorail station. They offer a huge variety of gourmet pizzas as well as Italian favorites. Patrons recommend the original Barbecue Chicken Pizza and the Carne Asada Pizza for a good change of pace from regular pizza.

Hard Times Café (IN)
Clarendon
3028 Wilson Blvd
Arlington VA 22201
703-528-2233
www.hardtimes.com
Metro: Clarendon (Orange line)

This local chain specializes in chili dishes from regions across the USA. The family will also appreciate the Wild West décor. The original location is on King Street in Old Town Alexandria, VA.

Goody's (IN)
Clarendon
3125 Wilson Blvd.
Arlington, VA 22201
Metro: Clarendon (Orange line)

This local favorite is a small, family owned establishment that offers tasty pizza, sandwiches and salads.

Bob and Edith's Diner (IN)
2310 Columbia Pike and 4707 Columbia Pike
Arlington, VA 22204
703-920-6103
www.bobandediths.com

This popular diner is found at two locations in Arlington. It is a classic American diner open 24 hours offering a huge selection of good food and desserts.

Red Hot and Blue (IN)
Rosslyn
1600 Wilson Boulevard
Arlington, VA 22209
(703) 276-7427
Metro: Rosslyn (Blue/Orange Lines)

This local chain offers Southern-style barbecue ribs, sandwiches and soul food.

Ray's Hell Burger (IN)
Rosslyn
1725 Wilson Boulevard
Arlington, VA 22201
703-841-0001
Metro: Rosslyn (Blue/Orange Lines)

This small restaurant has become a local institution with its amazing assortment of delicious burgers with all types of unusual toppings and combinations. President Obama made a visit here to enjoy one of Ray's specialty burgers.

Guapo's (M)
Shirlington
4028 Campbell Avenue
Arlington, VA 22206
703-671-1701
www.guaposrestaurant.com

This family owned Tex-Mex local chain offers tasty and authentic entrees. They also have locations in Upper Northwest D.C. and Bethesda, MD.

Bethesda, MD

BD's Mongolian Restaurant (M)
7201 Wisconsin Avenue
Bethesda, MD 20814
301-657-1080
www.gomongo.com
Metro: Bethesda (Red Line)

This do it yourself restaurant gives customers the chance to prepare their own stir fry creations with their choice of meat, fish, vegetables, noodles and sauces. Your unique mixture is placed on a huge 7-foot grill and expertly prepared by their chefs.

Café Deluxe (M)

4910 Elm Street
Bethesda, MD 20814
202-686-2233
www.cafedeluxe.com
Metro: Bethesda (Red Line)

Café Deluxe is an intriguing combination of a Parisian bistro with a neighborhood bar. Adults enjoy its eclectic menu, leather booths and mahogany bar and kids can choose from a diverse kid's menu. Additional locations are found in Tyson's Corner, VA, and in Upper Northwest Washington, D.C., near the National Cathedral.

The Original Pancake House (IN)

7703 Woodmont Avenue
Bethesda, MD 20814
301-986-0285
www.ophrestaurants.com
Metro: Bethesda (Red Line)

They serve up delicious pancake specialties, including their famous apple pancake and dutch baby, for breakfast, brunch and lunch. They also have locations in Rockville, MD, and Falls Church, VA.

Stromboli Family Restaurant (IN)

7023 Wisconsin Avenue
Bethesda, MD 20815
301-986-1980
www.strombolisrestaurant.com
Metro: Bethesda (Red Line)

This local classic offers tasty Italian food including a large variety of strombolis and pizzas. Patrons love the retro décor and comfy booths.

Moby Dick's House of Kabob (IN)

7027 Wisconsin Avenue
Bethesda, MD 20815
301-654-1838
www.mobysonline.com
Metro: Bethesda (Red Line)

This local favorite serves up big portions of Persian/Middle Eastern food featuring lamb, beef and chicken kebabs and fresh baked bread.

Bethesda Crab House (E)
4958 Bethesda Avenue
Bethesda, MD 20814
301-652-3382
www.bethesdacrabhouse.net
Metro: Bethesda (Red Line)

This is the place to go when you're ready to get messy enjoying some tasty steamed blue crabs and other seafood delicacies. Customers enjoy using small wooden mallets to get through the crab shells to the sweet crabmeat. They offer a covered outdoor patio and indoor seating and bibs on request. Call in ahead to get large crabs for your feast.

Rockville, MD

Cheeburger Cheeburger (IN)
14921 Shady Grove Road
Rockville, MD 20850
301-309-9555
http://cheeburger.com
Metro: Shady Grove (Red Line)

They offer a wide selection of oversized burgers and sandwiches as well as delicious milkshakes. Kids love the old fashioned soda fountain and neon lights.

La Brasa Latin Cuisine (M)
12401 Parklawn Drive
Rockville, MD 20852
301-468-8850
www.labrasalatincuisine.com
Metro: Twinbrook (Red Line)

Regulars rave about the big portions of Peruvian chicken, lomo saltado and carne asada at this Salvadorean/Peruvian restaurant.

Silver Spring, MD

Tastee Diner (IN)
8601 Cameron Street
Silver Spring, MD 20910
301-589-8171

7731 Woodmont Avenue,
Bethesda, MD 20814
301-652-3970
www.tasteediner.com
Metro: Silver Spring (Red Line) and Bethesda (Red Line)

Tastee Diner has been around since 1935 providing good diner food around the clock in a retro setting. An entertaining wait staff and jukeboxes with classic hits add to the experience.

Jackie's Restaurant (E)
8081 Georgia Avenue
Silver Spring, MD 20910
301-565-9700
www.jackiesrestaurant.com
Metro: Silver Spring (Red Line)

This trendy restaurant offers a diverse selection of delicious, organic American Entrees. The friendly staff serves the food up in a chic warehouse setting with exposed brick walls, roof rafters, handcrafted steelwork and soft pink lighting. Families particularly enjoy family night every Tuesday where children 10 and under eat free from an impressive children's menu until 7:30 PM. Jackie's is open daily for dinner and for Sunday brunch.

Thai at Silver Spring (M)
921 E. Ellsworth Drive
Silver Spring, MD 20910
301-650-0666
www.thaiatsilverspring.com
Metro: Silver Spring (Red Line)

This casual Thai restaurant serves up all your Thai favorites such as Pad Thai, drunken noodles, spring rolls and a variety of curry dishes in the middle of a busy pedestrian zone in Silver Spring. Friendly service and outdoor seating enhance the dining experience.

Mandalay Restaurant and Café (M)
930 Bonifant Street
Silver Spring, MD 20910
301-585-0500
www.mandalayrestaurantcafe.com
Metro: Silver Spring (Red Line)

This moderately priced restaurant is an interesting place to try for fans of Asian foods as it features Burmese cuisine. Customers love the variety of entrees, salads, spices, and desserts and describe the flavorful food as a hybrid of Thai, Indian and Chinese.

Mrs. K's Tollhouse Restaurant (E)
9201 Colesville Road
Silver Spring, MD 20910
301-589-3500
www.mrsks.com
Metro: Silver Spring (Red Line)

A Tudor style former toll house from the early 1900s, Mrs. K's has been serving classic American and international entrees and fine wine since 1930. Patrons enjoy the inn-like feel of the restaurant, which is furnished and decorated with antiques. There are also relaxing gardens around the house to explore.

Wheaton, MD

Nick's Diner (IN)
11199 Veirs Mill Road
Wheaton, MD 20902
301-933-5459
Metro: Wheaton (Red Line)

This local favorite provides classic diner food and Greek specialties for breakfast, brunch and lunch. Patrons love the old-school feel and friendly service. They accept cash payment only.

The Washington, D.C. Cupcake Craze

With the success of the TLC television show *D.C. Cupcakes*, the D.C. area has become a hotspot for cupcake aficionados. There are currently a host of stores around the area to satisfy cupcake fans. Expect lines at some of these locations, especially the two in Georgetown. One tip is to pre-order online to bypass the lines. Here are some local favorites:

Georgetown Cupcake
(Featured in television show *D.C. Cupcakes*)
3301 M Street NW
Washington D.C. 20007
202-333-8448
www.georgetowncupcake.com

Baked and Wired
1052 Thomas Jefferson Street NW
Washington, D.C. 20007
202-333-2500
www.bakedandwired.com

Sticky Fingers Bakery (Vegan)
1370 Park Road NW
Washington, D.C. 20010
202-299-9700
www.stickyfingersbakery.com

Sprinkles Cupcakes

3015 M Street NW
Washington, D.C. 20007
202-450-1610
www.sprinkles.com

Red Velvet Cupcakery

675 E Street NW
Washington, D.C 20004
202-347-7895
www.redvelvetcupcakery.com

Hello Cupcake!

1361 Connecticut Avenue NW 20036
Washington, D.C. 20036
202-861-2253
www.hellocupakeonline.com

Alexandria Cupcake

1022 King Street
Alexandria, VA 22314
703-299-9099
www.alexandriacupcake.com

Best Buns Bread Co.

4010 Campbell Avenue
Arlington, VA 22206
703-578-1500
www.greatamericanrestaurants.com/bestbuns

Curbside Cupcakes

Their mobile "Pinky" truck drives around Capitol Hill and Downtown offering cupcakes to go.
www.curbsidecupcakes.com

PART TWO:
Information About Main Attractions and Scavenger Hunts

In this section, I will provide useful information about the main attractions I recommend visiting combined with scavenger hunts for education and entertainment purposes at each site.

In order to complete the scavenger hunts, participants will have to find information or features onsite, pay attention to the essential information found in this guidebook (by reading it or listening to the group leader summarize some of the information) and/or ask rangers, docents and guides at the sites.

The scavenger hunt questions are coded by general age appropriateness. The questions with no letters next to them are designed for all ages. The "Y" represents a task best suited for children 9 and under. The "TW" represents a hunt question designed for tweens between ages 10-13. The questions marked with a "T" are designed for teenagers and more mature children. These codes are for approximate age categories, which **serve only as general guidelines**. Use your own judgment to decide which questions and tasks would be most interesting and appropriate for the child or children in your group. If the tasks seem too easy or difficult adjust accordingly.

These sections contain the scavenger hunt questions with room for the children to write an answer or indicate that they have completed the task. The page after each scavenger hunt contains a complete answer key with additional information on the attraction.

In my experience, children will have different methods and attitudes toward completing the scavenger hunt. Some kids insist on completing every task and are thrilled to get the answers and finish the hunt at each site. Other children have a great deal of interest in certain sites, but less so at different sites. Some kids like to take frequent breaks while others insist on working without stopping. Some kids love to work with an adult, some with a sibling or friend, and some prefer to complete tasks by themselves. You know the child or children who will be using the scavenger hunt and will quickly be able to gauge how they prefer to use it.

You will also know best when it's time to take a break from the hunt and let the kids explore on their own.

In short, there is no correct method of using the scavenger hunt. Use it in your own preferred method as a helpful tool to enhance your family or group's visit to our nation's capital. It should be educational, sometimes challenging and, ultimately, a fun experience for everyone.

National Mall Memorials and Monuments

Statue of Abraham Lincoln inside Lincoln Memorial.
Courtesy of the National Park Service.

Washington, D.C., is the capital city of the United States of America and, thus, is the location of a wide variety of national monuments and memorials to its most respected civilian and military leaders. There are also many memorials and monuments to the men and women of the U.S. Armed Forces, who fought and sacrificed for their country. These memorials and monuments come in all shapes and sizes and some inspire awe while others evoke sadness and deep contemplation. Most of these treasured sites are open 24 hours a day and elicit a different effect depending upon the amount of visitors, weather, or the time of day you visit.

The major monuments and memorials are operated by the National Park Service and staffed by park rangers. The rangers know their respective monuments and memorials well and they lead regular highlights tours. They will also tell you additional information about their site and help you answer any scavenger hunt questions upon polite request.

WASHINGTON MONUMENT

Address/Contact Information: 15th Street and Constitution Avenue NW, 202-426-6841, www.nps.gov/wamo/index.htm

Closest Metro Station: Smithsonian (Blue/Orange Lines)

Opening Hours/Ticketing: Interior is open 9 AM-5 PM (last tour before 4:45 PM), Memorial Day to Labor Day open 9 AM-10 PM (last tour before 9:45 PM). Timed tickets are required to ascend the monument and should be reserved well in advance, especially for the peak season of April-September. A set amount of same day tickets are available at the Washington Monument Lodge on 15th Street. This visitor center opens at 8:30 AM, but lines for tickets form at 7 AM during the peak season. Use the online reservation system at http://www.recreation.gov or call 877-444-6777 for tickets well in advance of your visit. Visitors can receive tickets in the mail or at the Will Call booth at the Washington Monument Lodge. Each online ticket has a reservation fee of $1.50. No food, drink or gum is permitted in the monument and there is metal detector security.

Essential Info: The Washington Monument dominates the District's skyline and honors the towering figure of the first U.S. President, George Washington. This immense monument was designed by Robert Mills to resemble an Egyptian obelisk. It stands 555 feet tall and is the largest freestanding masonry structure in the world. With visibility of up to 30-40 miles in clear weather, it offers the most impressive view in Washington, D.C., from its observatory level. The monument has a white marble façade supported by granite blocks and wrought iron columns with walls 15 feet thick at the base rising up to only 18 inches thick at the 500 foot level.

Construction on the monument began in 1848, but was halted at 156 feet when money ran out in 1854. The Civil War and a continuing lack of funds further delayed construction until 1876. During this time, critics derisively called the site "the beef depot monument" as cattle grazed unceremoniously around the isolated, unfinished structure. When construction resumed, marble from the original quarry in Maryland and from a different quarry in Massachusetts did not completely match with the original stone, resulting in a clear color distinction between the two sections. The monument was dedicated in 1884 complete with a small aluminum capstone on top.

There is a high-speed elevator to the observatory level at 500 feet, which is a vast improvement over walking the 898 steps to the top. On the elevator descent, visitors can observe some of the 192 memorial stones donated by U.S. states and other foreign and domestic organizations that helped financially support the building of the monument.

Refreshments: There are vendors on 15th Street between Constitution and Pennsylvania Avenues.

Bathroom Facilities: At Washington Monument Lodge on 15th Street and near the corner of 15th Street and Independence Avenue.

Scavenger Hunt:

No code letters-suitable for all ages
Y-designed for young children (under 10)
TW-designed for tweens ages 10-13
T-designed for teenagers

1. Y-Count the number of flags around the monument. What do the flags represent?

2. Spot where the marble changes color on the monument.

3. Why are there flashing red lights near the top of the monument?

4. Y, TW-Lie down and look all the way to the top of the monument.

5. Y-If it's windy, try to stand upright as you lean against the wind.

6. Y-Draw a picture of the Washington Monument.

7. How many steps would you need to climb on foot to get to the top?

8. TW-The monument is built as a huge obelisk. Which ancient civilization (which also built the pyramids) first constructed obelisks?

If you make the ascent to the top of the monument, please complete tasks 9-12:

9. Y-Find the statue of George Washington in the monument.

10. Find the Capitol Building, White House, Jefferson Memorial and Lincoln Memorial from the viewing windows.

11. Find the replica of the aluminum capstone that sits atop the monument.

12. T-Which commemorative stones did you see on the elevator ride down?

WASHINGTON MONUMENT SCAVENGER HUNT ANSWER KEY

No code letters-suitable for all ages
Y-designed for young children (under 10)
TW-designed for tweens ages 10-13
T-designed for teenagers

1. *There are 50 flags representing the 50 states in the USA.*

2. *About 1/3 of the way up the color changes-see essential information section for explanation.*

3. *The flashing red lights are there to warn planes from colliding with the monument.*

4. Y, TW-*Lie down and enjoy this new perspective.*

5. Y-*When it's windy it's a challenge to stand upright against this powerful force.*

6. Y-*You can draw this picture now or later in the day.*

7. *There are 898 steps to the top counting the ramp on the bottom.*

8. TW-*The ancient Egyptians built the pyramids.*

9. Y- *Across from the elevator you ascend to the top, you will see the bronze replica of a famous marble statue of George Washington by Jean-Antoine Houdon.*

10. *You can find each landmark through the viewing windows facing all 4 directions. For reference, use the photographs above each window which clearly mark all landmarks.*

11. *The capstone replica is found in the bookshop/exhibit area, one floor down from the observatory level.*

12. T-*The commemorative stones from states, countries, and other organizations can be seen during a couple stops the ranger makes in the elevator ride down to the base of the monument.*

WORLD WAR II MEMORIAL

Address/Contact Information: 17th Street, between Constitution and Independence Avenues SW, Washington, D.C., 202-619-7222, www.wwiimemorial.com

Closest Metro Station: Smithsonian (Blue/Orange Lines)

Opening Hours/Ticketing: 24 Hours a day. Park Service rangers are available every day 9:30 AM-8 PM

Essential Info: This long overdue memorial was dedicated in 2004 to honor the 16 million U.S. servicemen and women who served during history's largest conflict: World War II. The memorial also honors the heroic supporting efforts of the U.S. public on the home front during this trying time. The memorial was designed by Friedrich St. Florian, who did a masterful job of building a beautiful memorial with a descending center so as not to impede the view on the National Mall from the Lincoln Memorial to the Washington Monument. There are two flagpoles on either side of the entrance with granite and bronze bases with the military service seals of the different branches of the U.S. Armed Forces.

The 56 granite pillars in the memorial represent the U.S. states and territories during the war arranged in order of their entry into the Union. These pillars have wheat and oak wreaths on front and back symbolizing the agricultural and industrial contributions that these states and territories made during the war. There is a central Rainbow Pool celebrating and memorializing World War II veterans that unifies the design elements of the memorial.

Facing the memorial with your back to the Washington Monument there are two ceremonial walls with ramps leading down into the memorial pillars. These walls each have 12 individual bas relief panels sculpted by Ray Kaskey. The right hand side has panels on the wall depicting events in the Atlantic Theater with scenes of pivotal battles against Germany and Italy and from the home front. On the left hand side, there are similar panels on the wall depicting events from the fighting in the Pacific Theater against Japan and from the home front.

There are two large 43-foot tall victory pavilion arches marked Atlantic and Pacific representing the two main theaters of the wars. Major battles in these theaters are carved in the stone below each pavilion. The eagles holding the laurel wreaths in each pavilion symbolize the U.S. victory in both theaters of war. In the middle of the pillars, there is a cluster of 4,048 gold stars with each star honoring 100 Americans killed in the war.

As you exit the memorial through the Pacific Pavilion, the path leads to a visitor center where you can search an electronic register for all military service members who died during the war and other World War II veterans. The park rangers can also give you information on how to add the names of World War II veterans who served into the memorial's electronic register.

Refreshments: If you exit to the right through the Atlantic Pavilion, you can follow the path down toward Constitution Gardens where there is a refreshment kiosk.

Bathroom Facilities: On your left on the National Mall as you exit the memorial walking toward the Reflecting Pool and Lincoln Memorial.

Scavenger Hunt:

No code letters-suitable for all ages
Y-designed for young children (under 10)
TW-designed for tweens ages 10-13
T-designed for teenagers

1. Read the words found on the angled granite block Announcement Stone as you enter the memorial.

2. Y-Find a panel showing machinery or vehicles being built.

3. Going down the right hand ramp find the bas relief panel showing Russian troops and American troops meeting at the Elbe River. TW, T-What country is the Elbe River in and why was this meeting important?

4. Going down the left hand ramp, find the bas relief panel showing people listening to a radio during the war.

5. Find the Atlantic and Pacific pavilions. What do the names of the places around them represent?

6. TW, T-What do the eagles holding a laurel wreath at each pavilion represent?

7. Find the column of your home state.

8. Find the more than 4,000 gold stars in the Freedom Wall-What does each star represent?

9. TW, T-Find the graffiti carving of "Kilroy was here."

WORLD WAR II MEMORIAL SCAVENGER HUNT ANSWER KEY

No code letters-suitable for all ages
Y-designed for young children (under 10)
TW-designed for tweens ages 10-13
T-designed for teenagers

1. *This angled granite block sits at the front of the memorial when you are walking from the Washington Monument. Normally pedestrians take the crosswalk and walk to the left to the center of the monument just off the sidewalk on 17th street. The text places the importance of WW II veterans for the 20th century alongside Washington and Lincoln for the 18th and 19th centuries, respectively.*

2. *Y-There are panels on both walls showing America's massive industrial infrastructure producing machinery, armaments, and vehicles for the war effort.*

3. *This scene is found in the last panel at the end of the ramp heading downhill. TW, T-The Elbe River is located in Germany. This meeting was important because it was the meeting of the American troops (with British and French allies) pushing into Germany from the west with the Russian troops coming from the east. It signaled that the war was nearing its end.*

4. *From the carved dedication you can follow the friezes down the ramp on the left. These carvings depict events during the Pacific campaign including on the home front. In the first panel, the people are listening to a radio when Pearl Harbor was attacked on December 7, 1941, which brought the USA into WW II.*

5. *These names are the major battles fought against the Axis powers in WW II-Germany/Italy in the Atlantic-European Theater and Japan in the Pacific-Asian Theater of the war*

6. *T-The eagle is the symbol of the USA and the laurel wreath is an ancient symbol of victory. These sculptures represent the U.S. victory in both theaters of war.*

7. *The columns represent the states and territories in the USA during WWII.*

8. *Each of the 4,048 stars represents 100 U.S. soldiers who died fighting in World War II. The cost in human lives during World War II was staggering for the United States and all the countries involved.*

9. *TW, T-This interesting drawing of a soldier with a huge nose looking over a wall or fence is found by going to the exit near the Pacific Arch and walking to the right along the back of the monument. You will come to a metal gate and see the graffiti drawing on the granite wall behind it. The story about Kilroy is that a ship inspector named Kilroy had inscribed his name on many of the warships and transports sailors and soldiers were on in WW II. Soldiers and sailors saw his inscriptions and began putting their own "Kilroy was here" graffiti everywhere they went in the war. The drawing of the soldier with the big nose peaking over a wall became the representation of Kilroy.*

LINCOLN MEMORIAL

Address/Contact Information: 23rd Street between Constitution and Independence Avenues SW, 202-426-6841, www.nps.gov/linc

Closest Metro Station: Foggy Bottom (Blue/Orange Lines)-15-minute walk

Opening Hours/Ticketing: 24 Hours a day. Park Service rangers are available every day 9:30 AM-11:30 PM

Essential Info: The inspiring Lincoln Memorial honors the memory of the 16th President of the United States, Abraham Lincoln. Lincoln successfully led the country through its most trying period during the Civil War of 1861-1865 and a grateful nation built this grand memorial to honor him. Henry Bacon designed the memorial based on the Temple of Zeus in Greece. The memorial's 36 Doric pillars represent the states in the Union at the time of Lincoln's death in 1865. In the frieze circling the top of the memorial are the names of the 48 states in the Union at the time of the memorial's dedication in 1922. The names of the states are arranged in the order they entered the Union. Alaska and Hawaii are honored by an inscribed panel installed later at the base of the memorial.

More than 50,000 people attended a momentous dedication ceremony on Memorial Day 1922, including Lincoln's only surviving son, Robert Todd Lincoln. Also attending were President Warren Harding, former President William Taft, hundreds of Civil War veterans, and Dr. Robert Moton, principal of the Tuskegee Institute. The black attendees at the event were required to sit in a separate section during the ceremony because of Washington, D.C.'s segregation laws of the time.

The 19-foot seated statue of Lincoln on a throne, sculpted by Daniel Chester French, is one of the most famous statues in the United States. French studied photographs of Lincoln and actual casts of his hands to make the statue as realistic as possible. The final product was sculpted from 28 separate pieces of Georgian marble that were transported from his Massachusetts studio and assembled here on a grand pedestal. French portrays Lincoln's hands resting on the Roman Fasces (bundled birch rods), which symbolize the authority of the federal republic in the United States.

Above Lincoln's head you can read the art historian Royal Cortissoz's moving words carved into the wall: "In this temple, as in the hearts of the people for whom he saved the Union the memory of Abraham Lincoln is enshrined forever.

Lincoln's two most famous speeches-the 2nd Inaugural Address and the Gettysburg Address-are carved on the interior walls of the memorial. In the first column of Lincoln's second inaugural address, the word "Future" was initially misspelled as "Euture," before being repaired as much as possible by the carver. The murals above the speeches are by Jules Guerin and represent North-South unity and the freeing of the slaves, respectively.

Take the time to walk around to the rear of the memorial for a beautiful view of the Memorial Bridge symbolically linking North and South as it connects the Lincoln Memorial with Arlington National Cemetery, the former plantation home of Confederate General Robert E. Lee.

Two notable Civil Rights events occurred at the Lincoln Memorial. Renowned opera soprano Marian Anderson performed an Easter concert here in 1939 at the invitation of First Lady Eleanor Roosevelt. The black singer had earlier been prevented from singing at nearby Constitution Hall by the Daughters of the American Revolution organization. Martin Luther King, Jr. gave his famous "I Have a Dream" speech from the steps of the memorial during the 1963 March on Washington for Jobs and Freedom. This event took place on the 100th anniversary of Lincoln's Emancipation Proclamation, which freed the slaves in the rebellious states.

There are additional exhibits and interesting photographs in the museum area underneath concerning the historic gatherings at the memorial as well as the construction and dedication of the memorial.

The **Lincoln Memorial Reflecting Pool** powerfully reflects images of the Washington Monument and Lincoln Memorial in its shallow waters. The reflecting pool was also designed by Henry Bacon and was constructed after the dedication of the Lincoln Memorial. Its rectangular shape stretches 2,029 feet toward the World War II Memorial with a width of about 167 feet. Its deepest point is only about 30 inches at the center of the pool. Many well-known movies feature scenes here such as *Forrest Gump,* and *Night at the Museum II: Battle of the Smithsonian.* The reflecting pool was drained in the fall of 2010 for renovations through the fall of 2012.

Refreshments: There is a refreshment kiosk located on the road to the left when you are facing the Lincoln Memorial. There is another refreshment kiosk on Henry Bacon Drive across the street from the entrance to the Vietnam Veterans Memorial.

Bathroom Facilities: In the museum located at the beginning of the stairs on the left side of the memorial.

Scavenger Hunt:

No code letters-suitable for all ages
Y-designed for young children (under 10)
TW-designed for tweens ages 10-13
T-designed for teenagers

1.   Which bill and coin have the Lincoln Memorial on their flip sides?

2.   Find the name of your home state on the top of the memorial.

3.   Y, TW-Count the number of steps all the way to the top.

4.   Find the U.S. Capitol from the top step.

5.   TW, T-What two famous speeches are inscribed on the walls?

6.   T-Find the mural signifying the freeing of the slaves.

7.   Find the initially misspelled word in the first column of the 2nd Inaugural Address.

8.   Find the spot on the steps where Martin Luther King, Jr. gave his "I Have a Dream" speech in 1963. What was his dream?

9.   T-Ask a ranger about a special singing of "God Bless America" here in 1939.

10. Go around to the back of the memorial for a special view of the Potomac River and Memorial Bridge.

LINCOLN MEMORIAL SCAVENGER HUNT ANSWER KEY

No code letters-suitable for all ages
Y-designed for young children (under 10)
TW-designed for tweens ages 10-13
T-designed for teenagers

1. *Hold up the back of a penny and a five dollar bill to see the Lincoln Memorial.*

2. *The names of 48 states are inscribed on each side of the memorial at the top. Your state could be on any of the sides. Alaska and Hawaii are represented by a plaque at the beginning of the steps up to the memorial.*

3. *Y, TW-From the road level there are 57 steps and from the Reflecting Pool there are 98. An approximate count is fine!*

4. *The Capitol is directly across the National Mall in line with the Washington Monument.*

5. *TW, T-On the left side of the memorial is the Gettysburg Address, on the right side is Lincoln's Second Inaugural Address*

6. *T-There are two murals by Jules Guerin over the two inscribed speeches. The one located above the Gettysburg Address represents the freeing of the slaves, while the mural above the 2nd Inaugural Address represents the restoration of the union.*

7. *The word future was mistakenly carved as euture. The word is in the beginning of the second paragraph toward the right. The carver realized his mistake soon thereafter and corrected it as best he could, but the original mistake can still be seen.*

8. *Martin Luther King, Jr. gave his "I Have a Dream" speech in the middle of the landing before the final group of steps at the top of the memorial. Dr. King was the final speaker at the August 28, 1963 March on Washington for Jobs and Freedom, a pivotal event of the Civil Rights movement. In his speech, King spoke forcefully about his dream that his children would grow up in a country where they would be judged by the content of their character rather than the color of their skin. The spot where King stood was engraved in 2003 in recognition of the 40th anniversary of the event.*

9. *T-Famed black concert singer Marian Anderson was not allowed to sing at a performance at nearby Constitution Hall by the Daughters of the American Revolution because of her race. When First Lady Eleanor Roosevelt heard this news she cancelled her membership in that organization and organized a special Easter Sunday concert at the Lincoln Memorial featuring Ms. Anderson.*

10. *Take the time to walk around the memorial to see a beautiful view of the Memorial Bridge, Potomac River and Arlington National Cemetery. The Memorial Bridge symbolically represents the union between the North and South as it connects the Lincoln Memorial with the former Confederate state of Virginia and Confederate General Robert E. Lee's former home-now the site of Arlington National Cemetery.*

KOREAN WAR VETERANS MEMORIAL

Address/Contact Information: Independence Avenue SW across from Lincoln Memorial, 202-619-7222, www.nps.gov/kwvm

Closest Metro Station: Foggy Bottom (Blue/Orange Lines)

Opening Hours/Ticketing: 24 Hours a day. Park Service rangers are available every day 9:30 AM-11:30 PM.

Essential Info: This memorial honors the United States service personnel who fought in the Korean War from 1950-1953 alongside South Korean and United Nations forces against communist North Korea and China. The memorial was dedicated in 1995 by President Bill Clinton and South Korean President Kim Young Sam on the 42nd anniversary of the armistice that halted the war.

Frank Gaylord designed this visually appealing memorial which features the realistic scene of nineteen 7-foot tall steel servicemen on patrol. These men represent all branches of the military and are pictured patrolling in rainy weather somewhere in the wooded hills of Korea. The men wear uniforms and carry weapons and equipment authentic to the time. Some of the men appear to be talking to one another, but they all are on alert scanning different directions as they patrol. Gaylord sculpted their faces to reflect the main ethnicities who served in the war. The men's faces also look stressed and weary and their ponchos are billowing into a stiff wind as they march. Their reflection against the black granite wall doubles their number to 38, which is symbolic of the 38th parallel, the longitude that serves as the border between the two Koreas. This line was crossed by North Korea on June 25, 1950, to begin the war. After years of bloody fighting an armistice was signed, which established this line as the border, where it tenuously remains to this day. No formal treaty to end the war or to define permanent boundaries has ever been signed.

Walking along the path toward the wall, you will see the names of the 22 United Nations countries who participated in the war. The 164-foot polished black granite wall features laser etchings based on photographs of real U.S. servicemen and women who served in the conflict with a focus on support personnel. The 19 figures on patrol honor the frontline troops. On the east end of this wall there is an inscription that emphasizes the cost, purpose and unfortunate necessity of the war stating simply, "Freedom is not Free." The casualty figures of the U.S., South Korean and United Nations forces inscribed near the Pool of Remembrance reflect the terrible price of this conflict.

Refreshments: There is a refreshment kiosk located on the road to the left of the Lincoln Memorial.

Bathroom Facilities: In the lower area of the Lincoln Memorial.

Scavenger Hunt:

No code letters-suitable for all ages
Y-designed for young children (under 10)
TW-designed for tweens ages 10-13
T-designed for teenagers

1. Count the steel soldiers at the memorial. Do they look normal height?

2. Point out some of the different types of equipment they have. Why are they looking in different directions?

3. Y, TW-Touch a soldier's face that is etched on the black granite wall. Why do they look so real?

4. T-Was a formal treaty ever signed to officially end the Korean War?

5. Find the words "Freedom is not Free." What does this mean to you?

KOREAN WAR VETERANS MEMORIAL SCAVENGER HUNT ANSWER KEY

No code letters-suitable for all ages
Y-designed for young children (under 10)
TW-designed for tweens ages 10-13
T-designed for teenagers

1. *There are 19 soldiers representing the various U.S. service branches. The soldiers each stand 7 feet tall.*

2. *The soldiers are carrying weapons (rifles, mortars, machine guns) and equipment (radios, shovels, etc.) that soldiers used during the war. They are on patrol looking in different directions to guard against attack from those directions.*

3. *Y, TW-The 2,400 laser etched images are made from photos of actual service personnel during the war.*

4. *T-An armistice was signed in 1953 that ceased hostilities, but no official treaty to end the conflict has ever been signed. The 38th Parallel remains a tense, heavily mined and guarded border with thousands of soldiers stationed on both sides. The United States still has more than 37,000 troops stationed in South Korea.*

5. *This statement about the cost, purpose and unfortunate necessity of war is something to reflect on for adults and children.*

VIETNAM VETERANS MEMORIAL

Address/Contact Information: Constitution Avenue & Henry Bacon Drive NW, 202-634-1568, www.nps.gov/vive

Closest Metro Station: Foggy Bottom (Blue/Orange Lines)

Opening Hours/Ticketing: 24 Hours a day. Park Service rangers are available every day 8 AM-12 AM

Essential Info: The Vietnam Veterans Memorial was opened in 1982 and contains the names of more than 58,000 US servicemen who were killed or are still missing in action from the Vietnam War. Vietnam Veteran Jan Scruggs led the effort to raise private funds for the memorial in the late 1970s. Yale architect student Maya Lin's design is a V-shaped black granite wall with the inscribed names listed in chronological order by the day they were killed or went missing from 1959-1975. Known as "the Wall," it reaches its peak height of more than 10 feet in the middle corresponding to the late 1960s when the war was raging and casualties soared. Reference books near the entrance contain a list of the names inscribed on the Wall and instructions on how to find them.

Frederick Hart's sculpture called "Three Servicemen" was added in 1984 to meet the wishes of some veterans who disliked the Wall's foreboding appearance. The Three Servicemen honors all the servicemen who fought in the War and is notable for its attention to detail and its depiction of the three main races who served in the conflict. The servicemen's gazes look toward the Wall in solidarity with their lost brothers-in-arms. In 1993, Glenna Goodacre's moving statue of three field hospital nurses attending to wounded soldiers was added to honor the women who served in Vietnam.

Refreshments: There is a refreshment kiosk on Henry Bacon Drive across the street from the beginning of the Vietnam Veterans Memorial.

Bathroom Facilities: In the lower area of the Lincoln Memorial.

Scavenger Hunt:

No code letters-suitable for all ages
Y-designed for young children (under 10)
TW-designed for tweens ages 10-13
T-designed for teenagers

1. Find the statue of three soldiers. What do you notice about their faces? Where are they looking?

2. TW, T-Look up a name in the book and find it on the Wall. What does their name on the Wall represent? Why do some of the names have crosses next to them?

3. Look at your reflection in the Wall. Can you see the names in your reflection?

4. Y, TW-List some of the items you see at the base of the Wall honoring the fallen soldiers. What would you place there to honor them?

5. Ask a ranger or volunteer to help you do a rubbing of one of the names.

6. Find the statue honoring the women who served in Vietnam.

VIETNAM VETERANS MEMORIAL SCAVENGER HUNT ANSWER KEY

No code letters-suitable for all ages
Y-designed for young children (under 10)
TW-designed for tweens ages 10-13
T-designed for teenagers

1. *The statue represents the three main races of the US soldiers who fought in the war-White, African American, and Hispanic. They honor the men who served in Vietnam and are looking at the Wall where the names of their lost brothers in arms are inscribed.*

2. TW, T-*The vast majority of the names represent men who were killed in action, which is represented by a diamond after the name. Approximately 1,300 names have a cross after them representing that they are considered Missing in Action or a Prisoner of War.*

3. *Many people find the impact of seeing their own reflection among the thousands of names quite moving.*

4. Y, TW-*Visitors often find flags, letters, stuffed animals and other items of affection from loved ones. Please respect these items.*

5. *Rangers and volunteers will supply you with paper and a pencil for rubbings, but please be respectful of the name and what it represents.*

6. *This statue is located down the path to the right among the trees as you walk out of the Wall area away from the Lincoln Memorial.*

Tidal Basin Memorials and Monuments

T he Tidal Basin is a man-made lake located to the south of the National Mall. It acts as an overflow catch basin when the water in the Potomac River rises, helping to prevent extensive flooding of the National Mall. This area is particularly beautiful during the early spring as the cherry trees lining the Tidal Basin are in full bloom.

WASHINGTON, D.C. MARTIN LUTHER KING, JR. NATIONAL MEMORIAL

Address/Contact Information: 1964 Independence Avenue SW, 202-376-6704, www.nps.gov/mlkm

Closest Metro Station: Smithsonian (Blue/Orange Lines)

Opening Hours/Ticketing: 24 Hours a day. Park Service rangers are available every day 9:30 AM-11:30 PM.

Essential Info: This memorial was dedicated in fall 2011 and honors the famed Civil Rights leader, orator and advocate of non-violent change, Dr. Martin Luther King, Jr. The four-acre memorial site is located on a direct line between the Lincoln Memorial and the Jefferson Memorial. This site was selected to emphasize the leadership connection between Jefferson's Declaration of Independence, Lincoln's efforts to protect the Union and free the slaves, and King's mission to guarantee civil rights for all citizens.

Visitors enter the memorial through a narrow path cut through a huge boulder known as the *Mountain of Despair*, which symbolizes the struggles Dr. King endured throughout his life. Entering into the smooth plaza, visitors will see a large stone section cut from the boulder, which is called the *Stone of Hope*. On the first side of the stone, King's famous words from a 1963 speech are inscribed: "Out of the mountain of despair a stone of hope." On the other side there is an inscribed passage taken from a statement of how King wanted to be remembered: "I was a drum major for justice, peace and righteousness." A huge statue of Dr. King by Chinese sculptor, Lei Yixin, rises out of one side of the 30- foot tall stone. The statue has provoked controversy because of its large scale which makes seeing King's face difficult, its portrayal of King with his arms crossed, which some see as confrontational, and because the chosen sculptor was not American.

Fourteen of Dr. King's most memorable quotes are inscribed on the 450-foot crescent shaped Inscription Wall. A committee determined that these selected quotes were the most representative of his universal message of justice, democracy, hope and love. The designers planted 182 cherry trees and many crape myrtle trees in the memorial area for added beauty.

Refreshments: Refreshment kiosks are located near the Lincoln Memorial.

Bathroom Facilities: There are bathrooms at the beginning and end of the Franklin Delano Roosevelt Memorial.

Scavenger Hunt:

No code letters-suitable for all ages
Y-designed for young children (under 10)
TW-designed for tweens ages 10-13
T-designed for teenagers

1. Touch the *Mountain of Despair* as you walk through it.

2. How tall is the *Stone of Hope*?

3. Where did King give his "I Have a Dream" speech?

4. TW, T-How old was King when he was assassinated?

5. Find and read the inscriptions of King's quotes on the Inscription Wall. Which inscription of King's words do you find the most powerful?

WASHINGTON, D.C. MARTIN LUTHER KING, JR. NATIONAL MEMORIAL SCAVENGER HUNT ANSWER KEY

No code letters-suitable for all ages
Y-designed for young children (under 10)
TW-designed for tweens ages 10-13
T-designed for teenagers

1. *The "Mountain of Despair" is the huge boulder you walk through when you enter the memorial.*

2. *The "Stone of Hope" is about 30 feet tall.*

3. *King gave his famous "I Have a Dream" speech on the steps of the nearby Lincoln Memorial on August 28, 1963.*

4. *TW, T-Dr. King was only 39 years old when he was assassinated in Memphis, TN, on April 4, 1968.*

5. *There are 14 notable quotes from Dr. King on the Inscription Wall.*

FRANKLIN DELANO ROOSEVELT MEMORIAL

Address/Contact Information: 1850 West Basin Drive SW, 202-376-6704, www.nps.gov/fdrm

Closest Metro Station: Smithsonian (Blue/Orange Lines)

Opening Hours/Ticketing: 24 Hours a day. Park Service rangers are available every day 9:30 AM-11:30 PM.

Essential Info: This massive memorial to the nation's longest serving president, Franklin Delano Roosevelt (FDR), is more than 300 yards long. The memorial was designed by Lawrence Halprin and dedicated in 1997. Interestingly, FDR had asked only for a monument as big as his desk in front of the National Archives. This little noticed monument is still there today.

Halprin made the memorial out of red granite to resemble FDR's Hyde Park, NY, home and installed waterfalls to evoke FDR's many trips to Warm Springs, GA, for polio therapy as well as his service as Secretary of the Navy. At the beginning of the memorial, a statue of FDR in his wheelchair was added to show FDR as he normally appeared in private. After contracting polio at age 39, FDR never walked unaided again. FDR feared that the U.S. public and foreign allies and enemies would associate his disease with weakness, so he took steps to conceal his condition throughout his presidency. The president strictly controlled photographs of himself in his wheelchair. In public speeches he braced himself against the speaking rostrum and was primarily photographed sitting in cars or chairs. A model of his wheelchair is in the visitor center.

In the main area of the memorial, there are four outdoor "rooms" chronologically representing FDR's four terms as President. There are inspirational excerpts from FDR's speeches during his presidency inscribed on the granite walls. FDR was elected in the middle of economic uncertainty in the Great Depression where banks failed and there was 25% unemployment. He immediately offered a "New Deal for the American people" in the form of new government agencies and programs designed to offer jobs and assistance. He also addressed and reassured the American public on radio regularly in what became known as "fireside chats." A statue of a breadline for the poor and of Americans intently listening to a radio recalls this difficult time. A nearby waterfall represents the hydropower created by the Tennessee Valley Authority (TVA) and images on the walls and poles represent other New Deal work programs such as the Civilian Conservation Corps (CCC) and Works Progress Administration (WPA). Many of the public work projects constructed during this time included bridges, roads, dams, and theaters that still stand today. These programs also produced many excellent examples of public artwork.

In the next room is an impressive statue of a seated FDR with his beloved Scottish Terrier, Fala. Fala's ears are shiny because of the many hands that have touched them.

In addition to harsh economic challenges at home, FDR also faced the monumental challenge of leading the country through World War II. The broken rocks in the third room symbolize the devastation of war. In his 1941 State of the Union Address, as the nation prepared for war, President Franklin D. Roosevelt spelled out the "Four Freedoms" as a reminder of what was at stake in fighting the war. These four freedoms are inscribed on a wall in the last room. Roosevelt was elected to an unheard of 4th term in 1944, but died in office in April 1945 shortly before the end of the war. A wall engraving of FDR's funeral caisson captures the overwhelming sadness the nation felt upon losing their beloved, long-serving President. FDR served 12 years as president, a feat that will never be matched after the passage of the 22nd Amendment, which limits presidents to two 4-year terms in office.

In the last room there is also a statue of Eleanor Roosevelt, the only first lady honored at a presidential memorial. She revolutionized the role of first lady as a campaigner and advocate of political positions and was often the face and "legs" (her description) of the president because of his limited mobility. She later became the first United States Representative to the United Nations. First Lady Eleanor Roosevelt was a strong advocate for civil and human rights throughout her life.

Refreshments: Bottled water is available in visitor center.

Bathroom Facilities: At the beginning and end of the memorial.

Scavenger Hunt:

No code letters-suitable for all ages
Y-designed for young children (under 10)
TW-designed for tweens ages 10-13
T-designed for teenagers

1. Find the statue of FDR in his wheelchair. What disease did he suffer from?

2. TW, T-Why didn't FDR go out in public or let his picture be taken in his wheelchair?

3. Y-Find a replica of FDR's wheelchair in the visitor center.

4. TW, T-Stand in line at the breadline. What was the name of the economic event that happened that caused people to be so poor?

5. T-What were some of the "New Deal" programs called?

6. Y-Put your hand in one of the handprints of the working hands of America found on the columns.

7. Y, TW-Find the statue of FDR's dog and pet him. What type of dog was he and what was his name?

8. Find the biggest waterfall in the memorial.

9. What was the name of FDR's wife? Find her statue. Why are her hands so shiny?

10. TW, T-Find and read the "Four Freedoms," which FDR said people should enjoy throughout the world.

11. T-How many times was FDR elected President? Which amendment prohibits this from happening now?

FRANKLIN DELANO ROOSEVELT MEMORIAL SCAVENGER HUNT ANSWER KEY

No code letters-suitable for all ages
Y-designed for young children (under 10)
TW-designed for tweens ages 10-13
T-designed for teenagers

1. *The statue is to the right at the front of the memorial across from the gift shop. FDR contracted polio at 39 years of age. He could never walk again without the aid of crutches or a cane and got around normally in a wheelchair.*

2. TW, T-*FDR lived in an age when disabilities were considered a sign of weakness. He didn't want his political opponents at home or his enemies abroad to see him as weak. He was often photographed standing at podiums or sitting in chairs.*

3. Y-*The replica is displayed in the first room you enter.*

4. TW, T-*The Great Depression was an economic disaster that devastated the U.S. and much of the world economy starting with a stock market crash in the U.S. in 1929 and did not end until the outbreak of World War II in 1939. Unemployment rose to 25% in the U.S. As a result of these economic conditions, many people were forced to live off of the charity of others and many had to stand in breadlines for food.*

5. T-*Some well-known programs were the Civilian Conservation Corps (CCC) and the Public Works Administration (PWA), which put people to work building bridges, roads, parks, buildings, and dams and other public works projects. They also commissioned artists to produce public art such as murals, statues, and reliefs on buildings.*

6. Y-*These handprints represent the hands of the working people employed by New Deal programs.*

7. Y, TW-*Fala was a black Scottish Terrier.*

8. *It is either the TVA waterfall or the waterfall in the last room.*

9. *Eleanor Roosevelt was a groundbreaking first lady. She served as FDR's "legs" by representing him at many official events and by boosting morale among citizens and the troops. She also served as the first United States Ambassador to the United Nations, which was formed after World War II. Her hands are shiny because of people constantly touching them when they visit.*

10. TW, T-*FDR articulated the Four Freedoms in his State of the Union Address in Jan. 1941. They are: Freedom of Speech and Expression, Freedom of Worship, Freedom from Want, and Freedom from Fear. Famous American artist Norman Rockwell painted a representation of each Freedom in his Four Freedoms paintings series in 1943.*

11. T-*FDR was elected to President 4 times, serving 3 full terms and the beginning of a fourth before his death in April 1945. The 22nd amendment, passed in 1947, limits presidents to two 4-year terms.*

CHERRY TREES

Address/Contact Information: Located primarily around the Tidal Basin and in East Potomac Park SW, 202-426-6841, www.nationalcherryblossomfestival.org

Closest Metro Station: Smithsonian (Blue/Orange Lines)

Opening Hours/Ticketing: 24 Hours a day

Essential Info: The Mayor of Tokyo, Japan, gave 3,000 cherry trees to the United States in 1912 to foster good relations between the two countries. First Lady Helen Taft and the Japanese Ambassador's wife planted the first two trees on the banks of the Tidal Basin to symbolize and promote lasting friendship between the two countries. A ceremonial plaque marks this spot near the end of 17th Street, NW. The rest of the trees were planted nearby and in East Potomac Park. The main tree is the Yoshino variety, which produces a mainly white blossom, while the Akebono and Kwanzan varieties have the more famous pink blossoms. The peak blossom time is normally in the early spring. The combination of white and pink and the abundance of the blossoms against the backdrop of the Tidal Basin and memorials make a stunningly beautiful setting. Visitors from around the world come to enjoy this sight and participate in the annual National Cherry Blossom Festival, which started in 1935.

The older trees become thicker and bent with age and have gnarled branches and holes where squirrels and starlings nest. There are only a few original trees left.

At the end of the FDR Memorial, among the cherry trees, you will find an ancient stone Japanese pagoda. This 3,800 pound pagoda is thought to be from the Kamakura period of the 13th and 14th century and was a private gift from the Mayor of Yokohama to former District Commissioner Renah Camalier in 1957. The commissioner felt the gift belonged to the people and had it placed with the cherry trees for public display. In 1958 it was rededicated as a gift to all the people of the District of Columbia

Scavenger Hunt:

No code letters-suitable for all ages
Y-designed for young children (under 10)
TW-designed for tweens ages 10-13
T-designed for teenagers

1. When were the cherry trees first planted?

2. T-What is the main type of tree?

3. Find the Japanese pagoda near the exit of the FDR Memorial.

4. Find thicker, bent trees. Why do they look like this?

5. Find a knot/hole in a tree where starlings can nest.

6. Y-See if you can find a black squirrel at any point while walking on the Mall or near the Tidal Basin.

CHERRY TREES SCAVENGER HUNT ANSWER KEY

No code letters-suitable for all ages
Y-designed for young children (under 10)
TW-designed for tweens ages 10-13
T-designed for teenagers

1. *The cherry trees were a gift from the Mayor of Tokyo, Japan in 1912.*

2. T-*The main type of cherry tree is called Yoshino.*

3. *The pagoda is located at the end of the FDR Memorial heading toward the Jefferson Memorial.*

4. *The thick, gnarled trees are the oldest and contrast sharply with the thin, straight younger trees. A few of the oldest date back to the original group planted in 1912.*

5. *In the older trees, one can find many holes where starlings and squirrels nest.*

6. Y-*The black squirrels you might see in the Washington, D.C., area originated from a group of Canadian black squirrels that were released at the National Zoo in 1902. Keep your eyes open as you occasionally see some of them near the monuments and memorials.*

THOMAS JEFFERSON MEMORIAL

Address/Contact Information: South end of 15th Street SW on Tidal Basin, 202-426-6841, www.nps.gov/thje

Closest Metro Station: Smithsonian (Blue/Orange Lines)

Opening Hours/Ticketing: 24 Hours a day. Park Service rangers are available every day 9:30 AM-11:30 PM.

Essential Info: This picturesque memorial to the third president was dedicated in 1943 on the 200th anniversary of Jefferson's birth. John Russell Pope designed it in a classical style using a rotunda and 26 Ionic columns to evoke both the Pantheon in Rome as well as Jefferson's self-designed Monticello, Virginia, home. The 26 columns equal the number of states in the country at the end of Jefferson's presidency in 1809. President Franklin Roosevelt laid the Vermont marble cornerstone in 1939 with copies of the Declaration of Independence and the U.S. Constitution placed inside. During his presidency, Jefferson and the Congress negotiated the Louisiana Purchase with France, which added a huge amount of land to the United States in 1803. Stones from two states that eventually came from this purchase, Missouri and Minnesota, were used extensively in the construction of the memorial to honor this achievement.

The 19-foot high bronze statue of Jefferson was sculpted by Rudolph Evans and weighs five tons. The statue represents the Age of Enlightenment and Jefferson's prominent role as a philosopher, statesman, and champion of democratic principles. The statue features Jefferson holding a scroll (some say it's a copy of the Declaration of Independence) in his left hand as he addresses the Continental Congress. The memorial is positioned with Jefferson looking directly at the oval office in the White House. President Roosevelt asked the designers to maintain a clear view of the memorial from the White House for inspiration. Legend now says Jefferson is keeping a close eye on all future presidents. Because of wartime restrictions on metals, the original statue was made of plaster until its bronze replacement was installed in 1947.

On the walls of the rotunda there are excerpts from Jefferson's important writings including the Declaration of Independence and the Act for Religious Freedom, which represent some of his core principles. Above the main entrance is a marble pediment by Adolph Weinman called *The Drafting of the Declaration of Independence*, which features a standing Jefferson flanked by the four other committee members selected by the Continental Congress to write this powerful document in 1776 in Philadelphia. Benjamin Franklin and John Adams sit to Jefferson's left, while Roger Sherman and Robert Livingston sit to Jefferson's right.

There are additional exhibits and information on Jefferson's life and lasting influence in the gift shop area.

Refreshments: Snack vendors are sometimes located on paths leading to the memorial. There is also a refreshment kiosk at the paddle boat rental area located diagonally across the tidal basin.

Bathroom Facilities: In the lower section of the memorial.

Scavenger Hunt:

No code letters-suitable for all ages
Y-designed for young children (under 10)
TW-designed for tweens ages 10-13
T-designed for teenagers

1. Y-Count the columns around the memorial.

2. T-What famous building in Rome is this memorial modeled after?

3. What famous revolutionary document did Jefferson primarily write?

4. What famous residence is Jefferson directly looking at and why?

5. TW, T-Why was the first Jefferson statue made out of plaster and later replaced in bronze?

6. Find the marble sculpture above the entryway honoring the committee that drafted the Declaration of Independence with Jefferson. TW, T-Can you identify anyone besides Jefferson? Where and when was this document drafted and signed?

THOMAS JEFFERSON MEMORIAL SCAVENGER HUNT ANSWER KEY

No code letters-suitable for all ages
Y-designed for young children (under 10)
TW-designed for tweens ages 10-13
T-designed for teenagers

1. Y-*There are 26 columns matching the number of states at the end of Jefferson's presidency in 1809.*

2. T-*The Pantheon in Rome.*

3. *Thomas Jefferson was the main author of the Declaration of Independence.*

4. *The statue of Jefferson is staring at the White House. President Roosevelt wanted to preserve a clear view of the memorial from the White House for inspiration. Legend now says Jefferson is keeping an eye on the current occupant to make sure he is performing his duties well.*

5. TW, T-*The statue was made in plaster in 1943 because of wartime restrictions on the use of metal. Its bronze replacement is 19-feet tall and weighs 5 tons.*

6. *The sculpture is above the entryway.* TW, T-*Jefferson is in the middle with Benjamin Franklin and John Adams to his left and Roger Sherman and Robert Livingston to his right. The document was drafted and signed in Philadelphia during the summer of 1776.*

Federal Government

The White House decorated for Christmas. Courtesy of Destination DC.

As the capital of the United States, Washington, D.C., contains the iconic structures housing the federal government's three main branches: Executive, Legislative and Judicial. It also is the home of many massive neoclassical and modern office buildings serving as the headquarters for the various departments, agencies and organizations, which administer and support the tasks and duties of the federal government.

WHITE HOUSE AND LAFAYETTE SQUARE PARK AREA

Address/Contact Information: 1600 Pennsylvania Avenue NW, Visitor Center located at 1450 Pennsylvania Avenue, NW, 202-208-1631, www.whitehouse.gov

Closest Metro Station: McPherson Square and Federal Triangle (Blue/ Orange Lines), Metro Center (Blue/Orange Lines and Red Line)

Opening Hours/Ticketing: The White House Visitor Center is open 7:30 AM-4 PM.

Essential Info: The White House is one of the defining locations of Washington, D.C., and is both the home and office of the President of the United States. The White House was designed by Irish-born architect Thomas Hoban and finished in 1800. Originally known as the President's House it has served as the home and office for every president except George Washington. The White House has 132 rooms including 35 bathrooms. The house sits on 18 acres of grounds and occupies approximately 55,000 square feet. The president and his family reside on the second and third floors. For most visitors, a look at this beautiful mansion from the outside is well worth the trip.

In order to take a tour of the White House interior, you must contact one of your elected congressional representatives well in advance to get tickets. You will be required to submit personal information for security purposes.

The public tour of the interior includes the ground floor with the Library, Vermeil Room, China Room and the Diplomatic Reception Room. The tour also covers the first floor with the largest room in the White House known as the East Room, the Green, Blue, and Red Rooms and the State Dining Room. Also, be sure to take a look at the magnificent Grand Staircase near the East Room. The president and first lady, accompanied by official guests, descend on this staircase from the residence area to attend state dinners in the East Room. The artwork, furnishings and decorations in the White House are beautiful and provide insight into each president and his family.

The residence area on the two upstairs floors, the Oval Office, and other rooms for guests such as the Lincoln Bedroom are off limits to the public. If you couldn't secure a tour of the interior, go to www.whitehouse.gov for a virtual tour and more information. Whether you take an interior tour or not, I recommend a visit to the **White House Visitor Center** described below.

The **Eisenhower Executive Office Building**, formerly the Old Executive Office Building, is a huge granite Second Empire style office building located next to the White House at 17th Street and Pennsylvania Avenue, NW. This 1888 building's exterior architecture was designed by Alfred Mullet, with interior decorative elements and a modern fireproof cast-iron structure designed by Richard von Ezdorf. It was built to provide office space for some of the various agencies making up the Executive Office of the President and originally housed the Departments of State, War and Navy. The building currently contains the Office of the Vice President, the National Security Council, and parts of the Office of Management and Budget. Public tours are available on Saturday mornings with advance reservations. Call the Preservation Office at 202-395-5895 on Tuesday or Wednesday between 9 AM and 12 PM and be prepared to provide confidential personal information (legal name, citizenship, Social Security Number, and date of birth) for each visitor for security purposes.

The **Blair House** is a Federal Style townhouse built in 1824, which is located at 1651 Pennsylvania Avenue. The house serves as an official state guest residence for foreign visitors. Puerto Rican Nationalists tried to assassinate President Truman, while he was living here during White House renovations in 1950. Tragically, a White House police officer was killed in the gunfight along with one of the two assassins.

Lafayette Square Park is a seven-acre public park located north across from the White House designed by Andrew Jackson Downing in 1851. The park features four corner statues of foreign military advisors who assisted and trained Continental Army forces during the Revolutionary War. The four men honored are: General Marquis Gilbert de Lafayette and Major General Comte Jean de Rochambeau of France, General Thaddeus Kosciuszko of Poland, and Major General Baron Friederich Wilhelm von Steuben from Prussia. In the center of the park is an equestrian statue of President Andrew Jackson erected in 1853. The statue was made out of melted down cannons from the War of 1812 and sculpted by Clark Mills. The park is surrounded by beautiful houses as it was a fashionable residential area in the 19th Century. The park is now a frequent site of political demonstrations because of its proximity to the White House.

Located on the northwest corner of Lafayette Square Park is **Decatur House.** Commodore Stephen Decatur, famous and wealthy from his victories in the War of 1812 and the Barbary Wars, bought land on the northwest corner of Lafayette Square and commissioned famous architect Benjamin Henry Latrobe to build a fine home for entertaining. Latrobe built a classic three-story Federal style building made out of brick in 1818. The Decaturs entertained Washington society at the house until Commodore Decatur's death in a duel in 1820.

After Decatur's death, his wife Susan moved to Georgetown and rented the house to a succession of Secretary of States until the house was purchased by tavern and hotel owner, John Gadsby, owner of Gadsby's Tavern in Alexandria. A series of politicians and diplomats rented rooms in the house until it was purchased by General Edward Beale in 1872. The Beale family owned it for 84 years before bequeathing it to the National Trust for Historic Preservation in 1956. The house has been open to the public since the early 1960s.

Decatur House is located at 740 Jackson Place, NW. As of fall 2011, the house is currently undergoing renovations and closed for tours. The museum gift shop will remain open during the renovations Monday-Friday from 10 AM-5 PM. For more information go to www.decaturhouse. org or call 202-842-0915.

St. John's Church, known as "the Church of the Presidents," sits to the north of Lafayette Square Park at 16th and H Streets, NW. The yellow colored stucco-brick church has a beautiful golden cupola and dome and a 1,000-pound bell in the steeple cast by Paul Revere's son, Joseph. This still active Episcopal Church was built in 1816 by Benjamin Latrobe and was the place of worship for President James Madison and five succeeding presidents, who made the brief walk over from the White House. All the presidents worshipped in Pew 54, which was then set aside for all future presidents and became known as the "President's Pew." Since that time, many presidents have been members of the church or paid homage to the site with occasional visits. The church interior features 27 beautiful memorial windows, an 18th century prayer book autographed by many presidents, and silver and gold chalices encrusted with jewels. The church is open to the public Monday-Saturday from 9 AM-3 PM and during church services on Sunday. Admission is free.

The White House Visitor Center is located around the corner from the White House at 1450 Pennsylvania Avenue, NW. This facility offers displays, ranger talks, interactive exhibits and artifacts from the White House for visitors to gain insight into the history of the most famous house in the United States. The site features a continuously running 30-minute video called "Where History Lives-a Tour of the White House," which offers a great overview of the interesting history of this famous residence and its many memorable occupants and visitors. It also provides a unique look at the interior of the White House with views of the furnishings and decorations as well as a behind-the-scenes peek at the work the staff does to maintain the residence and to prepare for the many events occurring there.

The Visitor Center also has a **Kids Corner**, where kids can browse through picture and activity books, draw and color, and play games to test their knowledge of presidents and the White House. Pick up a copy of a National Park Service Junior Ranger activity booklet at the nearby information booth for more fun tasks.

Outside of the White House Visitor Center lies **Freedom Plaza** and **Pershing Park**. Freedom Plaza is on Pennsylvania Avenue between 13th and 14th Streets, NW, and features an inlaid stone version of Pierre L'Enfant's original city plan for the capital city. There are also famous quotes about the District inscribed in the stone on the plaza. The plaza was originally named as Western Plaza, but was renamed to honor Martin Luther King, Jr., who wrote his "I Have a Dream" speech at the nearby Willard Hotel in 1963. Freedom Plaza is a frequent site of events and political demonstrations.

On the other end of Freedom Plaza is a bronze equestrian statue honoring Kazimierz Pulaski, a Polish nobleman and famous military commander, who joined the fight against the British during the Revolutionary War. Pulaski used his formidable cavalry skills to help thwart British attacks against Revolutionary forces and reportedly saved General Washington's life. In recognition of his meritorious service, Washington promoted Pulaski to the rank of Brigadier General where he became known as the "Father of the American cavalry." He continued to serve skillfully and bravely until he was killed at the Siege of Savannah in 1779.

Pershing Park is located on Pennsylvania Avenue between 14th and 15th Streets, NW, and honors the celebrated American General John "Black Jack" Pershing. Pershing commanded the American Expeditionary Forces in World War I and is credited with shaping America's military into a modern, effective war machine. The park features a statue of General Pershing by Robert White, walls covered with quotes and descriptions of Pershing's many accomplishments, and a small pond and benches. The park normally offers outdoor ice skating in the winter.

Refreshments: Ellipse Visitor Pavilion at 15th Street and E St., NW, on the Ellipse and various vendors on 15th Street, NW.

Bathroom Facilities: Inside White House Visitor Center and at Ellipse Visitor Pavilion around 15th Street and E St., NW, on the Ellipse.

Scavenger Hunt:

No code letters-suitable for all ages
Y-designed for young children (under 10)
TW-designed for tweens ages 10-13
T-designed for teenagers

1. Y-Who lives in the White House now?

2. Who was the first president to live in the White House? When did he move in?

3. Who was the only president who didn't live in the White House?

4. How many rooms are in the White House?

5. TW-Who burned the White House in 1814? Where did President James Madison and First Lady Dolley Madison live after that?

6. T-Find the Blair House. What tragic event happened here in 1950?

7. Find the statue of Andrew Jackson on horseback in the park? What war and battle made him famous?

8. TW, T-Find the statue of General von Steuben in the park. Why is he famous?

WHITE HOUSE AND LAFAYETTE SQUARE PARK SCAVENGER HUNT ANSWER KEY

No code letters-suitable for all ages
Y-designed for young children (under 10)
TW-designed for tweens ages 10-13
T-designed for teenager

1. Y-*President Barack Obama and his family.*

2. *The first president to live in the White House was the 2ⁿᵈ president, John Adams, who moved into the White House in 1800.*

3. *The first president, George Washington, never lived in the White House.*

4. *132 rooms*

5. TW-*The British burned the capital city including the White House during the War of 1812 on August 24, 1814. The Madisons lived afterwards in a nearby building called the Octagon, which you can visit as well.*

6. T-*If you are on Pennsylvania Avenue facing away from the White House, you will find the Blair House on your left amidst the first cluster of town houses to your left at 1651 Pennsylvania Avenue. Puerto Rican Nationalists tried to assassinate President Truman, while he was living here during White House renovations in 1950.*

7. *The Andrew Jackson statue is in Lafayette Park directly across from the White House when you are standing on Pennsylvania Avenue looking away from it. Andrew Jackson, seventh President of the United States, was a hero of the Battle of New Orleans, which was fought during the War of 1812 against England. The battle took place in January 1815 and was a stunning American victory. Interestingly, the Treaty of Ghent to end the war had been signed about two weeks earlier, but word hadn't yet reached either side in New Orleans. Some of the metal used in the statue came from captured British cannons, which were melted down after the war.*

8. TW, T-*This Prussian General's statue is found in the northwest corner of the park. He is famous for training the inexperienced Continental Army in military tactics and drills and turning them into a formidable fighting force. His book "The Revolutionary War Drill Manual" served as the standard United States Army drill manual until the War of 1812.*

U.S. CAPITOL

Address/Contact Information: First Street and East Capitol Street NE, 202-226-8000, www. visitthecapitol.gov, interactive map of Capitol area available at www.aoc.gov.

Closest Metro Station: Senate side-Union Station (Red Line), House of Representatives side-South Capitol (Blue/Orange Lines), Visitor Center located closer to the South Capitol station.

Opening Hours/Ticketing: Visitor Center open Monday-Saturday from 8:30 AM-4:30 PM, tours offered from 8:20 AM-3:20 PM. Tickets are required for a guided tour of the Capitol Building, although you can explore the visitor center without a ticket. A limited number of same day tickets are available at the U.S. Capitol Visitor Center. During the high season, reserve tickets well in advance online or through your Senators' or Representative's Offices. Obtain Gallery passes for the Senate and House Chambers from your Senators' or Representative's Offices well in advance. Also, you can arrange private tours of the building with congressional staffers by contacting your Senators' or Representative's Offices well in advance. There are advantages in taking a private tour with one of these staffers: the group size is always small and they provide access to interesting areas in the building including the subway system used by congressional members and staff to travel between their offices and the legislative chambers. International visitors can get same day gallery passes at the visitor center by showing an international form of identification. To see when the legislative bodies will be in session, go to www.senate.gov and www.house.gov.

Essential Info: The impressive sight of the U.S. Capitol symbolizes the power of representative democracy in the United States of America. The cornerstone on the building was laid in 1793 by George Washington, and the North Wing was completed in 1805. The South Wing was added to house the Senate, but a planned dome was not constructed. The entire structure was severely damaged on August 24, 1814, when British soldiers burned much of the capital city. A 140- foot copper green dome with a stone interior and wood exterior designed by Charles Bulfinch stood in the center between the two wings from 1823 until 1855, when construction began on the current cast iron dome. The present exterior dome, weighing nearly 9 million pounds and standing 288 feet high (including the statue on top), was completed in 1863 and the decorations in the interior were finished in 1866. The statue of Freedom standing atop the dome is 19 ½ feet-tall and faces east as most mistakenly believed the city would expand in this direction. The East Front was also designed as the principal entrance to the Capitol Building as it was the only side on level ground. It is also said that the designers didn't want the sun to ever set on freedom.

You will start your visit at the massive underground U.S. Capitol Visitor Center, which has an exhibition hall, movie theaters, and a restaurant. The guided tour of the Capitol Building begins with an excellent 13-minute film called *Out of Many, One* and then features the crypt, the Rotunda, statuary hall, and sometimes the Old Supreme Court Chamber.

The Rotunda is filled with paintings of famous scenes of American history and statues of revered Americans. Italian American immigrant Constantino Brumidi brilliantly decorated the interior dome 180 feet above the rotunda with a fresco entitled *The Apotheosis of Washington*. This masterpiece shows Washington becoming a God surrounded by classical mythological figures. These figures were painted about 15-feet tall so they would appear life size to visitors standing in the rotunda. Brumidi also conceived the *Frieze of American History*, which depicts 19 famous scenes throughout the country's history. Brumidi slipped off his chair while working on the 8th panel of the frieze and dangled for 15 minutes from the scaffolding high above the Rotunda before being rescued. Brumidi wisely decided to let his assistant continue work on the frieze panels after this narrow escape at age 73.

The crypt area was designed to house the remains of George and Martha Washington, but they decided instead to be buried at Mount Vernon. It now holds many of the statues not currently being displayed in Statuary Hall.

Statuary Hall was the original House of Representatives chamber and now houses many of the statues given by each state to honor local or other heroes. Each state is allowed to send two statues of marble or bronze for display. One of the highlights of this room is experiencing the interesting acoustics which allowed Representative John Quincy Adams to covertly listen to his colleagues' discussions across the floor.

Time permitting, some tours visit the Old Supreme Court Chamber. This ornately furnished room is displayed as it was from 1810-1860 when the Supreme Court had its home here. From 1800-1806 this room was the lower half of the Senate chamber. Benjamin Latrobe's vaulted semi-circular ceiling is an impressive feature of the room.

Before or after the tour, take some time to visit Exhibition Hall in the visitor center, which features interactive displays, artifacts, documents, videos, theaters, and touchable models. One highlight of the hall is a 1:20 scale model of the U.S. Capitol Dome, which you are encouraged to touch. Visitors can use interactive kiosks to find the office locations of their congressional representatives where they can pay a visit and also pick up entry passes for the Senate and House of Representatives Galleries to view these legislative chambers in and out of session.

From the visitor center, visitors can also use an underground walkway, which provides easy access to the Library of Congress.

Refreshments: Restaurant onsite at lower level open 8:30 AM-4 PM.

Bathroom Facilities: Onsite

Scavenger Hunt:

No code letters-suitable for all ages
Y-designed for young children (under 10)
TW-designed for tweens ages 10-13
T-designed for teenagers

1. What do the flags flying over the two congressional wings signify?

2. TW, T-What is the name of the statue on top of the dome? How tall is it? Which direction does it face and why?

3. What is the name of the circular area directly underneath the dome?

4. What material is the exterior Capitol Dome made of?

5. What is the name of the rectangular land area stretching from the Capitol to the Lincoln Memorial?

6. Y-Find the large plaster model of the Statue of Freedom in the Visitor Center.

7. TW, T-Who was supposed to be buried in the Capitol Crypt?

8. Ask your tour guide to show you a statue from your home state in Statuary Hall.

9. TW, T-Find the spot in the Rotunda where presidents and national heroes have lain in state or lain in honor.

10. In the "Frieze of American History" find the scene depicting Columbus' landing in America.

11. Find Martin Luther King, Jr.'s statue in the Rotunda.

12. Listen to a message from the spot of John Quincy Adams former House desk located in Statuary Hall.

U.S. CAPITOL SCAVENGER HUNT ANSWER KEY

No code letters-suitable for all ages
Y-designed for young children (under 10)
TW-designed for tweens ages 10-13
T-designed for teenagers

1. *There is one flagpole over the Senate Chamber and one over the House of Representatives Chamber. When the flag is flying the legislative body is in session.*

2. *TW, T-The statue of Freedom is 19 ½-feet tall and faces east on the front of the Capitol Building. It faces east because the principal entrance was in the east wing, which was the only part of the building built on level ground. It was also mistakenly believed that the capital city would expand mostly eastward. It is also said that the designers did not want the sun to ever set on freedom.*

3. *The Rotunda is the circular area underneath the interior dome.*

4. *Cast Iron*

5. *The National Mall*

6. *Y-You can't miss this exact plaster replica of the 19 ½-foot statue in the Visitor Center.*

7. *TW, T-The Capitol Crypt was designed and built to house the tomb of George and Martha Washington, but they were interred instead at their beloved Mount Vernon home in Virginia.*

8. *Each state is allowed to send two statues to this hall to honor notable Americans hailing from their state.*

9. *TW, T-The circle directly under the rotunda is where Presidents Lincoln and Kennedy and other presidents have lain in state and national heroes have lain in honor. Hundreds of thousands of people have walked by the flag draped coffins of presidents and national heroes here to pay their respect.*

10. *This scene is depicted in the second panel above and to the right of the West door.*

11. *This statue is located near the entrance to the House of Representatives North Wing.*

12. *The tour guide will give you a demonstration of the unique acoustics in the chamber. Gather as close as you can to the plaque marking the location of John Quincy Adams' desk.*

LIBRARY OF CONGRESS

Address/Contact Information: 101 Independence Avenue SE, visitor entrance in Jefferson Building across from East Side of Capitol Building at First Street and Independence Avenue, (202) 707-5000, www.loc.gov

Closest Metro Station: South Capitol (Blue/Orange Lines)

Opening Hours/Ticketing: Thomas Jefferson Building is open Monday-Saturday 8:30 AM-4:30 PM. Tours are available Monday-Saturday 10:30 AM, 11:30 AM, 1:30 PM, 2:30 PM, and 3:30 PM. There is no 3:30 tour on Saturday. No tickets are required, but visitors often have to wait 15-45 minutes in line on the First Street side of the Jefferson Building to enter through the main doors. Groups can reserve tours in advance online.

Essential Info: The Library of Congress has served as the research arm of Congress since its founding in 1800 with about 3,000 volumes. The original library was housed in the Capitol Building, but was incinerated when the British set fire to the Capitol in 1814 during the War of 1812. Thomas Jefferson then sold his private collection of about 6,500 books at cost to start a new library. An Italian Renaissance style building was completed in 1897 to house the ever expanding library. This building, now known as the Thomas Jefferson Building, is currently part of a complex with two additional buildings that houses more than 144 million items. This collection includes: 33 million books, 63 million manuscripts, the largest rare book collection in North America, as well as an unmatched collection of films, photographs, maps, sheet music, sound recordings and legal materials. The library adds about 10,000 items to its collections daily and has approximately 745 miles of bookshelves.

Docents provide regular informative tours that feature the beautiful Great Hall, the main reading room and fascinating items such as one of three copies of the Gutenberg Bible, the world's first book printed on movable type. Thomas Jefferson's private library of books is also impressive. In addition, there is a multimedia interactive exhibit called "The Library of Congress Experience," which provides interesting information on the library and its many treasures.

Refreshments: There is a cafeteria with an excellent view on the 6th Floor in the James Madison Building open 9 AM-3 PM. This cafeteria is closed to the public 10:30 AM-12:30 PM. The Madison Building is accessible via underground walkway from the Jefferson building. Kids enjoy the journey through the lower hallways where visitors rarely venture. The restaurant at the lower level of the nearby U.S. Capitol Visitor Center is open 8:30 AM-4 PM.

Bathroom Facilities: Throughout the facility.

Scavenger Hunt:

No code letters-suitable for all ages
Y-designed for young children (under 10)
TW-designed for tweens ages 10-13
T-designed for teenagers

1. What happened to the first Library of Congress' set of 3,000 books?

2. From whom did the Congress purchase its next set of about 6,500 books to rebuild the Library of Congress in 1815?

3. T-How many miles of bookshelves are in the library?

4. TW, T-What was the first major book printed in moveable type on a printing press? Find a copy of it.

5. Y-Find a balcony overlooking the main reading room. Do you see anyone doing research?

6. Which mythological god is in the fountain in front of the library?

7. Which famous founding father can be seen above the entrance to the library

8. T-What movie featured "The President's Book" hidden in the Library of Congress?

LIBRARY OF CONGRESS SCAVENGER HUNT ANSWER KEY

No code letters-suitable for all ages
Y-designed for young children (under 10)
TW-designed for tweens ages 10-13
T-designed for teenagers

1. *These books were burned up along with most of the Capitol Building when the British burned much of the capital city on August 24, 1814, during the War of 1812.*

2. *Thomas Jefferson sold the government his huge private collection of nearly 6,500 books at cost.*

3. *T-There are approximately 745 miles of bookshelves.*

4. *TW, T-The Gutenberg Bible was printed by Johannes Gutenberg in Mainz, Germany, in the 1450s. A rare copy is on display on the first floor in the East Corridor just before the entrance to the Main Reading Room.*

5. *Y-From the Great Hall take the elevator up a couple levels for an interesting view of the main reading room.*

6. *Neptune, the mythological God of the Seas, is in the fountain.*

7. *Benjamin Franklin*

8. *T-"National Treasure II" starring Nicholas Cage*

U.S. SUPREME COURT

Address/Contact Information: One First Street NE, 202-479-3211, www.supremecourt.gov

Closest Metro Station: South Capitol (Blue/Orange Lines), Union Station (Red Line)

Opening Hours/Ticketing: Monday-Friday 9 AM-4:30 PM

Essential Info: The U.S. Supreme Court represents the Judicial Branch of the U.S. Government functioning as the highest and final court in terms of interpreting and passing judgment on U.S. law. The court consists of one Chief Justice and 8 Associate Justices. Each justice is appointed for life (or until voluntary retirement) by the president and approved by the Senate. The odd number of justices ensures that a decision on a contentious point of law will be made with a minimum vote of 5-4.

The U.S. Supreme Court met in the U.S. Capitol Building as well as in private homes, taverns and hotels before finally finding a permanent home in this beautiful marble neoclassical building in 1935. Designed by Cass Gilbert, the building features sculptures and friezes of real and fictional figures related to the history and importance of impartial justice in a free and democratic society. The engraved inscription above the west main entrance, "Equal Justice Under Law," emphasizes this. The east entrance has similar sculptures above it, but they are rarely viewed by visitors concentrating on the main entrance. The ornamental interior features a great hall with marble columns and busts of former chief justices of the court.

There are no guided tours, but visitors can take a self-guided tour, listen to a courtroom lecture, or attend an oral argument when the court is in session. All visitors should begin their visit by viewing the 24-minute film called *The Supreme Court*, which plays continuously from 9:15 AM-3:45 PM in the ground floor theater. The film relates the history of the Supreme Court and the building and features interviews with the Chief Justice and current and retired justices.

Docents lead the 30-minute courtroom lectures every hour on the half-hour when court is not in session or after it adjourns for the day. No tickets are necessary, but make sure to be in line in the great hall at least 15 minutes before the lecture is scheduled to begin.

Starting on the first Monday in October, the Court listens to two one-hour arguments a day, at 10 AM and 11 AM, with occasional afternoon sessions. Arguments are held on Mondays, Tuesdays, and Wednesdays through late April. Check their website for an updated schedule. For visitors wishing to listen to oral arguments, choose either the designated waiting line to listen to the entire argument or the three-minute line if you wish to briefly observe the court in session. Seating for the first argument begins at 9:30 AM and seating for the three-minute line begins at 10 AM.

Refreshments: The cafeteria onsite is open to the public from 9 AM-4 PM. Service for the public may be interrupted briefly at 12 PM and 1 PM to serve employees.

Bathroom Facilities: In the Visitor Center

Scavenger Hunt:

No code letters-suitable for all ages
Y-designed for young children (under 10)
TW-designed for tweens ages 10-13
T-designed for teenagers

1. What is the motto of the Supreme Court?

2. Y-Count the steps leading up to the entrance.

3. TW-When does the Supreme Court officially start its session?

4. How many justices are there? Who sits in the middle chair?

5. Y-What color are the justices' robes?

6. TW, T-Where did the Supreme Court meet before the construction of this building?

7. TW, T-Who is the only former president to serve as a justice here?

8. Who are the people represented by the busts in the great hall?

9. T-What was the first case to be decided by the Supreme Court? What exercise of practice did it begin for the Supreme Court?

10. T-What was decided in the *Dred Scott Decision* in 1857?

11. T-What was decided in the case of *Brown v. Board of Education* in 1954?

U.S. SUPREME COURT SCAVENGER HUNT ANSWER KEY

No code letters-suitable for all ages
Y-designed for young children (under 10)
TW-designed for tweens ages 10-13
T-designed for teenagers

1. *"Equal Justice Under Law". This motto is inscribed at the top of the West main entrance of the building.*

2. *Y-There are 44 steps, but an approximate amount is fine!*

3. *TW-The first Monday in October.*

4. *There are nine justices-eight Associate Justices and one Chief Justice. The odd number forces a final decision of 5-4 in their votes on contentious issues. The Chief Justice sits in the middle chair at the bench with the Associate Justices seated by order of seniority.*

5. *Y-Black. The robes are considered a reminder of the law and a symbol of neutrality.*

6. *TW, T-They met in the Old Supreme Court Chamber in the Capitol Building from 1819-1860. They have also met in private homes, taverns and hotels.*

7. *TW, T-President William Howard Taft was the 27th President (1909-1913) and later 10th Chief Justice of the Supreme Court (1921-1930).*

8. *The busts represent former Chief Justices.*

9. *T-The Supreme Court's first case heard was "Marbury vs. Madison" in 1803. Their decision in this case invalidated a law by determining it unconstitutional. This was the first implementation of "judicial review" in the United States as mentioned in Article III of the U.S. Constitution. This decision demonstrated clearly the use of "checks and balances" of power in the new federal government system.*

10. *T-This decision stated that neither people of African descent imported into the U.S. as slaves nor their descendants could become U.S. citizens nor were they afforded the protection of the U.S. Constitution. It further held that slaves were private property that could not be taken away from their owners without due process and that the federal government could not prohibit slavery in federal territories (overturning the Missouri-Maine Compromise of 1820). This controversial decision inflamed already high tensions over the issue of slavery and moved the nation closer to civil war.*

11. *T-This 1954 decision declared racially segregated education unconstitutional, overturning Plessy v. Ferguson (1896). Thurgood Marshall successfully argued this case and would later serve as an Associate Justice on the Supreme Court from 1967 until 1991.*

BUREAU OF ENGRAVING AND PRINTING

Address/Contact Information: 14th and C Streets SW, 202-874-3188, www.moneyfactory.com

Closest Metro Station: Smithsonian (Blue/Orange Lines)

Opening Hours/Ticketing: The best ticket option is to contact one of your congressional representative offices well in advance to schedule a tour. These special congressional tours take place Monday-Friday at 8:15 AM or 8:45 AM throughout the year. From May through August these special tours are also available every 15 minutes from 4 PM-4:45 PM.

During the peak season from March-August, you can obtain same day tickets starting at 8 AM on a first-come, first-served basis at the ticket booth on Raoul Wallenberg Place-formerly 15th Street, SW. The booth is open until all tickets for the day have been distributed. **Please note that lines form early and tickets are usually gone before 9 AM.** You should be in line by 7:45 AM to ensure getting tickets at the desired time. During the peak season tours run every 15 minutes from 9 AM-10:45 AM, 12:30 PM-3:45 PM and 5 PM-7 PM.

During the non-peak season from September-February tours run every 15 minutes from 9 AM-10:45 AM and 12:30 PM-2 PM. During this time no tickets are required, but you should still arrive early to ensure entry. Groups of 10 or more must schedule a tour well in advance by submitting a group reservation form found online or by calling the Tour Scheduler at 866-874-2330 or 202-874-2330. Groups of 10 or more take guided tours between 11 AM and 12:15 PM throughout the year. There is metal detector security at this facility.

Essential Info: The Bureau of Engraving and Printing (BEP) was established as part of the U.S. Treasury Department in 1863 and has been printing money in its current facility since 1914. Another site was opened in 1991 in Fort Worth, Texas. The BEP tour features a unique look at the various steps of currency production, beginning with large, blank sheets of paper, and ending with bills ready to use.

The BEP is responsible for the design, engraving and printing of all U.S. paper currency. The BEP also produces a variety of other items including: portions of U.S. passports, military identification cards, Immigration and Naturalization Certificates, and Treasury obligations and other U.S. Securities. The BEP also is responsible for all White House invitations. The BEP uses the most modern printing and engraving technology to ensure accuracy in the production process. They use various techniques including an embedded thread in the paper and special coloring to thwart counterfeiting.

The bills are printed on a special type of paper manufactured by only one company, the Crane Paper Company of Springfield, Massachusetts. This paper is more like fabric as it is made up of 75% cotton and 25% linen, which gives the bills their distinctive feel. Most of the bills printed here are used to replace worn out currency. For example, the life expectancy of a $1 bill is only between 18-22 months. If the workers find a mistake in the printing process using advanced laser scanners or visual inspection, they shred the defective bills. Bags containing some of these bills are available for purchase in the gift shop.

Some interesting production facts: the BEP is open 24 hours and produces about 26 million notes a day with a face value of nearly $1 billion. Both facilities use about 9 tons of ink per day. The largest bill denomination printed currently is the $100 bill. The largest notes ever produced were the 1934 $100,000 Gold Certificates, which were used for transactions between Federal Reserve banks and were unavailable to the general public.

Refreshments: Café at the annex of the Holocaust Museum next door.

Bathroom Facilities: Onsite

Scavenger Hunt:

No code letters-suitable for all ages
Y-designed for young children (under 10)
TW-designed for tweens ages 10-13
T-designed for teenagers

1. Find an example of an old money printing press.

2. How much money is printed here every day?

3. What type of bill or "denomination" are they printing today?

4. TW, T-What is the largest denomination of currency printed by the BEP today? What's the largest denomination they ever printed?

5. Y-Wave to a currency worker! Did he or she wave back?

6. T-Find out what the life expectancy of a $1 dollar bill is.

7. Find one of the laser devices that ensures the bills are printed correctly.

8. Y, TW-Find some funny sayings on signs above and on the machines. Which is your favorite?

9. Find a bag of shredded money in the gift shop. How much shredded money is in the bag?

10. Measure yourself against a stack of $100 bills in the gift shop. How much are you worth by height?

11. Find an engraving of a president and a White House invitation in the gift shop.

BUREAU OF ENGRAVING AND PRINTING SCAVENGER HUNT ANSWER KEY

No code letters-suitable for all ages
Y-designed for young children (under 10)
TW-designed for tweens ages 10-13
T-designed for teenagers

1. *In the visitors area before the tour begins, there are examples of old money printing presses and other historical artifacts.*

2. *They usually print about $26 million worth of currency.*

3. *The denomination will be one of the following: $1, $5, $10, or $100.*

4. TW, T-*The largest denomination they currently print is the $100 note. The largest denomination ever printed was the $100,000 Gold Certificate printed in 1934.*

5. Y-*Most of the workers are friendly and will wave back to you.*

6. T-*The life expectancy of a $1 bill is only between 18-22 months. Local banks turn in worn out currency, which is then replaced with the new bills printed here and in Fort Worth, Texas.*

7. *You can see a laser beam coming down from some of the machines that monitor the printing process.*

8. Y, TW-*On the machines and walls, there are some amusing sayings concerning depression on printing your lifetime salary in a matter of seconds, etc.*

9. *The amount of shredded money contained in these souvenir bags is both entertaining and a bit depressing.*

10. *There is a height chart on the wall that lets you know your worth by height when compared to stacks of $100 bills.*

11. *The BEP also produces beautiful engravings and prints official White House materials such as invitations and Christmas cards. Samples of all of these products are found in the gift shop.*

NATIONAL ARCHIVES

Address/Contact Information: 700 Pennsylvania Avenue NW, Visitor Entrance on Constitution Avenue near intersection with 8th Street NW, 202-357-5400, www.archives.gov

Closest Metro Station: Archives/Navy Memorial (Green/Yellow Lines)

Opening Hours/Ticketing: Day after Labor Day to March 14 10 AM-5:30 PM, March 15-Labor Day 10 AM-7 PM

Essential Info: This magnificent neoclassical building, designed by John Russell Pope, was opened in 1935 to house and catalog the most important papers and records of the United States of America dating back to 1774. The three most important documents: The Declaration of Independence, The Constitution, and The Bill of Rights are located in the Charters of Freedom Rotunda.

Begin your tour watching the short orientation film at the William G. McGowan Theater, which describes the mission and activities of the National Archives. On your way to the Rotunda, take some time to view the 1297 copy of the Magna Carta, the English document of rights which influenced the content of our own documents of freedom. Proceed to the Charters of Freedom Rotunda to view the three treasured documents, which are preserved in protective cases filled with Argon gas. Take note of Barry Faulkner's two large oil painting murals completed in 1936, which artistically portray the presentation of the Declaration of Independence and the Constitution. *The Declaration* mural (on the left) also hides a resting profile of Abraham Lincoln's head found above Thomas Jefferson, who is holding the Declaration in his hands.

After the Rotunda, proceed to the Public Vaults area where you can see more amazing original documents and use interactive devices to explore a treasure trove of artifacts and original records. The Boeing Resource Center provides additional hands-on activities for visitors. The Learning Lab provides opportunities for groups of middle school students to conduct onsite research-reservations are required. Look at the National Archives website for a schedule of temporary exhibitions and regular presentations that discuss interesting topics of U.S. History and their corresponding records.

Outside of the National Archives on the Pennsylvania Avenue side, you will find the original **Memorial to President Franklin Delano Roosevelt**. When asked what kind of memorial he wanted by his friend, Supreme Court Justice Felix Frankfurter, FDR answered that he would like a modest stone memorial no bigger than his desk located outside the National Archives. His preferred memorial was placed at the corner of Pennsylvania Avenue and 9th Street in 1965. It is little noticed now that there is a grand memorial to him on the Tidal Basin.

Tickets are not required for entry to the National Archives, but expect a wait of 30-90 minutes during the high season. Advance reservations are recommended during the high season and can be obtained online at a cost of $1.50 per ticket. Visitors can choose a guided tour or timed entry with these advance tickets and should report to the Special Events entrance at Constitution Avenue and 7th Street NW more than 10 minutes before the scheduled entry.

Refreshments: Charters Café onsite open Monday-Friday 10 AM-4 PM

Bathroom Facilities: Onsite

Scavenger Hunt:

No code letters-suitable for all ages
Y-designed for young children (under 10)
TW-designed for tweens ages 10-13
T-designed for teenagers

1. Find the William G. McGowan Theater and watch the short film.

2. Find the copy of the Magna Carta. T-In what country was it written and what was the document's significance?

3. Y-What color is the light in the display cases in the Charters of Freedom Rotunda?

4. Which three important documents are contained in the Charters of Freedom Rotunda?

5. Find the hidden resting profile of Abraham Lincoln's head in *The Declaration* mural in the Rotunda.

6. T-What movie featured the theft of the Declaration of Independence from the National Archives?

7. TW, T-In the Public Vaults, find military telegrams issued by President Lincoln.

8. Find a handwritten letter by George Washington.

NATIONAL ARCHIVES SCAVENGER HUNT ANSWER KEY

No code letters-suitable for all ages
Y-designed for young children (under 10)
TW-designed for tweens ages 10-13
T-designed for teenagers

1. *This orientation film gives an excellent perspective on the National Archives mission and its amazing collection.*

2. *This is a rare 1297 copy of the Magna Carta, which was originally signed by King John of England in 1215.* T-*The document was the first to challenge the authority of a monarch. By signing the document, King John admitted that his will was not arbitrary and that no freeman could be punished except through the law of the land. It was an important document acknowledging the freedom of the individual against tyranny. One must consider the power of monarchs at the time it was written to understand the significance of this document.*

3. *The green ultraviolet light preserves the documents from fading.*

4. *The three treasured documents are: The Declaration of Independence, The Constitution and The Bill of Rights.*

5. *The profile of Lincoln's head is located directly above Thomas Jefferson, who is holding the Declaration in his hands. The profile is in the clouds below the leaves of the tree.*

6. T-*The 2004 movie "National Treasure"*

7. TW, T-*Original telegrams from Lincoln are located in this area.*

8. *Original correspondence from George Washington is located in this area.*

Smithsonian Institution

Smithsonian Castle Building. Courtesy of Destination DC.

The Smithsonian Institution is the world's largest museum complex consisting of 19 museums and galleries (mostly in the District), the National Zoological Park and nine research facilities. Nicknamed "The Nation's Attic," the Smithsonian Institution has something of interest for all ages. The Smithsonian Institution has a vast collection of more than 140 million specimens, artifacts, records and works of art. Only a fraction of these items are on public display.

The initial grant for the museum came from an English scientist named James Smithson who willed his approximately $500,000 estate to establish an institution in Washington, D.C., for "the increase and diffusion of knowledge." Smithson willed this money for this purpose in the event his nephew died without an heir. Fortunately for future visitors to Washington, D.C., the nephew died without an heir and the Smithsonian Institution was established in 1846.

In my Scavenger Hunt section, I have listed the Smithsonian museums and locations that children and families usually find most enjoyable. There are additional museums and facilities which might also be of interest that I have listed in the "Additional Attractions in Washington, D.C.," section. Most of the museums are located on the National Mall, which makes it convenient to visit more than one in a day. I would not recommend visiting more than two in a day as it can lead to information overload, especially for children.

To see specific events scheduled during your visit at the various museums please go to their main website at www.si.edu. They have a useful section on this home page called "Visiting with Kids," which lists current exhibitions and scheduled events of interest to children and families. There is also an official Go Smithsonian Visitor Guide, which can be purchased for $2 at all their locations. Their website at www.gosmithsonian.com contains useful information including: a calendar of events, interactive maps, museum floor plans, and additional tips for visiting Washington, D.C.

Smithsonian Castle Building

1000 Jefferson Drive SW
Washington, D.C. 20056
202-633-1000
Metro: Smithsonian (Blue/Orange Lines)

Start your visit to the Smithsonian by going to the Smithsonian Institution Information Center located at the Smithsonian Castle Building on the National Mall, which opens daily at 8:30 AM. This building was the original location of the entire Smithsonian Institution, but now serves as an administrative headquarters and an orientation center. At this location you can find the latest schedules on special presentations, exhibitions, and events and can inquire as to any extended opening times. There is also an informative 12-minute video narrated by actor Ben Stiller, which runs continuously from 8:30 AM-4:30 PM in the Smithsonian Orientation Theater. This video gives a useful overview of the collections and highlights of the various museums as well as the important research and conservation work done throughout the Smithsonian Institution. The Castle Building also features a scale model of the city and an exhibit hall with a sampling of interesting artifacts from all the museums. The building also has public restrooms and a full service café.

Behind and to the side of the Castle Building and the Arts and Industries Building, you can relax in some beautiful gardens and fountains. Visitors can enjoy the flowers, plants and landscaping found in the Enid A. Haupt Garden, the Katherine Dulin Folger Rose Garden and the Mary Livingston Ripley Garden. Free guided garden tours with horticulturists are available May through September. These tours take place Tuesdays at 2 PM at the Ripley Garden (meet at the garden entrance sign between the Hirshhorn Museum and the Arts and Industries Building) and Wednesdays at 1 PM at the Haupt Garden (meet outside of the south entrance to the Castle Building).

While you're at the Castle Building, you can also pay your respects to James Smithson, whose tomb is near the front entrance. Interestingly, Smithson never visited the USA.

A good place to take a break from touring the museums is at the **Carousel on the Mall** located on the National Mall grounds across from the Smithsonian Arts and Industries Building. This vintage carousel was built in 1947 in Baltimore by Allen Herschell and has been at its present location since 1981. This beautiful carousel features 59 hand-carved and brilliantly painted horses and one green dragon. It is open daily 10 AM-6 PM with each ride costing $2.50. There is also a refreshment kiosk on the National Mall nearby.

NATIONAL AIR AND SPACE MUSEUM-National Mall Building

Address/Contact Information: Independence Avenue at 6th Street SW
Washington, D.C. 20560, 202-633-2214, www.nasm.si

Closest Metro Station: L'Enfant Plaza (Green/Yellow Lines and Blue/Orange Lines)

Opening Hours/Ticketing: 10 AM-5:30 PM. In the spring, summer and some holidays they are normally open until 7:30 PM.

Essential Info: This is the most visited museum in the world as more than 7 million people a year walk through its doors. It is a great place to visit for people interested in the history of air and space travel and for those fascinated by the technology that made these achievements possible. In its 22 galleries there are many stunning artifacts from aviation and space history including the original Wright Flyer-the first motor-powered airplane ever flown-and the Apollo 11 Command Module, which was in orbit during our first steps on the moon. You will also find plenty of hands-on exhibits that will entertain children, such as in the "How Things Fly" gallery, along with flight simulators, a multimedia planetarium, and an IMAX theater.

The highlights I have included in the scavenger hunt are on both floors but primarily to the left of the Milestones of Flight area with your back to the Jefferson Drive entrance. I recommend starting at the Milestones of Flight area as you enter, proceeding to your left on the first floor to the "How Things Fly" gallery, then heading up the stairs to the second floor and proceeding left to right to the galleries listed in the scavenger hunt.

The Einstein Planetarium is up the escalator on the second floor just to the right of the Milestones area and the flight simulators are on the first floor all the way to the right of the Milestones area in the far right corner. If your family or group is interested in military history, I would recommend visiting the Military Aviation galleries on the first and second floors to the right of the Milestones area. These galleries feature an amazing assortment of historic military aircraft from World War I to the Jet Age.

Before your visit, please consult the IMAX and Planetarium schedules to plan your time most effectively. Younger children will enjoy the free Friday 10:30 AM show called "One World, One Sky: Big Bird's Adventure" at the Planetarium, while older children prefer the regularly playing "Journey to the Stars" or "Cosmic Collisions" shows. If you are visiting during the high season, I recommend that you reserve your tickets to any shows in advance. The line for the flight simulators also gets long during the high season. The best time to come to avoid crowds anytime during the year is during the week and as early as possible.

The museum also has a Public Observatory featuring a 16-inch telescope for viewing the Solar System. The Observatory is open to the public on Wednesday and Thursday from 1 PM-3 PM and on Friday and Saturday from 11 AM-3 PM. The Observatory is occasionally open at night and can be reserved on Wednesdays for groups at 10:30 AM and 11:30 AM. Go to www. nasm.si.edu/exhibitions/popobservatory.cfm to learn more or to make a reservation.

Outside the museum there is an interesting permanent exhibition called "Voyage- A Journey through our Solar System," which presents our solar system at one ten-billionth actual size using 13 signs and models located along Jefferson Drive. These units represent the 9 planets, the Sun, and asteroids and comets with two introductory placards. The exhibition stretches 650 yards from the Air and Space Museum to the Smithsonian Castle Building. Walking along this exhibition gives visitors a better perspective on Earth's place in the Solar System.

Refreshments: There is a Food Court in Museum and vendors on Independence Avenue.

Bathroom Facilities: Onsite

Scavenger Hunt:

No code letters-suitable for all ages
Y-designed for young children (under 10)
TW-designed for tweens ages 10-13
T-designed for teenagers

Milestones of Flight-First Floor

1. Y-Stand in the middle of the great hall and count the airplanes and space capsules. Which is your favorite?

2. Touch the moon rock.

3. Find the Spirit of St. Louis airplane. Who flew it and where did they fly it?

4. Find the Apollo 11 space command module. Where did it fly?

5. TW, T-Find the replica of the first liquid-propelled rocket. Who developed this?

How Things Fly First Floor

6. What force keeps everything from floating off the Earth?

7. Y, TW-Find the scale. How much would you weigh on these various worlds compared to Earth?

8. Y-Hold the ball in the air with air pressure.

9. Y, TW-Climb into cockpit of a Cessna.

10. Test your reaction time by catching the ruler as fast as possible when it falls.

11. Y-Participate in hands-on activity if possible.

Explore the Universe-First Floor

12. Before entering this gallery, find the replica of the Lunar Module (outside this gallery near the food court). Where did the original land? Use the joystick camera to get a better look at it.

13. TW, T-Watch the short film explaining how the astronauts operated the Lunar Module.

14. In the gallery look through the replica of the telescope used by Galileo in the 1600s.

15. TW-Find the observing cage of the Mount Wilson Observatory. What was the diameter of the telescope used in this observatory?

16. Crank the wheel to see the effect of speed on the color of light.

17. See how you look illuminated by infrared light.

Apollo to the Moon-Second Floor

18. TW, T-How many men have walked on the moon? Were they all Americans?

19. TW, T-Find the model of the Lunar Rover Vehicle? During which Apollo Missions was it used?

20. Watch the film of an actual lunar landing.

21. Find the aft portion of the huge Saturn 5 rocket used in the lunar mission.

Space Race-Second Floor

22. Walk through the model of Skylab. How long do you think you could have lived in it?

23. T-Find the German V-2 missile.

The Wright Brothers and the Invention of the Aerial Age-Second Floor

24. What kind of shop did the Wright Brothers own?

25. Find a kite and gliders they used to test their theories on flight.

26. Find one of the original propellers of the 1903 Wright Flyer.

27. Find and read the original telegram sent when they achieved their first flight.

28. Use the computer simulator to get a feel for what is was like to fly the Wright Flyer at Kitty Hawk, N.C.

Pioneers of Flight-Second Floor

29. Find one of Amelia Earhart's planes. Why is she famous?

30. TW, T-What made the Tuskegee Airmen special? Find some of their flight gear.

NATIONAL AIR AND SPACE MUSEUM SCAVENGER HUNT ANSWER KEY

No code letters-suitable for all ages
Y-designed for young children (under 10)
TW-designed for tweens ages 10-13
T-designed for teenagers

Milestones of Flight-First Floor

1. *Y-The Milestones of Flight occupies the first large middle area as you enter the museum. Historic space capsules, rockets, space probes, satellites and planes are displayed on the floor and suspended from the ceiling.*

2. *In the great hall, there is a stand with an actual sliver of moon rock brought back by Apollo 17 that people are allowed to touch.*

3. *The silver airplane hangs in the great hall. Charles Lindbergh flew it from Long Island, NY, to Paris, France, in 1927. The 33 1/2 hour flight of 3,610 miles was the first successful solo flight across the Atlantic Ocean.*

4. *The Apollo 11 space command module is the capsule in the great hall fairly close to the information booth. This module orbited the moon with one astronaut while two others stepped on the moon for the first time on July 20, 1969.*

5. *TW, T-Near the Apollo 11 command module you will see a small rocket. This is a replica of the first liquid-propelled rocket launched in 1926 by the "Father of Modern Rocketry," Robert Goddard. This American physicist is credited with developing the first liquid-fueled and multi-stage rockets, which would eventually make spaceflight possible.*

How Things Fly First Floor

6. *Gravity*

7. *Y, TW-Weights are different on the Earth, Jupiter and the Moon because of their different sizes and the corresponding amount of gravitational force.*

8. *Y-Kids (and adults!) love using these air blowers to keep a ball suspended in the air.*

9. *Y, TW-The controls in the Cessna let you experience some of the basic controls needed to make a plane fly.*

10. *This test is across from the hands-on demonstration gallery on the right.*

11. Y-*The museum offers regular hands-on demonstrations in the gallery such as paper airplane contests.*

Explore the Universe-First Floor

12. *The exact replica of the Lunar Module is found at the end of the first floor near the food court. The original landed on the moon in the first landing in 1969 and is mostly still there on the moon's surface. The astronauts lifted off in the upper section to link up with the Apollo 11 command capsule orbiting above. They then flew this capsule back to Earth landing in the ocean for pick-up. This command capsule is displayed in the Milestones of Flight area.*

13. TW, T-*This fascinating short film is shown to the left of the Lunar Module.*

14. *The Italian scientist Galileo was one of the pioneers of astronomy. He improved telescopes through refraction to give higher magnification for looking at objects in space. He was the first to see the moons of Jupiter and the phases of Venus.*

15. TW-*You can find the huge observing cage in the walkway behind the Galileo telescope. The telescope had a diameter of 100 inches.*

16. *Continuing on past the Mount Wilson Observatory exhibit, you will see this hands-on crank area where you can experience the changing colors of light when you crank the wheel.*

17. *Continuing on to the left, you will find a large screen showing your body through an infrared camera. Your body will display different colors in this infrared light depending on the temperature.*

Apollo to the Moon-Second Floor

18. TW, T-*There were 11 manned Apollo missions (Apollo 7-17) with six of the missions landing on the moon. Twelve astronauts, all Americans, have walked on the moon.*

19. TW, T-*The LRV is in the display case on the left as you enter the exhibit. Three separate units were used on three missions-Apollo 15, 16, and 17.*

20. *This black and white film and audio gives you the feeling of being there.*

21. *You will find this imposing section used on the gigantic Saturn 5 rocket at the end of the exhibit.*

Space Race-Second Floor

22. *This is a full scale back-up model of the USA's first orbiting space station used for three extended manned research missions from 1973-1974. NASA planned to use the Space Shuttle to modify Skylab and keep it in orbit for additional missions into the 1980s. Unfortunately, NASA was not*

able to launch the shuttle in time and Skylab reentered the Earth's atmosphere in September 1979. Some fragments hit rural Australia, but fortunately there were no injuries.

23. *T-The huge black and white missile is located next to the back-up model of Skylab. Nazi Germany used these imposing missiles to terrorize civilians and allied personnel in England and Belgium at the end of World War II. Building on the research done by American physicist Robert Goddard and previous German scientists, the Nazis succeeded in launching over 3,000 of these missiles. The V-2 was the first ballistic missile that achieved sub-orbital spaceflight at unheard of speeds making any defensive measures impossible. The technology developed by German scientists in building and launching these missiles would later be used to help develop the rockets used in the space programs and the missile systems of the Soviet Union and the USA.*

The Wright Brothers and the Invention of the Aerial Age-Second Floor

24. *The Wright Brothers owned a bicycle shop in Dayton, Ohio.*

25. *There are kites and gliders the brothers used on the right hand side of the exhibit.*

26. *An original wooden propeller is in a case in the back left of the exhibit.*

27. *The telegram and additional artifacts are in the same case as the propeller.*

28. *Going behind the Wright Flyer on your left you will see computer simulators that demonstrate the Wright Brothers' four test flights using animated sequences.*

Pioneers of Flight-Second Floor

29. *Amelia Earhart set two records in this red Lockheed 5B Vega, which she owned from 1930-33. In 1932 she was the first woman to fly solo across the Atlantic and later was the first woman to fly nonstop across the entire United States. She went missing in 1937 over the Pacific Ocean as she attempted to circumnavigate the globe.*

30. *TW, T-The Tuskegee Airmen was the name given to the first black airmen who served in bomber and fighter units in the U.S. Army Air Corps during World War II- specifically the 332nd Fighter Group and the 477th Bombardment Group. Their stellar record in all their operations, particularly in combat missions escorting bombers, proved that race was not a factor in flying or fighting ability.*

NATIONAL AIR AND SPACE MUSEUM-STEVEN F. UD-VAR-HAZY CENTER

Address/Contact Information: 14390 Air and Space Museum Parkway, Chantilly, VA 20151, 703-572-4118, www.nasm.si.edu

Closest Metro Station: This museum is located 28 miles from its sister museum on the National Mall. There are no easy options to travel to this location using public transportation from Washington, D.C. In this instance using a car, cab, or the Washington Flyer private coach is the best option. If you must use public transportation, use a combination of Metrorail and Metrobus to get to Dulles International Airport or Dulles Town Center and then take a Virginia Regional Transit bus directly to the museum. Metrorail and Metrobus information is available at www.wmata.com. Virginia Regional Transit schedules, fares and information are available on the VRTA web site. For more information call 540-338-1610.

Opening Hours/Ticketing: 10 AM-5:30 PM. In the spring and summer they offer frequent extended hours until 6:30 PM. Public parking is $15 with **free parking available after 4:00 PM.**

Essential Info: Opened in 2003, this museum is built like a massive hangar and displays hundreds of historic aircraft and spacecraft that its sister museum on the National Mall cannot accommodate. Some of the highlights include an Air France Concorde, the SR-71 Blackbird, the B-29 Superfortress *Enola Gay* and the Space Shuttle *Enterprise*. The museum also boasts an observation tower with an unparalleled view of airplanes flying in and out of nearby Dulles International Airport. In addition, there are simulator rides and an IMAX theater.

The museum is over 10 stories high and has aircraft viewable from three different levels. Follow the scavenger hunt listed below to get a look at most of the highlights. There are also free 90-minute highlight tours given by museum staff at 10:30 AM and 1 PM starting at the Tours desk on the lower level.

Refreshments: McDonald's and McCafe onsite.

Bathroom Facilities: Onsite

Scavenger Hunt:

No code letters-suitable for all ages
Y-designed for young children (under 10)
TW-designed for tweens ages 10-13
T-designed for teenagers

Second Level

1. After entering on the second level, turn left on the walkway and find a Pilot's View touch screen. Find at least three pilot views of different airplanes.

2. Find the Nieuport 28c.1 airplane. Which war was it flown in and by what country?

3. TW-Find the Langley Aerodrome. Did it ever fly with a human onboard?

4. T-Find the famous WW II B-29 Superfortress bomber known as the *Enola Gay*. What weapon did it carry in WW II?

First Level

5. Find some artifacts used by Charles and Anne Lindbergh.

6. TW, T-Find some examples of aerial cameras.

7. Y, TW-Find Amelia Earhart's flightsuit.

8. Find the fastest passenger plane ever flown. Which airline used it and what was its name? What was its top speed?

9. Find another case displaying Charles Lindbergh's flight suit and gloves.

10. TW, T-Identify two Japanese and two German aircraft used in WW II.

11. Find the Lockheed SR-71 Blackbird. What makes it special?

First Level-Space Hangar

12. Find the Space Shuttle *Enterprise*. Did it ever fly in space?

13. Find the Gemini VII space capsule. How long was it in space?

14. In the space science area, find the Spacelab. Do you see any examples of experiments carried out using insects?

15. Find the Mars Pathfinder Lander. Was this mission manned?

16. T-In the Cold War aviation area, find the Bell UH-1H Iroquois "Huey" helicopter. What war was it primarily used in?

NATIONAL AIR AND SPACE MUSEUM-STEVEN F. UD-VAR-HAZY CENTER SCAVENGER HUNT ANSWER KEY

No code letters-suitable for all ages
Y-designed for young children (under 10)
TW-designed for tweens ages 10-13
T-designed for teenagers

Second Level

1. *The touch screens are found on the railings as you proceed down the walkway.*

2. *These airplanes were built by the French, but they were used by the United States in World War I.*

3. *TW-The Langley Aerodrome, built by Samuel Langley, had two successful unmanned flights, but his attempts at manned flight failed shortly before the Wright Brothers successful flight in December 1903. The Aerodrome is located hanging where the walkway bends to the right.*

4. *T-The Enola Gay carried the first atomic bomb used in warfare. This plane dropped the bomb called "Little Boy" on Hiroshima, Japan, on August 6, 1945. This large airplane is best viewed from this walkway. Continue to the end of the walkway and take the stairs on the left down to the first level and head to the right.*

First Level

5. *Coming out of the stairs go to the right and take another right until you come to the cases containing artifacts. Many of the artifacts came from the Lindberghs' two exploratory flights in 1931 and 1933 covering much of the world.*

6. *TW, T-A plastic case farther along on the right contains many examples of different cameras used in aircraft.*

7. *Y, TW-Head back to the area with the Lindbergh artifacts and take a right down the path until you see another plastic case where this famous woman aviator's items are displayed.*

8. *The Air France Concorde's top speed was 1,350 miles per hour. It could cross the Atlantic in between 3-4 hours.*

9. *After viewing the Concorde, turn around and head toward the Enola Gay. Just before you reach it on the left there is another case containing items that belonged to Lindbergh.*

10. *TW, T-The various WW II aircraft are on both sides of the path as you walk past the Enola Gay.*

11. *These high altitude reconnaissance aircraft hold the air speed record at 2,194 miles per hour.*

First Level-Space Hangar

12. *The Space Shuttle Enterprise was the first space shuttle orbiter built, but it was used only in ground and atmospheric testing. This vehicle did not have an engine or heat shields and was not capable of spaceflight. The information learned from its test flights proved invaluable for future space shuttles.*

13. *The Gemini VII spent 14 days in space in 1965 and provided critical research to help plan the future moon expeditions carried out by the Apollo missions.*

14. *In one of the cases in this area you can see spiders and butterflies used in experiments in space.*

15. *The model of the Mars Pathfinder Lander is near the exit on the left. Because of its vast distance from Earth, there have only been robotic exploratory missions to Mars.*

16. T-*After you exit the Space Hangar, go to the left to see more modern military aircraft. The Huey helicopter is located on the right at the end of this section. It was used extensively by US forces in the Vietnam War.*

NATIONAL MUSEUM OF THE AMERICAN INDIAN

Address/Contact Information: Fourth Street and Independence Avenue SW, 202-633-1000, www.nmai.si.edu

Closest Metro Station: L'Enfant Plaza (Green/Yellow Lines and Blue/Orange Lines)

Opening Hours/Ticketing: 10 AM-5:30 PM

Essential Info: Dedicated in 2004, the newest museum on the National Mall cuts an imposing figure. The museum celebrates the cultural diversity of the indigenous people throughout the Americas while emphasizing common areas of importance to Native Americans through its landscape and design. The building and site emphasize the American Indian peoples' connections to the earth and are filled with details, colors, and textures sacred to Native American culture.

The building's striking curved form evokes a wind/water-sculpted rock formation that demonstrates the eternal power and importance of nature. The landscaping is designed to portray the natural environment of the Americas before Europeans arrived. On separate sides there are various native plant types including a hardwood forest, wetlands and a meadow. There are also croplands featuring the "Three Sisters"-corn, beans, and squash- central to the Native American diet, as well as tobacco. A rippling creek and waterfall represent purification. Many ancient large boulders called "Grandfather Rocks" are strewn about representing Native American ancestors. The building is aligned perfectly in all four cardinal directions with stones from four representative tribes placed on the north-south and east-west axes on the grounds. These axes intersect in a circle of sandstone in the middle of the museum. The building design also incorporates specific celestial references, such as an east-facing main entrance and a dome that opens to the sky.

Upon entering the five level building, the theme of oneness between native cultures and nature continues as the walls are built as flowing, curving surfaces with no sharp corners. Copper bands on the walls represent Native American crafts using textiles and basketry. The importance of the sun is emphasized through the natural light shows provided by the prism window above.

Begin your visit watching the short multimedia presentation *Who We Are*, then proceed to the permanent exhibitions called "Our Universes," "Our Peoples," and "Our Lives." These exhibitions explore in order: spiritual relationships between Native Americans and the natural world, the struggle to maintain tradition and a unique identity in the face of severe challenges, and 21st century Native American life.

The sheer amount and variety of artifacts (just a fraction of the museum's collection is displayed) can be overwhelming. Take note of the many glass cases and metal drawers in the hallways that contain fascinating artwork, weapons, tools and other artifacts from a huge variety of American Indian cultures. The museum also features an extensive archive center, research facilities and unique gift shops. Be sure not to miss the wide variety of delicious Native American food from five geographic regions offered in the Mitsitam Café.

Refreshments: Mitsitam Café onsite offers a regional-based variety of Native American dishes and children's menus.

Bathroom Facilities: Onsite

Scavenger Hunt:

No code letters-suitable for all ages
Y-designed for young children (under 10)
TW-designed for tweens ages 10-13
T-designed for teenagers

1. Y, TW-Outside the museum, count the number of boulders in and around the water. What do they represent in Native American culture?

2. Y, TW-Find the circle in the center of the ground floor and look straight up into the sky.

3. Y-Which boat is your favorite on the ground floor?

4. Ride the elevator to the Fourth Floor. Find the Lelawi Theater and watch the film *Who We Are*. What was your favorite part?

Our Universes

5. Watch the animated feature that describes the legend of how Devil's Tower was formed.

6. Find the photo placard of the Lakota people that shows buffaloes or bison on the plains. TW, T-What was the Lakota word for buffalo or bison? Give two reasons why these animals were so important to the Lakota people.

7. Y-Find the toy buffalo in the Lakota Universe.

8. Step into the "Pueblo of Santa Clara."

9. After you exit the "Our Universes" area, find the statue of George Washington and Oneida Indians.

Our Peoples

10. Find examples of gold and silver taken from native peoples by the Spanish Conquistadors.

11. T-What were the 3 main reasons the Conquistadors were able to defeat and exploit the advanced native peoples of the Americas?

12. Find a famous pair of boots in the Apache area. Whose boots were they and why are they important?

13. Find a warrior's shield and a pipe in the Kiowa area. When was the pipe traditionally used?

14. TW, T-What was the name of the first American Indian newspaper?

15. TW, T-Did Sequoya use letters or symbols to write the Cherokee language?

16. In the Wixarika area find a quiver with a bow and arrows.

17. In the hallway display to the right, find five different types of animals in the artwork

18. In the hallway display across from the exit to "Our Peoples," find the biggest "Projectile Point" (arrow or spear head).

Our Lives

19. Before entering the exhibit, find the bald eagle feather that traveled to space.

20. In the Pamunkey area, drive the boat while watching the video.

21. Find the huge Bombardier vehicle in the St. Laurent area. What is it used for?

22. In the Chicago area, find a chi-town drum. When are these used?

23. Find the Yakama sweathouse. What is their favorite fish to eat?

24. Y-Find the Igloolik sled.

25. TW, T-Which Indian nation prides itself on being the best ironworkers, traditionally building skyscrapers and bridges?

26. TW-Watch the short film of the Kumeyaay Nation during their annual star gathering festival.

27. Choose your favorite three examples of beadwork in the case outside "Our Lives." Learn more about them using the interactive touch screens.

28. Find the huge totem pole in the Chesapeake Museum Store on the first level. Which state is it from?

29. Y, TW-Find some examples of different dwellings of Native American peoples outside the museum.

NATIONAL MUSEUM OF THE AMERICAN INDIAN SCAVENGER HUNT ANSWER KEY

No code letters-suitable for all ages
Y-designed for young children (under 10)
TW-designed for tweens ages 10-13
T-designed for teenagers

1. Y, TW-*There are about 40 of these huge boulders (approximate count is ok!), which are called grandfather rocks." With their advanced age (at least a billion years old) they represent the spirits of Native American ancestors.*

2. Y, TW-*This central circle is directly under the prism window, which provides brilliant and colorful natural lighting from the sun.*

3. Y-*Examples of boats from various cultures are found in the atrium area.*

4. *This 13-minute film provides an interesting introduction to the diverse native cultures living throughout the Americas.*

Our Universes

5. *In the middle of the exhibit area is a celestial theater area showing various animated features about some cherished Native American legends including the formation of Devil's Tower in Wyoming.*

6. *This placard is in the middle of the exhibit area.* TW, T-*The Lakota word for buffalo or bison is Tatanka. The Lakota people regarded the buffalo as a sacred gift from the Great Spirit. They viewed the buffalo as a relative whose sacrifice they honored. The Lakota used the buffalo for food and to make shelter, weapons, toys, containers and other items essential for life on the Great Plains.*

7. Y-*This is in a case in the exhibit area for the Lakota people.*

8. *This exhibit area gives you a feel of being in a pueblo.*

9. *This is in the hallway right before you enter the "Our Peoples" area. The statue features George Washington with prominent Oneida Indians who supported the colonists militarily and with supplies during the Revolutionary War.*

Our Peoples

10. *There are multiple examples on the right as you enter.*

11. T-*The three main reasons are explained farther into the exhibit on the right near examples of swords and other weapons. The Conquistadors had steel swords that easily cut through the shields of native*

peoples, they brought diseases that wiped out a huge percentage of the population, and they made clever alliances with less powerful enemy tribes opposed to the advanced peoples.

12. *These boots belonged to Apache scout Chatto, who worked with U.S. soldiers and led them to fellow Apache Geronimo's hideout in 1886. Geronimo had successfully resisted U.S. expansion into Apache lands in the U.S. Southwest for decades.*

13. *The pipe was used during discussions in an effort to get all participants to speak honestly.*

14. TW, T-*In the Cherokee area, you can find excerpts from the "Cherokee Phoenix" newspaper.*

15. TW, T-*Sequoya invented a syllabary, which was made up of 85 symbols representing syllables of the Cherokee's spoken language.*

16. *The Wixarika area is to the left near the exit to the exhibit.*

17. *There are multiple types of animals in the artwork.*

18. *There are a variety of projectile points in the case across from the exit.*

Our Lives

19. *Commander John Bennet Herrington, member of the Chicasaw Nation, brought this feather with him on the November 2002 mission of the Space Shuttle Endeavor.*

20. *This exhibit is found directly to the right as you enter.*

21. *These huge ice vehicles are used to transport people and equipment for commercial ice fishing on Lake Manitoba.*

22. *Following to the right you will find the Chicago area. These drums are used in Powwows.*

23. *Looping to the left you will find the Yakama area with its sweathouse. Their favorite fish to eat is salmon.*

24. Y-*Continuing to the left, you will find the Igloolik area with the sled in the middle.*

25. TW, T-*Continuing to the left you will find the exhibit on the Mohawk Nation, who pride themselves on their ironworking tradition.*

26. TW-*This film shows young tribal members participating in traditional games, dancing and singing during this annual festival.*

27. *This case is in the hallway near the ramp heading down to the next floor.*

28. *This huge totem pole was made by the Sayman Tlingit people in Alaska.*

29. Y, TW-*As you exit onto Independence Avenue, you will see examples of different Native American dwellings.*

NATIONAL MUSEUM OF NATURAL HISTORY

Address/Contact Information: 10th Street and Constitution Avenue NW, 202-633-1000, www.mnh.si.edu

Closest Metro Station: Smithsonian (Blue/Orange Lines)

Opening Hours/Ticketing: 10 AM-5:30 PM. In the spring and summer they are normally open until 7:30 PM.

Essential Info: This beautiful Beaux Arts style building with its impressive 125-foot dome opened in 1910 as the third Smithsonian museum. It was built to house the overflowing items of the original museum. Most of its collection is housed off-site including more than 126 million artifacts and specimens. The African Elephant dominating the Rotunda is one of the largest examples ever seen. It stood 14-feet high and weighed 8 tons. President Theodore Roosevelt collected many large animals on safari and had them preserved for the museum's collection.

By following the scavenger hunt, one can see many of the museum highlights, which are related to all aspects of our planet's history, including all its diverse forms of life. I recommend studying the floor plan and website to find additional areas of personal interest in this giant museum.

The museum has a **Discovery Room** with hands-on items and artifacts for kids to touch and investigate. This room is of interest primarily for children under 10 and is open Tuesday-Thursday from 12 PM-2:30 PM, Friday from 10:30 AM-2:30 PM and weekends from 10:30 AM-3:30 PM. School group programs from K-8th grade are also available October-May with advance reservations.

Children of all ages will enjoy a visit to the **Insect Zoo**, which contains many live specimens and opportunities to handle insects and watch feedings of tarantulas Tuesday-Friday 10:30 AM, 11:30 AM and 1:30 PM and on weekends 11:30 AM, 12:30 PM and 1:30 PM. Near the exit, there is a live butterfly pavilion where visitors can walk through a greenhouse type area with plants and live butterflies flying in all directions. Timed entry tickets for 30-minute visits are required at $6 for adults, $5.50 for seniors 60+ and $5 for children and can be purchased online, via phone or at the pavilion box office. On Tuesday admission is free, but timed tickets, available online or at the exhibit box office, are required.

The museum also has an **IMAX** theater featuring 40-45-minute shows and the Baird Digital Theater with shows running 20-25 minutes.

Refreshments: Two restaurants/cafes onsite offer a full selection of food and beverages. There is also a Gelato stand near the Atrium Café offering this Italian treat. In addition, there is a refreshment kiosk directly across from the Madison Drive entrance.

Bathroom Facilities: Throughout museum

Scavenger Hunt:

No code letters-suitable for all ages
Y-designed for young children (under 10)
TW-designed for tweens ages 10-13
T-designed for teenagers

On the Constitution Avenue entrance level

1. TW, T-Find the Moai Statue from Easter Island. What is the closet country to Easter Island? On what day do you think the island was discovered by Dutch explorers in 1722?

2. Find the huge totem poles from the Pacific Northwest.

Rotunda-First Floor

3. Y, TW-Find the butterflies and dung beetles near the big elephant in the rotunda.

4. Y-Find the Discovery Room. Do at least three fun activities there. Here are some examples: Find the huge pinecone. Put your hand in the crocodile's mouth. Someone from the group can play dress up with an outfit in the room.

Mammals Hall-First Floor

5. Y-Find a giraffe eating leaves off a tree.

6. Find a leopard and its prey in a tree.

7. TW, T-Find the small sculpture of "Morgie" near the Evolution Theater in the Mammals Hall. Why is she important? What theory do scientists use to describe her relationship with us?

8. Find a bronze chimpanzee "Harriet" watching a movie. Watch the movie with her!

9. Which three traits make an animal a mammal?

10. Y-Crawl into the cold world exhibit and touch a hibernating squirrel.

Human Origins Hall-First Floor

11. T-Watch the short film on the round screen about human origins. What percent of DNA do all humans share?

12. How many people currently live in the world?

13. TW, T-Play the "Keep Your Species Alive" game. Did you prevail?

14. Transform yourself into a Neanderthal at the video console.

Ocean Hall-First Floor

15. Find the replica of a huge whale in the Ocean Hall. What type of whale is it?

16. Watch the short movie about the undersea submarine exploring vessel ALVIN. Which undersea animal was your favorite?

17. Find the Giant Squid. Is it male or female? How long is it?

18. Y, TW-Find the coral reef aquarium with live fish. Can you find a fish similar to "Nemo" or "Dory?" Which fish is your favorite?

19. TW, T-Watch the Global Ocean System presentation featuring a spinning globe.

Insect Zoo-Second Floor

20. Find the huge prehistoric dragon fly. How wide was its wingspan?

21. Can you find the New Guinea Walking Stick insect in the case?

22. Y-Crawl through the termite mound.

23. Y, TW-Touch an insect shape to find out where it hides in a house.

24. Find the beehive in the Insect Zoo

25. What's growing in the infant nursery?

26. What is your favorite insect here?

27. Touch an insect or watch a tarantula feeding if possible.

Hall of Geology, Gems, and Minerals-Second Floor

28. Find the Hope Diamond. How many carats is it? What does legend say will happen if you own the Hope Diamond? Do you believe it?

29. TW, T-Find the iron meteorite that landed near Tucson, Arizona. How did local blacksmiths use it?

30. Find the huge crystal ball and look at your reflection in it.

31. TW, T-Find Marie Antoinette's (Queen of France from 1774-1792) diamond earrings. What happened to Marie Antoinette during the French Revolution?

In the Fossils area-First and Second Floors

32. Compare the jaws of the huge prehistoric shark to a shark living today.

33. Find the fossil of a large fish eating a small fish.

34. TW, T- Find an example of a "living fossil."

35. Find the fossil skeletons of a Tyrannosaurus Rex fighting a Triceratops.

36. Y-Touch the triceratops' horn.

37. Which fossils are the researchers working on in the Fossil Lab nearby?

38. Y-Touch the petrified wood outside the museum's Madison Drive entrance.

NATIONAL MUSEUM OF NATURAL HISTORY SCAVENGER HUNT ANSWER KEY

No code letters-suitable for all ages
Y-designed for young children (under 10)
TW-designed for tweens ages 10-13
T-designed for teenagers

On the Constitution Avenue entrance level

1. TW, T-*The Moai Statue is on the Constitution entrance level right after you pass through security. Chile is the closest country to Easter Island, which was discovered on Easter Sunday in 1722.*

2. *These beautiful huge totem poles are located in the back of this level and extend up through the stairway to the floors above. These totem poles are from the Haida and Tsimshian tribes in British Columbia.*

Rotunda-First Floor

3. Y, TW-*You will find examples of these insects that live off the waste of the elephant near his left rear leg and around the exhibit.*

4. Y-*The Discovery Room has great hands-on activities for younger kids. It is located on the northeast corner of the first floor between the Ocean Hall and African Voices exhibit. Please note that the Discovery Room is open Tuesday-Thursday from 12 PM-2:30 PM, Friday 10:30 AM-2:30 PM, and Saturday and Sunday 10:30 AM-3:30 PM. It is closed on Mondays.*

Mammals Hall-First Floor

5. Y-*The giraffe is found shortly after entering the Mammals Hall.*

6. *This display is found farther up the hall on the right.*

7. TW, T-*The small sculpture of Morgie is at the back of the Mammals exhibit in a special area with walls around it. Morgie is the nickname of what is considered our oldest mammalian ancestor. Scientists believe that all mammals, including humans, evolved from this small mammal that lived during the time of the dinosaurs. The theory scientists use to explain this is called the Theory of Evolution.*

8. *The Evolution Theater is at the back of the Mammals exhibit past Morgie. The movie runs continuously, so stick around to see the rest if you enter in the middle of the show.*

9. *As stated in the movie: hair, mothers provide milk for their young, and special ear bones.*

10. Y-*The hibernating squirrel is found in the wall of the cold world exhibit next to the Evolution Theater.*

Human Origins Hall-First Floor

11. T-*Humans share 99.9% of their DNA.*

12. *There is an automatic digital counter that shows the current world population as it steadily increases.*

13. TW, T-*Playing this game demonstrates that it's not easy satisfying all the needs and demands of a society.*

14. *This is a popular feature, so observe another participant if time is short.*

Ocean Hall-First Floor

15. *This is a life-sized model of a North Atlantic Right Whale.*

16. *There is a small theater continuously showing a fascinating movie on deep sea exploration.*

17. *This female Giant Squid was originally 36 feet long with tentacles of 22 feet. The preservation process has shrunk her size somewhat.*

18. Y, TW-*This small but beautiful aquarium is near the Global Ocean System presentation and contains plenty of colorful fish and sea life.*

19. TW, T-*This interesting high-tech presentation shows the effect of the world's oceans on weather and climate.*

Insect Zoo-Second Floor

20. *The dragon fly is on the left shortly after you enter the Insect Zoo. Its wingspan could reach up to 2 feet wide.*

21. *This insect looks like a stick and is hard to find among the branches in the case near the beginning of the insect zoo.*

22. Y-*You can't miss this huge brownish/red mound near the end of the exhibit.*

23. Y, TW-*Near the back of the exhibit you will find a model of a house with interactive displays showing where insect pests live.*

24. *At the back of the exhibit next to the model of the house you will find an active beehive. Don't break the glass!*

25. *Next to the beehive you will see a hatchery area with future occupants of the Insect Zoo.*

26. *Lots of interesting ones to choose from in this zoo!*

27. *The tarantulas are fed Tuesday-Friday at 10:30 AM, 11:30 AM, and 1:30 PM and 11:30 AM, 12:30 PM, and 1:30 PM on weekends. Volunteers also frequently display insects and let willing visitors hold and/or touch them.*

Hall of Geology, Gems, and Minerals-Second Floor

28. *The exquisite Hope Diamond was first bought by French King Louis XIV in 1668 from a French merchant who found it in India. At that time this gem was a staggering 112 carats! It eventually made its way to England and was resized to 45 ½ carats. It was purchased by the wealthy McLean family in USA in the 20ᵗʰ century. Its final owner, jeweler Harry Winston, donated it to the Smithsonian in 1958. Some legends say that if you own it you may suffer from a curse as some previous owners experienced terrible misfortune. However, the Smithsonian has had the biggest blue diamond in the world for more than 50 years without any problems.*

29. TW, T-*This huge meteorite is near the Hope Diamond. It landed in the desert in Arizona and was easy to find in the sand. In the 1700s, local blacksmiths used parts of it as iron anvils to help make horseshoes and other objects.*

30. *This amazing crystal ball is found in the National Gem Collection gallery located next to the Hope Diamond area.*

31. TW, T-*You can find these in the National Gem Collection gallery. Marie Antoinette and her husband King Louis XVI were both executed by the guillotine during the French Revolution in 1793.*

In the Fossils area-First and Second Floors

32. *On the second floor, the huge jaws of the prehistoric Megalodon are shown in comparison to a large Great White Shark of today, which pales in comparison.*

33. *On the second floor, you can find this amazing fossil of a large fish who died shortly after eating a smaller fish, which is seen inside its stomach.*

34. TW, T-*On the second floor, there is a section highlighting living fossils such as horseshoe crabs, which haven't changed in 445 million years!*

35. *On the first floor in the dinosaur area, you can see this amazing sight reconfigured with fossilized bones.*

36. Y-*On the first floor, you are allowed to touch a fossilized triceratops' horn.*

37. *Behind the dinosaur fossils area walking away from the rotunda, you will find a glassed in Fossil Lab area where researchers are working to study and preserve a huge variety of fossils.*

38. Y-*You can find examples of this outside of the Madison Drive entrance. These logs from Arizona are more than 180 million years old and have been cut and polished to show the amazing aging process that has turned all organic material in the tree to stone.*

NATIONAL MUSEUM OF AMERICAN HISTORY

Address/Contact Information: 14th Street and Constitution Avenue NW 202-357-3129, www.americanhistorysi.edu

Closest Metro Station: Smithsonian (Blue/Orange Lines), Federal Triangle (Blue/Orange Lines)

Opening Hours/Ticketing: 10 AM-5:30 PM. In the spring and summer they are normally open until 7:30 PM.

Essential Info: This recently renovated museum houses more than three million artifacts related to the unique history and culture of the United States of America. In the museum you will find national treasures such as: the original Star Spangled Banner, clothing and personal effects of U.S. Presidents and First Ladies, a gunboat from the American Revolution, Dorothy's ruby red slippers from *The Wizard of Oz* and other treasured pieces of American culture. The museum also features a hands-on science center called Spark!Lab where visitors conduct experiments and learn about technology.

The museum also offers an archives center, lectures, concerts and temporary exhibitions. Please check their website calendar to see the latest events. There are also ride simulators in the Lower Level West area. For groups interested in military history, do not miss the "Price of Freedom" Gallery which features military artifacts from our nation's conflicts.

Begin your visit at the Welcome Center near the Mall entrance and pick up a plan of the museum. Follow the scavenger hunt to see many of the highlights of the museum.

Refreshments: The Stars and Stripes Cafe is located in the museum and there are vendors outside of both entrances.

Bathroom Facilities: Throughout the museum

Scavenger Hunt:

No code letters-suitable for all ages
Y-designed for young children (under 10)
TW-designed for tweens ages 10-13
T-designed for teenagers

1. Find the original Star Spangled Banner. Which war made it famous? How many stars and stripes does it have?

2. TW, T-Near the entrance to 2 East, find the F.W. Woolworth lunch counter from the Greensboro store. What happened here?

3. Take the escalator up to 3 East and find the Appomattox Chairs in the Price of Freedom Gallery. Who sat in these chairs and what document were they signing?

4. T-Find George Armstrong Custer's buckskin coat. Where and how did he die?

5. Find a jeep used in World War II and a helicopter used in the Vietnam War.

6. Find the Gunboat *Philadelphia* in the next exhibit. What war was it used in? Touch the bar shot projectile fired to destroy sails and masts on ships. Can you find the hole where the cannonball hit and sank the *Philadelphia*?

7. In the American Presidency Gallery, find the top hat that President Lincoln wore to Ford's Theatre.

8. Find the portable desk Thomas Jefferson used. Which famous document did he write on it?

9. Act your most presidential at the presidential lectern.

10. T-Find the collection of locks of hairs from Presidents Washington to Pierce.

11. Y-Find Dumbo the Flying Elephant as you head toward 3 West.

12. Find a pair of ruby red slippers. Who wore these in which famous film?

13. Y-Find a famous green frog in this area. What's his name?

14. What is your favorite item in the popular culture area in comparison to the adults in your group?

15. In the musical instruments gallery find a Stradivarius violin. Play a Mozart musical piece using the push button system in the gallery.

16. Go down the escalator to 2 West and the First Ladies exhibit. Can you find First Lady Jacqueline Kennedy's and Michelle Obama's inaugural ball gowns? Which gown in the exhibit is your favorite and why?

17. Y-Touch the swatch of bison fur found near the stuffed bison in front of the "Communities in a Changing Nation" Gallery.

18. In the gallery find a typical slave cabin.

19. T-Go to the "Within these Walls" exhibit and explore how families lived from colonial times to World War II.

20. As you leave this wing, find a statue of George Washington. What makes it unusual?

21. Take the escalator down to 1 West and find a huge telescope. Who used it?

22. Y, TW-Try out windsurfing and other activities at the "Invention at Play" exhibit.

23. Find a handwritten recipe by the famous chef Julia Child.

24. In the "Science in American Life" exhibit use the cyclotron to smash an atom.

25. Do some experiments in the Spark!Lab.

26. Walk across to 1 East and find an early steam locomotive.

27. TW, T-In the "America on the Move" Gallery, find the interactive terminal demonstrating how the USA is a Nation of Immigrants. When did your ancestors come to the United States and where were they from?

28. Find three different types of vehicles traveling on Route 66. Where did this route go?

29. Experience a simulated ride in 1959 in a Chicago elevated railway car or the "L." What is the L short for?

NATIONAL MUSEUM OF AMERICAN HISTORY SCAVENGER HUNT ANSWER KEY

No code letters-suitable for all ages
Y-designed for young children (under 10)
TW-designed for tweens ages 10-13
T-designed for teenagers

1. *This huge garrison flag was flown over Fort McHenry at the Battle of Baltimore during the War of 1812 to signal a dramatic victory over British naval and ground forces in September 1814. Francis Scott Key, held captive on a British ship in the harbor, was inspired by the sight of the huge flag flying and wrote "The Star Spangled Banner," which would later become our national anthem. These same British troops had routed American forces and burned the capital city of Washington, D.C., a few weeks earlier. The flag has 15 stars and 15 stripes. Mary Pickersgill was paid $544.74 for sewing this flag, which took 6 weeks to make with the help of other workers.*

2. TW, T-*Throughout the South after the end of the Civil War and into the 1960s, there was a policy of segregation, which denied blacks the same level of services as whites and mandated separate eating and lodging facilities. These laws also made voting difficult and sometimes impossible for African Americans. These discriminatory state and local laws were known as "Jim Crow" laws. On February 1, 1960, four young African-American men sat down at this lunch counter at Woolworth's and asked for service. After they were denied service, these men and others staged a long-running passive sit-in that ultimately led to the desegregation of Woolworth stores. This was a pivotal moment in the Civil Rights Movement, which eventually resulted in the overturning of segregation and "Jim Crow" laws. The nearby "African American History and Culture" gallery deals with similar themes and serves as a preview gallery for the Smithsonian National Museum of African American History and Culture, scheduled to open in 2015.*

3. *These chairs were used by Confederate General Robert E. Lee and Union General Ulysses S. Grant to sign the surrender document that ended the Civil War.*

4. T-*Custer was killed at the Battle of the Little Bighorn in Montana in 1876. He and five companies from the 7th Cavalry were annihilated by a combined force of thousands of Sioux and Cheyenne Indians.*

5. *There are a Willys Jeep from World War II and a UH-1H Huey helicopter used during the Vietnam War in the exhibit.*

6. *In October 1776 during the Revolutionary War, a hastily constructed collection of small gunboats under the command of Benedict Arnold fought a far superior force of British ships to a standstill on Lake Champlain, NY. The Gunboat Philadelphia was sunk by a 24-pound cannonball during the battle. The well-preserved boat was raised from the bottom in 1935 with much of its equipment intact.*

7. *The gallery features the top hat that Lincoln wore on his fateful visit to Ford's Theatre on April 14, 1865.*

8. *This small desk is in a glass display case in the middle of the gallery. He wrote the Declaration of Independence and many other important documents on this desk.*

9. *There is a presidential lectern where you can imagine yourself as the president.*

10. T-*This strange collection of locks of hair is in a glass display case near the "Presidency in the Popular Imagination" area. Locks of hair were a popular keepsake in the 19th century.*

11. Y-*This purple Dumbo comes from the famous "Dumbo the Flying Elephant" ride at Disneyland.*

12. *The ruby red slippers were worn by Judy Garland when she played Dorothy in the 1939 classic film "The Wizard of Oz." They are located in the "National Treasures of Popular Culture-1939" section.*

13. Y-*Kermit the Frog from "Sesame Street" and "The Muppet Show" is located in the National Treasures of Popular Culture section.*

14. *The adults might appreciate Archie Bunker's chair or Fonzie's jacket, while the kids will like the Simba Mask from the Lion King musical or Michael Jackson's hat.*

15. *These priceless instruments are found throughout the gallery. Listen to a few musical pieces using the push button system.*

16. *These exquisite gowns are in their own display cases in the exhibit.*

17. Y-*Touch the sample, but please don't touch the stuffed bison!*

18. *This cabin shows a typical slave residence and furnishings and is found near the end of the exhibit.*

19. T-*This fascinating exhibit shows how families lived throughout much of the history of America.*

20. *The statue of George Washington by Horatio Greenough from 1832 is unusual because he is seated and is bare-chested. Some appreciated the artistry and symbolism of the work, while others found it inappropriate.*

21. *Maria Mitchell, the first U.S. woman astronomer, used this telescope in the mid-late 1800s.*

22. Y, TW-*There are many hands-on activities in this fun and educational exhibit.*

23. *This recipe and Julia Child's entire kitchen are found in a nearby exhibit.*

24. *The cyclotron is found near the end of this exhibit.*

25. *This hands-on area offers interesting scientific experiments for children of all ages. It is open from 10 AM-4 PM with lab bench experiments conducted on the hour from 11 AM-3 PM.*

26. *This John Bull steam locomotive was built in 1831.*

27. TW, T-*This terminal is near the beginning of the exhibit.*

28. *Route 66 went 2,000 miles from Chicago to Los Angeles.*

29. *This car is found near the end of the exhibit. The "L" stands for "elevated."*

NATIONAL POSTAL MUSEUM

Address/Contact Information: 2 Massachusetts Avenue NE, 202-633-5555, www.postalmuseum.si.edu

Closest Metro Station: Union Station (Red Line)

Opening Hours/Ticketing: 10 AM-5:30 PM

Essential Info: This museum is located in a beautiful Beaux Arts building, which formerly served as a post office building for the city. Its galleries display artifacts and exhibits related to the history of the U.S. Postal Service featuring many original transportation vehicles used to carry the mail. The museum houses the National Philatelic Collection, which features a priceless collection of postage stamps from around the world. The National Postal Museum also has a wide variety of interactive exhibits where kids can learn about the various tasks and delivery methods of the U.S. Postal Service.

The museum is expanding significantly in the future to include: a new gallery that will permanently display its priceless stamp collection, an exhibit on the importance of mail to troops in wartime, and an exhibit called "Systems at Work," which recreates the path mail travels from sender to recipient.

Interactive games are available at the Ford Education Center in the museum and you can also play them at home before and after your visit at: www.postalmuseum.si.edu/activity/8_activity.html

If your group would like to see some of the museum's most prized stamps such as the 1918 "Inverted Jenny" airplane stamp or the 1847 George Washington first federal postal stamp, please contact the museum ahead of time to schedule an appointment.

Please follow the scavenger hunt to experience many of the main highlights of the museum.

Refreshments: Food Court and restaurants are at Union Station next door.

Bathroom Facilities: Onsite

Scavenger Hunt:

No code letters-suitable for all ages
Y-designed for young children (under 10)
TW-designed for tweens ages 10-13
T-designed for teenagers

1. In the museum foyer, find the statue of Ben Franklin? Why is he honored in this museum?

2. What is your favorite mail-carrying vehicle displayed in the main area of the museum?

3. Find the dogsled used to transport mail. Where was it used?

4. Y-Climb into the front cab of a postal delivery truck.

5. Y, TW-What kind of animal was the mascot of the Postal Service? Learn his story. Can you find him near the rail car?

6. In the "Binding the Nation" Gallery, how did the first postal riders find their way along the Native American trails from Boston to New York City? Find evidence of their methods.

7. TW, T-Look in the mail pouch. Why are there more newspapers than letters?

8. In the "Post Haste" area, use the terminal to see the various vehicles and routes needed to transport mail across the country before air mail service.

9. Y-Climb into the Concord Coach to feel what it was like to ride with the mail.

10. Find the exhibit on the Pony Express. TW, T-When was this system used and where did it begin and end? How many horses would one rider use in a shift?

11. In the "Postal Inspectors" Gallery, find an original Thompson submachine gun.

12. Find the mailbag used for President Franklin Delano Roosevelt's mail.

13. Match the suspect with the wanted poster.

14. T-Try to forge a signature.

15. In the "Customers and Communities" Gallery, find the pneumatic tube service canister used to transport mail beneath city streets in the early to mid 20th century. How fast did a letter travel when using this system?

16. Find all the ways the mail is being delivered in the large mural.

17. Explore the interactive exhibits in the "Systems at Work" gallery that shows how a letter gets from sender to receiver.

18. Go to the Ford Education Center and play the matching game and other games. Send stamps to an email account.

19. In the Stamp Gallery inside the vault area, find the rare Graf Zeppelin stamp.

20. In the US & International Stamp Gallery, find stamps from Japan, Ireland, and France and any other countries you choose. Which are your favorites?

NATIONAL POSTAL MUSEUM SCAVENGER HUNT
ANSWER KEY

No code letters-suitable for all ages
Y-designed for young children (under 10)
TW-designed for tweens ages 10-13
T-designed for teenagers

1. *Ben Franklin was the founder of the U.S. Postal Service and the first Postmaster General of the United States.*

2. *A variety of planes, trucks, cars, coaches, and a dogsled are displayed at the beginning of the museum.*

3. *The dogsled is found in the area near the stagecoach. Dogsleds used to regularly transport mail in Alaska. In recent years commemorative mail has been carried on some dogsleds during races to pay tribute to this tradition.*

4. Y-*At the beginning of the museum, there is a large postal delivery truck where visitors can climb into the front cab.*

5. Y, TW-*Owney the Dog, was an abandoned dog adopted by workers at a postal office in Albany, NY, in 1888. He began traveling on wagons and then trains with the mail and the postal workers adopted him as an unofficial good luck mascot. The workers noted that no railway trains he rode on ever crashed. He soon traveled on a tour by train and steamship wearing medals and tags jingling from a jacket given to him by the Postmaster General. After he died, his body was preserved by the Smithsonian Institution and is now on display at the Postal Museum.*

6. *The postal riders would occasionally notch a tree with their axe so they could find their way back home along this 268-mile route.*

7. TW, T-*The federal government gave cheaper rates to newspapers than letters so that it would be easier to keep the public informed of important news. The postal service still charges a lesser rate for shipping "media," such as magazines, books and printed materials.*

8. *Letters traveled via coach, railroad, and steamship to get across the country.*

9. Y-*Imagine how cramped it would have been to travel in these coaches with bags of mail packed inside with the passengers.*

10. *The Pony Express exhibit is in the "Binding the Nation" area.* TW, T-*This private mail service only ran from 1860-1861 and featured a relay system of riders, horses and stations on a 1,966 mile route stretching from St. Joseph, MO, to Sacramento, CA. One rider's shift averaged 75-100 miles with a change of horses every 10 miles (8-10 horses).*

11. *This weapon is found in the glass display case at the beginning of the exhibit.*

12. *In the same display case you can see the White House mail bag used to collect the president's mail.*

13. *This seemingly simple task is more complicated than it looks when the suspects look alike.*

14. *T-This is one of the interactive exhibits used to demonstrate the criminal activities postal inspectors are trained to stop.*

15. *This canister is located next to the large mural at the beginning of the gallery. Letters traveled up to 35 mph through the pneumatic tubes.*

16. *The 17 postal workers are using a variety of methods to deliver the mail.*

17. *These interactive exhibits demonstrate the amazing complexity involved in delivering the mail. The amount of steps needed to accomplish this task is eye-opening.*

18. *These games are challenging and interesting for any age. Take the time to play a variety of them for fun and education.*

19. *This rare stamp was one of three types issued in 1930 to subsidize the German airship Graf Zeppelin's special flight from Germany to South America and the United States.*

20. *Pull out the metal drawers and enjoy the amazing varieties of colors and styles of stamps from around the world.*

NATIONAL ZOOLOGICAL PARK

Address/Contact Information: 3001 Connecticut Avenue NW, 202-633-4800, http://nationalzoo.si.edu

Closest Metro Station: Cleveland Park is a .5 mile level walk south, Woodley Park is a .4 mile uphill walk north (Red Line). Take bus L1 or L2 from Cleveland Park direction Dupont Circle or McPherson Square or bus L2 or L4 from Woodley Park in direction Chevy Chase Circle. Paid parking available onsite-but the garage is generally filled by late morning in high season. Parking costs $15 for the first 3 hours and $20 for more than 3 hours.

Opening Hours/Ticketing: April 2-October 29 exhibits and concessions open every day 10 AM-6 PM, October 30-April 1 open every day (except Dec. 25) 10 AM-4:30 PM. **The grounds are open from 6 AM to 8 PM and 6 AM to 6 PM, respectively.** Free admission. Visitors can park at the zoo beginning at 8:30 AM. The Visitor Center and Panda Plaza open at 9 AM.

Essential Info: This 163-acre zoological park is part of the Smithsonian Institution and is located in Rock Creek Park. This location features more than 2,000 individual animals representing almost 400 different species. The star attractions of the zoo are its two giant pandas, Tian Tian and Mei Xiang. More than two million people a year visit the zoo to enjoy the animals, wander among its peaceful gardens, and learn useful information about the protection of wildlife.

Pick up or download a zoo map to plan your visit as there is a lot of ground to cover in this huge zoo. Be prepared for a lot of walking on hilly terrain to see and learn about a wide variety of animals. The website also has some activity sheets and scavenger hunts families can use during a visit. **Please note that families looking for an early morning destination can enter and walk the zoo grounds starting at 6 AM, although the zoo's enclosed exhibits and concessions don't open until 10 AM.**

The National Zoo also offers special educational programs for kids including classes and camps featuring close contact with the animals. They also offer the unique "Snoar and Roar" overnight program where an adult and children can camp out overnight at the zoo. Call or go online to reserve spots in these programs.

Refreshments: Various restaurant and refreshment stands are found throughout the park.

Bathroom Facilities: Onsite

Scavenger Hunt:

No code letters-suitable for all ages
Y-designed for young children (under 10)
TW-designed for tweens ages 10-13
T-designed for teenagers

1. Find the cheetahs. How many can you count?

2. TW-Do you see any black squirrels on the grounds? Find out the story about where they came from.

3. Find animals from Africa, Asia, and South America. Which continent has the biggest animals?

4. Y-Can you find the meerkats? What is the name of the most famous meerkat of all and the movie he was in?

5. Find the Giant Pandas. Are they inside or outside or both? What are their names?

6. What is the Giant Panda's favorite meal?

7. Find three types of tropical birds in the Bird House.

8. Find the elephants. Are they Asian or African?

9. Go to the Great Ape House and try to see a western lowland gorilla from Africa. T-What are some differences between a monkey and an ape?

10. TW, T-Who rides on the O Line in the zoo?

11. Find tigers and lions. Which cat is bigger?

12. Y-Visit the Kids' Farm and touch 3 different animals.

13. Find a type of mammal, fish, amphibian, reptile and insect in the Amazonia Habitat.

14. Find a bald eagle in beaver valley.

15. Y-Which animal was the noisiest?

16. Which animal ate the most?

17. Which animal was your favorite and why? TW, T-Are they endangered or safe in their native habitat?

18. Y-Draw a picture of your favorite animal.

19. T-Find "Uncle Beazley." What is he?

NATIONAL ZOO SCAVENGER HUNT ANSWER KEY

No code letters-suitable for all ages
Y-designed for young children (under 10)
TW-designed for tweens ages 10-13
T-designed for teenagers

1. *There are currently 1 female and 3 male cheetahs at the Cheetah Conservation Center.*

2. *TW-The black squirrels you see running around the grounds and throughout the area came about from an exchange of black and gray squirrels between the Smithsonian Institution and Ontario, Canada's Superintendent of Parks in 1902. Eight black squirrels were released on the zoo grounds and have since expanded well into neighboring regions. The only difference between the black squirrels and the native gray variety is their pigmentation, although some area residents complain that the black squirrels are more aggressive.*

3. *Use your map to mark down when you have seen animals from these continents. At the zoo, the Asian elephants are the largest animals, although African elephants are the largest land animals on Earth.*

4. *Y-The meerkats live in a colony near the Giant Panda Habitat. The most famous meerkat is Timon from "The Lion King."*

5. *The Giant Pandas, Mei Xiang and Tian Tian, live in the Giant Panda Habitat, which is designed to be similar to their native habitat in China.*

6. *The Giant Pandas love to eat bamboo.*

7. *The Bird House is located down a path near the Giant Pandas.*

8. *The elephants are located near the pandas. They are Asian as you can tell from their small ears and overall smaller size compared to African elephants.*

9. *T-The Great Ape House features 6 western lowland gorillas and 6 orangutans. Monkeys, apes and humans are all primates. The most obvious differences between apes and monkeys are that apes don't have tails and are normally bigger than monkeys.*

10. *TW, T-The orangutans travel between the Great Ape House and the Think Tank on the Orangutan Transport System known as the O Line. This system involves about 500 feet of plastic-coated steel cables connecting eight 50-foot high towers that allow animals to move between these two buildings. The best time to see the orangutans using this system is on warm days between 11 AM and 11:30 AM.*

11. *You can see lions and tigers and learn information at the Great Cats Exhibit and Lion/Tiger Hill. Tigers are normally bigger than lions.*

12. Y-*The Kids' Farm features an interactive area with goats, alpacas, donkeys, pigs, rabbits and cows. There is also an exhibit, which teaches kids where pizza ingredients originate.*

13. *This amazing exhibit replicates the Amazon River habitat with its rich variety of life.*

14. *These majestic animals symbolize America and are found in the Beaver Valley area.*

15. Y-*Likely candidates include some of the birds and monkeys.*

16. *Likely candidates include the elephants, big cats, and great apes.*

17. TW, T-*The information placards for most animals at the National Zoo educate you about their status in the wild.*

18. Y-*This task can be completed at the zoo or later in the day*

19. T-*Uncle Beazley is a 27-foot long fiberglass model of a triceratops dinosaur found at the zoo. Ask an employee for help finding this model of a giant from the past.*

National Park Service Historic Sites

Ford's Theatre in 1865 after the Assassination of President Lincoln.
Courtesy of the Library of Congress.

Washington, D.C., also has some important historic sites that are operated by the National Park Service and staffed by park rangers. The rangers know their respective sites inside and out, so feel free to ask them for any help on the scavenger hunts or for any other information you would like to know.

FORD'S THEATRE

Address/Contact Information: 511 10th Street NW, 202-426-6924, www.nps.gov/foth

Closest Metro Station: Gallery Place/Chinatown (Green/Yellow Lines and Red Line)

Opening Hours/Ticketing: 9 AM-5 PM. The last entry to the theatre is at 4:30 PM, and the last entry to the museum is at 4 PM. Timed tickets are required and are valid for Ford's Theatre, Ford's Theatre Museum and the Petersen House. Same day tickets are available onsite, but advance tickets are recommended. Go online or call (202) 297-SEAT and pay a small reservation fee for your timed tickets.

Essential Info: Ford's Theatre is the site of one of the most tragic moments in U.S. history: the assassination of President Abraham Lincoln on April 14, 1865. The theater was built in 1863 and had only been in service for two years when this great crime occurred. The U.S. government bought it shortly after the assassination and used it for administrative purposes and to house the Army Medical Museum. The National Park Service took the building over in 1933 and restored it to its original appearance in 1968. It currently operates as both a national historic site and a working theater.

On April 14, 1865, only five days after the end of the Civil War, President and First Lady Mary Todd Lincoln attended a play at the theater called *Our American Cousin*. They were in a joyous mood after the end of the long war that cost so many American lives. They arrived after the play started and upon entering the orchestra played "Hail to the Chief." The audience gave the president a long standing ovation for his impressive service. It took the president about a half hour to get to the presidential box because everyone wanted to personally congratulate him on his successful service to the country.

During a scene in the play where only one actor was on the other side of the stage and directly after another actor uttered a humorous line, the terrible event occurred: a famous Southern actor and Confederate sympathizer named John Wilkes Booth assassinated President Lincoln by firing a single shot from behind into the president's temple with a .44 caliber Deringer pistol. The 26-year-old Booth was an ardent supporter of the Southern cause who had meticulously planned a conspiracy with like-minded accomplices to simultaneously kill Lincoln and other top officials of the U.S. Government. They hoped their efforts would gain some time for the defeated Confederacy to recover, regroup and continue fighting. The sofa in the President's Box and the portrait of George Washington are original to that fateful night.

After the shot, President Lincoln slumped forward mortally wounded and First Lady Mary Todd Lincoln screamed in horror. One of the president's guests in the box, Major Henry Rathbone, wrestled with Booth who stabbed him with a dagger and then jumped dramatically to the stage below. Rathbone managed to grab hold of Booth briefly as he started to jump from the box forcing him off balance. Booth's foot then got tangled in the U.S. Treasury flag in front of the President's box on the way down and he landed awkwardly on the stage 15 feet below. The fall resulted in a broken bone in his leg. Booth shuffled to the middle of the stage, held his bloody dagger over his head and yelled "Sic Semper Tyrannus!" This Latin phrase means "So thus always to Tyrants!" and is the State motto of Virginia. Some accounts say he also said "The South is avenged" when he jumped from the box. Booth then made his way off the stage out the back door where an unwitting theater worker waited with a horse. He managed to escape the city, but after an intense 12-day manhunt he was killed while hiding in a tobacco barn in Virginia. Soon after the fateful shot from Booth, Lincoln was carried across the street to the Petersen Boarding House, where he died the following morning.

National Park rangers give regular informative talks in Ford's Theatre describing the details of the assassination. There is also a one act play that runs regularly called "One Destiny" that explores the events of that day from two eyewitnesses' viewpoints. Tickets for this play and for other performances at the theater can be purchased online at www.fordstheatre.org or at the box office onsite.

Be sure to visit the renovated **Ford's Theatre Museum**, which features interesting artifacts and interactive exhibits about Lincoln's life and presidency. The museum contains such fascinating artifacts as the clothes Lincoln was wearing the evening he was shot, the weapons of the assassin, and Mrs. Lincoln's opera glasses case. There are also interactive terminals, videos and other interesting artifacts from Lincoln's presidency.

For a detailed look at the events of the assassination of President Lincoln, including the conspiracy and Booth's escape route go to the National Park Service's online brochure at: www.nps.gov/history/history/online_books/hh/3a/hh3j.htm.

You can also pick up a National Park brochure and map at the visitor information center.

Refreshments: There are various restaurants on 10th Street.

Bathroom Facilities: In the museum.

Scavenger Hunt:

No code letters-suitable for all ages
Y-designed for young children (under 10)
TW-designed for tweens ages 10-13
T-designed for teenagers

1. TW, T-What special day did President and Mrs. Lincoln attend the play? Was the Civil War over yet?

2. Find out the name of the play the Lincolns were watching that night.

3. TW, T-What song did the orchestra play when the Lincolns entered the theater?

4. What was the name of the assassin? What was his profession?

5. How far did Booth jump to the stage after he shot the president?

6. TW, T-Go outside the theater and find the alleyway where Booth escaped. Did anyone see him during his escape?

FORD'S THEATRE SCAVENGER HUNT ANSWER KEY

No code letters-suitable for all ages
Y-designed for young children (under 10)
TW-designed for tweens ages 10-13
T-designed for teenagers

1. TW, T-*They attended the play on Good Friday April 14, 1865. The Civil War had effectively ended on April 9, 1865, with the surrender of General Lee's Army of Northern Virginia, although various Confederate units continued to resist.*

2. *"Our American Cousin"*

3. TW, T-*The Lincolns arrived late to the play. When they came in, the play was halted and the orchestra played "Hail to the Chief." A standing ovation ensued and it took the Lincolns about 30 minutes to make it to their seats through the crowd of well-wishers.*

4. *John Wilkes Booth was a famous actor of the time from Maryland and a fierce supporter of the Confederacy. He was able to freely walk throughout the theater prior to the assassination because he was so well-known.*

5. *The stage was about 12 feet below the box, but Booth jumped from the top of the railing, which made it a 15-foot leap.*

6. TW, T-*At the end of your visit, proceed out of the theater to the right and take a right onto F Street. About ¾ of the way down the block near 918 F Street you will find an alleyway marked by a historical sign describing Booth's escape. One young boy witnessed Booth escaping down the alleyway on horseback. For an interesting historical perspective walk down the alleyway and go to the right to see the back of Ford's Theatre complete with various historic doors used by actors and entrances used by theater workers to transport stage materials.*

FORD'S THEATRE MUSEUM

Next door to Ford's Theatre

Scavenger Hunt:

No code letters-suitable for all ages
Y-designed for young children (under 10)
TW-designed for tweens ages 10-13
T-designed for teenagers

1. Was the Capitol Dome finished when Lincoln was inaugurated in 1861?

2. Measure yourself against the life-sized statue of President Lincoln. How tall was he?

3. T-What is the name of the plan the Union would use to defeat the Confederacy?

4. Y-In "Life in the White House" section, find the toy sword owned by Lincoln's son Tad.

5. Find Lincoln's white gloves worn at a White House reception.

6. T-Was there another attempt on Lincoln's life before Ford's Theatre?

7. TW, T-Watch the short film *We Cannot Escape History*.

8. Who are the people reading "The Gettysburg Address" in the video?

9. TW, T-In the Surratt Boarding House area, find the gun Booth used. How many shots could it fire before reloading?

10. Find the diary Booth used during this time.

11. T-Did Booth act alone or were there other conspirators acting against Lincoln and the U.S. Government?

12. In the "Lincoln's Day April 14, 1865" area, find the plaster life mask of Lincoln from 1865.

13. Find the playbill from Ford's Theatre from that night.

14. Find the Treasury Flag that Booth caught is spur on after his attack.

15. Find actual theater tickets used that night.

16. Find Mary Todd Lincoln's opera glasses case, which she dropped on that night.

17. Find the clothes that Lincoln wore that fateful night.

18. TW, T-Find a pillow. What is on it?

19. Find the wooden door wedge used by Booth.

FORD'S THEATRE MUSEUM SCAVENGER HUNT ANSWER KEY

No code letters-suitable for all ages
Y-designed for young children (under 10)
TW-designed for tweens ages 10-13
T-designed for teenagers

1. *When you first enter the museum, you will see a picture of Lincoln's first inauguration with the half-finished Capitol Dome in the background. Lincoln insisted they continue working on the Capitol Dome during the Civil War to reassure the country that the Union and the necessary business of the nation would continue on despite the rebellion.*

2. *The statue is in "The Working White House" section. Lincoln remains our tallest president at 6'4", which was exceptionally tall for that time period.*

3. *T-In the "Improvised Plan" area, there is a small placard that describes the successful "Anaconda Plan." This plan devised by General Winfield Scott and implemented by subsequent Union generals focused on the blockading of the South by sea, dividing their states at the Mississippi River and then squeezing the life out of the Confederacy like a giant Anaconda snake.*

4. *Y-You can find this sword in one of the middle cases in this section.*

5. *These are in the case near Tad's sword.*

6. *T-Yes. There is a placard near Lincoln's gloves describing a near fatal assassination attempt in 1864 when Lincoln was riding to his beloved summer Soldier's Home cottage. The family frequently went to this house about three miles from the White House to escape the Washington, D.C. heat. On this night, Lincoln was riding alone on a horse when a sniper shot a hole through his tall stovetop hat. Lincoln joked about it and asked that the matter be kept quiet, but after that he only rode to the cottage in a carriage protected by mounted soldiers.*

7. *TW, T-This film discusses the relationship between Lincoln and the famed black leader, Frederick Douglass.*

8. *This video reading of Lincoln's most famous speech features U.S. Presidents Jimmy Carter, George H.W. Bush, Bill Clinton, and George W. Bush.*

9. *TW, T-The gun is a .44 caliber Deringer that is only capable of firing a single shot before reloading. Booth dropped it after shooting the president.*

10. *This diary was kept in an appointment book and is found in a case in the "Surratt Boarding House" area.*

11. *T-The "Surratt Boarding House" area shows the conspirators that worked with Booth to kill Lincoln and simultaneously attempted to do the same to other high-level members of the U.S.*

Government. Their goal was to put the Union into chaos in order to buy time for the Confederacy to rebuild its strength and keep fighting.

12. *This plaster mask shows the effects of stress on Lincoln's face after years of war.*

13. *This is located near the life mask.*

14. *This blue flag is in the background of the case with the playbill and life mask.*

15. *These tickets are in the same case near the life mask.*

16. *This opera glasses case is near the life mask.*

17. *Lincoln's clothes are in the next case in the same area.*

18. TW, T-*The pillow is bloodstained from the president's head resting on it as he lay dying at the Petersen House.*

19. *This is in the same case. It was used by Booth to prevent easy access to the president's box area after his attack.*

PETERSEN HOUSE-The House where Lincoln Died

516 10th Street NW (across from Ford's Theatre)

The Petersen Boarding House sits across from Ford's Theatre and is known as "The House where Lincoln Died." After being shot the night of April 14, 1865, at Ford's Theatre, the president was too critically wounded to survive a rough carriage ride to a hospital or back to the White House, so a nearby house was sought. Through the commotion, the people attending Lincoln spotted a boarder at the Petersen Boarding House across the street holding a lantern and yelling for them to bring him there. The house was owned by a German tailor, Mr. William Petersen, who built the row house in 1849. Soldiers and physicians carried Lincoln through the hysterical mob on 10th Street into the house. They laid the president on a small bed being used by a boarding soldier, William Clark, who was out celebrating the end of the war. The soldiers had to lay Lincoln diagonally across the small bed to accommodate his 6'4" frame.

Lincoln was primarily attended to by 23-year-old Dr. Charles Leale, who had begun helping him at Ford's Theatre. Dr. Leale, with other physicians assisting, made Lincoln as comfortable as possible and held his hand throughout the night. Members of the Lincoln administration and the first lady held vigil in the front rooms of the house until he died at 7:22 AM the next morning. When he died, Secretary of War Edwin Stanton remarked famously "Now he belongs to the ages" (some witnesses thought he said "angels.") Ironically, Booth had stayed in this very boarding house about a month earlier as he plotted the conspiracy. Some accounts say he even slept on the same bed where Lincoln would later die.

After the event, souvenir seekers went brazenly through Ford's Theatre and the Petersen House to find relics. Mr. Petersen was so angry at the trashed condition of the room and the rest of his building that he threw one of the bloodstained pillows out the window into the alleyway. Shockingly, the soldier whose room and bed were used by the dying president slept in the same bed later that night.

Timed tickets, which are also valid for Ford's Theatre and Museum, are needed for entry into the Petersen House. Park rangers onsite do not give presentations, but will answer any questions about the site.

Scavenger Hunt:

No code letters-suitable for all ages
Y-designed for young children (under 10)
TW-designed for tweens ages 10-13
T-designed for teenagers

1. Stand at the top of the staircase to the house and look at Ford's Theatre. Imagine what the scene was like in the street the night of April 14, 1865.

2. T-What was the profession of the man who owned the boarding house?

3. Find the room where the cabinet met to plan to catch the assassin and other conspirators.

4. How did President Lincoln fit on the small bed?

5. What did Secretary of War Stanton say when Lincoln died?

6. TW, T-What did Mr. Petersen do with one of the blood-stained pillows on the bed?

7. T-Did anyone use the bed after President Lincoln's body was removed?

PETERSEN HOUSE SCAVENGER HUNT ANSWER KEY

No code letters-suitable for all ages
Y-designed for young children (under 10)
TW-designed for tweens ages 10-13
T-designed for teenagers

1. *From this spot a boarder at the house, Henry Safford, held a lantern aloft and called for the soldiers and doctors carrying Lincoln to "bring him in here." Take a moment to imagine the confusion of the scene as the men carried Lincoln through the mob of people gathered in the street after news of the assassination attempt quickly spread.*

2. *T-William Petersen was a tailor, who had originally emigrated from Germany.*

3. *The backroom parlor area is where Secretary of War Edwin Stanton coordinated efforts to hunt down the assassin and other conspirators. First Lady Mary Todd Lincoln kept vigil in the front parlor.*

4. *Lincoln's 6' 4" frame had to be placed diagonally to fit on the bed.*

5. *"Now he belongs to the ages." Some accounts say he said "angels."*

6. *TW, T-He angrily threw the pillow out a window into an alleyway.*

7. *T-The soldier whose room it was continued using the bed after the tragedy.*

THE OLD POST OFFICE PAVILION AND CLOCK TOWER

Address/Contact Information: 1100 Pennsylvania Avenue NW, 202-289-4225, Clock Tower information-202-686-8691, www.oldpostofficedc.com

Closest Metro Station: Federal Triangle (Blue/Orange Lines)

Opening Hours/Ticketing: Clock Tower Schedule: Memorial Day to Labor Day Monday-Saturday 9 AM-8 PM, Sunday 10 AM-6 PM, Labor Day-Memorial Day Monday-Saturday 9 AM-5 PM, Sunday 10 AM-6 PM

Essential Info: This 1899 granite building with a steel frame is the former U.S. Postal Service headquarters and boasts a clock tower soaring 315 feet high. The observatory at 270 feet provides a unique 360 degree view of downtown Washington and all the area's famous landmarks. Visitors can also get a close up look at the 10 Congress Bells, which were a gift from a private foundation in Britain to celebrate the U.S. Bicentennial in 1976. The bells are replicas of the four hundred-year-old bells in Westminster Abbey in London and were cast by Whitechapel Foundry, the same company who made the original bells. There are videos of volunteers playing these bells and visitors can occasionally watch live performances.

Some people prefer this location's vantage point surrounded by downtown buildings and the National Mall to the higher view from the Washington Monument. One great advantage of this location is that it rarely gets too crowded and no reserved tickets are required for entry. The courtyard area provides frequent live entertainment and has a variety of food court restaurants and shops.

Refreshments: Food court onsite

Bathroom Facilities: Onsite

Scavenger Hunt:

No code letters-suitable for all ages
Y-designed for young children (under 10)
TW-designed for tweens ages 10-13
T-designed for teenagers

1. Find the statue of a famous American outside the Old Post Office. What was his profession?

2. Y-Stand against the side of the glass elevator as it rises up the tower.

3. Find the Congress Bells and the ropes used to pull them.

4. Find five famous D.C. landmarks from the observation deck.

THE OLD POST OFFICE PAVILION AND CLOCK TOWER SCAVENGER HUNT ANSWER KEY

No code letters-suitable for all ages
Y-designed for young children (under 10)
TW-designed for tweens ages 10-13
T-designed for teenagers

1. *There is a statue of Benjamin Franklin with his profession "Printer" engraved on it. Franklin was the first postmaster general of the U.S. Postal Service.*

2. *Y-Don't do this if you have a fear of heights as it's quite an eye-opening view.*

3. *The ropes are visible on the 9th floor when you arrive and the bells are between that level and the observatory level.*

4. *The spectacular view features many famous D.C. landmarks including the U.S. Capitol, Smithsonian museums, and the memorials and monuments on the National Mall.*

FREDERICK DOUGLASS NATIONAL HISTORICAL SITE

Address/Contact Information: 1411 W Street SE, 202-426-5961, www.nps.gov/frdo

Closest Metro Station: Anacostia (Green Line), take B2 bus in the direction of Mt. Ranier. There is a bus stop directly in front of the Douglass home at the corner of 14th and W streets. Continue along the sidewalk in the direction the bus is traveling until you reach the visitor center (15th and W Streets, SE). **I recommend taking a cab or driving to visit this site. Please be alert and cautious as some areas of Anacostia are economically depressed and can be dangerous. It is not advisable to visit this area at night or alone. Contact the site for more specific information.**

Opening Hours/Ticketing: April 16-October 15 from 9 AM-5 PM, October 16-April 15 from 9 AM-4:30 PM

Essential Info: The Frederick Douglass National Historic Site features "Cedar Hill," the mansion where famed black leader Frederick Douglass lived the last 18 years of his life until his death in 1895. Douglass' amazing life is chronicled in the short film *A Fighter for Freedom* in the visitor center. The film recounts how Douglass was born a slave in Maryland in 1818 and received some schooling from a kindly mistress as a boy. After his lessons were prohibited, he self-taught himself to become an excellent reader, writer and orator. Douglass eventually escaped to freedom at age 20 and then became a fierce advocate for the abolition of slavery. He published newspapers and his famous autobiography to help further this noble cause. He also used his masterful oratory skills to speak for the abolitionist cause throughout the U.S. and in Europe.

During the Civil War, Douglass pushed for the right of escaped slaves and free blacks to fight on the Union side and recruited many soldiers to the cause. First Lady Mary Todd Lincoln gave him President Lincoln's walking stick after the president's assassination in recognition of Douglass' efforts. After the Civil War, he remained a champion of black civil rights and also fought for the rights of women and oppressed people around the world. During his time at Cedar Hill, Douglass was appointed U.S. Marshall of the District of Columbia, and later was made the U.S. Minister to Haiti.

Tours of the mansion are offered throughout the day. The house and museum are much busier during Black History Month in February and during the summer. In the mansion, take note of the well-stocked library of Douglass' books, a period checker board, and his favorite musical instrument-the violin. On the second floor, you will see the room of Anna Murray, his wife of 44 years until her death in 1882, and the room of his second wife, Helen Pitts. His marriage to the white Helen Pitts in 1884 sparked controversy. Douglass answered critics that he would be the worst hypocrite if he did not marry a woman he loved simply because of her race. Ms. Pitts would go on to tirelessly lead the efforts to preserve Cedar Hill as a memorial to Douglass after his death. The beautiful view from the second floor features many of Washington, D.C.'s famous landmarks.

Behind the house, you will find a replica of "The Growlery," the small wooden cabin where Douglass would retreat to write and read privately and feel like the king of his own "lion's lair."

Refreshments: N/A

Bathroom Facilities: In visitor center

Scavenger Hunt:

No code letters-suitable for all ages
Y-designed for young children (under 10)
TW-designed for tweens ages 10-13
T-designed for teenagers

1. What skills, which Douglass learned secretly, were forbidden for most slaves to master?

2. TW, T-What was the name of the groups of people who wanted to eliminate slavery?

3. T-What was the name of the book that inspired Douglass?

4. T-What was the name of Douglass' anti-slavery newspaper?

5. What was the name of the woman who was the leader of the Underground Railroad and became a friend of Douglass?

6. TW, T-Who gave Douglass President Lincoln's walking stick after he was assassinated? Why?

7. Y-Find the statue of Douglass in the visitor center.

8. Find the excerpts of Douglass' speeches/writings on the wall. Which is your favorite and why?

9. Y-What was Douglass' favorite game to play with his guests? Can you find the game in the house?

10. Which instrument did Douglass like to play? Find this instrument in the house.

11. Find the bust of Douglass in the house. Who gave it to him?

12. Look out the window near Douglass' bedroom on the second floor. Which famous buildings can you see that Douglass would have also seen?

13. TW, T-What was the nickname of the small cabin behind the house where Douglass liked to work and relax privately?

FREDERICK DOUGLASS NATIONAL SITE SCAVENGER HUNT ANSWER KEY

No code letters-suitable for all ages
Y-designed for young children (under 10)
TW-designed for tweens ages 10-13
T-designed for teenagers

1. *Most slaves were not allowed to learn reading and writing. One of Douglass' mistresses taught him some reading and writing as a young boy, but this ended abruptly after the master discovered it. Douglass then self-taught himself these skills and became a masterful orator and writer.*

2. *TW, T-They were called Abolitionists.*

3. *T-The book called "The Columbian Orator" inspired Douglass. Douglass' favorite story was about a slave who debated the ills of slavery so convincingly with his master that he was freed as a result.*

4. *T-It was called "The North Star," which referred to the star that slaves followed on the Underground Railroad heading north.*

5. *Harriet Tubman was the leader of the Underground Railroad. Douglass' house in Rochester, NY, was a stop on this fugitive slave route.*

6. *TW, T-First Lady Mary Todd Lincoln gave Douglass this walking stick in recognition of Douglass' efforts to recruit black soldiers to fight for the Union during the Civil War.*

7. *Y-The statue is in the back of the visitor center.*

8. *These excerpts are on the wall near the statue of Douglass.*

9. *Y-Douglass liked to play checkers with his guests. A period checkers table is in the first room on the left.*

10. *Douglass loved to play violin. A violin is on the piano in the first room on the right.*

11. *The bust in Douglass' bedroom is a plaster copy of the bust of him found in Rochester, NY. His friends in Rochester, NY, sent this bust to Douglass for display in his Cedar Hill home.*

12. *From the window near Douglass' bedroom on the second floor, you can see the Washington Monument, the U.S. Capitol, and the Library of Congress. All of these buildings were in existence during Douglass' residence at Cedar Hill.*

13. *TW, T-Douglass thought of it as his "lion's lair" and nicknamed it the Growlery.*

OLD STONE HOUSE

Address/Contact Information: 3051 M Street NW, 202-895-6070, www.nps.gov/olst

Closest Metro Station: Foggy Bottom (Blue/Orange Lines). Take blue Georgetown shuttle bus from station.

Opening Hours/Ticketing: Wednesday-Sunday 12 PM-5 PM

Essential Info: The Old Stone House is the oldest standing structure in Washington, D.C., and is 85% original. This simple but impressive house provides a unique view into middle-class colonial life in the 18th century. The house was built by cabinetmaker Christopher Layman in 1765 for use as both a residence and a shop. After Layman's death shortly after the building was finished, it was bought by Cassandra Chew who added a wing to the house in 1767. The house boasts period artifacts and a beautiful English garden that provides a rare bit of tranquility on bustling M Street in Georgetown.

Refreshments: There are many excellent restaurants on M Street.

Bathroom Facilities: N/A

Scavenger Hunt:

No code letters-suitable for all ages
Y-designed for young children (under 10)
TW-designed for tweens ages 10-13
T-designed for teenagers

1. How tall were the average men and women in colonial times compared to today? Use the chart on the wall to see how you and your family compare.

2. Y, TW-Pick up and try out some of the colonial era toys. Do any look familiar to present day toys?

3. In the dining room, can you find sheet music and a deck of cards?

4. TW, T-What was the original color of the dining room?

5. TW-What was the linen spinning wheel used for in the small bedroom?

6. What is in the basket near the large spinning wheel in the large bedroom?

7. What material was used to stuff mattresses in all the bedrooms?

8. Y-Find the pick-up sticks game in the upstairs children's bedroom.

9. T-Why weren't there many closets in houses during colonial times?

10. Find the bench farthest away from the house in the garden and sit on it. How noisy is it here compared to walking on M Street?

OLD STONE HOUSE SCAVENGER HUNT ANSWER KEY

No code letters-suitable for all ages
Y-designed for young children (under 10)
TW-designed for tweens ages 10-13
    T-designed for teenagers

1. *You will find a chart and explanation of varying average heights on the left as you enter the first room. The difference in height from the present day to the colonial era is not as great as one might think.*

2. Y, TW-*A basket in the room contains examples of colonial toys. Some toys look familiar including a yo-yo.*

3. *Playing music and games such as cards were some of the ways families would amuse themselves during this time. The sheet music is on the wooden stands and the cards are in the open drawer of a table to the right of the entrance.*

4. TW, T-*To the right of the dining room entrance near the floor, you will find an exhibit showing the many layers of paint applied during the long life of the house. The original maroon color layer of the dining room is on the bottom.*

5. TW-*The women in the family would use spinning wheels such as this to make clothing and other household textile needs.*

6. *This basket contains naturally dyed wool yarn.*

7. *The mattresses are stuffed with straw.*

8. Y-*This game and others are found in front of the bed.*

9. T-*As explained by the placard next to the entrance, the British Crown had a law designating closets as additional rooms that were subject to a closet tax. As a result, closets were rare until the American victory in the Revolutionary War.*

10. *One can enjoy a tranquil moment while sitting on this bench near the end of the garden.*

Private Museums

International Spy Museum. Courtesy of Destination DC.

Washington, D.C., has an excellent variety of privately owned museums showcasing items as diverse as spy equipment and artifacts from the Holocaust. These museums provide even more interesting destinations for the city's visitors to explore.

INTERNATIONAL SPY MUSEUM

Address/Contact Information: 800 F Street NW, 202-654-0950, www.spymuseum.org

Closest Metro Station: Gallery Place-Chinatown (Green/Yellow Lines and Red Line)

Opening Hours/Ticketing: 9 AM-7 PM Memorial Day to Labor Day, 10 AM-6 PM rest of year, but hours may vary. Tickets, without tax, cost $18 for ages 12-64, $17 for 65+, and $15 for kids ages 5-11. Reserve in advance online during the high season. Group discounts are available.

Essential Info: This is the only public museum in the world dedicated specifically to espionage and its impact on world events. The museum is located in the building housing the former head-quarters of the American Communist Party, The museum contains the world's largest display of spy artifacts as well as interactive exhibits that introduce you to the skills and techniques necessary to succeed in espionage.

By following the hunt below, you will be able to experience many of the highlights of this museum. Start by assuming an "alias" and remembering the accompanying details until you leave-you will be quizzed upon exiting at an interactive terminal if so desired. After watching a brief video orientation on spying, you will enter a section where there are a variety of interactive exhibits-such as spotting spies in disguise. Take your time in this section as children especially will enjoy it.

The rest of the museum is interesting if a bit overwhelming as you will see thousands of examples of spy devices and tools from ancient times to today. A good understanding of history will help visitors enjoy the museum even further. If your kids are too young and/or not history buffs you can breeze through some of the sections that go into great detail on the Cold War and other time periods. Take the time to listen to some of the presentations such as: spying during Washington's time, the World War II documentaries in the old theater, the portrayal of spies in movies and television, and the final video on the need for intelligence in the modern world.

The museum also offers a wide variety of lectures and additional programs for kids such as "Operation Spy," a one hour program where participants have to find a missing nuclear trigger before it's too late. Additional fees apply for these programs. Visit their website for the latest schedule of special events.

Refreshments: There are restaurants throughout the area including the Spy Café next to the Museum.

Bathroom Facilities: In the museum.

Scavenger Hunt:

No code letters-suitable for all ages
Y-designed for young children (under 10)
TW-designed for tweens ages 10-13
T-designed for teenagers

1. T-Find out which organization had their headquarters in this building in the 1940s.

2. Assume an "alias"-an alternate identity-and remember the key facts when you exit the museum.

3. Play the interactive video game where you try and spot an agent in disguise.

4. Find three hidden transmitter devices. Which one do you like the most?

5. Y-Crawl through the museum's ductwork and spy on the people below.

6. Find Agent 007 James Bond's car. Don't leave until it does something special.

7. Find three weapons hidden in objects.

8. Find a life-sized Japanese Ninja warrior in a glass case.

9. Find the camera-carrying homing pigeon.

10. Find George Washington's letter.

11. Step inside the "Father of the KGB's" office. Which country used the KGB as their spy agency?

12. Y-Find the old war and spy toys near the theater. What's your favorite?

13. Watch a World War II documentary or cartoon in the old theater.

14. TW, T-Play the interactive game showing how the "Enigma" decoding device worked.

15. TW, T-Crack the Navajo Code Talkers code.

16. T-Find information about a baseball player and entertainer who were also spies.

17. In the downstairs "War of the Spies" Gallery, pick up the receiver and listen to a recording in the telephone booth.

18. T-What was the name of the feared East German intelligence agency during the Cold War?

19. Find a section of a tunnel that was under Berlin.

20. Find a section of the Berlin Wall. T-How long did this barrier divide the city of Berlin?

21. Find some Washington, D.C., landmarks on the spy satellite photo.

22. Watch the video clip showing fictional spies including Austin Powers. TW, T-What was Austin's favorite catchprase?

23. TW, T-In the "Wilderness of Mirrors" exhibit, find two double agents and learn what the consequences of their actions were.

24. TW, T-In the "21st Century" Gallery watch the movie "Ground Truth" discussing the challenges facing modern espionage.

25. Complete your debriefing and cross the border without any problems.

INTERNATIONAL SPY MUSEUM SCAVENGER HUNT ANSWER KEY

No code letters-suitable for all ages
Y-designed for young children (under 10)
TW-designed for tweens ages 10-13
T-designed for teenagers

1. T-*The American Communist Party had its headquarters in this building from 1941-48.*

2. *At the beginning of the museum in the "Covers and Legends" Gallery everyone is given an "alias" and some key facts to remember about their alternate identities. Remember these facts as you will be quizzed at an interactive terminal as you exit the museum.*

3. *In the first area you enter in the "School for Spies" gallery, you will find this interactive video game and others.*

4. *In the "School for Spies" gallery, you will see many examples of transmitter devices hidden in ingenious ways to gather information.*

5. Y-*In the "School for Spies" gallery on the right hand side you will find an entryway for crawling in the air ducts above your fellow museumgoers.*

6. *At the end of the "School for Spies" gallery, you will find James Bond's stylish and formidable 1964 Aston Martin DB5. Every few minutes you will hear a familiar music theme and see an example of the car's defensive equipment and the firing of its front machine guns.*

7. *In the "School for Spies" gallery you will find guns, knives, and explosives hidden in a variety of common objects.*

8. *In the "Secret History of History" gallery you will find a life-sized model of a Japanese Ninja in an aggressive battle stance.*

9. *In a room on the left in the "Secret History of History" gallery, there is an exhibit on aerial reconnaissance. The homing pigeon with a camera was a World War I innovation.*

10. *In the parlor style room on the right in the "Secret History of History" gallery, you will find a letter written by George Washington in 1777. In the letter, Washington discusses the formation of a spy network in British-occupied New York City. As visitors to Mount Vernon know, Washington understood the importance of intelligence gathering in achieving victory in the Revolutionary War.*

11. *This intimidating office is found at the end of the "Secret History of History" gallery and belonged to legendary spymaster Feliks Dzerzhinsky. The KGB was the spy agency of the Soviet Union, which was the United States main enemy during the Cold War era. This era existed after World War II until the end of the Soviet Union in 1991.*

12. Y-*There is an interesting collection of vintage metal and plastic toys outside the theater.*

13. *The theater continuously plays morale-boosting cartoons and interesting World War II era documentaries about enemy spy rings.*

14. TW, T-*In the "Spies Among Us" gallery there is an interactive game showing how the German "Enigma" decoding device worked during World War II.*

15. TW, T-*In the "Spies Among Us" gallery visitors can play an interactive game to try and crack the Navajo Code Talkers code. The Navajo Code Talkers were Navajo American Indians who created an unbreakable code from the Navajo language. They operated throughout the Pacific Theater and communicated vital battlefield information over the radio. The Japanese were never able to break their code.*

16. T-*Moe Berg was a professional baseball player who also gathered intelligence about the research efforts of Nazi scientists developing the Atom Bomb. Famed entertainer Josephine Baker also provided valuable intelligence working with the French Resistance.*

17. *You will find the red telephone booth near a car in Cold War Berlin, Germany.*

18. T-*The East German intelligence agency, the Ministry for State Security was known as the "Stasi." This agency ruthlessly and efficiently controlled and monitored the lives of millions in socialist East Germany (the German Democratic Republic). The Stasi used all types of spying technology and a vast network of informants at home and abroad to gather intelligence, repress democratic opposition and enable the ruling Socialist Unity Party of Germany (SED) to maintain firm control of East Germany.*

19. *The U.S. and British intelligence agencies built this tunnel in Berlin to tap Soviet communication lines and gather information.*

20. *The museum has a section of the notorious Berlin Wall.* T-*This ugly barrier divided East and West Berlin from 1961 to 1989 and was a powerful symbol of the Cold War.*

21. *On the floor of this exhibit there is a huge spy satellite photo of Washington, D.C., with many famous landmarks visible.*

22. *This interesting exhibit with toys, books and video clips shows the impact of espionage on popular culture and how spies are portrayed dramatically and comically in literature, movies and television.* TW, T-*Austin Powers' famous catchphrase was "Oh behave!"*

23. TW, T-*During the Cold War there were many double agents who betrayed their home countries for material gain. Notorious examples include Kim Philby and Robert Hanssen.*

24. TW, T-*This sobering movie illustrates the many challenges the world faces with modern terrorism and other threats.*

25. *In the last room there is an interactive terminal where you answer questions about your alias and recent visit. Make sure you get the answers right so you can avoid being detained!*

NEWSEUM

Address/Contact Information: Pennsylvania Avenue and 6th Street, NW, 888-639-7386, www.newseum.org

Closest Metro Station: Archives/Navy Memorial (Green/Yellow Lines), Judiciary Square (Red Line)

Opening Hours/Ticketing: 9 AM-5 PM, Tickets, without tax, cost $21.95 for ages19-64, $12.95 for ages 7-18, $17.95 for ages 65+, military and students. There is also a Family Four Pack ticket for $49.95 and an online purchase discount of 10%. Groups of 10 or more get an additional discount per ticket of $15.95 for adults and seniors and $10.95 for ages 7-18. Groups also receive a complimentary chaperone ticket for every 10 tickets. Tickets are valid for two consecutive days.

Essential Info: This massive 250,000-square-foot marble and glass museum celebrates the Freedom of the Press in grand style. This museum opened in 2008 and offers visitors five centuries of news history artifacts combined with interesting interactive and multimedia exhibits. Visitors also get a chance to simulate the work of reporters including an opportunity to do a live report in front of a camera. Don't miss the 4-D multimedia presentation called "**I-Witness,**" which recounts the career experiences of three legendary journalists.

Download or pick up a copy of their 2-Hour Highlights Tour brochure to guide you through the main attractions. Start in the concourse and then take the elevator to the top level and proceed down following the scavenger hunt questions below. These questions will cover many of the museum highlights. There are also temporary exhibitions and a large variety of interactive terminals to explore.

The Newseum also offers customized private group tours for an additional fee with reservations in advance.

Refreshments: The Food Section restaurant is on the lower level.

Bathroom Facilities: Onsite

Scavenger Hunt:

No code letters-suitable for all ages
Y-designed for young children (under 10)
TW-designed for tweens ages 10-13
T-designed for teenagers

1. Before entering the museum find a newspaper from your home state.

Concourse Level

2. Watch the introductory film "What's News?"

3. Y- What is the latest news on the big screen in the Great Hall of News area?

4. T-Find the Unabomber's cabin.

5. Find the sections of the Berlin Wall and the East German guard tower. T-What year did the Berlin Wall fall symbolizing the beginning of the end of the Cold War?

Level 6

6. Go to the Pennsylvania Avenue terrace and enjoy the view of the Capitol and National Mall.

7. Try and find your hometown newspaper in "Today's Front Pages."

Level 5

8. In the "News History" section find the headline "Man lands on the Moon." What year did this happen?

9. Stop in the small theater showing a film about the press and Hollywood.

10. T-Find the door from the Watergate office complex break-in. Whose presidency ended because of this scandal?

11. Find the first pamphlet printing of the U.S. Constitution in the "Great Books Gallery."

Level 4

12. In the 9/11 Gallery find the large antenna mast. Where did this once stand?

13. Find newspaper headlines from three countries about the 9/11 attack.

14. Walk to the front side of the building to the "First Amendment" Gallery and listen to Bart Simpson's thoughts on his First Amendment rights. Which freedom in the First Amendment to the U.S. Constitution does the Newseum primarily celebrate?

15. TW, T-In the "World News" section find some examples of countries without freedom of the press on the World Press Freedom Map.

Level 3

16. In the "Internet, TV, and Radio" section, use the touch-screen to listen to coverage of John Glenn's historic orbiting of the Earth.

17. Find a microphone used by President Franklin Delano Roosevelt. T-What did Roosevelt call his radio addresses to the American people?

Level 2

18. In the "Interactive Newsroom" section, pretend to be a reporter using the touch-screen system.

19. If you have time, give a live news report on camera.

20. TW, T-In the "Ethics Center," team up with an adult to answer tough questions and assemble a newspaper front page while racing the clock.

Level 1

21. Find the Pulitzer Prize winning photographs for the year you and your parents were born. TW, T-Which photograph shows the earliest event you can remember? **Please note that some of these pictures are graphic and may not be appropriate for children under 12.**

22. Find the Annenberg Theater and watch the 4-D presentation "I-Witness!" Which journalist did you find most impressive?

NEWSEUM SCAVENGER HUNT ANSWER KEY

No code letters-suitable for all ages
Y-designed for young children (under 10)
TW-designed for tweens ages 10-13
T-designed for teenagers

1. *Newspapers from every state line the front of the building.*

Concourse Level

2. *This 7-minute introductory film explores the role news plays in people's lives and how it unites people from around the world.*

3. *Y-In the Great Hall area news reports run continuously on the big screen and all around you.*

4. *T-The cabin of this mentally unstable killer who made homemade bombs and mailed them to his victims is found in the "G-Men and Journalists" Exhibit.*

5. *These huge exhibits are found behind the glass elevators. T-The Berlin Wall came down in 1989. Take the glass elevator to level 6 to continue the hunt.*

Level 6

6. *This terrace with an amazing view is to the left of the elevator.*

7. *Walk through this gallery and down the stairs to Level 5.*

Level 5

8. *The United States landed on the moon on July 20, 1969.*

9. *There are five theaters behind the cases along each wall. The various depictions of the press by Hollywood over the years are entertaining.*

10. *T-The scandal arising from the politically motivated break-in of the Democratic National Committee Headquarters at the Watergate office complex in 1972 led to the resignation of President Richard Nixon in 1974.*

11. *After looking through some of these incredibly influential works, exit into the Big Screen Theater for a show and then head down the stairs to Level 4.*

Level 4

12. *This was part of the antenna that stood atop the North Tower of the World Trade Center in New York City before both towers were destroyed on September 11, 2001.*

13. *This gallery has more than 100 front pages of global coverage of the attack.*

14. *The Newseum celebrates the Freedom of the Press. Walk down the staircase that crosses the atrium to Level 3 and the "World News" section.*

Level 3

15. *TW, T-The map is color coded by the amount of freedom of the press. Countries with no freedom of the press are colored red and are found around the world.*

16. *Touch-screens in this section play news coverage about this fascinating event and other historic moments.*

17. *TW, T-FDR used to give occasional "Fireside Chats" on the radio to inform and comfort citizens during the tumultuous years of his presidency. Go down the staircase to Level 2 to the "Interactive Newsroom" section.*

Level 2

18. *This system gives you an idea about what it takes to be a good reporter.*

19. *There are multiple stations with cameras where visitors can give a simulated news report. After doing your report you can save it electronically and share it with friends and family.*

20. *TW, T-These simulated scenarios will test your ethics. Take the stairs down to Level 1 and head to the "Pulitzer Prize Photographs" section.*

Level 1

21. *These photos capture moving moments in the history of our world. Please note that some of these pictures are graphic and may not be appropriate for children under 12.*

22. *Don't miss this unique presentation, which shows the experiences of three famous American journalists and other historic moments in an entertaining and realistic setting.*

NATIONAL MUSEUM OF CRIME & PUNISHMENT

Address/Contact Information: 575 7th Street, NW, 202-621-5550, www.crimemuseum.org

Closest Metro Station: Gallery Place/Chinatown (Green/Yellow Lines and Red Line)

Opening Hours/Ticketing: From September-May 20th open Sunday-Thursday 10 AM-7 PM, Friday-Saturday 10 AM-8 PM. From May 21st- August, open Monday-Saturday 9 AM-9 PM, Sunday 10 AM-7 PM. Last entry is always one hour before closing. For adults ages 12-59 online tickets, without tax, cost $17.95, gate tickets cost $19.95. For children 5-11 online and gate tickets cost $14.95. Children under age 5 are free. For seniors 60+, military and law enforcement online tickets cost $14.95 and gate tickets cost $16.95. Order tickets online or by phone at 202-651-5567. Groups of 20 or more require advance reservations. Group ticket prices are reduced to $15.25 for adults and $12.75 for students and all other categories.

Essential Info: This huge new museum has more than 25,000 square feet of exhibit space over its three levels and contains a multitude of informative placards, artifacts and interactive exhibits focused on the intriguing topic of crime and punishment. The museum provides a history of crime and its consequences using actual and simulated artifacts from infamous criminals and crimes, driving and shooting simulators and a detailed look at real Crime Scene Investigation (CSI) procedures. The filming studio for the hit television show *America's Most Wanted* is also located on the premises.

This is a museum for crime and history buffs and features many interesting artifacts and replicas along with a lot of information to read on placards. The scavenger hunt follows the suggested visitor's path to the museum and captures many of the highlights.

Please note that some of the exhibits contain disturbing images, artifacts and themes, which are not suitable for young children or sensitive people in general. Monitor your family or group closely when visiting this museum and when necessary skip certain age appropriate sections, such as the CSI examination area.

Refreshments: There are beverages, candy, and ice cream in the gift shop.

Bathroom Facilities: Onsite

Scavenger Hunt:

No code letters-suitable for all ages
Y-designed for young children (under 10)
TW-designed for tweens ages 10-13
T-designed for teenagers

1. Find the stocks. What were some of the crimes people committed to suffer this punishment?

2. Find the model of Blackbeard the pirate. Was his treasure ever found?

3. Explore the Cochise County Jail.

4. Find the Confederate flag carried by Jesse James.

5. Spin the "Legends of the Old West" wheel and find one hero and one villain.

6. T-Find the bullet-riddled 1934 Ford from the movie *Bonnie and Clyde*.

7. Find a prop machine gun used in the film *Scarface*.

8. TW, T-Try your hand at cracking a safe.

9. Go to the "Booking Officer" area and get fingerprinted.

10. Stand in a line-up. What are these used for?

11. Y-Try to escape from a jail cell.

12. Find Al Capone's prison cell. Is it a typical cell?

13. Y- Find yourself on the heat seeking camera monitor.

14. Try out the shooting and driving simulators.

15. Find the names of a few famous television crime shows.

16. Visit *America's Most Wanted* studio. View yourself as a most wanted suspect.

NATIONAL MUSEUM OF CRIME AND PUNISHMENT SCAVENGER HUNT ANSWER KEY

No code letters-suitable for all ages
Y-designed for young children (under 10)
TW-designed for tweens ages 10-13
T-designed for teenagers

1. *Relatively minor offenses such as petty thievery and "offensive" behavior in public could have resulted in you ending up in the stocks.*

2. *This terrifying pirate's treasure was never found.*

3. *Get the feel of Old West Justice as you read about some famous outlaws and their fates.*

4. *This interesting artifact is to the left of the Cochise County Jail area.*

5. *This wheel gives interesting information on many heroes and villains of the old west.*

6. T-*This vehicle was used in the hit 1967 movie starring Warren Beatty and Faye Dunaway.*

7. *A case in the exhibit area on gangsters contains this prop used by Al Pacino in the 1983 movie.*

8. TW, T-*In the "Silent Criminals" area you will find an interactive exhibit where you can learn how to crack open a safe.*

9. *There is an interactive terminal in this area where you can view your electronic fingerprints.*

10. *These line-ups are used by police to help witnesses identify crime suspects.*

11. Y-*There is a large hole in the jail cell, which you can crawl out of into the next exhibit area.*

12. *Al Capone's luxurious cell was a symbol of the gangster's power even when he was incarcerated.*

13. Y, TW-*This monitor is found at the end of the exhibits on this floor near the simulators.*

14. *These interesting simulators test your judgment along with your shooting and driving ability.*

15. *The names of many famous television crime shows along with various props are on the wall.*

16. *There is a green screen area where you can picture yourself as a most wanted suspect.*

UNITED STATES HOLOCAUST MEMORIAL MUSEUM

Address/Contact Information: 100 Raoul Wallenberg Place SW, 202-488-0400, www.ushmm.org

Closest Metro Station: Smithsonian (Blue/Orange Lines)

Opening Hours/Ticketing: 10 AM-5:20 PM, entry passes are required for permanent exhibition from March-August. Visitors can obtain free same day passes on a first-come, first-served basis. Visitors can also obtain passes in advance for a $1 processing fee on their website or by calling 877-80-USHMM.

Essential Info: Perhaps the most solemn site in Washington, D.C., the U.S. Holocaust Memorial Museum was dedicated in 1993 to honor the millions of Jewish people and other groups persecuted by Nazi Germany and its allies. Inside there are also tributes to the allied liberators of the concentration camps as well as to those who helped hide and protect people from the Nazis. Architect James Ingo Freed designed the building to make people uncomfortable and feel oppressed to remind visitors of the victims' suffering. The interior is reminiscent of a prison with industrial metalwork such as steel plates, rivets and exposed beams.

The permanent exhibition takes up four levels with visitors beginning the tour by taking an identification card of an actual victim of the Holocaust. **Because of its graphic nature, this main part of the museum is not recommended for children under 11.** Visitors begin on the top level and follow the historic progression of this terrible time from the rise of the Nazis to power to the final liberation of the concentration camps in 1945. Throughout the museum are videos and visual aids explaining this time period. More disturbing is seeing actual artifacts such as prison uniforms, confiscated personal items, and an actual boxcar used to transport hundreds of people crowded on top of one another. The many artifacts and images reflecting an unimaginable cruelty will leave a lasting impression on any visitor.

Visitors can light a candle in tribute to the victims at the Hall of Remembrance on the first floor. There is also a Children's Tile Wall and special exhibits on the bottom level. On the second level is The Wexner Center, which is a multimedia encyclopedia on the history of the Holocaust, featuring video recollections of Holocaust survivors and camp liberators.

On the first level is an exhibit designed for children 8 and older called **"Remember the Children: Daniel's Story."** This exhibit follows the life of a fictional boy, Daniel (a composite of the millions of children affected by the Holocaust), as he struggles to understand what is happening to his family and friends during this tragic period. Photographs and simulated artifacts combined with a spoken narrative tell Daniel's heartbreaking story. At the end of the exhibit, children are invited to share their reflections on what they have experienced. This exhibit is a good alternative for children too young or too sensitive for the disturbing permanent exhibition.

Refreshments: Museum café in the annex next door.

Bathroom Facilities: Throughout the museum.

Scavenger Hunt: The permanent exhibition is not appropriate for a scavenger hunt, but the "Daniel's Story" exhibition provides an opportunity for younger children to carry out this activity.

Daniel's Story

1. Can you find Daniel's diary? What is a diary?

2. What did the Nazi's make Daniel wear to show he was Jewish?

3. Look in the cookie box-whose name is there?

4. Push a button to light up the country where they live. Which country is it?

5. Open the "windows" of the house.

6. What happened to Jewish stores and synagogues on "Kristallnacht?" Can you find broken glass?

7. Find the ghetto area. Who was forced to live there?

8. Look through the door to find people eating soup. Was there much food in the ghetto? Does it look very good?

9. Climb into the wall area and see where Daniel and Erika lived in 1942.

10. Find the train car. Where did it take the Jewish people?

11. Which groups of people were imprisoned in the "concentration camps?"

12. Can you find barbed wire and a watchtower at the camp?

13. What happened to Daniel's diary? How did he keep a diary going in the camp?

14. Listen to the phone to learn more about what happened during this terrible time.

15. How do you feel after hearing about Daniel's story?

16. How do you feel about living in a country like America compared to Nazi Germany?

17. Write your feelings down and read how other children have reacted to this exhibit.

18. Find the Hall of Remembrance and light a candle to honor those who suffered during the Holocaust.

UNITED STATES HOLOCAUST MEMORIAL MUSEUM SCAVENGER HUNT ANSWER KEY

Daniel's Story

1. *A diary is a book people use to record personal thoughts and experiences. Daniel's fictional diary gives readers a sense of what many millions of children experienced during this terrible time.*

2. *Jewish people were forced to wear golden yellow stars with the word "Jude" meaning Jew printed on them. These stars signified that the wearers were Jewish and considered different and inferior.*

3. *The name Erika is on the cookies. Erika is Daniel's sister.*

4. *Daniel's family originally lived in Germany.*

5. *There is more to see when you open the windows of the house.*

6. *Gangs of Nazis destroyed and burned down Jewish stores and synagogues on Kristallnacht, which means "night of broken glass" in German.*

7. *The Nazis forced the Jewish people to live together in these dirty and crowded neighborhoods called ghettos.*

8. *Nutritious food was hard to come by in the ghetto, especially as time passed.*

9. *The whole family lived in one room in the ghetto.*

10. *These cramped train cars took many Jewish people to concentration camps in Germany and other countries.*

11. *The Nazis kept Jewish people, political opponents, and anyone else they considered inferior or dangerous in these terrible camps.*

12. *These camps were surrounded by barbed wire and patrolled by guards to prevent people from escaping.*

13. *The Nazis took Daniel's diary when he got to the camp. He kept his diary going in his mind.*

14. *The phones have recordings talking about more experiences during this awful period.*

15. *Daniel's tragic story shared by so many is hard for anyone of any age to comprehend.*

16. *This exhibit and the museum make people appreciate their freedom and safety even more.*

17. *Many children write moving tributes to the people who suffered during the Holocaust.*

18. *This somber hall is nearby on the same level and allows visitors a chance to pay tribute to the people who suffered through this terrible event in world history. It also allows visitors a chance to reflect on how lucky they are to live in a free country.*

Other Main Attractions in Washington, D.C.

T he District has additional main attractions of interest, which do not fall into clearly defined categories. Each of these sites offers visitors a unique educational and entertaining experience.

NATIONAL GALLERY OF ART

Address/Contact Information: Buildings and sculpture garden located on the National Mall between 3rd and 9th Streets NW, and along Constitution Avenue NW, 202-737-4215, www.nga.gov

Closest Metro Station: Judiciary Square (Red Line), Archives/Navy Memorial (Green/Yellow Lines), Smithsonian (Blue/Orange Lines)

Opening Hours/Ticketing: Monday to Saturday 10 AM-5 PM, Sunday 11 AM-6 PM

Essential Info: In 1937 the United States Congress created the National Gallery of Art with a Joint Resolution that accepted a generous gift from financier Andrew Mellon. This noted art collector and public servant donated his extensive art collection along with the funds for the construction of an art gallery to house it. John Russell Pope designed the original impressive neoclassical building (now called the West Building), which opened in 1941. Mellon was a former Secretary of the Treasury and Ambassador to Britain and his collection included many European masterpieces with a large amount coming from the famed Hermitage Museum in Russia. Mellon's hope that his generous contribution of famous paintings and sculptures would inspire other wealthy individuals to donate was soon realized. After Mellon's gift, huge donations of cash and artwork poured into this new center of the arts in America, making it a truly world class museum.

The West Wing focuses on the development of Western art from medieval times to the 19th century and also features works from pre-20th century American artists. This gallery displays paintings, sculptures and other artwork by such giants as Rembrandt, Van Gogh, Raphael, Monet, Rodin and Hopper as well as the only Leonardo Da Vinci painting in the Americas.

In 1978 the modern East Building, designed by I.M. Pei, opened to accommodate the National Gallery's ever expanding collection of precious art. This building contains 20th century paintings, sculptures, drawings and prints by masters such as Picasso, Dali, Pollock, and Matisse. This building also houses the world's largest mobile hanging from the ceiling, created by Alexander Calder. In addition, the building contains space for frequent temporary exhibitions, research facilities and auditoriums for public events.

The two buildings are connected by an underground concourse area featuring a moving walkway decorated with *Multiverse*, the largest and most complex light sculpture created by American artist Leo Villareal. This work features 41,000 computer programmed LED (light emitting diodes) nodes that illuminate channels throughout the 200-foot-long moving walkway. The concourse area also features a gift shop and café area where you can enjoy gelato and other treats while a waterfall cascades on the windows in front of you.

In 1999, a 6-acre sculpture garden was added in the land across from the National Archives and between the West Building and the Museum of Natural History. This popular spot features 17 unusual public sculptures by famous artists such as Lichtenstein, Oldenburg, and Bourgeois. In the summer, locals and tourists alike flock to free Friday evening "Jazz in the Garden" concerts. You can enjoy ice skating (rentals available) at the same location in the winter. The Pavilion Café offers food and refreshments including hot chocolate in the winter.

Start your visit at the information center near the West Building National Mall entrance, where you can obtain a useful Map and Visitor's Guide, find information about temporary exhibits and daily programs, and also browse the vast art collection on computer terminals. The information center also offers equipment for audio tours for adults and children, as well as regularly scheduled highlights tours with museum staff. The scavenger hunt will explore many of the highlights of the National Gallery by building/gallery area, but please refer to the Visitor's Guide and plan your visit according to your time constraints and preferences.

The National Gallery also offers regularly scheduled art-related films for children of all ages. In addition, every Sunday there is a hands-on investigative activity exploring one work of art. Sign-up begins on Sunday at 11 AM for 60-minute programs throughout the day for children ages 4-7. Before and after your visit, children can play online games and complete interactive activities to learn more about the art at the National Gallery at www.nga.gov/kids/kids.htm.

Refreshments: Various cafeterias/restaurants onsite

Bathroom Facilities: Onsite

Scavenger Hunt:

No code letters-suitable for all ages
Y-designed for young children (under 10)
TW-designed for tweens ages 10-13
T-designed for teenagers

West Building

1. Find the statue of Mercury when you enter the West Building.

2. Find the Leonardo Da Vinci painting. What is on the back?

3. Across the hall in the Dutch Masters area find a painting of a man surrounded by lions.

4. In the Dutch masters area find a small painting of a red-haired girl wearing a red hat.

5. If time, descend to the ground floor on the west side and find the wax statuette of a little dancing girl in Gallery 3.

6. T-Go to the East side of the West Building. Find busts of the French philosopher Voltaire with a wig (perruque) and without one sculpted by Houdon in Gallery 53. What famous Americans did Houdon also portray in sculptures and busts?

7. Find a frightening portrayal of a shipwreck in Gallery 55.

8. In which room is the French Emperor Napoleon standing in the famous painting by Jacques-Louis David in Gallery 56?

9. Find a family portrait of the Washingtons.

10. TW, T-In which city's harbor did a shark attack occur, which was later captured in a painting in Gallery 60B?

11. Y-How many paintings of American bisons (buffaloes) can you find in Gallery 65?

12. TW, T-In which war did the soldiers portrayed in the Shaw Memorial fight?

13. Go to the Ground Floor, Gallery 42, and find two different paintings of the same cathedral.

Concourse

14. Y, TW-Ride both ways on the walkway with flashing lights.

East Wing

15. Look up to find the huge multi-colored mobile hanging from the ceiling.

16. On the Mezzanine Level, find a modern art depiction of the Last Supper with Jesus and the Apostles. Who is the only one showing his face in the painting?

17. On the Upper Level, find a painting containing an image of the Statue of Liberty.

18. What instrument is the musician playing in Picasso's *Harlequin Musician*?

19. T-On the Ground Floor in the Small French Paintings area, find a painting by Vincent van Gogh.

Scultpure Garden

Located between the West Building and the National Museum of Natural History. Enter from Seventh Street and proceed on the circular path to the right.

20. Y,TW-What type of animal is thinking deeply on a rock?

21. Find a polished marble chair to sit in and take a break.

22. Find a gigantic spider.

23. T-Find a massive typewriter eraser. What were these used for before the personal computer age?

24. Find a subway or metro station from another city. Can you guess the city?

25. Find a silver-colored tree.

26. Find a house that a cartoon character might live in. Can you spot a similar colored sculpture when looking across the National Mall?

NATIONAL GALLERY OF ART SCAVENGER HUNT ANSWER KEY

No code letters-suitable for all ages
Y-designed for young children (under 10)
TW-designed for tweens ages 10-13
T-designed for teenagers

West Building

1. *This statue is prominently displayed under the rotunda as you enter the West Building from the National Mall.*

2. *This painting entitled "Ginevra de' Benci" is the only Da Vinci painting in the Americas and was completed in the late 1400s. It is located in Gallery 6. On the reverse of the painting there is a wreath made of laurel and palm around a sprig of juniper and a scroll with a Latin phrase meaning "Beauty adorns virtue."*

3. *"Daniel in the Lion's Den" by Dutch painter Peter Paul Rubens is located in Gallery 45.*

4. *"Girl with Red Hat" by Johannes Vermeer is located in Gallery 50A.*

5. *This famous statuette entitled "Little Dancer Aged Fourteen" by Edgar Degas is in Gallery 3 on the ground floor.*

6. *T-The famed French sculptor, Jean Antoine Houdon, sculpted these busts located in Gallery 53. Houdon also sculpted likenesses of Washington, Jefferson and Franklin and many other famous Americans and Europeans of the time.*

7. *"The Shipwreck" by Claude Joseph Vernet is located in Gallery 55.*

8. *David's "The Emperor Napoleon in his Study at the Tuileries" is located in Gallery 56. This is a unique portrait as it portrays the famous French leader standing in his military uniform not on a battlefield or in a regal setting, but in his private study.*

9. *"The Washington Family" by Edward Savage is located in Gallery 62.*

10. *TW, T-The oil painting of "Watson and the Shark" by John Singleton Copley depicts a shark attack in the harbor of Havana, Cuba. The painting is located in Gallery 60B.*

11. *Y-There are a couple of these among the fascinating paintings of Native Americans and the Old West by George Catlin found in Gallery 65.*

12. TW, T-*The Shaw Memorial by Augustus Saint-Gaudens is located in Gallery 66. It portrays members of the Massachusetts Fifty-fourth Regiment, the first unit of black soldiers to fight in the Civil War, led by Colonel Robert Shaw.*

13. *Claude Monet's "Rouen Cathedral, West Façade," and "Rouen Cathedral, West Façade, Sunlight," are excellent representations of the French Impressionist movement, which changed accepted concepts on color and light. Many other impressive paintings are in this gallery.*

Concourse

14. Y, TW-*This walkway, described in the introduction, is both practical and an entertaining work of art.*

East Wing

15. *This multi-colored mobile by Alexander Calder is the largest in the world and hangs from the ceiling.*

16. *This stunning painting "The Sacrament of the Last Supper" by Salvador Dali is located on the Mezzanine Level near the elevator. Jesus is the only one whose face can be seen as the Apostles all appear bowed in prayer.*

17. *In the hallway on the Upper Level, there is a brightly colored painting entitled "Painting with Statue of Liberty," by Roy Lichtenstein.*

18. *This painting is found in Gallery 404C on the Upper Level. It appears that the musician is playing a violin or fiddle.*

19. T-*The painting "Roulin's Baby" is located in Gallery 103C near the end of this exhibit.*

Scultpure Garden

Located between the West Building and the National Museum of Natural History. Enter from Seventh Street and proceed on the circular path to the right.

20. Y, TW-*The sculpture "Thinker on a Rock" by Barry Flanagan features a skinny rabbit in deep thought.*

21. *The chairs in the work entitled "Six-Part Seating" by Scott Burton are a rarity in the art world and this sculpture garden as visitors are encouraged to touch and sit on them.*

22. *This massive bronze "Spider" is a work by Louise Bourgeois*

23. T-*"Typewriter Eraser, Scale X" was done by Claes Oldenburg. Typewriter erasers were used to correct mistakes when typing with typewriters before the age of computers and delete keys.*

24. *This sculpture by Hector Guimard is entitled "An Entrance to the Paris Metropolitain."*

25. *The stainless steel "Graft" is a work by Roxy Paine.*

26. *Roy Lichtenstein's "House I," looks like an ideal residence for your favorite cartoon character. Another Lichtenstein work entitled "Brushstroke" sits in front of the Hirshhorn Museum directly across the Mall and a little to the left from the "House I" sculpture point of view. The Hirshhorn Museum also features a sculpture garden in front of it if your group would like to see additional interesting works of outdoor art.*

WASHINGTON NATIONAL CATHEDRAL

Address/Contact Information: 3101 Wisconsin Avenue NW, 202-537-6200, www.nationalcathedral.org

Closest Metro Station: Cleveland Park (Red Line), then take any 30 Series Metrobus.

Opening Hours/Ticketing: The cathedral is open on Monday-Friday from 10 AM-5:30 PM with tours available from 10 AM-11:30 AM and 12:45 PM-3:30 PM. On Saturdays the cathedral closes at 4:30 PM. On Sundays the cathedral is open 8 AM-5 PM, but tours are only available 1 PM-2:30 PM. In the summer the Nave level is open Tuesday and Thursday evenings until 8 PM. The requested donation for visiting the Washington National Cathedral is $5.

Essential Info: Soaring majestically on Mount Saint Alban overlooking Washington, D.C., sits the world's 6th largest cathedral. The cathedral is officially an Episcopal Church known as the Cathedral Church of St. Peter and St. Paul. The cathedral has traditionally served as a church for national events such as the site of state funerals for U.S. presidents.

President Theodore Roosevelt laid the first cornerstone, (a rock brought from Bethlehem), starting construction in 1907. The completion of the west towers marked the end of construction in 1990. The building was constructed primarily of Indiana limestone using traditional mason techniques and is shaped like a cross with a 517-foot-long nave and two shorter transepts. The cathedral was built in Gothic architectural style characterized by its massive height, pointed arches, boss stones, ribbed vaulting, large stained glass windows, and majestic flying buttresses. The exterior is decorated by grotesques and gargoyles designed to deflect rainwater away from the building. One unique gargoyle, designed by a school child, was built to resemble Darth Vader's head!

Outside of the main entrance, take the time to look at the West Façade with magnificent tympana and sculptures by Frederick Hart exploring the movement of humankind from creation to redemption along with brilliant statues of Peter, Adam, and Paul. The three huge bronze gates show scenes from the lives of Peter, Abraham and Moses, and Paul.

The interior of the cathedral is full of amazing stained glass windows in bays or transepts, and a wide variety of chapels and ornate altars decorated with exquisite wood and stone carvings. Through the religious artwork and architecture, the theme of redemption through faith is told as you move from west to east. Highlights include the tomb and bay for President Woodrow Wilson, the Space Window containing a piece of moon rock brought back by Apollo 11 and the amazing Rose Windows. The beautiful pulpit at the main altar is where Reverend Martin Luther King, Jr. gave his last sermon.

The lower level is known as the Crypt and contains more peaceful and beautifully decorated chapels including the Chapel of St. Joseph of Arimathea. This Romanesque style chapel contains the remains of Helen Keller and her teacher, Anne Sullivan. After walking through the cathedral, take the elevator up to the Pilgrim Observation Gallery for a great view of the District and beyond. This is the highest spot in Washington, D.C., at 676 feet, as the building was built upon Mount Saint Alban resulting in a higher elevation than the Washington Monument. The cathedral is an active place of worship so always remain respectful during your visit.

Docents lead regular guided highlight tours of the cathedral with a donation requested. Self-guided and audio tours are also available. In addition, they offer special art and architecture tours, garden tours, a behind-the-scenes tour and a popular "Tour with Tea."

The cathedral also offers an organ demonstration on Mondays and Wednesdays at 12:30 PM and an organ recital on Sundays at 5:15 PM. Carillon bell recitals are played on Saturdays at 12:30 PM. The Washington Ringing Society performs the art of change ringing on the Central Tower peal bells every Sunday around 12:30 PM and rehearses on Tuesday evenings from 7 PM-9 PM. The best place to listen to these performances is the Bishop's Gardens. Cathedral Choirs sing at the Sunday service and daily at Choral Evensong. The Cathedral Choral Society is the resident symphonic choir performing four concerts each year in the cathedral nave.

They also have a downloadable brochure, available at the information table called "Explore the Cathedral with Children." This brochure provides a self-guided tour of the cathedral and gardens with useful information and a scavenger hunt for kids.

The cathedral also offers special gargoyle tours from April-October on Sundays at 2 PM. These tours meet at the 7th floor auditorium and begin with a slide show of the interesting gargoyles and grotesques decorating the cathedral. The tour then ventures outside for a closer look at them including the famous Darth Vader example. Admission for this tour is $10 for adults and $5 for children ages 12 and under or $30 per family. The cathedral also offers the Gargoyle's Den program on Saturdays from 10 AM-2 PM, where kids ages 6-12 can participate in hands-on arts and crafts activities to learn about the construction techniques used to build the cathedral. During the program, kids can make clay models of gargoyles and try to build arches and stained glass windows. These programs cost $5 for a family of 4 and $1 for each additional person. No reservation is required for this program.

The cathedral also offers Family Saturdays once a month for kids ages 4-8. These programs include a special tour of the cathedral and arts and crafts projects. The Family Saturdays cost $6 per child and take place from 10 AM- 11:30 AM and 12 PM-1:30 with reservations required.

There is also an annual **National Cathedral Flower Mart** that takes place over the first Friday and Saturday in May on the cathedral grounds. This event features floral displays, plants, herbs, puppet shows, antique carousel rides, vendors and entertainment for the whole family. Visit www.allhallowsguild.org/fm for a full schedule of events.

Refreshments: Food and drinks are available at the Cathedral Store located on the south side of the lower level. There are also multiple restaurants across the street on Wisconsin Avenue.

Bathroom Facilities: Onsite

Scavenger Hunt:

No code letters-suitable for all ages
Y-designed for young children (under 10)
TW-designed for tweens ages 10-13
T-designed for teenagers

1. Find the statues of Washington and Lincoln near the front of the cathedral. Find where the word "soldier" is engraved on Washington's statue.

2. Y-As you sit in the chairs waiting for the tour to start, find the flags above. What are they representing?

3. TW-When you are at the top of the cathedral why are you at the highest point in the city?

4. Observe the light shadows coming from the West Rose window over the cathedral entrance. What colors is it casting onto the stone?

5. Where does the rock in the middle of the stained glass window with a space theme come from and why was it given to the cathedral?

6. Who is the only president buried here and why? Find his tomb in the cathedral.

7. T-Staring at the Last Judgment stained glass window in the transept or great crossing area near the pulpit, try to determine how big the figure of Jesus is in the center.

8. What famous minister gave his last Sunday sermon from this pulpit?

9. T-Find the Pentagon Cross. What makes it special?

10. In the Freedom Windows, find the depiction of the flag raising on Iwo Jima during WW II.

11. Y-Find 3 different types of animals in the iron doors leading to the Children's Chapel.

12. T-Find the tomb of the American pilot killed during World War I. What country was he fighting for when he died in 1916?

13. In the choir area, find the Bishops chair. What is it called?

14. TW, T-In the choir area, where does the altar stone come from?

15. Find a wooden carving of a lion eating the head of a snake in the oak choir benches.

16. TW, T-In St. Mary's chapel, what is the biblical story represented on the 450-year-old tapestries?

17. TW, T-What biblical figure is represented in the three stained glass windows with ancient Egyptian characteristics?

18. In the Crypt area find the Chapel of St. Joseph of Arimathea. What famous woman is buried here along with her teacher and friend?

19. Take the elevator to the Pilgrim Observatory Level and identify three famous Washington sites.

20. Find some flying buttresses from the observatory. What is their function?

21. Find examples of gargoyles and grotesques on the cathedral. TW, T-What is the difference between them?

WASHINGTON NATIONAL CATHEDRAL SCAVENGER HUNT ANSWER KEY

No code letters-suitable for all ages
Y-designed for young children (under 10)
TW-designed for tweens ages 10-13
T-designed for teenagers

1. *The statues are in the front right and left corners of the nave (main level) area. The word "soldier" is engraved on the side of the pediment on Washington's statue.*

2. *Y-These are some of the 50 U.S. state flags.*

3. *Y-Even though the Washington Monument is taller than the cathedral, the cathedral is on a hill making the top of it the highest point in the city at 676 feet.*

4. *Depending upon the time of day and season, you will see a variety of colors cast through this beautiful stained glass window.*

5. *There is a moon rock from the Apollo 11 mission in the middle of the space themed stained glass window in the middle of the windows on the right side. The rock was given to the cathedral because one of the Apollo 11 astronauts, Michael Collins, had a son attending the private school on the cathedral grounds-St. Albans School.*

6. *Woodrow Wilson is the only president buried in the cathedral and in all of Washington, D.C. Wilson's grandson was a longtime Dean of the National Cathedral and was instrumental in having him interred here. Wilson's tomb is on the right side a little past the moon rock stained glass window.*

7. *T-This beautiful window is on the upper left side as you stand in the great crossing area near the pulpit. The window is so huge and high up that the 6 ft. tall figure of Jesus appears small.*

8. *The Reverend Dr. Martin Luther King, Jr. gave his last Sunday sermon from this exquisitely carved pulpit four days before he was killed in Memphis, TN, on April 4, 1968.*

9. *T-The Pentagon Cross is found near the entrance to the Children's Chapel. It is made out of Pentagon building fragments resulting from the attacks of 9/11.*

10. *These windows are near the Children's Chapel and depict many famous battles and leaders in U.S. history. The raising of the flag on Iwo Jima is depicted in the first window at the bottom left from the viewer's perspective.*

11. *Y-The intricate ironwork on these doors features multiple types of animal heads.*

12. T-*The American pilot, Norman Prince, was a founding member of the Escadrille Lafayette, a fighter squadron of American pilots fighting for France against Germany before the U.S. entrance into WW I in 1917. The pilot's parents had him interred here and they were later buried in the crypt below. This tomb is located on the right before you enter the Choir area.*

13. *This stone chair is similar to a throne and is on the left in the altar area. A church becomes a cathedral when a bishop has a seat or "cathedra" there.*

14. *The Jerusalem Altar comes from stones originally used in building the Temple of Solomon in Jerusalem.*

15. *This wooden carving is located in the first chair of the 2nd row of benches on the left side of the choir. The artist carved the head of the snake to resemble Hitler.*

16. TW, T-*This chapel is directly after the choir. The Flemish tapestries show the biblical story of David defeating Goliath.*

17. TW, T-*These windows are behind St. Mary's chapel as you exit into the nave. They represent Moses in three different periods of his life.*

18. *The Chapel of St. Joseph of Arimathea is located on the right side of the Crypt area before you reach the gift shop. Going down the stairs on your left you will find a plaque marking the area where Helen Keller and her teacher, the "Miracle Worker" Anne Sullivan are interred.*

19. *Walk through the Cathedral Store and up the stairs and take the elevator to the 7th floor observatory level. You will see many famous Washington, D.C., landmarks from this observatory including the U.S. Capitol Building and the Washington Monument.*

20. *The huge curved arches are known as flying buttresses and are used to support the massive weight of the cathedral.*

21. *From the observatory level you can see many examples of gargoyles and grotesques-basically ugly faces carved on the side of the building.* TW, T-*Gargoyles have an opening in their mouth and serve as waterspouts to guide rainwater away from the building and preserve the stone. Grotesques do not drain water and are mainly for decoration. Sometimes they are used as corbels to help support weight. The most famous gargoyle came from a contest where kids sent in ideas. The winner's design selection: Darth Vader. Ask the docent how to see this gargoyle.*

NATIONAL AQUARIUM

Address/Contact Information: 1401 Constitution Avenue NW (Lower level of Commerce Building between Constitution and Pennsylvania Avenues. Entrance is on 14th Street close to Pennsylvania Avenue.), 202-482-2825, http://nationalaquarium.org

Closest Metro Station: Federal Triangle (Blue/Orange Lines)

Opening Hours/Ticketing: 9 AM-5 PM, last admission at 4:30 PM.

Essential Info: The National Aquarium in Washington, D.C., is the nation's first public aquarium. Established in 1873 in Woods Hole, MA, the National Aquarium was relocated to a series of holding ponds at the current site of the Washington Monument in 1878. The National Aquarium was originally run by the Federal Fish Commission, which later became part of the Department of Commerce in 1903 and changed its name to the Bureau of Fisheries. For this reason, the National Aquarium was incorporated into its present location in the lower level of the Department of Commerce building when it was constructed in 1932. This aquarium formed a partnership with the much larger National Aquarium in Baltimore in 2003 and began an extensive renovation and modernization of its facilities that was completed in 2008.

Despite its small size, the National Aquarium contains 250 species and more than 1,500 specimens. The aquarium features fish, reptiles, and amphibians from throughout the world along with seldom seen invertebrate sea dwellers such as chambered nautiluses. The main exhibits of the National Aquarium are organized into a 45-minute tour called *America's Aquatic Treasures*, which highlights the animals and habitats preserved and protected by our National Marine Sanctuaries Program.

The aquarium also features a touch tank for those who want to touch live sea creatures. A highlight of the aquarium is the daily feeding of some of the world's scariest predators along with an aquarist talk. The sharks are fed Monday, Wednesday and Saturday at 2 PM, and the piranhas are fed on Tuesday, Thursday, and Sunday at 2 PM. The alligators are fed on Friday at 2 PM.

Refreshments: No food or drinks are allowed in the main exhibit area of the aquarium.

Bathroom Facilities: Onsite

Scavenger Hunt:

No code letters-suitable for all ages
Y-designed for young children (under 10)
TW-designed for tweens ages 10-13
T-designed for teenagers

1. Y, TW-Touch a sea urchin in the touch pool

2. Find one type of fish from the Atlantic, Pacific, and Indian Oceans.

3. Find a freshwater fish native to North America.

4. Find the chambered nautilus. Is this animal a fish or something else?

5. Find a freshwater electric eel. What continent are they from?

6. Find your favorite predator: an alligator, shark, or piranha and observe feeding time if possible.

7. Y, TW-Find an example of an invasive species. Do they help or harm their new homes?

NATIONAL AQUARIUM SCAVENGER HUNT ANSWER KEY

No code letters-suitable for all ages
Y-designed for young children (under 10)
TW-designed for tweens ages 10-13
T-designed for teenagers

1. Y, TW-*There are sea urchins, starfish and many other living animals to experience in the touch pool.*

2. *A few examples include: the Guineafowl Puffer from the Pacific Ocean, the Longsnout Seahorse from the Atlantic, and the Red Lionfish from the Indian and Pacific Oceans.*

3. *There are many North American species found in the American Freshwater Ecosystems Gallery.*

4. *The chambered nautilus is an invertebrate, not a fish.*

5. *Found in the Amazon River Basin Gallery, these electric eels are native to South America.*

6. *You can find these predators' locations using the aquarium plan. They are fed on alternating days at 2 PM.*

7. Y, TW-*The National Aquarium has the following invasive species on display: Cane Toad, Northern Snakefish and Red Lionfish. These animals were introduced to non-native environments and have harmed the ecological balance of their new homes. One main problem is that these invasive species do not normally have predators in their new homes. Without predators, the non-invasive species reproduce too rapidly and upset the balance for native animals and plants.*

UNION STATION

Address/Contact Information: 40 Massachusetts Avenue NE, 202-289-1908, www.unionstationdc.com

Closest Metro Station: The Union Station (Red Line) Metrorail station is located within the Union Station complex.

Opening Hours/Ticketing: Station open 24 hours, **Retail stores**: Monday -Saturday, 10 AM-9 PM, Sunday, 12 PM-6 PM, **Food Court**: Monday-Saturday, 7 AM-9 PM, Sunday, 7 AM-6 PM, some hours may vary. **Sit Down Restaurants**: Times vary-contact restaurant. **Outdoor Market**: April-October, Monday-Saturday, 7 AM-7 PM

Essential Info: This beautiful 1907 Beaux Arts building is made of white granite and still serves as Washington's main train station. The architect Daniel Burnham's design was inspired by classical Roman Baths such as the Diocletian Baths. Arrow vaulted ceilings reach 96 feet at their highest point and are decorated with more than 70 pounds of 22 karat gold leaf. In 1909 President William Howard Taft was the first of many presidents to use its Presidential Suite to officially welcome international leaders to Washington, D.C.

Union Station operated at its peak during World War II facilitating the movement of critical equipment, supplies, and as many as a 100,000 civilian and military passengers a day. In the Post War Era, the railway station had fallen into disrepair until a major renovation in 1988 restored it to its former glory. The building now houses many upscale retail shops and restaurants as well as a food court.

Visitors enjoy the architecture inside and out the building. Louis St. Gaudens' statues of Roman Centurions line the upper reaches. St. Gaudens also sculpted six large statues on the front of the building and entitled them *The Progress of Railroading*. These statues depict three male and three female gods representing fire, electricity, freedom, imagination, agriculture and mechanics.

Exiting the station, visitors immediately see the inspiring sight of the U.S. Capitol Dome. In front of the station there is an elaborate fountain dedicated to Christopher Columbus that was designed by Lorado Taft. The fountain features sculptures of a globe of the new hemisphere, the figure of discovery on the prow of a ship, and an old European man and Native American, representing the old and new worlds, respectively. Nearby there are three flagpoles representing Columbus' three ships from his maiden voyage to the Americas and an oversized replica of the Liberty Bell.

Refreshments: Restaurants are located throughout the facility and there is an underground food court.

Bathroom Facilities: In the station area the Men's room is located at Gate A and the Women's restroom is located at Gate G. Restrooms are also located in the food court area downstairs.

Scavenger Hunt:

No code letters-suitable for all ages
Y-designed for young children (under 10)
TW-designed for tweens ages 10-13
T-designed for teenagers

1. T-Who was the first president to use Union Station?

2. Who is the explorer in the statue in front of the station?

3. What do the three flag poles in front of Union Station represent?

4. TW, T-What do the Native American and the old man in the memorial represent?

5. Find a replica of a famous bell in front of Union Station. What is the name of the famous bell it copies? T-Where is the original bell located?

6. What is the building with a dome across the street from Union Station?

7. T-Find the six statues high up on the front of the building. Can you find one holding a lightning bolt representing electricity?

8. Can you find any Roman centurions inside Union Station?

9. Y-Find a schedule showing when trains depart and arrive. Can you find a train heading to New York City?

10. Find a clock with the mistakenly written Roman numeral IIII instead of the correct IV.

11. T-Find a memorial to A. Philip Randolph. Why is he famous?

UNION STATION SCAVENGER HUNT ANSWER KEY

No code letters-suitable for all ages
Y-designed for young children (under 10)
TW-designed for tweens ages 10-13
T-designed for teenagers

1. T-*President William Howard Taft first used the Presidential Suite at Union Station in 1909 to entertain arriving international leaders. This suite is now defunct with the space occupied by a restaurant.*

2. *This statue honors the namesake of the District of Columbia, Christopher Columbus.*

3. *The three flagpoles represent Columbus' three ships on his maiden voyage to the Americas: The Niña, the Pinta, and the Santa Maria.*

4. TW, T-*The Native American represents the new world (for Europeans!) that Columbus found. The old man represents the old world of Europe.*

5. *There is an oversized replica of the Liberty Bell in front of the station.* T-*The original is located in Philadelphia.*

6. *This famous building is the U.S. Capitol Building.*

7. T-*Louis St. Gaudens sculpted six large statues on the front of the building and entitled them "The Progress of Railroading." These statues are three male and three female gods representing fire, electricity, freedom, imagination, agriculture and mechanics. The statue of Thales representing electricity is the second from the left. Thales is clearly holding a lightning bolt in his left hand against the middle of his chest.*

8. *Look up when inside the building's Main Hall to see the centurions. The shields were installed later to shield the pelvic areas because some worried the naked bodies of the centurions would offend sensibilities.*

9. Y-*There is a large digital screen in the Main Hall of Union Station showing the arriving and departing trains.*

10. *The huge clock over the entrance to the East Hall has this mistake. There is also a similar clock with the same mistake found over the exit out to First Street/Metro.*

11. T-*The memorial is located in the Gate A area next to the Starbucks. A. Philip Randolph was an African American Civil Rights and Labor leader. One main organization he founded was the Brotherhood of Sleeping Car Porters, which fought for the rights and benefits of these railway workers. He also was the initiator and leader of the August 28, 1963, "March on Washington for Jobs and Freedom," a pivotal event of the Civil Rights movement. Martin Luther King, Jr. gave his "I Have a Dream" speech at this event.*

Arlington, Virginia Sites

The Marine Corps War Memorial in Arlington, VA. Courtesy of Destination DC.

Located directly across the Potomac River in Virginia, is the city of Arlington, VA. This city contains our nation's military headquarters at the Pentagon, the country's most important national cemetery and a variety of beautiful memorials. You will also notice a skyline of residential and commercial buildings in the Crystal City, Ballston, Clarendon, Shirlington and Rosslyn neighborhoods in contrast to Washington, D.C., where there are strict height limits on buildings. Washington Reagan National Airport is also located here as well as the huge shopping area at the Pentagon City Mall, which families enjoy visiting. For helpful visitor information about Arlington, VA, go to www.stayarlington.com.

ARLINGTON NATIONAL CEMETERY

Address/Contact Information: Located southwest of the Pentagon in Arlington, VA. Vehicles enter from Washington, D.C., by driving south across the Memorial Bridge through a traffic circle to the cemetery grounds and Visitor Center. 877-907-8585, www.arlingtoncemetery.mil.

Be mindful of your group's stamina, the weather and the length of your visit when visiting the cemetery and bring bottled water. It is a 5-10-minute uphill walk from the visitor center to the Kennedy Gravesite and about a 15-20-minute hilly walk from the visitor center to the Tomb of the Unknowns. Vehicle passes are available for disabled visitors. **Use the site map found in the Visitor Center as an essential reference guide for finding important graves and memorials.**

Closest Metro Station: Arlington National Cemetery (Blue Line), parking lot/garage available.

Opening Hours/Ticketing: 8 AM-7 PM April-September and 8 AM-5 PM October-March. Free admission.

Essential Info: Nearly four million people a year visit this shrine to our nation's military and civilian heroes. The impressive mansion on the hill, Arlington House, and the more than 200 acres surrounding it, once belonged to famed Confederate General Robert E. Lee. At the outbreak of the war in 1861, the Lee family left the property and it was quickly occupied by the Union Army, who made use of the land as a cemetery. In 1864 it was officially dedicated as a military cemetery and it now contains more than 300,000 graves. Veterans of every American war and conflict are buried here-veterans from earlier wars were reinterred here after 1900. There is also a large columbarium for the cremated remains of veterans not meeting the strict criteria for burial. Arlington National Cemetery is still an active cemetery with an average of 28 burials a day.

The cemetery holds the remains of two presidents, John F. Kennedy and William Howard Taft, famous military leaders, Supreme Court Justices, and a variety of American heroes such as heavyweight champion boxer Joe Louis and polar explorers Robert Peary, Matthew Henson and Richard Byrd. There are also many markers and monuments honoring military units and special memorials to the space shuttle crews who died in flight.

The Women in Military Service for America Memorial

Located near the entrance of the cemetery, this is the only major national memorial exclusively honoring women who have served in the country's military. The memorial was dedicated in 1997 and features an exhibit gallery, theater, and a computerized register containing more than 250,000 interesting military women's stories.

Kennedy Gravesite

President John. F. Kennedy once remarked on a visit to Arlington House, that the view of Washington, D.C., was so perfect that he could stay there forever. After his assassination in 1963, the president was buried at a gravesite on the hillside below Arlington House marked by a specially designed and natural gas operated Eternal Flame. Because of the large amount of visitors, the gravesite was remodeled and enlarged in 1967 and paved with stones of Cape Cod granite. First Lady Jacqueline Bouvier Kennedy Onassis and their deceased children are also buried at the gravesite. Excerpts from inspirational Kennedy speeches are inscribed on the walls nearby. The president's brothers, Senators Robert and Edward Kennedy, are buried nearby with each grave marked by a simple white cross.

Arlington House

At the top of the hill above the Kennedy Gravesite sits the impressive Greek Revival mansion that was the home of famed Confederate General Robert E. Lee and his family for 30 years. The mansion and outbuildings (including slave quarters) are open 9:30 AM-4:30 PM (6 PM in the high season). The house is currently unfurnished as the original furnishings are undergoing renovation. For more information about the site go to www.nps.gov/arho.

The Tomb of Unknowns

This memorial to the unknown dead from America's conflicts was dedicated on Memorial Day 1921 to honor an unknown soldier from World War I. The white marble sarcophagus has three Greek figures sculpted in its east panel facing Washington, D.C., which represent Peace, Victory and Valor. In front of the sarcophagus are markers honoring unknown soldiers from World War II, Korea and the Vietnam War. The remains of the Unknown Soldier from the Vietnam War were identified through DNA testing in 1988 and returned to the family for reinterment near their home.

The Tomb of the Unknowns is guarded by a special army unit 24 hours a day. Members of this unit participate in a stirring Changing of the Guard ceremony every hour or half hour depending upon the season. Note that the guards march exactly 21 steps, then wait for 21 seconds and then walk another 21 steps. This is symbolic of the 21-gun salute, the military's highest honor.

Refreshments: Bottled water is available in the Women in Military Service for America Memorial. Food and beverages (except for bottled water) are not allowed on the cemetery grounds.

Bathroom Facilities: In the Visitor Center and near the Tomb of Unknowns/Memorial Amphitheater.

Scavenger Hunt:

No code letters-suitable for all ages
Y-designed for young children (under 10)
TW-designed for tweens ages 10-13
T-designed for teenagers

1.   Who owned this land when the Civil War began?

2. In the Women in Military Service for America Memorial, find the computerized register displaying interesting servicewomen's stories. Whose story was most inspiring?

3. Y-Look sideways down a row of graves to see how straight they are.

4. TW, T-During your visit find graves displaying 2 different religions.

5. Find the "Eternal Flame." Which president is buried there and honored by this flame?

6. Can you find Robert F. Kennedy's grave marked by a simple cross?

7. TW, T-Which presidents are buried at Arlington?

8. Climb the hill and view Washington, D.C., from Arlington House.

9. T-Who is buried at the top of the hill near Arlington House?

10. Find the slave quarters behind Arlington House.

11. Find the way to the Tomb of the Unknowns.

12. During "The Changing of the Guard" ceremony at the Tomb of the Unknowns, how many steps do the soldiers take in each direction before stopping?

13. T-Why did they remove the remains of the unknown soldier from the Vietnam War from the Tomb of the Unknowns?

14. Y-Sit in the memorial amphitheater used for special events.

15. TW, T-Find Audie Murphy's grave? Why is he special?

16. Find the monuments to the Space Shuttle *Challenger* and *Columbia* crews. TW, T-Can you find the name of the astronaut Christa McAuliffe on the Challenger Memorial? What made her special?

17. T-Find the ship's mast of the USS *Maine*. What war did the sinking of the USS *Maine* spark?

18. TW, T-Find the grave of the heavyweight champion boxer Joe Louis.

ARLINGTON NATIONAL CEMETERY SCAVENGER HUNT ANSWER KEY

No code letters-suitable for all ages
Y-designed for young children (under 10)
TW-designed for tweens ages 10-13
T-designed for teenagers

1. *Confederate General Robert E. Lee owned this land in 1861. It originally belonged to his wife Mary Custis' family and became his after their marriage and the death of her father George Washington Parke Custis (George Washington's step grandson). The house they lived in called Arlington House still sits on the top of the hill overlooking the cemetery.*

2. *This large memorial is found near the cemetery entrance and features this computerized register and exhibits honoring American servicewomen.*

3. *Y-These graves are lined up with military precision.*

4. *The graves are marked by crosses for Christians and Stars of David for those of the Jewish faith. Other religions are also represented. Be respectful of the graves and the cemetery when viewing graves.*

5. *President John F. Kennedy was buried here after being assassinated in November 1963.*

6. *Robert F. Kennedy's grave is down the path to the left of the Eternal Flame.*

7. *Presidents John F. Kennedy and William Howard Taft are the only presidents buried in the cemetery.*

8. *This amazing view from this hill impressed President Kennedy and inspired First Lady Jacqueline Kennedy to have his final resting place nearby.*

9. *T-Pierre L'Enfant, one of the main designers of Washington, D.C., is buried at the top of the hill.*

10. *These modest quarters are located in the outbuildings behind the Arlington House.*

11. *Signs direct you there as you walk along the main paths. It's about a five to ten-minute walk first downhill then uphill from Arlington House.*

12. *The soldiers take 21 steps, pause for 21 seconds and then repeat the process. This is symbolic of the 21-gun salute, which is the military's highest honor.*

13. *T-New developments in DNA research enabled officials to identify the airman killed during the Vietnam War. His family requested his remains be reinterred near their family home in Missouri.*

14. *Y-This beautiful structure is directly behind the Tomb of the Unknowns.*

15. TW, T-*Audie Murphy, who was turned down by the Marines for being too small, was the most decorated soldier of World War II. Fighting with the U.S. Army in Europe, he earned the nation's highest award for valor, the Medal of Honor, and 32 additional U.S. and foreign awards and citations. Murphy's grave is directly behind the Memorial amphitheater. Cross the road and go to your left to the small tree. The grave is found where the path forms a right angle and is usually marked by a small American flag.*

16. *These monuments to the shuttle crews are behind the amphitheater, across the road to the right and near the ship's mast of the USS Maine.* TW, T-*Christa McAuliffe was chosen to be the first teacher in space and would have been the first American civilian to go into space. Her alternate, Barbara Morgan, finally made it into space on a shuttle mission in 2007.*

17. T-*This huge mast is visible when you come out behind the Memorial amphitheater across the road to your right. This battleship sank in the harbor of Havana, Cuba, in 1898 after an explosion of still undetermined cause. The tensions from this event contributed to the beginning of the Spanish-American War between the United States and Spain.*

18. TW, T-*Joe Louis was world heavyweight boxing champion from 1937-1949. His grave is found as you walk downhill on the path from the Tomb of the Unknowns. Actor Lee Marvin's grave is found next to the Louis grave. He was a decorated U.S. Marine in World War II.*

U.S. MARINE CORPS WAR MEMORIAL AND NETHERLANDS CARILLON

Address/Contact Information: Adjacent to Arlington National Cemetery on George Washington Parkway, 703-289-2500, www.nps.gov/gwmp/marinecorpswarmemorial, www.nps.gov/gwmp/nethcarillon

Closest Metro Station: Arlington National Cemetery (Blue Line), Rosslyn (Blue/Orange Lines), parking lot available until midnight.

Opening Hours/Ticketing: Open 24 hours a day. Free admission.

Refreshments: N/A

Bathroom Facilities: There are portable toilets in the memorial area and indoor restrooms in Arlington National Cemetery Visitors Center during opening hours.

Netherlands Carillon

Essential Info: This bell tower and carillon is a gift from the people of the Netherlands to the people of the United States in gratitude for their assistance during and after World War II. The carillon of 49 bells was given as a gift in 1954 and then installed in the 127-foot-tall steel bell tower in 1960. An additional bell was added after renovations in 1995 on the 50th anniversary of the liberation of Holland. The total weight of the bells is 28 metric tons, with the largest weighing almost 13,000 pounds. There is a glass booth and observatory about 80 feet up where visitors can get a great view of the area and observe musicians known as carillonneurs playing the bells during performances. The carillon is tuned to the chromatic scale with its 50 bells providing it with two notes more than four octaves. In the playing cabin are the wooden levers and pedals of the clavier, which connect directly to the movable inner clappers of the hanging bells.

Two bronze lions designed by Dutch sculptor Paul Konig guard the entrance to the area. The lions represent the Coat of Arms of the Kingdom of the Netherlands. In the spring, visitors to the site can enjoy the bloom of thousands of tulips, the national flower of the Netherlands.

From April to September there are concerts on Saturdays from 2 PM-4 PM Throughout the year, 18 of the bells are programmed to play "Westminster Chimes" and other songs hourly.

Scavenger Hunt:

No code letters-suitable for all ages
Y-designed for young children (under 10)
TW-designed for tweens ages 10-13
T-designed for teenagers

1. What country donated the bell tower and carillon to the US and why?

2. How many bells are in the carillon?

3. Climb the bell tower and look at the view of Washington, D.C. Can you identify some of the monuments and buildings?

4. During a performance were you able to see the musicians at work? TW, T-What are these musicians called?

NETHERLANDS CARILLON SCAVENGER HUNT ANSWER KEY

No code letters-suitable for all ages
Y-designed for young children (under 10)
TW-designed for tweens ages 10-13
T-designed for teenagers

1. *The Netherlands gave this gift in gratitude for U.S. assistance during and after World War II.*

2. *There are 50 bells in the carillon.*

3. *The observation area has a beautiful view of Washington, D.C., and the surrounding area.*

4. TW, T-*The professional musicians who play the carillon are called carillonneurs.*

U.S. Marine Corps War Memorial (Iwo Jima)

Essential Info: Located adjacent to Arlington National Cemetery, this memorial serves to honor all U.S. Marine Corps personnel who have died in defense of their country since the Marine Corps founding in 1775. The memorial, designed by Horace Peaslee, has a Swedish granite base listing the major engagements the Marine Corps has been involved in since 1775 and a quote from Fleet Admiral Chester Nimitz about the men who fought on Iwo Jima: "Uncommon valor was a common virtue."

The bronze statue sculpted by Felix de Weldon is based on Joe Rosenthal's Pulitzer Prize winning photograph of the historic flag raising on Mount Suribachi at the Battle of Iwo Jima during WWII in February 1945. The sculptor modeled the forms exactly on the five Marines and one Navy corpsman in the photograph conducting personal sitting sessions with the two surviving Marines and the corpsman. He used photographs of the three other marines who had died during later phases of the battle. The statues of the men stand 32-feet high. The bronze flagpole is 60-feet high and must have a U.S. flag flying on it continuously by virtue of a presidential proclamation from President Eisenhower in 1954.

Three of the Marines in the flag raising died in later phases of the battle. The Marines killed in action were: Mike Strank, Harlon Block, and Franklin Sousley. The two surviving Marines were Rene Gagnon and Ira Hayes, a Pima Indian. The surviving Navy corpsman was John Bradley. These three surviving men, famous from the photograph, participated reluctantly in a nationwide war bond tour to raise funds for the war effort. They would also all attend the dedication of this memorial in 1954. To their deaths these men steadfastly maintained that the real heroes of the war were their fallen and wounded buddies and all the other servicemen who didn't come home.

The Marine Silent Drill Team, Color Guard and Drum and Bugle Corps hold a one-hour **Sunset Parade** every Tuesday at 7 PM from the last Tuesday in May to the third Tuesday in August. There is no public parking at the site during these evening performances. Guests may park at the Arlington National Cemetery Visitor Center and then ride a free shuttle bus service from the visitor center to the war memorial grounds from 5:30 PM-6:30 PM before the parade and from 7:30 PM-8:30 PM following the parade. For additional information call 202-433-6060.

Scavenger Hunt:

No code letters-suitable for all ages
Y-designed for young children (under 10)
TW-designed for tweens ages 10-13
T-designed for teenagers

1. Y-How many servicemen are helping to plant the flag?

2. How tall are the statues of the men?

3. TW, T-What was the name of the battle the U.S. Marines fought in where they raised the flag?

4. TW, T-How many of the men involved in the flag raising survived the battle?

5. Name three conflicts the U.S. Marines have fought in over the years.

6. T-What was the name of the photographer who took the famous picture that inspired this monument?

7. T-What was the name of the Clint Eastwood-directed movie that was made about the men involved in the flag raising?

U.S. MARINE CORPS WAR MEMORIAL (IWO JIMA) SCAVENGER HUNT ANSWER KEY

No code letters-suitable for all ages
Y-designed for young children (under 10)
TW-designed for tweens ages 10-13
T-designed for teenagers

1. *Y-There are five Marines and one Navy corpsman planting the flag portrayed exactly as they were in the famous photograph during World War II.*

2. *The statues of the men are 32 feet high.*

3. *TW, T-The Battle of Iwo Jima was a pivotal and costly battle fought against Japan near the end of World War II in February 1945.*

4. *TW, T-Two of the Marines and the Navy corpsmen survived the battle and were sent back to the home front. The government organized a nationwide tour with the men, now famous because of the photograph, to increase the sale of war bonds for the war effort. These men would also attend the dedication of this memorial in 1954 led by President Eisenhower.*

5. *On the base of the memorial, there is a list of the wars and conflicts where the U.S. Marines have fought.*

6. *T-Joe Rosenthal won the Pulitzer Prize for this photograph in 1945.*

7. *T-The movie was called "Flags of our Fathers," based on the book of the same name.*

PENTAGON MEMORIAL

Address/Contact Information: Just southwest of the Pentagon in Arlington, VA, at 1 Rotary Road, 703-697-7351, www.whs.mil/memorial

Closest Metro Station: Pentagon (Blue/Yellow Lines)

Opening Hours/Ticketing: 24 hours a day. Free admission.

Essential Info: The Pentagon building is the headquarters for the United States Department of Defense and the world's largest office building by floor area. The Pentagon memorial honors the 184 victims of the terrorist attack on the Pentagon on September 11, 2001, and was dedicated on the seventh anniversary of the event. Beckman and Kaseman designed the memorial, which is situated directly across from where the plane was intentionally crashed into the Pentagon on that terrible day. As you enter the memorial area you will see the date of September 11, 2001, etched into a stone that was scorched from the attack. There are 184 illuminated benches representing each victim, which are organized according to their ages ranging from 3 to 71. The name of each victim is engraved on an individual memorial bench. The benches representing the 125 victims inside the Pentagon are arranged so that those reading the names will face the Pentagon's south façade where the plane impacted. The benches dedicated to the 59 victims aboard American Flight 77 are arranged so those reading the engraved name are facing skyward along the path the plane traveled.

During your visit please show appropriate respect for the memory of the people who perished in this tragic event.

Refreshments: N/A

Bathroom Facilities: N/A

Scavenger Hunt:

No code letters-suitable for all ages
Y-designed for young children (under 10)
TW-designed for tweens ages 10-13
T-designed for teenagers

1. Why is this building called the Pentagon? What department has their headquarters here?

2. Is this the largest office building in the world?

3. TW, T-On what day and year was the Pentagon attacked? Find the burnt stone with this date inscribed.

4. Ask the adults in your group where they were on September 11, 2011.

5. Why are the benches organized by year?

6. T-Why are some of the benches pointing toward and some away from the Pentagon?

PENTAGON MEMORIAL SCAVENGER HUNT ANSWER KEY

No code letters-suitable for all ages
Y-designed for young children (under 10)
TW-designed for tweens ages 10-13
T-designed for teenagers

1. *This building is called the Pentagon because of its 5-sided geometric shape. It houses the headquarters for the Department of Defense.*

2. *The Pentagon is the largest office building in the world by floor area. It has about 6.5 million square feet of floor area with about 3.7 million square feet used as office space.*

3. TW, T-*September 11, 2001. The stone burnt from the attack is at the beginning of the memorial.*

4. *Everyone old enough to remember will have a unique story about their own personal experience on this day.*

5. *The benches each represent a victim of the attack and are grouped by their birth year.*

6. T-*The benches each have a victim's name at the end coming out of the ground. The benches pointing toward the Pentagon represent the victims in the plane as the designers wanted the person reading the name to be looking toward the sky. The benches pointing away from the Pentagon represent the victims in the Pentagon as the designers wanted the person reading the name to be looking toward the Pentagon.*

U.S. AIR FORCE MEMORIAL

Address/Contact Information: Intersection of Columbia Pike and South Joyce Street at One Air Force Memorial Drive in Arlington, VA, 703-979-0674, www.airforcememorial.org

Closest Metro Station: Pentagon (Blue/Yellow Lines)

Opening Hours/Ticketing: From April-September 8 AM-11 PM and from October-March 8 AM-9 PM. Free admission.

Essential Info: Visible from across the Potomac River in Washington, D.C., the three soaring spires of the U.S. Air Force Memorial have become an impressive landmark of the area. Designed by famed architect James Ingo Freed, the memorial was dedicated in 2006 to honor all veterans of the U.S. Air Force and its predecessor organizations. The three curving stainless steel spires, one reaching a height of 270 feet, evoke a command of the sky in the form of the signature "bomb burst" maneuver of the Air Force's Thunderbird Demonstration Team. This famous flight team performs aerial wizardry at events around the world. The three spires also represent the three core values of the Air Force- integrity first, service before self, and excellence in all that is done.

Beneath the three spires is the Air Force "star," which is found on Air Force aircraft and serves as the rank insignia of all enlisted members of the Air Force. Additional elements of the memorial include a paved Runway to Glory at the entrance, two granite inscription walls located at each end of the central lawn and a Glass Contemplation Wall to honor fallen Air Force service members. Celebrated sculptor, Zenos Frudakis, created the Honor Guard statue with four eight-foot tall bronze figures, which is found in front of one of the inscription walls.

Refreshments: N/A

Bathroom Facilities: N/A

Scavenger Hunt:

No code letters-suitable for all ages
Y-designed for young children (under 10)
TW-designed for tweens ages 10-13
T-designed for teenagers

1. Y-Which metal spire is the tallest?

2. What type of flying maneuver do the metal spires represent?

3. TW, T-What are the three core values of the Air Force?

4. How tall are the figures in the Honor Guard statue?

5. T-During World War II what was the official name of the military air units which would later become the U.S. Air Force?

U.S. AIR FORCE MEMORIAL SCAVENGER HUNT ANSWER KEY

No code letters-suitable for all ages
Y-designed for young children (under 10)
TW-designed for tweens ages 10-13
T-designed for teenagers

1. Y-*The middle spire is 270 feet tall.*

2. *The spires are meant to show the signature "bomb burst" maneuver of the Thunderbird demonstration team.*

3. TW, T-*Their three core values are "Integrity first, service before self, and excellence in all that is done."*

4. *The bronze statues are each 8-feet tall.*

5. T-*The organization was called the United States Army Air Force (USAAF) during World War II and was officially a combat arm of the United States Army. In 1947 the U.S. Congress officially created a new service branch renaming it the United States Air Force.*

Alexandria and Mount Vernon, Virginia Sites

Across the Potomac River about five miles south from Washington, D.C., lies the historic city of Alexandria, VA. The first English settlement was in 1695 and the area had different names before being officially incorporated in 1779 as Alexandria. Portions of the town were part of the original District of Columbia but were retroceded to Virginia in 1846.

The city is rich in history as the scavenger hunts listed below will demonstrate. George Washington, who lived at nearby Mount Vernon, was often in Alexandria on business and for social calls. He also worshipped regularly at Christ Church and kept a townhouse here. Robert E. Lee grew up in Old Town and also worshipped at Christ Church. The first casualties on both sides of the Civil War happened here in 1861 when Union troops occupied the city.

The picturesque Old Town section features historic sites and buildings, antique and specialty stores and fine dining. This area is Metrorail-accessible from Washington, D.C., and warrants a visit. Mount Vernon, VA, with George Washington's home and other attractions is about 8 miles south from Old Town, but is not easily Metro accessible.

There is a free trolley service from the King Street Metrorail station that will bring you to the Alexandria Visitors Center and near to the attractions listed below.

Start your visit at the Alexandria Visitors Center at Ramsay House located at 221 King Street for the latest information on current exhibits and events throughout the city. The recommended sites listed here are all within walking distance from King Street. At the visitor center you can also purchase a "Key to the City," which covers admission to nine historic sites and offers discounts at area attractions, shops, and restaurants. Pick up a free "Ask Alex Cell Tours" brochure provided by the Office of Historic Alexandria and you can use your cell phone as a convenient audio guide to the main attractions. For additional information visit: http://visitalexandria.com.

GADSBY'S TAVERN MUSEUM

Address/Contact Information: 134 North Royal Street, Alexandria, VA, 703-746-4242, www.gadsbystavern.org

Closest Metro Station: King Street (Blue/Yellow Lines), Take free King Street Trolley up King Street to Royal Street.

Opening Hours/Ticketing: From November-March they are open Wednesday-Saturday from 11 AM-4 PM, and Sunday from 1 PM-4 PM. From April-October they are open Tuesday-Saturday from 10 AM-5 PM, and on Sunday from 1 PM-5 PM. Last tours begin 15 minutes before closing. Adult tickets cost $5, children ages 5-12 cost $3, and children under 5 are free.

Essential Info: Gadsby's Tavern Museum consists of a tavern built around 1785 and the city hotel built in 1792. Owner John Gadsby's tavern and hotel were the center of Alexandria's social and political life and played host to George Washington's annual Birthnight Ball-a formal celebration with much dancing and merrymaking. Washington was a frequent guest at Gadsby's Tavern and even attended two of the balls held in his honor. Other notable patrons were Thomas Jefferson, John Adams, James Madison, James Monroe and the Marquis de Lafayette. Visitors can tour the historic building and also enjoy 18th century dining at the Gadsby's Tavern Restaurant, where they can sample authentic colonial dishes served by wait staff in period costumes.

Refreshments: At Gadsby's Tavern Restaurant next door.

Bathroom Facilities: At Gadsby's Tavern Restaurant next door.

Scavenger Hunt:

No code letters-suitable for all ages
Y-designed for young children (under 10)
TW-designed for tweens ages 10-13
T-designed for teenagers

1. Which President was honored by a ball here and why?

2. Were women allowed in the Tap Room?

3. Y, TW-Find the sugar nipper. Which sugar was more expensive when the tavern was operating- brown or white?

4. Who prepared and served the food and drinks and kept the tavern clean?

5. Did guests usually sleep alone in beds at colonial inns?

6. TW, T-Where does the phrase "sleep tight" come from?

7. How did the musicians get up to the musicians gallery?

GADSBY'S TAVERN MUSEUM SCAVENGER HUNT ANSWER KEY

No code letters-suitable for all ages
Y-designed for young children (under 10)
TW-designed for tweens ages 10-13
T-designed for teenagers

1. *President Washington's birthday was celebrated by a formal Birthnight Ball. This tradition began at Gadsby's in 1797 and has continued to the present day.*

2. *It was not considered proper for women to be in the bar area.*

3. Y, TW-*The sugar nipper is in the Tap Room area. White refined sugar was more expensive than brown sugar-the opposite of today.*

4. *Slaves did most of the work at the tavern.*

5. *Guests normally slept with others of the same sex in one bed-often strangers. The guests would sleep next to each other with their heads and feet alternating.*

6. TW, T-*Before there were springs in bed, the mattresses would be suspended on ropes. People used to tighten the ropes to keep the mattresses firm.*

7. *There is a retractable staircase that pulls down to let the musicians gain access to the musicians gallery.*

GEORGE WASHINGTON MASONIC MEMORIAL

Address/Contact Information: 101 Callahan Drive, Alexandria, VA, 703-638-2007, www.gwmemorial.org

Closest Metro Station: King Street (Blue/Yellow Lines)

Opening Hours/Ticketing: From October-March 31 Monday-Saturday 10 AM-4 PM, Sunday 12 PM-4 PM. From April-September Monday-Saturday 9 AM-4 PM, Sunday 12 PM-4 PM. **Admission is not included in the "Key to the City" ticket.** First and Second Floor exhibits are free. Tower exhibits and observation desk- Adult tickets cost $5, children 12 and under are free. Family ticket for 5 or more costs $20. Guided Tower tours are available Monday-Saturday at 10 AM, 11:30 AM, 1:30 PM and 3 PM, and Sundays at 12 PM, 1:30 PM and 3 PM. Groups of 10 or more should reserve spots online at least two weeks in advance.

Essential Info: George Washington is perhaps the most famous member of the fraternal organization known as Freemasonry, which originated in Scotland. The organization's members seek to improve themselves as they improve the communities in which they live. To join one must believe in a Supreme Being, be upright, moral and honest in character, and be recommended by a Mason.

Freemasons from throughout the United States and abroad privately donated money for the construction of this impressive memorial for George Washington. Freemasons value and honor classical architecture and knowledge from the Egyptians, Greeks and Romans. Elements from these three great civilizations are found in this memorial. For example, the lighthouse design of the memorial comes from the Lighthouse of Alexandria, one of the Seven Wonders of the Ancient World that was located in Egypt.

The memorial was dedicated in 1932 on the hilly site originally recommended as a perfect location for the U.S. Capitol Building by Thomas Jefferson. The memorial contains many artifacts related to George Washington and to the history of Freemasonry in the United States. On the ninth floor about 300 feet up, there is an outdoor observatory area giving impressive views of the Potomac River, Alexandria and Washington, D.C.

Refreshments: Bottled war and candy is available in the administrative room where you purchase tickets.

Bathroom Facilities: Onsite

Scavenger Hunt:

No code letters-suitable for all ages
Y-designed for young children (under 10)
TW-designed for tweens ages 10-13
T-designed for teenagers

1. TW, T-What Wonder of the Ancient World does the memorial building resemble?

2. Y-Find a large statue of Washington. How tall is the statue?

3. In the lodge area, find the chair once used by George Washington.

4. TW, T-Why is the clock in the case stopped at 10:20?

5. Find the sash worn by the Marquis de Lafayette on his visit to Alexandria in 1825.

6. T-On the fifth floor, find the replica of the Ark of the Covenant.

7. On the eighth floor, find the sword that belonged to a Crusader.

8. On the ninth floor observatory level, identify some of the famous landmarks of Washington, D.C.

9. In the fourth floor museum, find the Washington family bible and some bills with his signature.

10. Find a trunk and desk used by Washington during military campaigns.

11. Find the key to the Bastille Prison from France given to Washington. Who gave it to him? Do you know where there is another key just like it also given to Washington?

12. Sit in the Memorial Theater on the ground level. T-What popular movie with a plot centered on finding historical treasures filmed a scene here?

13. Y, TW-Find and operate the Shriners parade mechanical exhibit on the ground level.

GEORGE WASHINGTON MASONIC MEMORIAL SCAVENGER HUNT ANSWER KEY

No code letters-suitable for all ages
Y-designed for young children (under 10)
TW-designed for tweens ages 10-13
T-designed for teenagers

1. TW, T-*The memorial is modeled after the Lighthouse of Alexandria in Egypt.*

2. Y-*This bronze statue by Bryan Baker is 17 feet tall and weighs more than 7 tons.*

3. *The chair came from Washington's home at Mount Vernon. It is protected by a hard plastic case and was once used by the Master of the Alexandria Lodge during meetings.*

4. TW, T-*This clock was in the bedroom when Washington died at Mt. Vernon on December 14, 1799. One of the attending physicians, Dr. Elisha Dick, cut the catgut chord of the clock right after Washington passed away to forever mark the time of this historic moment.*

5. *Lafayette was a French officer who fought with the colonists against the British during the Revolutionary War. He became good friends with Washington and other colonial leaders and made a triumphant return tour of the United States in 1825. His sash is in the first room of artifacts near the gift shop.*

6. T-*There is a replica of the Ark of the Covenant on this floor, emphasizing the importance of the Ten Commandments as well as other symbols of religious significance in the memorial.*

7. *On the wall on your left coming out of the elevator is an actual sword used by a Crusader fighting in the Holy Land in the Middle East during the Crusades.*

8. *Some landmarks in view are the Washington Monument and the U.S. Capitol Dome.*

9. *You can find Washington's family bible and bills in the "Virginia Planter" area.*

10. *You can find the trunk and desk in the "Military Officer" section.*

11. *This artifact from the French Revolution in 1789 is in the "Military Officer" section. Lafayette gave Washington this key as well as another that is displayed at Mount Vernon.*

12. *The impressive semicircular Memorial Theater is located on the second floor.* T-*This theater was used in the opening scene of the movie "National Treasure II." On the upper level is an impressive collection of plaques commemorating the large number of presidents who were also Freemasons.*

13. Y, TW-*Kids enjoy watching the mechanical model of a Shriners parade found in the Shriners exhibit area on the ground level. The Shriners, a branch of the Masons, traditionally organize parades, circuses and other events to help children who are burn victims and to raise money for other charitable causes.*

CHRIST CHURCH

Address/Contact Information: 118 North Washington Street, Alexandria, VA, 703-549-1450, www.historicchristchurch.org

Closest Metro Station: King Street (Blue/Yellow Lines), Take free King Street Trolley up King Street to where it intersects with Washington Street. Walk one block to the left (north) and you will see the church on your left.

Opening Hours/Ticketing: Gift shop open Tuesday-Saturday 10 AM-4 PM, Sunday 8:45 AM-1 PM. Tours of church available Monday-Saturday 12 PM-4 PM, Sundays 2 PM-4 PM. Last tour begins 20 minutes before closing. Donation is suggested.

Essential Info: Christ Church was built in 1773 by John Carlyle as the first Episcopal Church in Alexandria. Designed by James Wren in the colonial Georgian style, the church has had many important regular worshippers including George Washington and Robert E. Lee. President Franklin Roosevelt and British Prime Minister Winston Churchill attended services here on the World Day of Prayer for Peace on January 1, 1942. Docents onsite offer regular guided tours pointing out architectural features and the pews where the Washington and Lee families worshiped.

The churchyard has many old tombstones of prominent citizens with interesting inscriptions. At the front of the churchyard near Washington Street, there is a mound covered with ivy marked by a stone slab commemorating the mass burial of 34 Confederate prisoners of war. These men died during the Civil War in Federal hospitals in occupied Alexandria. Some of the churchyard's gravestones were taken over the years to be used as steps and walkways in front of nearby Old Town residences.

Please remember to be respectful as this church is an active house of worship.

Refreshments: There is candy available in the gift shop. There are nearby restaurants on King Street.

Bathroom Facilities: In adjacent Parish House.

Scavenger Hunt:

No code letters-suitable for all ages
Y-designed for young children (under 10)
TW-designed for tweens ages 10-13
T-designed for teenagers

1. Sit in the Washington Family pew. Who are some of the famous people to have sat and worshipped in this pew?

2. TW, T-What is the function of the sounding board above the pulpit?

3. T-Why are their hand-lettered wooden tablets on the wall behind the pulpit showing important prayers?

4. Find the Lee family pew and sit in it.

5. In the churchyard, find the mound where Confederate soldiers were buried.

6. Try to read an inscription on one of the tombstones. What years are visible?

CHRIST CHURCH SCAVENGER HUNT ANSWER KEY

No code letters-suitable for all ages
Y-designed for young children (under 10)
TW-designed for tweens ages 10-13
T-designed for teenagers

1. *George Washington purchased this pew for 26 British pounds in 1773. Many presidents, first ladies and other notable people have worshipped from this spot including President Franklin Roosevelt, Prime Minister Winston Churchill, President Ronald Reagan and both Bush Presidents.*

2. TW, T-*The wooden structure above the pulpit is called a sounding board. It is designed to distribute and amplify the voice of the speaker at the pulpit to the parishioners sitting above and below.*

3. T-*Many parishioners could not afford prayer books, so many Episcopal churches would write important prayers on large wooden tablets displayed for the congregation's use in worshipping.*

4. *The famous Confederate General, Robert E. Lee, was a young volunteer at the church and would eventually rent a family pew. He and two of his daughters were confirmed on the same day here.*

5. *Pick up a map of the churchyard and the listing of some of the inscriptions from the docent. Follow the main path in the churchyard straight back toward Washington Street and then go left just before you reach the exit. There is mound with a large bush covering it and a stone slab marking the spot. 34 Confederate prisoners of war, who died in federal hospitals in Alexandria, were reinterred here in 1879.*

6. *There are many old tombstones in the churchyard. Use the pamphlet listing inscriptions from the tombstones for assistance.*

STABLER-LEADBEATER APOTHECARY MUSEUM

Address/Contact Information: 105-107 South Fairfax Street, Alexandria, VA, 703-746-3852, www.alexandriagov/Apothecary

Closest Metro Station: King Street (Blue/Yellow Lines), Take free King Street Trolley up King Street to Fairfax Street. The museum will be on the right.

Opening Hours/Ticketing: From November-March they are open Wednesday-Saturday from 11 AM-4 PM, and on Sunday from 1 PM-4 PM. They are open in April-October on Tuesday-Saturday from 10 AM-5 PM, and on Sunday from 1 PM-5 PM. Last tours begin 15 minutes before closing. Adult tickets cost $5, children ages 5-12 cost $3, and children under 5 are free. Discounts are available online and for AAA members. Schedule group tours of 10 or more at least two weeks in advance. Mandatory 30-minute guided tours are available 15 minutes before and 15 minutes after the hour.

Essential Info: Both a pharmacist and historian's dream attraction, this pharmacy opened in 1792 and didn't close its doors until 1933. The owners left the contents of the pharmacy behind in pristine condition including a huge collection of bottles, papers, medicines and herbs.

There is a customer pharmacy area on the first level and a large storage space upstairs. Both areas are impressively stocked with original shelves, drawers, bottles, cans and actual medicinal ingredients dating back at least to 1933 with some items originating much earlier. Fortunately, preservation minded owners bought the building and turned it into a museum in 1939, which was extensively renovated in 2006. Some of the pharmacy's notable customers included Martha Washington and Robert E. Lee as well as Union soldiers who occupied Old Town at the beginning of the Civil War. The historic business Day Book has notations concerning sales to these famous customers.

Adult groups of up to 8 people can also arrange special "Behind the Counter" tours to see items not normally on display to the public. The museum also offers special birthday party events for children ages 7 and up, where kids can learn the basics of making and marketing their own brand of medicine. Call or go online to make reservations.

Refreshments: There is soda and candy in the gift shop and a water cooler upstairs.

Bathroom Facilities: Onsite

Scavenger Hunt:

No code letters-suitable for all ages
Y-designed for young children (under 10)
TW-designed for tweens ages 10-13
T-designed for teenagers

1. Find the biggest mortar and pestle in the first floor pharmacy area. What were they used for in the pharmacy?

2. Who is the most famous customer in the Day Book, which recorded transactions at the store?

3. Find the letter from Martha Washington at Mount Vernon. What product did she want?

4. Y-Find the bottle that contained cinnamon.

5. On the second floor, ask the docent to open the trap door. What was it used for in the pharmacy?

6. Find the drawer containing the medicinal material known as "Dragon's Blood."

7. Find a can containing mandrake roots.

8. TW, T-Find the Tanglefoot paper. What was it used for and where?

9. Find the drawer containing watermelon seeds.

10. Find the old mimeograph copy machine and the pencil sharpener.

11. T-What part of an animal was hung above the entrance to the storage area for luck?

STABLER-LEADBEATER APOTHECARY MUSEUM SCAVENGER HUNT ANSWER KEY

No code letters-suitable for all ages
Y-designed for young children (under 10)
TW-designed for tweens ages 10-13
T-designed for teenagers

1. *There are a variety of mortar and pestles, but the biggest one is displayed on top of one of the glass cases. They used these to crush ingredients to make medicine for customers.*

2. *Robert E. Lee, the famous Confederate General, was a frequent customer and his name is visible in this book.*

3. *Martha Washington ordered Castor Oil.*

4. *Y-The bottle of cinnamon is among the bottles displayed on the shelf area behind the historic Day Book.*

5. *There is a trap door covering a hoist used to move large products from the storage area upstairs to the pharmacy store area below.*

6. *There are a few drawers of this strange medicine in the main storage area. It is a latex like material that comes from trees in the Amazon. It has antiviral and wound healing effects.*

7. *This can is above the section of drawers containing dragon's blood.*

8. *TW, T-Tanglefoot paper was a type of flypaper designed to catch insects and other pests while you slept in bed.*

9. *There is a section of drawers containing various seeds to the right of the door as you walk into the storage area.*

10. *There is an office area across from the entrance when you walk into the storage area.*

11. *T-There is an old turkey foot (claw) hung by previous occupants for good luck.*

CARLYLE HOUSE HISTORIC PARK

Address/Contact Information: 121 North Fairfax Street, Alexandria, VA, 703-746-3852, www.nvrpa.org/park/carlyle_house_historic_park

Closest Metro Station: King Street (Blue/Yellow Lines), Take free King Street Trolley up King Street to Fairfax Street. Take a left on Fairfax Street and walk less than a block to the house on the right.

Opening Hours/Ticketing: Tuesday-Saturday 10 AM-4 PM, Sunday 12 PM-4 PM. Adult tickets cost $5, children ages 11-17 cost $3, and children under 11 are free. Guided tours are available on the hour and half hour. Schedule group tours of 10 or more in advance. Special school tours, including one from a house slave's perspective, are available with advance notice. Scout tours and hands-on archaeology programs are also offered with advance notice.

Essential Info: The Carlyle House provides an interesting window into the gentry lifestyle of a merchant family and their attending servants and slaves in colonial America. British merchant John Carlyle built this stone, mid-Georgian style house with Virginia Palladian design for his bride, Sarah Fairfax, in 1753. This type of house, common in Carlyle's British homeland, was a rare jewel in the rapidly growing trade center of Alexandria. Carlyle was a leading merchant in Alexandria and his home rapidly became a hub of social and political activity for the community.

British General Edward Braddock made Carlyle's house his headquarters and residence when he assumed command of British and colonial forces in the French and Indian Wars. In Carlyle's dining room, Braddock conducted his famous Congress of Alexandria meeting with 5 colonial governors on April 15, 1755, to plan a war strategy to fight the French and their American Indian allies. Braddock tried unsuccessfully to convince the governors to levy additional taxes in their colonies to support the war effort. Braddock and his colleagues displayed an arrogant and dismissive attitude toward the Carlyle family and other important colonists that left a lasting negative impression. Braddock's disastrous defeat and death at the Battle of the Monongahela in Pennsylvania shortly thereafter diminished the reputation of Britain further among influential colonists. Braddock's defeat and other signs of British incompetence in ruling the colonies would lead to a growing feeling of an independent American identity in many colonists including John Carlyle.

Refreshments: Light refreshments available onsite, restaurants on King Street.

Bathroom Facilities: Onsite

Scavenger Hunt:

No code letters-suitable for all ages
Y-designed for young children (under 10)
TW-designed for tweens ages 10-13
T-designed for teenagers

1. Watch the short movie introducing the original owner of the house, John Carlyle. Which country did he come from in Europe?

2. T-What was buried in the wall of the building and why?

3. TW, T-What made the house special at that time in Alexandria?

4. In the first bed chamber, find the bed warmer and closed stool. What was the closed stool used for at night?

5. Y-Find a wig in the bedroom. Whose was it?

6. In Carlyle's study find the old map of the United States. Why doesn't it look the same as today?

7. What was the white feather used for at the desk?

8. What is the name of the musical instrument in the parlor?

9. T-What famous meeting happened in the dining room as discussed in the short film?

10. Whose wedding dress is replicated in the room? Why isn't it white?

11. TW-What material protects the knife holder in the dining room?

12. T-On the second floor, find the mourning jewelry. What memento is found in them?

13. TW, T-What beautiful wedding gift is found in this area?

14. Why are there mattresses on the floor in this hall?

15. TW, T-How many pieces of clothing did women in the family have to wear?

16. Y, TW-Find the embroidery sample made by 8-year-old Sarah Carlyle. Which letters are missing?

17. In young George William Carlyle's room, find a hat with a revolutionary slogan on it.

18. What did George have to bring with him to boarding school besides his clothes?

19. T-What war did George fight in and what happened to him?

20. TW, T-In the room showing the architectural aspects of the building, find an exposed beam and the keystone.

21. Find the door with graffiti on it. What is the oldest writing on the door?

CARLYLE HOUSE HISTORIC PARK SCAVENGER HUNT ANSWER KEY

No code letters-suitable for all ages
Y-designed for young children (under 10)
TW-designed for tweens ages 10-13
T-designed for teenagers

1. *Carlyle came from England, but he was of Scottish descent.*

2. *T-A dead cat was entombed in the wall of the building in a superstitious attempt to protect the house and family from evil.*

3. *TW, T-The house was made of stone as in Scotland. Most houses in Alexandria were made of wood.*

4. *The bed warmer is near the fireplace and the closed stool is the chair with the hole near the bed. Wealthier people used these at night for more comfort when relieving themselves.*

5. *Y-The wig belonged to John Carlyle.*

6. *The old map was drawn at a time well before the U.S. had 50 states.*

7. *People used feathers as quills for writing.*

8. *It is called a spinet and is more similar to a harpsichord than a piano.*

9. *T-British General Braddock conducted his famous Congress of Alexandria meeting here with 5 colonial governors on April 15, 1755.*

10. *A similar style of dress belonged to John Carlyle's bride, Sarah Fairfax. A fragment is found upstairs. Wedding dresses didn't become white until Queen Victoria's reign in the 19th century.*

11. *TW-Shark skin protects the knife holder.*

12. *T-Hair from the deceased relative is kept as a memento in the mourning jewelry.*

13. *TW,T-A silver tankard*

14. *Depending on the number of visitors at the house, the house slaves and indentured servants would sometimes have to sleep on mattresses on the floor.*

15. *TW, T-There are 4 or 5 pieces of clothing the women would have to put on every day.*

16. *Y, TW-The embroidery sample is on the wall and is missing the letters J and U.*

17. *There is a red hat with "Give me liberty or give me death," a famous line which came from a speech given by Patrick Henry.*

18. *The custom of the time was that students had to bring their beds with them to school.*

19. T-*George was killed at age 16 in one of the last battles of the Revolutionary War.*

20. TW, T-*The keystone is the large stone displayed on the left hand side of the room and the beam is in the middle of the floor.*

21. *There is a wooden door in the room with graffiti dating back to 1798.*

LEE-FENDALL HOUSE MUSEUM AND GARDEN

Address/Contact Information: 614 Oronoco Street, Alexandria, VA, 703-548-1789, www.leefendallhouse.org

Closest Metro Station: King Street (Blue/Yellow Lines), Take free King Street Trolley up King Street to Washington Street, then walk 4 blocks north on Washington Street to Oronoco Street.

Opening Hours/Ticketing: Wednesday-Saturday 10 AM-3 PM, Sunday 1 PM-3 PM. The last tour begins at 3 PM. Adult tickets cost $5, children ages11-17 cost $3, and children under 11 are free. Mandatory 30-minute guided tours are available at the top of the hour. Schedule group tours of 10 or more in advance.

Essential Info: Revolutionary War hero Henry "Light Horse Harry" Lee, father of Robert E. Lee and great friend of George Washington, bought this corner plot of land among others and sold it to his cousin Philip Fendall in 1785. Fendall built this beautiful wooden frame house, which served as a home to 37 different members of the Lee family from 1785 until 1903. George Washington was a frequent visitor to the house and Robert E. Lee grew up in the brick house (now a private residence) diagonally across Oronoco Street.

Union soldiers seized the Lee-Fendall House in 1863 and used it as a military hospital and headquarters for their head surgeon. A prominent Alexandria haberdasher, Robert Downham, bought it from the Lee family in 1903 and lived there for 31 years. Downham sold the house to the famous and controversial President of the United Mine Workers, John L. Lewis, who lived in this house until his death in 1969. The house is now owned and operated by the Virginia Trust for Historic Preservation.

The house has been restored to its early Victorian elegance and is interpreted as a Lee family home during the 1850-70 time period. The rooms are filled with period furniture and premier decorative arts including Lee family heirlooms and other historical artifacts. The house exhibits the largest public collection of furniture manufactured by the famous Green Furniture Company from Alexandria, VA, in the 19th century.

Behind the house there is a beautiful half-acre garden featuring roses and herbs and magnificent old black walnut, magnolia and ginkgo trees. Beneath the huge magnolia tree, you will find the tombstone of Philip Fendall's mother Eleanor who died in 1759. This stone was brought here from her gravesite to avoid destruction, but her remains were not transferred here. In the garden and surrounding area, you will likely see many squirrels. These gray squirrels are the symbol for the Lee family, which is found on many of the items in the house.

Refreshments: There are nearby restaurants on Washington and King Streets.

Bathroom Facilities: Onsite

Scavenger Hunt:

No code letters-suitable for all ages
Y-designed for young children (under 10)
TW-designed for tweens ages 10-13
T-designed for teenagers

1. In the formal parlor, find the portraits of "Light Horse" Harry Lee and his son, Robert E. Lee.

2. Find the servant bell.

3. In the family parlor, take a look through the stereoscope.

4. T-What made the two Lee brothers, Richard Henry and Francis famous?

5. Find the Lee family coat of arms. What animal is in it?

6. TW, T-In the dining room, find the original newspaper containing Lighthorse Harry's eulogy for George Washington. Can you find a famous line from the eulogy?

7. T-Why did most houses built in the 18th century not have kitchens attached to them?

8. TW, T-Why were many of the containers designed to hold canned goods?

9. Find an original signature from George Washington in the house.

10. In the master bedroom, find the lock of hair from Henry Clay.

11. T-Why were portraits sometimes done in profile as in this room?

12. Y, TW-In the girls' bedroom, find a squirrel in the doll house.

13. TW-Why is the sewing machine in the girls' bedroom?

14. What modern convenience did John Lewis install in the house? Can you find any evidence of this device now?

15. In the garden, find the gravestone of Philip Fendall's mother, Eleanor.

LEE-FENDALL HOUSE MUSEUM AND GARDEN SCAVENGER HUNT ANSWER KEY

No code letters-suitable for all ages
Y-designed for young children (under 10)
TW-designed for tweens ages 10-13
T-designed for teenagers

1. *The father's portrait is over the fireplace and the son's portrait is directly across on the wall.*

2. *To the left of the fireplace on the wall is a servant bell.*

3. *This device provided 3-D views of famous locations and can be found on the table to the left of the entry door.*

4. *T-These two brothers were the only brothers to sign the Declaration of Independence. Richard Henry's portrait along with his brother Arthur's portrait hang in the family parlor.*

5. *A frame next to the back porch contains an example of the Lee family coat of arms featuring a squirrel and the Latin motto of "Ever mindful of the future."*

6. *TW, T-The newspaper contains the powerful eulogy with the famous line- "First in war, first in peace, and first in the hearts of his countrymen…"*

7. *T-The Lee-Fendall house is a rarity because of its attached kitchen. Houses in this time period normally had kitchens in outbuildings to prevent fires. The dining room originally served as a fire break to help stop a fire from reaching the main house.*

8. *TW, T-During the Victorian era, serving items using the new technology of canned goods was a symbol of wealth.*

9. *You can find this signature near the Grandfather Clock when you walk up the stairway. This signature is found on a document concerning Lighthorse Harry Lee's acceptance into the prestigious Society of Cincinnati.*

10. *A frame containing a lock of hair from the famous Kentucky politician, Henry Clay, is on the wall next to the fireplace.*

11. *T-The portrait of Jonathan Hite Lee is a profile. Portraits were done in this manner as a less expensive alternative to a regular portrait.*

12. *Y, TW-The squirrel is in the bathtub in the doll house.*

13. *TW-Girls were expected to know how to knit and sew in an era when making and repairing family clothing was a necessity.*

14. *John Lewis, the famous labor leader and final private owner of the house, installed an elevator. This elevator was removed when the house was restored back to its Victorian appearance, but you can still see some of its infrastructure on the upper levels of the stairway.*

15. *Eleanor's Fendall's gravestone was brought here to avoid possible destruction at the original gravesite, but her remains were not transferred here. The gravestone without a grave is located beneath the large magnolia tree in the upper right hand section of the garden.*

ALEXANDRIA ARCHAEOLOGY MUSEUM

Address/Contact Information: Torpedo Factory Art Center, 3rd Floor, 105 North Union Street, Studio #327, Alexandria, VA, 703-838-4399, www.alexandriava.gov/Archaeology

Closest Metro Station: King Street (Blue/Yellow Lines), Take free King Street Trolley up King Street to final stop at Union Street, then walk 1 block north to entrance in Torpedo Factory Art Center

Opening Hours/Ticketing: Tuesday-Friday 10 AM-3 PM, Saturday 10 AM-5 PM, Sunday 1 PM-5 PM. Free admission. Contact the museum in advance for site tours, public dig days and special events and to schedule school/group tours.

Essential Info: This museum provides a glimpse into how archaeologists do their work and shows examples of Alexandria's rich history from its earliest inhabitants to today. Kids will enjoy their hands-on activities including piecing together pottery shards. Highlights of the museum include a 13,000-year-old Clovis spear point, artifacts from a drummer boy in the Civil War, and a 19th century musket. They also offer a scavenger hunt, which kids can complete to learn more about the museum's artifacts.

On the second Saturday of October **the Arts Safari** takes place in the Alexandria Archaeology Museum. This festival features a host of hands-on arts and crafts and archaeology activities for children.

Refreshments: There are vending machines on the first floor, a food pavilion next door and multiple restaurants on King Street.

Bathroom Facilities: Onsite and at the food pavilion next door.

Scavenger Hunt:

No code letters-suitable for all ages
Y-designed for young children (under 10)
TW-designed for tweens ages 10-13
T-designed for teenagers

1. Y-Try to piece a ceramic plate back together in the hands-on area.

2. Guess what kind of animal skeleton is on display.

3. Find the oldest artifact in the museum. How old is it and what was it used for?

4. Find the historic smoking pipes. What did they do to people's teeth?

5. Find the letter and drum stick from a drummer boy in the military. What war did he serve in? What was the minimum age for boys to become drummer boys?

6. Where was the Wickham Musket found?

7. Find an old plow blade used on a farm.

8. TW, T-Find the model of an archaeological dig and identify some of their tools.

9. Find an actual torpedo on the first floor of the Torpedo Factory building.

ALEXANDRIA ARCHAEOLOGY MUSEUM SCAVENGER HUNT ANSWER KEY

No code letters-suitable for all ages
Y-designed for young children (under 10)
TW-designed for tweens ages 10-13
T-designed for teenagers

1. Y-*A few samples are in the hands-on area.*

2. *The small dinosaur-looking skeleton is actually from a dog.*

3. *The museum displays a Native American Clovis spear point, which is estimated at 13,000 years old. This hand-shaped and sharpened stone projectile point would normally be used on the end of a spear for hunting and/or fishing.*

4. *The pipes are on display in the case to the right of where the Clovis spear point is located. The smoke from the pipes stained and weakened people's teeth.*

5. *These artifacts are in a case on the left as you enter the museum. This boy served in the Civil War when there was a minimum age requirement of 12 for drummer boys.*

6. *This musket was found cocked and loaded in the remains of a privy or outhouse. Many items were disposed of in this fashion before landfills became common. Privies are a great resource for artifacts that archaeologists like to study.*

7. *A rusty plow blade is displayed in front of the Wickham musket area.*

8. TW, T-*There is a model of an archaeologist excavating to the right as you enter the museum. A variety of tools they use on archaeological digs is displayed there.*

9. *This building once housed a torpedo factory making these weapons for use in World War II. A green Mark XIV torpedo made here in 1945 is on display on the ground level in the main hall.*

THE LYCEUM

Address/Contact Information: 201 South Washington Street, Alexandria, VA 22314, 703-838-4994, http://alexandriava.gov/Lyceum

Closest Metro Station: King Street (Blue/Yellow Lines), Take free King Street Trolley up King Street to Washington Street, then walk south on Washington Street 1 block to the Lyceum.

Opening Hours/Ticketing: Monday-Saturday 10 AM-5 PM, Sunday 1 PM-5 PM, permanent museum exhibition admission is $2.

Essential Info: In 1839 a group of distinguished gentlemen from Alexandria called the Alexandria Lyceum joined with the Alexandria Library Company to build this beautiful Greek Revival hall. Their goal was to provide a permanent location for lectures, concerts, special events and scientific experiments as well as a place to study and read. After service as a hospital in the Civil War, and time as a private residence and office building it now serves as a museum for the city of Alexandria containing more than 5,000 items. It also features an interesting gift shop with specialty items related to Alexandria's history.

The permanent exhibition features two galleries of interesting artifacts including Native American tools and weapons, a parlor from a historic residence, ceramics, civil war weapons and currency, period furniture, and artifacts related to Alexandria's commercial history. There are also temporary exhibitions and frequent special lectures and events.

Refreshments: Bottled water and candy is available in the gift shop. Nearby restaurants are on King and Washington Streets.

Bathroom Facilities: Onsite

Scavenger Hunt:

No code letters-suitable for all ages
Y-designed for young children (under 10)
TW-designed for tweens ages 10-13
T-designed for teenagers

1. Which family was the town Alexandria named after?

2. Y-Touch the deer hide. What did Native Americans use to hunt deer?

3. Smell the tobacco leaves. How many pounds of them are in the barrel or "hogshead?"

4. Find what looks like a cannon. TW, T-What is this weapon called and where was it primarily used?

5. Find the baby's rattle and toothbrush found during archaeological excavations.

6. Y-Find the old street sign. What is the name of the street on it?

7. Find the 1863 Springfield musket from the Civil War. How many shots could a good soldier fire in a minute?

8. Find the Confederate money. How much was it worth after the war?

9. T-Find the memorial/commemorative card for Colonel Elmer Ellsworth. Why was he important to people in the Union during the Civil War?

10. TW, T-What was the Lyceum used as during the Civil War?

11. TW, T-What were two of the main industries of Alexandria after the Civil War?

12. Find the World War I uniform.

13. T-Why were five men arrested at the Alexandria Library in 1939? What happened as a result of Samuel Tucker's successful defense of them?

14. For which war did the torpedo factory in Alexandria produce torpedoes?

15. While standing outside in front of the Lyceum, find the statue of the Confederate soldier at a nearby intersection. Which direction is he facing and why?

THE LYCEUM SCAVENGER HUNT ANSWER KEY

No code letters-suitable for all ages
Y-designed for young children (under 10)
TW-designed for tweens ages 10-13
T-designed for teenagers

1. *The Alexander family*

2. *Y-Native Americans used a bow and arrow to hunt deer.*

3. *The barrel could contain about 1,000 pounds of this valuable export.*

4. *This weapon is called a carronade. TW, T-It was primarily used on ships because of its size, mobility and ease in reloading.*

5. *In a case diagonally to the right of the carronade you will find these items.*

6. *Y-As you exit the first gallery to the next gallery, you will see this old stone King Street sign lying on the floor.*

7. *Good soldiers could fire three shots in one minute.*

8. *The Confederate money is in the same case as the musket. This money was worthless after the war and is now valued as a historical artifact.*

9. *T-The card and other mementos are in the case across from the musket case and behind you as you stare at the musket. Ellsworth was the first Union officer to be killed during the Civil War. He took down a Confederate Flag flying over the Marshall House in Alexandria and was killed by the owner of the house, James Jackson. Jackson was then shot and killed by Union troops and both men became martyrs to their respective causes. The Marshall house stood at the corner of South Pitt and King Streets, which is now occupied by the Hotel Monaco.*

10. *TW, T-Interesting photos show the Lyceum being used as a Federal hospital during the Civil War.*

11. *TW, T-Photos and exhibits show the importance of the railroad and the Portner Brewery for Alexandria.*

12. *The World War I uniform is near the end of the exhibit.*

13. *T-Segregation between the races existed at this time in Virginia. The men were arrested for trespassing in a whites only library. After Tucker's vigorous defense, the charges were dropped and the city built a new library for blacks called the Robert Robinson Library.*

14. *The torpedo factory made torpedoes for use in World War II.*

15. *The "Confederate Statue" or "Appomattox" was dedicated in May 1889 to the memory of the 99 men from Alexandria, who died in the Civil War. This statue was dedicated by their surviving comrades. The figure is based on a photograph of an unarmed Confederate soldier with head bowed during the surrender of the Army of Northern Virginia at Appomattox Court House, VA, in 1865. The statue marks the spot where Confederate soldiers departed the city to fight in the war in 1861 and faces south along the route they travelled. It is located at Prince Street and South Washington Street.* Do not attempt to view the statue up close as it is located in the middle of a busy intersection.

FRIENDSHIP FIRE HOUSE MUSEUM

Address/Contact Information: 107 South Alfred Street, Alexandria, VA, 703-838-3891, http://alexandriava.gov/FriendshipFirehouse

Closest Metro Station: King Street (Blue/Yellow Lines), Take free King Street Trolley up King Street to Alfred Street, then walk south 1 block to Firehouse.

Opening Hours/Ticketing: Friday-Saturday 10 AM- 4 PM, Sunday 1 PM-4 PM, suggested donation is $2.

Essential Info: For an interesting look back into the history of firefighting in the 18th and 19th centuries, stop by the Friendship Fire House Museum. The Friendship Fire Company was established in 1774, possibly by George Washington himself, and was the first volunteer fire company in Alexandria. The firehouse at this location was built in 1855 and restored in 1992. The first floor features historic firefighting equipment including buckets, hose, axes and hand drawn fire engines.

On the second floor, you can see the company's meeting room and ceremonial objects associated with the history of the organization. Of particular note, are the many letters from famous individuals accepting honorary membership into the company including President Eisenhower and Prime Minister Winston Churchill.

Refreshments: There are nearby restaurants on King Street.

Bathroom Facilities: Onsite

Scavenger Hunt:

No code letters-suitable for all ages
Y-designed for young children (under 10)
TW-designed for tweens ages 10-13
T-designed for teenagers

1. Find the hose reel cart.

2. Find the fire engine used before steamers. How many men were needed to operate it?

3. T-Which tragic event demonstrated the importance of using riveted leather hose vs. buckets to fight fires?

4. Why was the steam fire engine, known as a "steamer," more efficient than the hand-pumper?

5. TW, T-Walk upstairs and find the framed letters concerning honorary membership in the fire company from Charles Lindbergh, President Eisenhower, and Prime Minister Winston Churchill.

6. Find the black parade hat used by fire company members. What is the symbol for friendship they used in their regalia?

7. Why is there a bust of President George Washington in the room?

FRIENDSHIP FIRE HOUSE MUSEUM SCAVENGER HUNT ANSWER KEY

No code letters-suitable for all ages
Y-designed for young children (under 10)
TW-designed for tweens ages 10-13
T-designed for teenagers

1. *This type of cart was used for the transportation of hose to fight fires. Rival fire companies would often race these carts for bragging rights.*

2. *16-20 men were needed to operate this engine.*

3. *T-Fire companies from Georgetown and Washington, D.C., demonstrated the effectiveness of using hose when they assisted Alexandria fire companies in fighting the devastating Green Furniture Company fire in 1827. The speed and effectiveness of hose were far superior to buckets.*

4. *The steamer, which came into service in the second half of the 19th century, only needed 4 men to operate vs. 15-30 men for the hand-pumper.*

5. *TW, T-These framed letters are in the first room upstairs on the wall to the left. There are additional interesting letters from honorary members found in the white plastic binders below the frame.*

6. *The symbol they use for friendship is a pair of clasped hands.*

7. *Tradition says that George Washington helped start the Friendship Fire Company in 1774.*

OLD PRESBYTERIAN MEETING HOUSE

Address/Contact Information: 323 South Fairfax Street, Alexandria, VA, 703-549-6670, www.opmh.org

Closest Metro Station: King Street (Blue/Yellow Lines), Take free King Street Trolley up King Street to Fairfax Street, then walk 3 blocks south.

Opening Hours/Ticketing: Monday-Friday 8:15 AM-4:15 PM.

Essential Info: This church is famous for being the location of George Washington's memorial services. It also has a cemetery containing the graves of notable Alexandria residents. The original church was established in 1772 with the first building constructed in 1774 and destroyed by fire in 1835. The current church was built soon after on the site of the original church.

George Washington was a member of the local Church of England, Christ Church, about 8 blocks northwest of this site, which was considered rural at this time. During the week of his memorial services the roads to Christ Church were muddy and snowy and virtually impassable, so officials decided to have his services at this more accessible location. In addition, Washington's personal physician and close friend, Dr. James Craik, was a member here and Washington was also a close friend of the Pastor, James Muir. Washington was a mason with these men in the local Masonic lodge and had often worshipped at this meeting house.

In the cemetery, you will find the Tomb of the Unknown Revolutionary War Soldier with the inscription "Here lies a soldier of the Revolution whose identity is known but to God." In 1821, workers digging a foundation for a new Catholic chapel behind the Meeting House found the unmarked grave with an ammunition box serving as a coffin. Newspaper reports noted his tattered revolutionary war uniform and buttons that showed he came from Kentucky. The man was reinterred and a permanent marker was installed in 1929. The graves of Dr. Craik and the owner of the Carlyle House, John Carlyle, are also located in the cemetery.

Refreshments: There are nearby restaurants on King Street.

Bathroom Facilities: N/A

Scavenger Hunt:

No code letters-suitable for all ages
Y-designed for young children (under 10)
TW-designed for tweens ages 10-13
T-designed for teenagers

1. TW, T-Why do the pews in the meeting house have small doors?

2. T-Why is this church called a "meeting house?"

3. Find the Tomb of the Unknown Revolutionary War Soldier.

4. Find the graves of Dr. James Craik and John Carlyle.

OLD PRESBYTERIAN MEETING HOUSE SCAVENGER HUNT ANSWER KEY

No code letters-suitable for all ages
Y-designed for young children (under 10)
TW-designed for tweens ages 10-13
T-designed for teenagers

1. TW, T-*Parishioners would bring warm stones and bricks wrapped in cloth and place them near their feet to ward off the cold. The doors helped keep the heat in the pew.*

2. T-*In colonial times the Church of England was the official church and only their places of worship could be called "churches." Other denominations could worship in public places called "meeting houses."*

3. *The tomb is marked by an American flag and is surrounded by an iron fence.*

4. *Dr. Craik's grave is on the path near the stairs when you exit the meeting house. John Carlyle's grave has a large marker to the left of center at the beginning of the main part of the cemetery.*

ALEXANDRIA BLACK HISTORY MUSEUM

Address/Contact Information: 902 Wythe Street, Alexandria, VA, 703-746-4356, http://alexandriava.gov/BlackHistory

Closest Metro Station: Braddock Road (Blue/Yellow Lines), Walk .1 mile on West Street and take a left on Wythe Street, walk .3 mile to museum. Alternatively take 10 A/B Bus toward Hunting Towers and get off at Pendleton Street and Alfred Street and walk one block north to the museum on Wythe Street.

Opening Hours/Ticketing: Tuesday-Saturday 10 AM-4 PM, suggested donation is $2.

Essential Info: The Alexandria Black History museum is dedicated to exhibiting local and regional black history and to fostering appreciation of the diverse African American experience. The museum itself is located in the former Robert H. Robinson library, which was constructed in 1940 following a historic sit-in protest at the segregated main library of Alexandria. This groundbreaking protest is believed to be one of the first successful events in the early Civil Rights movement.

The museum combines historic artifacts from black life in Virginia in the 1600s to the present. You will also find informative placards describing the horrors of the "Middle Passage" from Africa, slave and free black life in Alexandria, and the achievements of free African American Benjamin Banneker. Banneker was a mathematical genius who produced impressive almanacs and helped survey the new capital city.

Don't miss the miniature model of 18th century Alexandria, which shows historic Alexandria buildings along with the sobering reality of the slave trade taking place at Market Square. The museum also offers temporary exhibitions and films about black culture. The Watson Reading Room next door is a research repository focusing on issues of African-American history and culture.

Follow the hunt in a circle from left to right to get a good overview of the artifacts and information in the museum.

Refreshments: Nearby restaurants are located on North Henry and King Streets.

Bathroom Facilities: Onsite

1. Y-Find the wooden hair comb in the "Kingdoms of Africa" section.

2. Find the stringed instrument from Africa.

3. TW, T-In the "Immigrants against their will" section, find the diagram of a slave ship. What was the terrible sea voyage made from Africa to the Americas called?

4. When did the first Africans arrive in Virginia?

5. For which valuable crop did Virginia planters need slave labor?

6. Find artifacts from the Lee Plantation laundry.

7. TW, T-Find the slave shackles and bill of sale for a slave.

8. TW, T-Find the slave sales going on at Market Square in the miniature model of Alexandria in the 18th century.

9. T-What was the paradox of early America highlighted throughout the museum?

10. TW, T-Find the life-sized figure of a slave drinking water. What important industry did he work at in Alexandria?

11. Find the woodcut art showing a free black neighborhood in Alexandria.

12. Y-Find some ceramics from both slave and free black households in Alexandria in the 1800s.

13. What was the name of the famous free black man who excelled in math and astronomy and published his own almanac in 1791?

ALEXANDRIA BLACK HISTORY MUSEUM SCAVENGER HUNT ANSWER KEY

No code letters-suitable for all ages
Y-designed for young children (under 10)
TW-designed for tweens ages 10-13
T-designed for teenagers

1. Y-*The wooden comb used by women in Liberia is at the top of the exhibit case.*

2. *This instrument is in the exhibit case on the right. Many instruments in the U.S., including the banjo, originated in Africa-along with the roots of gospel, jazz and the blues.*

3. TW, T-*The placards in this area show these gut-wrenching diagrams and feature quotes from slaves and crew onboard about the horror of these journeys. This hellish voyage was known as "the middle passage."*

4. *The first Africans arrived against their will in 1619. These first few were treated as indentured servants with a chance for freedom in the future.*

5. *Tobacco*

6. *In a small plastic case you will find buttons, thimbles, and pins recovered from an archaeological dig on this plantation.*

7. TW, T-*These shocking artifacts are displayed in a case across from the miniature exhibit.*

8. TW, T-*This depressing scene is captured in one small area of this beautifully detailed miniature of Old Town Alexandria in the 18th century.*

9. T-*One placard sums it up succinctly "How could one group of people searching for freedom in the New World deprive another group of the very same rights?" There are quotes to this effect from famous Americans throughout the museum.*

10. TW, T-*This figure depicts a slave who worked at the sugar refinery in Alexandria.*

11. *This drawing is to the right of the life-sized model of the slave as you are walking toward the exit. Groups of free blacks in Alexandria began buying houses in the outskirts of Alexandria, which eventually became free black neighborhoods. The Miller family, a Quaker family who were strong abolitionists, were actively involved in renting and selling lodging to free blacks in Alexandria,*

12. Y-*These artifacts are located in an exhibit case near the woodcut art.*

13. *Benjamin Banneker, who is well-known for his work in surveying and planning the new capital city, is also celebrated for his impressive almanacs. He sent a copy of one almanac to Thomas Jefferson in an effort to demonstrate the intellectual capabilities of his race.*

GEORGE WASHINGTON'S MOUNT VERNON ESTATE AND GARDENS

Address/Contact Information: 3200 Mount Vernon Highway, Mount Vernon, VA 22121, 703-780-2000, www.mountvernon.org

Closest Metro Station: Huntington Station (Yellow Line), then take Fairfax Connector Bus #101 (Fort Hunt Line) for a 20-minute bus ride. Free parking available onsite. Spirit Cruises offers boat transportation from Washington, D.C., to Mount Vernon from March-October. See their website for rates and schedule at www.cruisetomountvernon.com. The Potomac Riverboat Company offers boat tours from Old Town, Alexandria, and National Harbor, MD, to Mount Vernon from April-October. Check rates and schedule at www.potomacriverboatco.com/mount-vernon-cruise-rates.php.

Opening Hours/Ticketing: Open 365 days a year, April-August 8 AM-5 PM, March, September and October 9 AM-5 PM, November-February 9 AM-4 PM. The historic area is cleared a half hour after closing, while the museum and education center is cleared one hour after closing. Tickets cost $15 for adults, $14 for seniors 62+, $7 for children ages 6-11, and children under 6 are free. Annual passes cost $25 for adults and $10 for children.

Essential Info: A visit to Mount Vernon is a celebration of the incredible life of the "Father of our Country," George Washington. The millions of visitors that have come to this honored location are a testament to the powerful, enduring influence Washington had on forming the United States of America. There is much to see and do at this location so plan to spend between 3-5 hours here.

When Washington died in 1799 he had developed his estate from 500 acres and a small mansion to 8,000 acres and a 21-room mansion with many outbuildings, farms and gardens. However, by the time it was purchased by the Mount Vernon Ladies Association in 1858, much of the grounds had been sold off and the mansion and outbuildings had deteriorated badly. The women of this association solicited a huge amount of private donations from across the country and around the world to restore the area to its former glory. The organization continues to successfully restore and manage Mount Vernon, which is the most visited private estate in the world.

Begin your visit by entering the visitor center and greeting the bronze life-sized sculptures of George and Martha Washington and her two grandchildren. Take your time appreciating the 1/12th size exact replica of the mansion and the beautiful stained glass window featuring five scenes from Washington's life. Watch the orientation film *We Fight to Be Free* (some violent battle scenes could be too much for younger children) and then proceed to the stirring sight of Washington's beloved Mount Vernon mansion home.

After a 20-minute guided tour of the mansion, take your time exploring the grounds and buildings. Sit on the piazza and enjoy the view of the Potomac. Visit some of the outbuildings surrounding the mansion including the kitchen, a blacksmith shop, slave quarters, a greenhouse, and stables containing historic carriages. You will also find a variety of gardens and walking paths to enjoy. Visit the paddock to view sheep from the same heritage line as Washington's own animals, and then make your way to the tomb where the remains of George and Martha Washington are interred. A memorial to the slaves that lived and worked at Mount Vernon is located near the tomb at the site of the slave burial ground.

If you have additional time and are visiting sometime between April-October, visit the "George Washington: Pioneer Farmer" area. This site features a 4-acre working farm and a recreation of one of Washington's most ingenious creations: a 16-sided treading barn where Washington's animals would walk over the wheat straw and break the grain out to be captured below. This grain was then transported to his nearby gristmill to be ground into flour. There are many hands-on children's activities and farming, cooking and craftwork demonstrations at this site that will illuminate how difficult and time-intensive life working on a pioneer farm was. The wharf providing boat access on the Potomac River is adjacent to this area.

After you have finished exploring the grounds, visit the Donald W. Reynolds Museum and Education Center, which features theaters, life-sized models, interactive exhibits, and amazing artifacts that tell the story of Washington's life as a surveyor, farmer, military commander, and the first president. I have included many of the highlights in the scavenger hunt, but there is plenty more to see and do that will satisfy even the most enthusiastic visitor. Be sure to visit the **Revolutionary War Theater**, which depicts three famous battles of the war with realistic audio, visual, and sensory effects including artificial snowflakes falling on the audience.

Mount Vernon does an excellent job of providing children-friendly information and activities. When you purchase your ticket, ask for an "Adventure Map for Kids," which children can use to solve nine puzzles by exploring the outbuildings and mansion. In the education center, there is a Hands-on History room where children ages 3-8 can dress up in period clothes, play with replicas of toys and tools, and learn about the farm animals at Mount Vernon. Before and after your visit, kids can go online at www.washingtonsworld.org to play games and view animated features about the Battle of Yorktown and Washington's life at Mount Vernon.

If you have additional time and interest, you can visit reconstructions of **George Washington's Whiskey Distillery and Gristmill**. Both of these businesses provided additional revenue to supplement Washington's farming activities. This site is located on Route 235, 3 miles south of Mount Vernon and is open daily from 10 AM-5 PM from April through October. This site features production demonstrations of both facilities by workers in period costumes. There is also a gift shop offering colonial themed toys, games, and giftware as well as stone ground cornmeal that is milled onsite. Tickets cost $2 for adults and $1.50 for children ages 6-11 when combined with Mount Vernon admission or $4 and $2, respectively, when purchased individually.

Refreshments: There is a food court in the gift shop area and fine dining available at the adjacent Mount Vernon Inn.

Bathroom Facilities: Onsite

Scavenger Hunt:

No code letters-suitable for all ages
Y-designed for young children (under 10)
TW-designed for tweens ages 10-13
T-designed for teenagers

Mansion and Grounds

1. Is the mansion made of wood or stone?

2. Y-In the large dining room, find the animals carved on the fireplace mantle.

3. Stare into the same large mirror that the Washington family once used.

4. Sit in one of the wooden chairs on the piazza and appreciate the same view the Washington family enjoyed.

5. T-Find the original swamp chestnut oak tree that Washington planted.

6. Find the key to the Bastille prison in Paris that was given to Washington by his friend Lafayette.

7. T-Which room was Washington's favorite in the house?

8. Find the harpsichord in one of the rooms.

9. What is the Washington family having for dinner in the dining room?

10. TW-Did the Washington family normally have many visitors to Mount Vernon? Where did the visitors sleep?

11. Find a bed warmer and the crib Martha gave to her granddaughter when she was expecting a child.

12. TW, T-How old was Washington when he died?

13. In the study find the snout of a sawfish.

14. Which chair would you prefer: the fan chair or his presidential swivel chair?

15. Find a colonial carriage.

16. Visit the sheep in the paddock area.

17. Pay your respects to George and Martha Washington at their tomb.

18. Find the memorial to the slaves who lived at Mount Vernon.

19. T-What was Washington's main cash crop?

20. TW, T-Find the slave quarters.

21. Observe a blacksmith making tools for the plantation.

Museum

22. Find the famous Houdon bust and get a close up look at how Washington really looked.

23. Find a sword owned by George Washington.

24. Find the original weathervane that sat atop the mansion.

25. Find General Washington's shaving case that he used when in the field.

26. Find original letters signed by George and Martha Washington.

Education Center

27. What was Washington's first job? Find a model of him performing this work.

28. TW, T-How long was George married to Martha?

29. What was the name of General Washington's horse as depicted in the life-sized model of the General on horseback?

30. TW, T-Did Washington win or lose more battles during the war?

31. T-After visiting the immersive Revolutionary War Theater, take a moment to view the video in the hallway demonstrating the importance of effective spying in the war.

32. TW, T-What animal did Washington breed and use extensively as a work animal on his plantation?

33. T-What happened to Washington's slaves after his death?

34. Find Washington's dentures. Were any of his teeth wooden?

35. Take the presidential oath of office with President Washington.

36. T-Find some of Washington's cabinet members. What is the phrase used to describe the importance of Washington's presidential actions in determining the future accepted behavior of his successors?

37. On your way out of the education center, find some photos of past important visitors to Mount Vernon. Do you or your family recognize any of them?

GEORGE WASHINGTON'S MOUNT VERNON ESTATE AND GARDENSSCAVENGER HUNT ANSWER KEY

No code letters-suitable for all ages
Y-designed for young children (under 10)
TW-designed for tweens ages 10-13
T-designed for teenagers

Mansion and Grounds

1. *The house is made of wood, but it resembles stone. The builders cut long pine boards into stone shapes then sanded and painted them to look like stone. While the paint was wet, they then threw fine sand on the boards to make it look more realistic.*

2. *Y-The animals are found carved at the top of the beautiful marble fireplace mantle in the room.*

3. *This huge mirror is found on the wall on the left hand side as you are exiting the room.*

4. *The land across from Mount Vernon is protected, preserving the view the Washington family enjoyed. Depending upon how crowded the tour is, it might work better to come back and sit in these chairs after you finish your tour of the mansion.*

5. *T-This tree is to the left of the piazza on the crest of the hill sloping down to the Potomac.*

6. *In the central passage area you will see this large key in a glass container on the wall between the blue guest room and dining room. This artifact from the French Revolution in 1789 was a treasured gift from the Marquis de Lafayette. This French officer assisted the colonial army during the American Revolutionary War and was a close friend and advisor to Washington.*

7. *T-The first parlor was Washington's favorite room and is decorated with portraits and images of his many famous friends.*

8. *The harpsichord is similar to a piano and is found in the second parlor.*

9. *The sample meal displayed alternates depending upon the season, but is always authentic to what the family ate.*

10. *TW-George Washington became a living legend after the war and his presidency. As a result guests flocked to Mount Vernon continuously. One year the family hosted 677 overnight guests who stayed primarily in these 2nd floor guest bedrooms.*

11. *Bed warmers are found in all the rooms and look something like a shovel with an oval end. The bed warmer was filled with hot coals and placed in the bed to keep the occupant warm. The crib is found in the bedroom on the far right.*

12. TW, T-*Washington was 67 years old when he died on December 14, 1799, in his bedroom at Mount Vernon.*

13. *This interesting oddity is hard to miss. Wealthy people of the time prided themselves on collecting unusual artifacts such as this.*

14. *Washington used the fan chair to keep cool. He made many important and precedent setting decisions in his presidential chair, including the decision not to seek a third term.*

15. *You can find carriages and other riding vehicles in the coach house and stable area on the right as you are heading downhill toward the tomb.*

16. *These Hog Island Sheep come from the same heritage line of Washington's sheep.*

17. *The Washington family tomb is found as you continue walking down the road to the right.*

18. *This memorial is found behind the tomb area at the site of their former burial area.*

19. T-*Mount Vernon's main cash crop was wheat.*

20. TW, T-*As you walk back toward the entrance you can visit additional outbuilding and gardens that are to the left of the mansion. The slave quarters are found near the greenhouse.*

21. *The blacksmith shop is near the greenhouse in the outbuildings to the left of the mansion.*

Museum

22. *This famous bust by French sculptor Jean Antoine Houdon is said to be perhaps the best likeness ever done of George Washington.*

23. *There are several of these ceremonial and combat swords in the museum thought to be owned by Washington.*

24. *This weathervane is featured prominently in the "At Home with the Washingtons" room.*

25. *This case and other objects are found in the "Life in Camp" area dominated by the field bed.*

26. *There are original letters from the Washingtons in the Gilder Lehrman Gallery.*

Education Center

27. *Washington's first job was as a surveyor. A model portrays him as a surveyor in the third room of the education center.*

28. TW, T-*Their marriage lasted 40 years from 1759-1799. If you have time, watch the film in the aptly named theater describing their 40 year romance.*

29. *This horse was named Blueskin. Another horse he often rode in battle was named Nelson. Both horses were retired to Mount Vernon after the war.*

30. TW, T-*Near the horseback model is a map on the wall with the title "Perseverance." When you push these buttons you can see that Washington lost more battles than he won, especially in the beginning of the war when his poorly trained troops were fighting crack British regulars. However, Washington learned from his mistakes, trained his men relentlessly, and would go on to win the most important battles that turned the tide to ultimate victory.*

31. T-*The important role espionage played in winning the war is documented in this interesting video.*

32. TW, T-*Washington bred American mules for their strength, endurance and intelligence. He introduced them to American agriculture and his methods were soon copied throughout the country.*

33. T-*In his will Washington arranged to free his 123 slaves after the death of himself and Martha. However, he had no power over the "dower slaves" that originally belonged to Martha Washington. Find out more information by watching the videos and looking at the exhibits in "The Dilemma of Slavery" area.*

34. *Washington had many sets of dentures. The dentures displayed are made of human and cow teeth and elephant ivory. Others contained other animal teeth and hippopotamus ivory, but no wood.*

35. *There is a button you can push to recite the presidential oath of office next to the historical representation of Washington's first presidential oath taking.*

36. T-*Washington picked an able cabinet to help him perform his job as the first president. He was well aware that his behavior as the first president would "set precedent" for his successors.*

37. *On the walls here and in the restroom area near the gift shops, you will find many photos of famous visitors to Mount Vernon.*

PART THREE

Additional Sites Of Interest

The Corcoran Gallery of Art. Courtesy of Destination DC.

In this section, I have included information on additional attractions of interest in Washington, D.C., and in the nearby area. All of these sites have something special to offer visitors. Take some time to read through this diverse list to find attractions appealing to your family's unique interests.

Additional Attractions in Washington, D.C., by Neighborhood

National Mall Area

The Freer and Sackler Galleries
1100 Jefferson Drive SW
Washington, D.C. 20001
202-633-4880
www.asia.si.edu
Open daily 10 AM-5:30 PM
Metro: Smithsonian (Blue/Orange Lines)

These Smithsonian Institution galleries display an outstanding collection of Asian art from China, Japan, Korea and the ancient Near East and Islamic world. The Freer Gallery also houses the world's most extensive collection of works by American artist James McNeill Whistler, including his masterpiece called *The Peacock Room*. Whistler painted and decorated this opulent London Dining Room to highlight the owner's collection of Asian ceramics in 1876-77.

The Sackler Gallery features 9,917 Asian art objects, with more than 1,000 pieces donated by Arthur Sackler in 1987 including Chinese bronzes, jades and sculpture from South and Southeast Asia. The two galleries also house the largest Asian art research gallery in the United States, which is open to the public 5 days a week without appointment.

The National Museum of African Art

950 Independence Avenue SW
Washington, D.C. 20560
202-633-4600
http://africa.si.edu
Open daily 10 AM-5:30 PM
Metro: Smithsonian (Blue/Orange Lines)

This Smithsonian Institution museum houses a wide range of African visual arts and other cultural treasures including mosaics, textiles, sculptures, musical instruments, and masks. The massive amount of art objects highlights the diverse cultures in Africa. The museum is connected underground to the Freer and Sackler Galleries.

The Hirshhorn Museum and Sculpture Garden

Independence Avenue at 7th Street SW
Washington, D.C. 20013
202-633-4674
http://hirshhorn.si.edu
Museum Open daily 10 AM-5:30 PM
Plaza open daily 7:30 AM-5:30 PM
Sculpture Garden open daily 7:30 AM-dusk
Metro: Smithsonian (Blue/Orange Lines)

The Smithsonian Institution Hirshhorn Museum building's space age cylindrical shape is a stark contrast to the traditional architecture on the National Mall and signals that this museum is displaying non-traditional art objects. Art collector Joseph Hirshhorn donated money and his extensive modern art collection to help start this unique museum, which opened in 1969. The museum offers three floors of gallery space displaying a wide range of modern art from the late-nineteenth century to the present. Artists from around the world have created these works. Art objects include works on traditional media such as paper, painting, photography, and sculpture as well as works using digital and video art.

Visitors also enjoy outdoor sculptures and art in the plaza surrounding the building. In addition, there are interesting art pieces, such as works by Rodin, in the bi-level Sculpture Garden in front of the building. The Hirshhorn Museum Sculpture Garden is a peaceful place to take a break while walking along the National Mall.

Constitution Gardens and Declaration of Independence Memorial

Along northern edge of National Mall near intersection of 17th Street and Constitution Avenue NW
Washington, D.C. 20006
202-426-6841
www.nps.gov/coga/index.htm
Metro: Farragut West (Blue/Orange Lines)

This beautiful 52-acre park area is located between the World War II Memorial and the Vietnam Veterans Memorial running adjacent to Constitution Avenue. This relaxing setting features a

6 ½-acre man-made lake and island. The water, woods and animals inhabiting this area make it a more tranquil path to get to the Vietnam Veterans and Lincoln Memorial from the WW II Memorial.

The Declaration of Independence Memorial is on a small island in the lake. This memorial honors the 56 signers of the Declaration of Independence. Information on each signer and facsimiles of their signatures are etched into 13 groups of red marble stones, representing the 13 original colonies. While crossing the wooden bridge to the island to visit the memorial, look for koi and other fish in the water as well as various types of waterfowl.

Old Lockkeepers House
Intersection of 17th Street and Constitution Avenue NW
Washington, D.C. 20006
Metro: Farragut West (Blue/Orange Lines)

At this busy intersection sits a historic building from when the Chesapeake & Ohio Canal connected with the Washington Canal in the 19th century. The canal ran in the District along where Constitution Avenue now stands. The C & O Canal stretched 184.5 miles from Washington, D.C., to Cumberland, Maryland, from 1831 until 1924. The lockkeeper's house was near the eastern end of the C & O Canal where it emptied into the Potomac River and Tiber Creek. It was also near the western end of the Washington Canal. The Washington Canal connected the Anacostia River to Tiber Creek, the Potomac River and the C & O Canal.

The Washington Canal opened in 1815 and was the first major thoroughfare in the capital city before the railroads. The portion that is now Constitution Avenue was filled in and made into a road in the1870s. The lockkeeper and his family lived in this house from the 1830s and collected tolls and kept business records on this important extension connecting the two canals.

Albert Einstein Memorial
2101 Constitution Avenue NW
Washington, D.C. 20037
202-334-2000
www.nasonline.org/about-nas/visiting-nas/nas-building/the-einstein-memorial.html
Metro: Foggy Bottom (Blue/Orange Lines)

A striking 21-foot tall bronze statue of the famous physicist, Albert Einstein, lies at the front of the National Academy of Sciences building. Many people visit this site after viewing the nearby Vietnam Veterans Memorial. The statue was sculpted by Robert Berks in 1979 and portrays a seated Einstein holding a notebook of his famous mathematical equations, while studying thousands of celestial bodies. Children and adults love to climb this statue, which makes for a great photo.

District of Columbia War Memorial
National Mall on north side of Independence Avenue, SW, between the World War II Memorial and Lincoln Memorial
Washington, D.C. 20006
202-426-6841
www.nps.gov/nama/planyourvisit/dc-war-memorial.htm

Walking from the top of the Reflecting Pool toward Independence Avenue and the Tidal Basin, you will see a 48-foot tall dome peristyle temple with Doric pillars that commemorates the 26,000 citizens of Washington, D.C., who served in World War I. Before World War II, this war was referred to as "The Great War" and "The War to End All Wars."

The names of the 499 Washington, D.C., men who died in the conflict are inscribed in the base of the memorial. The memorial was designed by Frederick Brooke and dedicated on Armistice Day in 1931. There is currently an effort to expand and rededicate this memorial to serve as a national memorial for all the Americans who served in the First World War.

Tidal Basin Area

George Mason Memorial
In West Potomac Park near intersection of Ohio Drive and East Basin Drive, SW
Washington, D.C. 20024
202-426-6841
www.nps.gov/gemm/index.htm
Metro: Smithsonian (Blue/Orange Lines)

Walking from the FDR Memorial toward the Jefferson Memorial, you will pass over a small bridge. To the right of this bridge there is a small, but attractive memorial to George Mason, known as the "forgotten founder." The memorial was dedicated in 2002. Mason wrote the Virginia Declaration of Rights, which influenced the formation of the Declaration of Independence and the U.S. Constitution. He was a delegate to the Constitutional Convention in Philadelphia in 1787, but refused to sign the Constitution because it did not abolish slavery nor provide enough protection for the individual from the federal government. Some of the protections were later added in the Bill of Rights. The memorial features a 72-foot long stone wall, circular pool and a slightly larger than life sculpture of George Mason. Wendy M. Ross sculpted Mason sitting in a relaxed pose on a bench with his legs crossed.

Penn Quarter/Gallery Place

The National Portrait Gallery and Smithsonian American Art Museum
Eighth and F Streets NW
Washington, D.C. 20001
202-633-8300 and 202-633-7970
www.npg.si.edu and http://americanart.si.edu
Open daily 11:30 AM-7 PM
Metro: Gallery Place-Chinatown (Green/Yellow Lines and Red Line)

These two museums are located in a beautifully restored 19th century Greek Revival building, which was originally designed to house the U.S. Patent Office. The National Portrait Gallery contains a huge amount of artistic portrayals of famous Americans and other notables and features an impressive gallery of presidential portraits. Gilbert Stuart's masterful Lansdowne portrait of George Washington is a famous highlight of the collection.

The Smithsonian American Art Museum contains a magnificent array of artwork by American artists including Bierstadt's stunning *Among the Sierra Nevada*, O'Keeffe's modern masterpiece *Manhattan*, and Paik's video installation of televisions called *Electronic Superhighway: Continental U.S., Alaska, Hawaii*.

Visitors also enjoy relaxing in the enclosed **Kogod Courtyard**, which features an elegant glass canopy covering 28,000 square feet.

Mary Surratt's Boarding House
604 H Street NW
Washington, D.C. 20001
Metro: Gallery Place (Green/Yellow Lines and Red Line)

Conspirators led by John Wilkes Booth met here in 1865 to formulate a plan to initially kidnap and then kill President Lincoln and prominent members of his administration. The owner of the boarding house, Mary Surratt, became the first woman executed by the U.S. government after being convicted for her involvement in the conspiracy. The role of Surratt in the conspiracy is still a matter of debate and is the subject of a film called *The Conspirator*, directed by Robert Redford.

National Building Museum
401 F Street NW
Washington, D.C. 20001
202-272-2448
www.nbm.org
Metro: Judiciary Square (Red Line) and Gallery Place (Green/Yellow Lines and Red Line)

This beautiful Pension Building housing the museum was built with more than 15 million red bricks. The building opened in 1887 as the Pension Bureau to help serve U.S. war veterans, primarily from the U.S. Civil War. Its exterior features a 1,200-foot terra cotta frieze that encircles the building depicting Union forces during the Civil War. Its spacious interior features a Great Hall and eight 75-foot high Corinthian columns made of faux marble. This hall is a featured location for presidential inaugural balls and other glamorous events. The museum features hands-on models, interactive displays and permanent and temporary exhibitions that focus on architecture and the built environment and its impact on people's lives.

The National Building Museum offers Family Tool Kits to help families explore the architecture of the building and learn by seeing, moving, touching and completing activities. There are also Discovery Carts throughout the museum with additional activities. They also offer an opportunity to build a 7-foot tall, soft-block arch with the Amazing Arches program. The museum also has a "Treasure Hunt Activity Booklet" available at the Information Desk, which is designed to teach and entertain kids ages 6 and up about architectural subjects.

The museum offers an exhibition called "The Building Zone," which is designed for kids ages 2-6. This area encourages kids to build using legos and building blocks and to dress up as a craftsperson with tools and a hard hat. There are also trucks to play with and picture books to enjoy. This exhibit costs $2 per child ages 2 and up and is open Monday-Saturday from 10 AM-4 PM and 11 AM-4 PM on Sunday.

They also offer Family Tours of the museum conducted by Junior Docents. These 30-minute tours take place on Saturdays at 10:30 AM and 11 AM and Sundays at 1 PM. To reserve space for groups of 10 or more or for more information call or go online.

National Law Enforcement Officers Memorial

E Street-between 4th and 5th Streets NW
Visitor Center
400 7th Street NW
Washington, D.C. 20004
202-737-3213
www.nleomf.org/memorial
Metro: Judiciary Square (Red Line) and Gallery Place (Green/Yellow Lines and Red Line)

This memorial honors all law enforcement officers in the United States who have died in the line of duty. It was dedicated in 1991 and features two curving 304- foot-long memorial walls with nearly 19,000 names of fallen officers inscribed on it dating back to 1791. New names are added to the memorial in a somber ceremony each spring. Each of the pathway entrances is decorated by a powerful statue of an adult lion protecting its cubs. Construction has begun on a museum near the memorial that will tell the story of the nation's law enforcement officers with a scheduled opening date of fall 2013.

Marian Koshland Science Museum

525 E Street NW
Washington, D.C. 20001
202-334-1201
www.koshland-science-museum.org/index.jsp
Metro: Gallery Place (Green/Yellow Lines and Red Line)

The museum's mission is to engage the general public in current scientific issues that impact their lives. The museum features state-of-the-art interactive exhibits, public events, and educational programs to educate the public and provide insight into how scientific research supports policy decision-making.

The United States Navy Memorial and Naval Heritage Center

701 Pennsylvania Avenue NW
Suite 123
Washington, D.C. 20004
202-737-2300
www.navymemorial.org
Metro: Archives-Navy Memorial (Green/Yellow Lines)

Located in the plaza behind the National Archives, the United States Navy Memorial consists of an outdoor paved granite map 100 feet in diameter showing the vastness of the seas in the world. The paved map is surrounded by fountains, pools, flagpoles and sculptural panels showing historic achievements at sea. The famous statue by Stanley Bleifeld, *The Lone Sailor*, honors all sailors from the U.S. Navy and other sea services.

In a building flanking the memorial is the Naval Heritage Center. Another statue by Bleifeld is in the entrance called *The Homecoming*. It depicts the happy reunion of a family with a sailor returning from a long voyage at sea. Inside the center there are exhibits showcasing the various work and duties of the U.S. Navy such as the dangerous tasks of the Explosive Ordnance Disposal unit. The center also shows an interesting 35-minute movie about high tech naval operations around the world called *At Sea*. Daily showings are at 10 AM, 12 PM, and 2 PM. The U.S. Navy Band performs regularly at this site in the spring and summer. The outdoor memorial is open around the clock and the Naval Heritage Center is open daily from 9:30 AM-5:30 PM. Admission is free.

Dupont Circle

Woodrow Wilson House
2340 S Street NW
Washington, D.C. 20008
202-387-4062
www.woodrowwilsonhouse.org
Metro: Dupont Circle (Red Line)

The 28th president moved into this Georgian Revival house in 1921 after he left the White House. Weakened by a serious stroke in 1919, the president spent the last three years of his life here under the care of his wife Edith. The house is preserved as it was in these years with many artifacts from Wilson's presidency including interesting gifts from world leaders. Guests are encouraged to make online reservations for a guided tour, but drop-in tours are sometimes available. The house is open 10 AM-4 PM from Tuesday-Sunday. Admission is $10 for adults, $8 for seniors, and $5 for students.

The Textile Museum
2320 S Street NW
Washington, D.C. 20008
 202-667-0441
www.textilemuseum.org
Metro: Dupont Circle (Red Line)

This private museum was founded by collector George Hewitt Myers in 1925 with the mission to expand the public's knowledge and appreciation of the artistic and cultural importance of the world's textiles. The museum's 18,000 objects are housed in two historic buildings, which also host temporary exhibitions and special events.

One Saturday a month the museum hosts an "Arts for Families" program, which invites families to explore exhibitions and conduct hands-on activities. Call to register for this and other programs. The museum is open 10 AM-5 PM Tuesday-Saturday and 1 PM-5 PM on Sunday with an $8 suggested donation. The museum will move to a new location at George Washington University in 2014.

The Phillips Collection
1600 21st Street NW
Washington, D.C. 20009
202-387-2151
www.phillipscollection.org
Metro: Dupont Circle (Red Line)

The Phillips Collection is the nation's first museum of modern art and is located within the family home of its founder, Duncan Phillips, and in some extensive new galleries. The permanent collection contains impressive works by Renoir, Rothko, Bonnard, van Gogh and Diebenkorn as well as artwork by talented contemporary artists. The museum also offers temporary exhibits, lectures, and special Conversations with Artists.

They offer musical concerts on Sundays from October-March at 4 PM and the After Five program on the first Thursday of the month, which includes jazz performances, films and gallery talks. These programs require admission fees with a recommended online reservation. The museum also produces an educational outreach program for students and teachers.

The Phillips Collection is open from Tuesday-Saturday 10 AM-5 PM, Sundays from 11 AM-6 PM and until 8:30 PM on Thursday. Admission to the permanent collection Tuesday-Friday is by donation. Weekend visitors pay a special exhibition fee or $10 for adults and $8 for students and seniors 62+. There is no charge for children under 18.

Andersen House
2118 Massachusetts Avenue NW
Washington, D.C. 20008
202-785-2040
www.societyofthecincinnati.org/visits.htm
Metro: Dupont Circle (Red Line)

This magnificent 50-room Beaux Arts mansion was completed in 1905 as the winter home of famous American diplomat Larz Anderson III and his wife Isabel. The Andersons entertained many prominent guests at their home, which is adorned with marble floors, carved wooden walls, and ornate iron staircases. The mansion houses a world class collection of paintings, sculpture, furniture, ceramics, and tapestries. When Larz died in 1937 without an heir, Isabel donated the house and most of its artwork and furnishings to the Society of Cincinnati. This venerable organization, originally led by George Washington, uses the building as its headquarters and offers free tours to the public. Guided tours are available at 1:15 PM, 2:15 PM and 3:15 PM Monday-Saturday and by appointment at other times.

Mahatma Gandhi Memorial
Metro: Dupont Circle (Red Line)

In the middle of Massachusetts Avenue at 21st Street, NW, is a larger than life bronze statue on a red granite pedestal honoring Indian political and spiritual leader Mahatma Gandhi. The nearly

9-foot tall statue created by Gautam Pal is located near the Indian Embassy and depicts Gandhi in stride using a walking stick.

The Buffalo Bridge
Metro: Dupont Circle (Red Line)

This bridge at the 2700 block of Q Street, NW, is officially known as the Dumbarton Bridge, but locals call it the Buffalo Bridge because of the four sculptures of buffaloes (American Bison) on it. The bridge was erected in 1915 to connect Dupont Circle area to Georgetown across Rock Creek Park. The sculptor was Alexander Phimister Proctor, one of the nation's most highly regarded "animaliers." An animalier is an artist skilled at realistically portraying animals in art.

Christian Heurich House Museum
The Brewmaster's Castle
1307 New Hampshire Avenue NW
Washington, D.C. 20036
202-429-1894
www.brewmasterscastle.com
Metro: Dupont Circle (Red Line)

This architectural wonder was built in 1894 by German immigrant, Christian Heurich, who made a fortune as a brewery owner and real estate magnate. This beautiful late Victorian house has 31 rooms with ornately hand-carved wood features, 15 fireplaces, painted ceilings, and luxuriously furnished rooms showcasing original Heurich family collections. This house also incorporated modern technology with features such as indoor plumbing, electricity and fire-proof construction materials.

Walk-in tours of the mansion are available Thursday-Saturday at 11:30 AM and 1 PM with a 2:30 PM tour on Saturday as well. Group tours and reserved tours can be arranged by calling the main number. There is a suggested donation of $5 for entry. There is a relaxing Victorian garden on the grounds, which is open to the public weekdays from spring through the fall from 10 AM-4 PM.

St. Matthews Cathedral
1735 Rhode Island Avenue NW
Washington, D.C. 20036
202-347-3215
www.stmatthewscathedral.com
Metro: Farragut North (Red Line)

This majestic Roman Catholic cathedral was inspired by Italian churches and designed by C. Grant Lafarge in 1893. It has an impressive red brick exterior with an exquisite copper ribbed dome soaring over the area. Its eclectic interior features ornate stained glass windows, religious artwork and beautiful chapels. Pope Pius XII made St. Matthews the cathedral of the archdiocese of Washington, D.C., in 1939.

This cathedral was the site of President Kennedy's funeral in November 1963. A memorial near the altar marks where the president's casket was placed during the service. Outside the cathedral's main entrance is where a famous scene during the funeral procession occurred: young John F. Kennedy Jr. saluted his father's casket as the procession passed by the cathedral.

Downtown (Near the White House)

Renwick Gallery
1661 Pennsylvania Avenue NW
Washington, D.C. 20006
202-633-7970
http://americanart.si.edu/renwick
Open daily 10 AM-5:30 PM
Metro: Farragut West (Blue/Orange Lines)

The Renwick Gallery, a branch of the Smithsonian American Art Museum, is located in a French Second Empire style building designed by architect James Renwick Jr. The building was completed in 1861 and opened as an art gallery in 1873. It eventually became the home of the Smithsonian American Art Museum's contemporary craft program in 1972. The Renwick Gallery houses one of the finest collections of American craft objects and decorative arts from the 19th century to the present. The museum features unique art and craft objects created from materials such as clay, fiber, glass, metal, and wood.

Corcoran Gallery of Art
500 17th Street NW
Washington, D.C. 20006
202-639-1700
www.corcoran.org
Metro: Farragut West (Blue/Orange Lines)

In 1869 William Corcoran opened an impressive private art gallery with his extensive collection "for the purpose of encouraging American genius." The expanding collection outgrew the original building (which now houses the Renwick Gallery) and moved into the present Beaux Arts building in 1897. The collection now includes a multitude of diverse artwork from renowned American artists from the 18th century to the present. It also holds many works by European masters and hosts frequent temporary exhibitions in its ornate setting. Newer additions to the collection include photographs and African American artwork.

On the third Saturday of every month, the gallery hosts themed 90-minute workshops for children ages 5-7 and 8-12. There are also many youth artist programs designed to develop young talent. The gallery is open Wednesday- Sunday from 10 AM-5 PM. Admission is $10 for adults, and $8 for seniors 62+ and students. Children ages 12 and under and active military and their family members do not require admission. There is free general admission on Saturdays in the summer. Regular highlights tours are included with admission. Purchase tickets onsite, online or by calling 800-745-3000. School and group tours with optional workshops for 8-75 people are available Wednesday-Friday with advance reservations.

The Octagon House

1799 New York Avenue NW
Washington, D.C. 20006
202-638-3221
www.nps.gov/nr/travel/wash/dc22.htm
Metro: Farragut West (Blue/Orange Lines)

This architectural masterpiece was designed by Dr. William Thornton, the architect of the U.S. Capitol, and constructed between 1799 and 1801 as a D.C. family residence for Virginia plantation owner, Colonel John Tayloe. Colonel Tayloe offered this house as a temporary "Executive Mansion" to President James Madison and First Lady Dolley Madison after the British burned the White House during the War of 1812 in August 1814. The Madisons enjoyed their stay there until the White House was ready for their return. President Madison used the circular room above the entrance as a study where he signed the Treaty of Ghent to end the War of 1812. The three-story brick house represents a sharp break with Georgian and Federal architecture as its unique structure combines a circle, two rectangles and a triangle to fit into its irregularly shaped lot.

The American Architectural Foundation now owns the Octagon House and offers pre-arranged group tours by appointment. The foundation also offers an architectural museum with exhibits and an architectural bookstore. Call 202-638-3221 or visit www.archfoundation.org/aaf/aaf to arrange a tour.

National Museum of Women in the Arts

1250 New York Avenue NW
Washington, D.C. 20005
202-783-5000
www.nmwa.org
Metro: Metro Center (Blue/Orange Lines and Red Line)

This is the only museum in the world dedicated exclusively to recognizing the contributions of women artists. The museum is located in an impressive 1908 Renaissance Revival building with nearly 79,000 square feet of space. The building was formerly used as a Masonic temple. The permanent collection is comprised of more than 3,000 works that provide a comprehensive survey of art by women from the 16th century to the present, with new artwork added regularly. The work in the collection represents a wide range of styles and media from the Renaissance paintings of Elisabetta Sirani to modern photographs by Barbara Morgan and Louise Nevelson's contemporary sculptures. NMWA also has several important special collections, including silverwork by 18th and 19th-century Irish and English women silversmiths.

The museum is open Monday-Saturday from 10 AM-5 PM and Sunday 12 PM-5 PM. Admission for adults is $10 and $8 for seniors 65+ and students. Ages 18 and under enter free. The museum offers free general admission the first Sunday of the month. Guided tours and educational programs for groups and schools, including some with lunch and tea, are available with reservations at least a month in advance. Contact them online or call 202-783-7996.

Daughters of the American Revolution Museum
Memorial Continental Hall
1776 D Street, NW
Washington, D.C. 20006
202-628-1776
www.dar.org/museum
Metro: Farragut West (Blue/Orange Lines)

The Daughters of the American Revolution (DAR), an organization whose members have ancestors who aided in the fight for independence, operate this museum located in Memorial Continental Hall. They also offer theatrical and musical performances in nearby Constitution Hall. Their extensive collection of period artifacts includes: furniture, art, ceramics, quilts, and jewelry, as well as guns and swords. They also display 31 "Period Rooms" furnished with furniture, decorations and other interior items by historical period from colonial times through the early 20th century. Some of their famous items include presidential china from George Washington, a pair of Dolley Madison's earrings, Thomas Jefferson's socks and slippers, silver items made by Paul Revere and many personal and ceremonial objects related to President Benjamin Harrison and his wife Caroline. An extensive revolutionary period research library is also available for visitors.

The DAR Museum is open free of charge Monday-Friday from 9:30 AM-4 PM and from 9 AM-5 PM on Saturday. Docent led tours are available every 30 minutes from 10 AM-2:30 PM Monday-Friday and from 9 AM-4:30 PM on Saturday. Groups of 10 or more should reserve a tour at least a month in advance with a $3 per person fee. School programs are available Monday-Friday 10 AM-2:30 PM with reservations required two weeks in advance.

The museum also offers a special "Colonial Adventure" where children ages 5-7 learn about the life of an early American child through dressing up in period costumes and participating in an interactive tour. This free program occurs the first and third Saturdays of the month from September-May. Call 202-879-3240 to reserve up to 12 places at least two weeks in advance.

The DAR Museum offers "Fun Family Saturdays" every third Saturday from September-June where the whole family can participate in hands-on activities such as crafts and games and receive a tour of the museum. Call to reserve a spot.

Organization of American States Main Building
19th Street and Constitution Avenue NW
Washington, D.C. 20006
202-458-3000
www.oas.org
Metro: Farragut West (Blue/Orange Lines)

This architectural gem was built in 1910 to house the headquarters of the world's oldest regional organization, the Organization of American States, whose mission is to foster peace, understanding and good relationships in the Americas region. The building has an architectural harmony reflecting the cultural influences found in the organization's 35 members. The three monumental bronze entrance gates represent North, Central, and South America with two friezes depicting North and South America as an Eagle and Condor staring at each other respectfully. The interior features a tropical patio with a sliding glass roof and exotic plants and flowers from around the Americas.

The interior also boasts a massive Hall of Flags and Heroes featuring busts of national heroes from the member states, colorful national flags and Corinthian columns. The building also houses the Columbus Memorial Library containing information, records, and artifacts from the member states and a mural-covered tunnel connecting headquarters with the administration building. Outside the great hall's stained windows, visitors can view the impressive Aztec gardens complete with statues, a fountain and reflecting pool connecting the building to the OAS Art Museum of the Americas.

Tours are available Monday-Friday from 9:30 AM-5 PM. Visitors are required to complete a Tour and Briefing Request Form, available online, and either fax it to 202-458-6319 or email it to their Coordinator of the Public Tour and Briefing Program, Betty Arevalo at barevalo@oas.org. A guided tour for groups up to 20 people costs $100, while a guided tour and briefing for groups up to 20 people costs $200.

Mary Mcleod Bethune Council House

1318 Vermont Avenue NW
Washington, D.C. 20005
202-673-2402
www.nps.gov/nr/travel/wash/dc62.htm
Metro: Mcpherson Square (Blue/Orange Lines)

Mary Mcleod Bethune, a famed educator, political leader and founder of the National Council of Negro Women, lived at this Victorian townhouse from 1943-1955. Bethune's organization's main goal was to promote unity of action among women's groups to achieve a better cultural, economic, political and social life in America and to eliminate all forms of discrimination. Ms. Bethune used this building as the group's headquarters and received many important national and international leaders here. The house now serves as a museum for Ms. Bethune's life and hosts the National Archives for Black Women's History, which contains a huge amount of historic materials pertaining to black women and their respective advocacy organizations. The house is open year round Monday-Saturday from 9 AM-5 PM with the last tour starting at 4 PM. Free admission.

National Geographic Society Museum

1145 17th Street NW
Washington, D.C. 20036
800- 647-5463, 202-857-7588
www.nationalgeographic.com/society/ngo/explorer
Metro: Farragut North (Red Line), Farragut West (Blue/Orange Lines)

The headquarters of this renowned organization and its famous magazine features an interesting museum with changing exhibits that celebrate the geography, history and cultural diversity of our world. The museum offers artifacts, photographs, videos, and interactive displays to entertain visitors and educate them about the world. The museum has a section with exhibits and interactive devices open to the public free of charge as well as temporary exhibits on special topics normally requiring paid tickets.

The National Geographic Society also offers performances, lectures and presentations from fascinating speakers on a wide variety of topics in the Grosvenor Auditorium. Go online to see their latest schedule and reserve tickets to special exhibits. The museum is open 9 AM-5 PM from Monday-Saturday and 10 AM-5 PM on Sundays. Special exhibits usually stay open later.

Foggy Bottom

U.S. Department of State
2201 C Street NW
Washington, D.C. 20520
202-647-4000
www.state.gov
Metro: Foggy Bottom (Blue/Orange Lines)

The U.S. Department of State's mission is to advance freedom for the benefit of the American people, represent U.S. interests around the globe, and help build a more secure, democratic and prosperous world through the development and execution of U.S. foreign policy goals. Guided tours are available of the Diplomatic Reception Rooms of the Department of State. These 45-minute tours take place Monday-Friday at 9:30 AM, 10:30 AM, and 2:45 PM. The Diplomatic Reception Rooms are used for official functions hosted by the Secretary of State and other high level government officials. The rooms are exquisitely decorated with 18th century American furniture, paintings and decorative arts. **This is primarily a fine arts tour and is not recommended for children under 12.** Reserve your tour online or by phone at 202-647-3241 at least 90 days in advance.

U Street Corridor/Shaw

The U Street Corridor in the Shaw neighborhood was known as the "Black Broadway," in its cultural heyday in the first half of the twentieth century. Famed black performers, including locally raised Duke Ellington, were featured at the jazz club called the **Bohemian Caverns**, the **Lincoln Theatre** and other nearby clubs. These two famous venues have been restored to their former glory and host regular musical and theatrical performances.

African American Civil War Memorial and Museum
1925 Vermont Avenue NW
Washington, DC 20001
202-667-2667
www.afroamcivilwar.org
Metro: U Street (Green/Yellow Lines)

This memorial and museum honor the more than 209,000 black Americans who fought for the Union in the U.S. Civil War. More than 36,000 of these soldiers were killed in action. In the museum, the Gladstone Collection contains priceless artifacts and replicas of period uniforms, weapons and clothing, newspaper articles, photographs and records telling the story of African

Americans in the Civil War. There are also interactive kiosks with documents, photographs and music with additional information on this theme. The museum has also started a Descendants Registry to trace the descendants of the soldiers who served in the United States Colored Troops during the Civil War. More than 2,000 descendants have already been found using this system. The museum also features a permanent exhibit exploring African Americans' struggle for freedom from the Civil War to Civil Rights.

The striking African American Civil War Memorial is across the street from the museum at the intersection of U Street and Vermont Avenue, NW, outside the U Street Metrorail station. On the five granite walls, known as the Wall of Honor, there are stainless steel plaques listing the more than 209,000 names of the former slaves and freemen who fought in the war and the more than 7,000 white officers who served with these troops. The 9 ½ foot tall *Spirit of Freedom* statue, sculpted by Ed Hamilton and unveiled in 1998, depicts three soldiers and a sailor preparing for combat. On the back, there is a relief of a family group saying farewell to a son departing for war.

The memorial is open 24 hours a day and the museum is open Monday-Friday from 10 AM-5 PM and Saturday from 10 AM-2 PM. Admission is free but donations are appreciated.

Capitol Hill

Ulysses S. Grant Memorial
Below West Front of U.S. Capitol
Washington, D.C. 20001
Metro: Union Station (Red Line)

This impressive memorial honoring the 18th U.S. president and famed Civil War general is located below the west front of the U.S. Capitol Building at the beginning of the National Mall. The memorial features a central bronze statue of Grant on his horse Cincinnatus and depictions of infantry units on frieze panels on the large marble pedestal. Grant's statue is flanked by realistic bronze statues of fighting Union artillery and cavalry units. Grant's statue is the third largest equestrian statue in the world. Sculptor Henry Merwin Schrady spent 20 years working on this masterpiece and died shortly before its dedication in 1922.

On either side of the Grant Memorial below the west front of the U.S. Capitol Building are the **Peace Monument** and the **Garfield Monument**. These monuments stand in the middle of traffic circles. The white marble Peace Monument was sculpted in 1878 by Franklin Simmons to honor the U.S. Navy sailors who died during the Civil War. The bronze Garfield Monument to honor James Garfield, our 20th president, was sculpted by John Quincy Adams Ward and the monument was dedicated in 1887. President Garfield was the second president to be assassinated, shot only four months into his administration by a mentally unstable man. The assassin had been denied a diplomatic position with the new Garfield administration.

National Japanese American Memorial To Patriotism During World War II
Louisiana Avenue and D Street NW
Washington, D.C. 20001
Metro: Union Station (Red Line)

This memorial, dedicated in 2000, honors the sacrifice and patriotism of Japanese-American soldiers and the more than 100,000 Japanese-American citizens who were forced to spend the war in relocation camps. The memorial features a granite wall with inscriptions of the famous battles fought by legendary Japanese American units, the names of soldiers who died in the war, writings by Japanese American authors, and the names of the ten infamous internment camps. At the center of the memorial is a bronze sculpture of a Japanese crane by Nina Akamu above a wall with barbed wire symbolizing rising above limitations.

Robert A. Taft Memorial

Constitution Avenue, between New Jersey Avenue and First Street NW
Washington, D.C. 20001
Metro: Union Station (Red Line)

Located one block north and west from the capitol is a 100-foot marble bell tower with a 10-foot bronze statue honoring the service of former Senate Majority Leader Robert A. Taft. Senator Taft, son of President William Howard Taft, served as senator from Ohio from 1939 until his death in 1953. Taft was highly regarded for his honesty and principles and was honored by his senate colleagues with this memorial dedicated in 1959.

Sewall-Belmont House and Museum

144 Constitution Avenue NE
Washington, D.C. 20002
202-546-1210
www.sewallbelmont.org
Metro: Union Station (Red Line)

This Georgian mansion is the working headquarters for the National Woman's Party and a museum celebrating the efforts of people fighting for women's voting rights. The museum contains an extensive collection of historic artifacts and archives documenting the efforts to achieve voting rights and equality for women. Highlights of the museum include Susan B. Anthony's desk and a banner used during the first protests calling for women's suffrage. The museum is open Tuesday-Friday 11 AM-3 PM and Saturday from 12 PM-4 PM. Admission is free and tours are self-guided. Guided tours can be scheduled with advance notice.

Folger Shakespeare Library

201 East Capitol Street SE
Washington, D.C. 20003
202-544-4600
www.folger.edu
Metro: Capitol South (Blue/Orange Lines)

Wealthy industrialist and benefactor Henry Folger founded this private research institution which opened to the public in 1932. He donated the world's finest collection of Shakespeare artifacts and printed materials and hired architect Paul Phillipe Cret to design the beautiful neoclassical library building. The exterior of the marble building includes nine bas-reliefs by John Gregory depicting memorable scenes from Shakespeare's plays. A sculpture of Shakespeare's famous character "Puck" by Brenda Putnam is found on the grounds along with a relaxing Elizabethan garden. The interior of the building was constructed in Tudor style and features oak wood paneling.

Although much of the work of the institution is devoted to research on Shakespeare, the Renaissance and the early modern age, the library also seeks to educate and entertain the public. The library contains changing exhibitions with rare manuscripts, books and artwork and a permanent multimedia exhibit in the Shakespeare Gallery. The Folger Theatre regularly presents Shakespeare plays and other productions and the Folger Consort performs period music pieces. The library also features lectures and readings by contemporary poets and authors. The library also supports numerous programs designed to develop the literary and dramatic talents of students. The Folger Shakespeare Library is open to the public Monday-Saturday from 10 AM-5 PM. Admission is free. Call the main number or reserve tickets online for performances and special events.

Eastern Market

225 7th Street SE
Washington, D.C. 20003
202-698-5253
www.easternmarket-dc.org
Metro: Eastern Market (Blue/Orange Lines)

Eastern Market is the city's oldest continually operated fresh food market and a community hub for the lively Capitol Hill neighborhood. The South Hall market building, open daily except Monday, features a range of indoor merchants offering fresh produce, flowers, meat, poultry, bakery, cheese and dairy products. On weekends the outside area becomes a farmer's market combined with a market where vendors sell art, crafts and antiques.

Capitol Hill Lincoln Park

Emancipation Memorial and Mary Mcleod Bethune Memorial located within the park
East Capitol Street and 11th Street NE
Washington, D.C. 20002
Metro: Eastern Market (Blue/Orange Lines)

Emancipation Memorial

This bronze statue by Thomas Ball was dedicated in 1876 to honor Abraham Lincoln's role as the emancipator of the slaves. The monument depicts Lincoln standing over a crouching slave who is shirtless and shackled. Lincoln holds a copy of the Emancipation Proclamation in his right hand. The freed slave was modeled after Archer Alexander, the last person captured under the Fugitive Slave Act. Even though the monument was paid for by African Americans, there was controversy over the depiction of the freed slave portrayed in an inferior position.

Mary Mcleod Bethune Memorial

At the west end of the park is a statue honoring the famous educator and civil rights activist Mary Mcleod Bethune. The statue depicts an elderly Mrs. Bethune with a cane (a gift from President Franklin Roosevelt) handing a copy of her legacy to two black children. The modern statue was sculpted by Robert Berks. The memorial was dedicated in 1974 with funds raised by the organization Mrs. Bethune founded in 1935, the National Council of Negro Women.

Congressional Cemetery
1801 E Street SE
Washington, D.C. 20003
202-543-0539
www.congressionalcemetery.org
Metro: Potomac Avenue (Blue/Orange Lines)

This historic cemetery was the first national cemetery and is the oldest in the District of Columbia, first opening in 1807. The still active cemetery occupies more than 35 acres with more than 55,000 people interred in its grounds. This is the final resting place for many notables including: Apache Chief Taza-the son of Cochise, Civil War photographer Matthew Brady, composer John Philip Sousa, FBI Director J. Edgar Hoover and more than 80 congressmen. The cemetery is also noteworthy for its display of 165 cenotaphs, which primarily honor former members of Congress who served in the 19th century. These memorials look like bulky, cube-shaped stones with a small dome on top. These cenotaphs, which means "empty tomb," are normally memorial structures with no graves beneath and were designed as a new form of funerary art by the Architect of the U.S. Capitol, Benjamin Henry Latrobe.

The cemetery is open every day from dawn to dusk and open to the public for self-guided tours. Pick up a copy of the tour at the gatehouse or download it from their website. Docents lead free tours on Saturdays from April-October at 11 AM starting at the cemetery chapel. There are also free Civil War-related tours from April-October on the third Saturday of the month starting at 1 PM. Go to their website to find out about additional tours and special events offered throughout the year.

National Museum of the U.S. Navy and Navy Yard and the USS *Barry*
6th and M Streets SE gate-pedestrian entrance
With car or bus enter at 11th and O Streets, SE gate
Buses should enter at 6th and M Streets, SE gate on weekends/holidays
Washington, D.C. 20003
Museum: 202-433-4882
USS Barry: 202-433-3377
www.history.navy.mil
Metro: Navy Yard (Green Line), Eastern Market (Blue/Orange Lines)

A large museum located in the Navy Yard chronicles the history of the U.S. Navy from its origin in the Revolutionary War to the present day. The museum contains historic vessels, artifacts, weapons, documents and models as well as interactive exhibits detailing heroes, battles and the U.S. Navy's role in exploration and humanitarian missions. Highlights of the museum include: a simulated submarine command center with touch screens and displays, an interactive exhibit on the Battle of Leyte Gulf in World War II, and uniforms, hats, and weapons from throughout the Navy's history. In Willard Park outside the museum, visitors can view different types of naval ordnance, a World War I railway gun, and a PCF "Swift Boat," used in the Vietnam War.

With advance reservations the museum offers guided tours and special hands-on educational programs for children to learn about naval operations and history.

At the river dock area nearby, visitors can explore the decks of a decommissioned destroyer, the USS *Barry*, and get a feel for life as a sailor during war and peacetime. The USS *Barry* was on active duty in the 1950s and 60s.

Please note that the Navy Yard is an active military base with correspondingly strict security and unannounced closings. **Adults and children over 16 must bring official photo identification to gain entry.** Check their website or call before your visit to ensure the facilities are open to visitors and to comply with any security requirements.

The museum is open Monday-Friday from 9 AM-5 PM and weekends and holidays from 10 AM-5 PM. The USS *Barry* is closed on Sunday.

Southwest Waterfront

Titanic Memorial
Washington Channel Park
4th and P Streets SW
Washington, D.C. 20024
Metro: Waterfront-SEU (Green Line)

The ocean liner RMS *Titanic* sank tragically on its maiden voyage across the Atlantic in 1912 after striking an iceberg. This moving statue commemorates the many men who gave their lives so that more women and children could be saved in the lifeboats of the *Titanic*. The red granite statue was designed by Gertrude Whitney and sculpted by John Horrigan. The 13-foot statue depicts a partially clothed anonymous male figure with arms outstretched in sacrifice.

The statue was commissioned by the Women's Titanic Memorial Association and was dedicated by former First Lady Helen Taft in 1931 in Rock Creek Park. The memorial was removed in 1966 to make way for the Kennedy Center and erected at its present location in 1968.

Anacostia

The Anacostia Community Museum
1901 Fort Place SE
Washington, D.C. 20020
202-633-4820
http://anacostia.si.edu
Open daily 10 AM-5 PM
Metro: Anacostia (Green Line), use Local exit and transfer to Metrobus W2 or W3

This museum provides visitors with material evidence of the African American experience from a community perspective. With its changing temporary exhibitions, the museum strives to challenge perceptions and deepen understanding about the ever-changing concepts and realities of "community," while still maintaining its strong connection to Anacostia and the D.C. area. The permanent collection of the museum features artifacts, photographs, archival documents, media, and art objects that document family and community locally, regionally, nationally, and internationally.

I recommend taking a cab or driving to visit this museum. Please be alert and cautious as some areas of Anacostia are economically depressed and can be dangerous. It is not advisable to visit this area at night or alone. Contact the museum for more specific information.

Brookland

Basilica of the National Shrine of the Immaculate Conception
400 Michigan Avenue NE
Washington, D.C. 20017
202-526-8300
www.nationalshrine.com
Metro: Brookland/CUA (Red Line)

The area around Catholic University is known as "Little Rome" because of the wide variety of Catholic churches, monasteries, orders and related organizations that have their national headquarters there. The most impressive building in the area is the Basilica, which is the National Catholic Shrine. This is the biggest Roman Catholic Church in North America and one of the 10 biggest churches in the world.

The Basilica is dedicated to the Blessed Virgin Mary and is an architectural masterpiece with intricate mosaics, stained glass windows, and an amazing collection of modern ecclesiastic art. The interior features more than 70 chapels and oratories relating to the peoples, cultures and traditions of the Catholic faith. Its hybrid Romanesque-Byzantine architecture complete with a massive dome pays tribute to the Catholic Church's architectural history, while remaining uniquely American. The shrine was finished in 1959 and has been visited by Pope John Paul II and Pope Benedict XVI.

The Basilica is open free of charge year round from 7 AM-6 PM and until 7 PM from April-October. 1 hour guided tours are available with docents Monday-Saturday on the hour from 9 AM-3 PM (except noon) and on Sunday at 1:30 PM, 2:30 PM and 3:30 PM. The Basilica is an active place of worship, so please behave respectfully when visiting.

Franciscan Monastery of the Holy Land in America
1400 Quincy Street NE
Washington, D.C. 20017
202-526-6800
www.myfranciscan.org
Metro: Brookland/CUA (Red Line)

The Franciscan Monastery of Mount Sepulchre has been a place of worship and pilgrimage since it was dedicated in 1899. It was declared a National Historic Site in 1991. Its copies of sacred Holy Land Shrines are interesting to both Roman Catholics and visitors of other faiths. The

Main Church consists of an Upper and Lower Church. The Upper Church is a copy of the Holy Sepulchre in Jerusalem and contains beautiful chapels, stained glass windows, marble altars and narrative wood carvings. The Lower Church contains a copy of the catacombs, the underground tunnels in Rome where early Christians had to worship in secret. Children find the dark, winding catacombs especially fascinating. In the Lower Church there is a reproduction of the Nativity Grotto found in Bethlehem. The grounds contain magnificent upper and lower gardens with a Cloister Walk and reproductions of Holy Land shrines.

Guided tours of the Upper Church and the Lower Church with its catacombs are offered on the hour Monday-Saturday from 11 AM-3 PM (except for 12 PM) and on Sunday from 1 PM-3 PM. Tours of the beautiful, peaceful gardens are self-guided. Advance reservations are required for groups of 5 or more. The Franciscan Friars offer an annual Youth Day for 7th and 8th graders in the fall, which includes a tour and discussions. They also offer Student Lenten Pilgrimages to elementary and high school students. Please contact them to make arrangements for these special events. Admission is free, but donations are appreciated.

Lincoln Cottage and Soldier's Home
Eagle Street Gate
Rock Creek Church Road and Upshur Street NW
Washington, D.C. 20011
202-829-0436
www.lincolncottage.com
Metro: Georgia Ave/Petworth (Green/Yellow Lines)-1 mile from site. Take H8 Metrobus to Eagle Street Gate entrance at Rock Creek Church Road and Upshur Street, NW

From June to November in 1862-1864, President Abraham Lincoln and his family sought relief from the heat and stress of downtown Washington at this stately but comfortable residence about three miles north of the White House. The cottage is located on the grounds of the Armed Forces Retirement Home or Soldiers Home, which has provided lodging for retired and disabled veterans since 1851 to the present. The renovated cottage and new visitor center were opened to the public in 2008 and have become must see attractions for visitors interested in Lincoln and Civil War history.

Lincoln spent about a quarter of his presidency at this beautiful cottage where he relaxed and enjoyed the cool breezes, received visitors and officials, and formulated the ideas and strategies that would define his presidency.

Visitors can tour the cottage on one hour docent-led tours, which also feature images and "historical voices" presentations using multimedia technology. At the Robert H. Smith Visitor Education Center, visitors can learn interesting information about Lincoln's presidency and his time at the cottage by exploring galleries of historical artifacts and interactive exhibits. Tickets are required for entry and cost $12 for adults, $10 for active military and $5 for children ages 6-12. Purchase tickets in advance online or call ETIX at 1-800-514-ETIX. Onsite tickets are subject to availability.

Georgetown

C & O Canal Mule-Drawn Barge Rides

Georgetown Visitor Center
1057 Thomas Jefferson Street NW
Washington, D.C. 20007
202-653-5190
Great Falls Tavern Visitor Center
11710 MacArthur Boulevard
Potomac, MD 20854
301-767-3714
www.nps.gov/choh/planyourvisit/publicboatrides.htm
Metro: Foggy Bottom (Blue/Orange lines) with Georgetown shuttle bus for Georgetown location

Journey back to the 1870s with a ride down the Chesapeake and Ohio Canal on a barge pulled by mules. The boats depart for one hour tours from two locations: Georgetown in Washington, D.C., and from Potomac, MD. The barges make a scenic journey down this formerly busy working canal. Guides in period dress provide expert and interesting commentary and provide musical entertainment during the pleasant ride. The Georgetown location is open from April 1-August 15, and the Potomac location from May 15-October 31. The boats leave from Wednesday-Sunday at 11 AM, 1:30 PM and 3 PM. Tickets cost $8 for adults, $6 for seniors 62+, and $5 for children ages 4-14.

Dumbarton Oaks

1703 32nd Street NW
Washington, D.C. 20007
202-339-6401
www.doaks.org
Metro: Foggy Bottom (Blue/Orange lines), then take Georgetown shuttle bus

Dumbarton Oaks is a former 53-acre hilltop estate with a Federal mansion and landscaped woods and gardens purchased by the Bliss family in 1921. They donated portions of the grounds to Harvard University for research use and to the U.S. Government for use as a public park in the 1940s. Visitors can now tour the mansion, which houses a museum containing Byzantine and Pre-Columbian art as well as European masterpieces.

Visitors also can walk through the beautiful landscaped gardens and woods. By appointment visitors can make use of the Dumbarton Oaks Research Library, which collects materials to support scholarship in Byzantine studies, Pre-Columbian studies, and garden and landscape studies. The museum is open daily 2 PM-5 PM except Monday with free admission. The gardens are open daily 2 PM-6 PM except Monday from March 15-October 31, and 2 PM-5 PM the rest of the year. Admission to the gardens is $8 for adults and $5 for seniors, students and children ages 2-12. Admission to the gardens is free from November 1-March 14.

Tudor Place Historic House and Garden

1644 31st Street NW
Washington, D.C. 20007
202-965-0400
www.tudorplace.org
Metro: Foggy Bottom (Blue/Orange lines), then take Georgetown shuttle bus

Martha Washington's granddaughter, Martha Custis and husband Thomas Peter used an $8,000 legacy from George Washington to purchase this land in 1805. They hired the famous architect of the U.S. Capitol and the Octagon, Dr. William Thornton, to design this grand neoclassical mansion with its circular domed portico and beautifully landscaped gardens. Generations of the Peter family lived there until 1983, entertaining important guests such as the Marquis De Lafayette, Daniel Webster, Henry Clay and John Calhoun.

The public can now visit the immaculately preserved house, which has an impressive collection of European and American decorative arts and more than 100 objects formerly belonging to George and Martha Washington. Visitors can also tour the 5 ½-acre garden, which maintains its unique Federal period design and features a Bowling Green and Japanese Tea House. Docents lead tours of the house on the hour from 10 AM-3 PM Tuesday-Saturday, and 12 PM-3 PM on Sunday. Admission is $8 for adults, $6 for seniors and military, and $3 for students ages 7-18. Children 6 and under are free. The garden is open Monday-Saturday from 10 AM-4 PM and Sunday from 12 PM-4 PM. A self-guided garden tour costs $3 per person.

Dumbarton House

2715 Q Street NW
Washington, D.C. 20007
202-337-2288
www.dumbartonhouse.org
Metro: Foggy Bottom (Blue/Orange lines), then take Georgetown shuttle bus

Construction began on the Dumbarton House in 1791 and it serves as an excellent example of Federal period architecture. The house is displayed during its time as a residence of the Nourse family from 1803-1814 offering visitors a look at period architecture, furniture and decorative arts. Owner Charles Carroll hosted First Lady Dolley Madison at the house during her flight from the British, who burned the White House on August 24, 1814.

In 1915, the house was moved 100 feet from its original location to accommodate the construction of the Dumbarton Bridge (Buffalo Bridge) and extension of Q Street into Georgetown. The National Society of The Colonial Dames of America restored this house in 1932 and now uses the building as their headquarters. Tours are offered year round from Tuesday-Sunday from 11 AM-3 PM with the last museum entry at 2:45 PM. Admission is $5 for adults and free for children and students with ID.

John F. Kennedy Residences

1528 31st Street NW
1400 34th Street NW
3321 Dent Place NW
2808 P Street NW
3307 N Street NW

John F. Kennedy lived at various addresses in the Georgetown area from his time as a Congressman, Senator and as President-Elect. Some of his notable addresses are listed above. Congressman John F. Kennedy lived with his sister Eunice at the first address from 1947-50 and at the 34th Street address after that. Senator John F. Kennedy and new wife Jackie lived at Dent Place in 1953-54 and then at the P Street house for less than a year in 1957. They lived at the N Street residence from 1958-60; this was their residence when John F. Kennedy was elected president.

Please be respectful when viewing these houses as they are private property.

Upper Northwest

Hillwood Estate Museum and Gardens
4155 Linnean Avenue NW
Washington, D.C. 20008
202-686-5807
www.hillwoodmuseum.org
Metro: Van Ness-UDC (Red Line)

Post Cereal heiress Marjorie Merriweather Post willed her beautiful 25-acre estate to the public upon her death in 1973. Visitors can tour her art-filled mansion, which features a world famous collection of Russian imperial art and eighteenth-century French decorative art and furnishings. Some of the collection highlights include Fabergé eggs, Russian porcelain, Russian Orthodox icons, Beauvais tapestries, and Sèvres porcelain.

Visitors can also explore the wooded grounds of the estate and enjoy 13 acres of formal gardens. The museum is open year round except the month of January. Opening hours are Tuesday-Saturday from 10 AM-5 PM and select Sundays from 1 PM-5 PM. Suggested donation for admission is $15 for adults, $12 for seniors, $10 for college students and $5 for children ages 6-18.

Kreeger Museum
2401 Foxhall Road NW
Washington, D.C. 20007
202-337-3050, Reservations-202-338-3552
www.kreegermuseum.org

This private art museum is located at the former Kreeger residence, a building designed by renowned architect Philip Johnson. The building grounds feature more than five acres of gardens with sculptures and peaceful wooded areas. The museum focuses on 19th and 20th century paintings by masters such as Monet, Picasso and Chagall and also features traditional African and Asian art. The museum is open year round, except for the month of August, on Saturday 10 AM-4 PM with optional guided tours at 10:30 AM, 12 PM, and 2 PM. Reservations are required for visiting Tuesday-Friday for 10:30 AM or 1:30 PM tours. Admission is $10 for adults and $7 for students and seniors 65+.

The Kreeger Museum offers special story time programs for children ages 3-5 on select Saturdays and Thursdays and art workshops for children ages 8-12 on select Saturdays.

Additional Attractions in Maryland

Glen Echo Park
7300 MacArthur Boulevard
Glen Echo, MD 20812
301-634-2222
www.nps.gov/glec

This historic park just outside Washington, D.C., was the premier amusement park in the area from 1900 to 1968. The park now offers year-round activities in dance, theater, and the arts for adults and children. The 1921 Dentzel carousel is a favorite of children operating May through September. The Spanish Ballroom and Bumper Car Pavilion offer dance events and classes in all types of dance throughout the year. The park offers an annual Family Day in the spring with special entertainment events, hands-on art activities and refreshments. On the grounds of the park there are a variety of activities listed below:

The Adventure Theatre provides entertaining children's theater throughout the year. 301-634-2270, www.adventuretheatre.org.

The Puppet Company offers regular puppet shows designed to entertain families. They also put on the entertaining **Nutcracker Puppet Show** during the Christmas season. 301-320-6668, www.thepuppetco.org.

There is also a small children's museum located in the former Stables building called **Living Classrooms of the National Capital Region**. At this innovative museum kids can explore nature, history, and the arts through interactive exhibits. 202-488-0627 ext. 243, www.living-classroomsdc.org.

Clara Barton National Historic Site
5801 Oxford Road
Glen Echo, MD 20812
301-320-1410
www.nps.gov/clba

Adjacent to Glen Echo Park is the Clara Barton National Historic Site, run by the National Park Service. Clara Barton was a tireless nurse, morale booster and logistical supporter of soldiers and others in need. During the Civil War, she was known affectionately as the "Angel of the Battlefield." After the war she was a fierce advocate for victims from natural disasters and war and eventually formed the American Red Cross in 1881. Clara Barton lived in this house for the last 15 years of her life and used it as a residence as well as a headquarters and warehouse for the American Red Cross.

The house is open all year with no admission required, but it is accessible by guided tour only. Tours are offered daily and begin on the hour from 10 AM-4 PM. The site offers an interesting and educational Junior Ranger program for kids called "Traveling Clara Barton."

National Museum of Health and Medicine
2500 Linden Lane
Silver Spring, MD 20910
301-319-3300
http://nmhm.washingtondc.museum
Metro: Silver Spring (Red Line), then take Bus #4 from Metro station which runs only on weekdays at 9:36 AM and then in afternoon starting at 1:36 PM. There is no bus service on weekends.

This museum of medical history and oddities is not for the squeamish. The museum features a huge collection of artifacts and specimens with a focus on medical pathologies and the effects of weapons on the human body. The exhibit "To Bind up the Nation's Wounds" displays specimens related to Civil War medicine and human anatomy. The featured specimen is the preserved amputated leg of Union General Daniel Sickles. The general had the unusual habit of visiting his leg on the anniversary of its amputation. The exhibit "Visibly Human: Health and Disease in the Human Body" includes diseased organs and a leg horribly swollen from the parasitic infection called Elephantiasis.

Other specimens and artifacts include: pieces of President Abraham Lincoln's skull and the bullet that killed him in 1865, a giant hairball ingested by a compulsive hair eating 12-year-old girl, abnormal organs, giant tumors, a complete brain and spine, mummies and skeletons. There are also sections devoted to modern medicine and equipment.

The museum also houses a huge collection documenting changes in medical technology and an anatomical collection made up of bones and body parts not open to the public.

The museum is open daily from 10 AM-5:30 PM. There is no admission fee, but donations are appreciated.

Beall-Dawson Historic House Museum
111 West Montgomery Avenue
Rockville, MD 29850
301-340-2825
www.montgomeryhistory.org/beall-dawson-historic-park
Metro: Rockville (Red Line)

The Beall-Dawson House was built around 1815 for Upton Beall and his family. Beall was the Clerk of the Court of the county and wanted an impressive residence in line with his important position. This Federal style house remained in private hands until the 1960s when it was purchased by the city and became the Montgomery County Historical Society's headquarters.

The house is interpreted in the early 19th century period as the home of the upper class Beall family and their African American slaves. The house retains most of its original architectural features including the indoor slave quarters. Two rooms on the second floor are used by the historical society to exhibit their collections.

They offer self-guided tours Wednesday-Sunday from 12 PM-4 PM and guided tours with docents Friday-Sunday at quarter past the hour from 12:15 PM-3:15 PM.

Stonestreet Museum of 19th Century Medicine

Located on the grounds of the Beall-Dawson House, this museum displays the one-room doctor's office of Dr. Edward Stonestreet built in 1852. Dr. Stonestreet served as one of Rockville's doctors until his death in 1903. He incorporated many new developments in medical technology and knowledge into his practice. This museum displays medical and pharmaceutical tools and technology, furniture, books and journals from the 19th to the early 20th century. A first person interpreter portrays Dr. Stonestreet on the second Sunday of each month.

Regular tours of the Beall-Dawson House include this museum. Tickets for the tour to both facilities cost $5 for adults and $3 for seniors and children ages 6 and up.

Josiah Henson Historic Site
11420 Old Georgetown Road
North Bethesda, MD 20852
301-650-4373
www.montgomeryparks.org/PPSD/Cultural_Resources_Stewardship/heritage/josiahhensonsp.
shtm

Josiah Henson was an escaped slave whose autobiographical stories describing life as a slave inspired Harriet Beecher Stowe's famous abolitionist novel *Uncle Tom's Cabin*. Henson lived as a slave on the Isaac Riley property from 1795-1830. The structure still standing at the site is the former home of Isaac and Matilda Riley. Henson escaped to Canada in 1830 and established a fugitive slave community called "Dawn." He became an influential minister, writer, and speaker for the anti-slavery movement and returned to the United States often as a conductor on the famous escape route north called the Underground Railroad.

The site is being renovated into a historic park and house museum, which will feature an interpretive program to honor Henson.

College Park Aviation Museum
1985 Corporal Frank Scott Drive
College Park, MD 20740
301-864-6029
www.collegeparkaviationmuseum.com
Metro: College Park-U of MD (Green Line)

This modern museum is located on the grounds of the world's longest continuously operating airport. The airport was founded in 1909 when Wilbur Wright came to the area to give flight instruction to the first military aviators. The 27,000 square foot facility displays historic aircraft and unique artifacts and offers hands-on activities and interpretive programs designed for children of all ages. There are also opportunities to ride in simulators and to dress up as pilots.

The museum offers special school programs for grades K-6 with advance reservations and an afternoon hands-on program for kids ages 5 and up on Fridays at 2 PM. There is also a demonstration of the construction of a 1909 Wright aircraft rib on the fourth Tuesday of every month at 3 PM. The museum is open daily from 10 AM-5 PM with admission costing $4 for adults, $3 for seniors, and $2 for children.

Visitor Center at NASA's Goddard Space Flight Center
880 Greenbelt Road
Greenbelt, MD 20771
301-286-0691
www.nasa.gov/centers/goddard/visitor/home

NASA's Goddard Space Flight Center is the nation's largest organization of scientists and engineers who develop technology to study the universe. The Visitor Center offers guests a window into this exciting scientific world with interactive exhibits and presentations on astrophysics, planetary science, climatology and heliophysics. A new exhibit called "Science on a Sphere" uses computers and video projection to display animated data on a large suspended sphere. Children especially enjoy putting on kid-sized spacesuits and climbing into a model of a Gemini space capsule. There is also an exhibit focused on the amazing discoveries of the Hubble Space Telescope.

Outside there is a space garden featuring actual rockets and space vehicles and the Goddard Moon Tree, whose seeds were flown to the moon and back. On the first Sunday of the month at 1 PM, there are demonstrations of rocket model launches. Visitors can purchase and assemble model rockets from the gift shop. There is also a monthly Family Science Night designed for middle school age children and parents to work together on hands-on scientific activities.

The Visitor Center is open September-June on Tuesday-Friday from 10 AM-3 PM and weekends from 12 PM-4 PM. In July and August the center remains open on weekdays (except Monday) until 5 PM. Admission is free. Special school tours and tours of the research facilities are available with advance reservations.

National Cryptologic Museum
Street Highway 32 and Street Highway 295
Annapolis Junction, MD 20701
301-688-5849
www.nsa.gov/about/cryptologic_heritage/museum

Run by the top secret intelligence organization, the National Security Agency (NSA), this is the first and only public museum featuring artifacts from the intelligence community. The museum features exhibits about the history of cryptology, which is the science that deals with secret communications using codes and ciphers. The museum focuses on the history of cryptology in the United States and contains information on some of the legendary figures in this science and examples of the machines and techniques they developed. There are also interactive devices for visitors to use to learn more about cryptology and to try their hand at cracking secret codes.

The museum library also holds an amazing assortment of declassified documents, monographs, oral histories and historic books that provide more insight into the history of cryptology. Outside the museum is the National Vigilance Park, which honors the contribution of aerial reconnaissance by displaying two aircraft used in secret missions: the RU-8D used by the U.S. Army in Vietnam and the C-130 used by the U.S. Air Force during the Cold War era.

The museum is free to the public and open Monday-Friday from 9 AM-4 PM, and the 1st and 3rd Saturdays of the month from 10 AM-2 PM. The museum library hours vary so please call 301-688-2145 to inquire about availability.

Oxon Cove Park/Oxon Hill Farm

6411 Oxon Hill Road
Oxon Hill, MD 20745
301-839-1176
www.nps.gov/oxhi

This huge 512-acre park offers hiking and biking trails and features a working 19th century farm for families to explore. The Debutts family owned this land in the 19th century and established the Mount Welby Plantation. There are self-guided tours and guided tours of the farm buildings with visits to the resident cows, chickens, sheep and horses. There are also wagon rides, educational programs with living history interpreters and seasonal hands-on activities such as sheep shearing and apple pressing to make cider.

Groups of five or more should call at least two weeks in advance to make reservations for these special programs. The park and farm are open daily from 8 AM-4:30 PM. Admission is free.

Thomas Stone National Historic Site

6655 Rose Hill Road (Near Junction of MD 225 and 6)
Port Tobacco, MD 20677
301-392-1776
www.nps.gov/thst

This 322-acre national historic site features the restored mansion and farmland of Maryland's youngest signer of the Declaration of Independence, Thomas Stone. Stone was a prominent lawyer and politician in Maryland. The site features 1840s outbuildings, hiking trails and the burial sites of Thomas Stone, family members, and their slaves and servants. Park rangers give regular 30-minute tours of the Stones' restored mansion, "Haberdeventure," featuring fine examples of interior colonial architecture and furnishings. There is also a visitor center with an orientation film and exhibits about colonial Maryland and Stone's life. The site is open from Memorial Day to Labor Day daily 9 AM-5 PM and the rest of the year from Wednesday-Sunday from 9 AM-5 PM with the last tour at 4:30 PM. Admission is free.

Belair Mansion and Belair Stable Museum

12207 Tulip Grove Drive
Bowie, MD 20715
301-860-0269
www.cityofbowie.org/leisureactivities/museum/belair_mansion.asp

This magnificent five-part Georgian plantation home was built around 1745 for the Provincial Governor of Maryland, Samuel Ogle. The mansion was enlarged in 1914 and in the first half of the century served as the home of famous horseman William Woodward. The house features furniture, silver pieces, paintings and other artwork from the Ogle and Woodward families. The grounds feature beautiful gardens and Tulip Poplar trees. The mansion is open from Tuesday-Sunday from 12 PM-4 PM. Schedule a group tour for 10 or more people by calling 301-809-3089. A donation is requested for admission.

The **Belair Stable Museum** is located on the original plantation grounds about 1000 feet from the Belair Mansion at 2835 Belair Drive. This stable was part of the famous "Belair Stud," owned and operated by William Woodward. It was one of the premier racing stables from the 1930s to the 1950s. The stable was the oldest continually operated horse farm in the country when it closed in 1957. Such famous horses as Gallant Fox, Omaha and Nashua were bred and trained here. The Belair Stable has been restored and is now open to the public as a museum. It is open free of charge from Tuesday-Sunday from 12 PM-4 PM. For more information call 301-809-3089 or visit www.cityofbowie.org/LeisureActivities/Museum/belair_stable.asp.

John Wilkes Booth Escape Route Sites
Sites in Maryland and Virginia

After John Wilkes Booth shot Abraham Lincoln at Ford's Theatre on the night of April 14, 1865, he escaped justice for 12 days. Booth and an accomplice, David Herold, hid at various sites in Southern Maryland and then crossed the Potomac River seeking safety in Virginia. Ultimately, they were tracked down by a unit from the 16th New York Cavalry at a tobacco barn on the Garrett Farm, where Herold surrendered. Booth refused to give up and the Union forces set the barn on fire to force his surrender. After observing Booth aiming his carbine, a Union soldier shot Booth through the neck severing his spinal cord. Booth died shortly afterwards looking at his paralyzed hands and exclaiming "Useless! Useless."

I have included two intact sites below that are open to the public. Some of the sites on the escape route are on private property or marked only by signs. The Surratt House Museum offers 12-hour guided tours called "The Original John Wilkes Booth Escape Route Tour" in the spring and fall. Go to www.surratt.org/su_bert.html for more information and to make advance reservations. Another escape route tour is available from the Civil War & Military Tours of Washington, D.C. Company. Go to www.cwmhtwdc.com for more information.

Go to www.civilwartraveler.com/about/maps/JWBMap.pdf for a map of the escape route locations. Using this information, visitors can take their own self-guided driving tour.

There is also a National Park Service brochure that visitors can use for more information on the events surrounding the assassination of Lincoln, including Booth's escape route available at: www.nps.gov/history/history/online_books/hh/3a/hh3j.htm.

Surratt House Museum
9118 Brandywine Road
Clinton, MD 20735
301-868-1121
www.surratt.org

Since the release of Robert Redford's film, "The Conspirator," interest in the Lincoln Conspiracy and of Mary Surratt's role in it has increased. After being convicted for participating in the conspiracy, Surratt became the first woman executed in the United States.

This middle-class plantation house was built in 1852 and was Mary Surratt's country home. During the decade leading up to the Civil War it served as a tavern, hotel, post office and polling place. During the war, it was a safe house for the Confederate underground. John Wilkes Booth and an accomplice rode to this home around midnight on the night of the assassination to pick up two Spencer carbines, ammunition and other supplies that had been hidden there earlier. The men did not retrieve one of the hidden carbines, which is still on display at the Surratt House.

In addition to the ten-room house, the museum also has an adjacent visitor center with permanent exhibits on the Surratt family and Booth's escape route. The museum is open from mid-January through mid-December from 11 AM-3 PM on Thursdays and Fridays and from 12 PM-4 PM on weekends with the last tour beginning 30 minutes before closing. In July and August the museum is also open on Wednesdays from 11 AM-3 PM. Tickets cost $3 for adults, $2 for seniors and for groups with 10 or more adults, and $1 for children ages 5 and up. Group tours can also be arranged with advance reservations by calling the museum.

Dr. Samuel A. Mudd House Museum

3725 Dr. Samuel Mudd Road
Waldorf, MD 20601
301-645-6870, 301-274-9358
www.somd.lib.md.us/MUSEUMS/Mudd/location.html

John Wilkes Booth and his accomplice, David Herold, came to this house in the early morning after the assassination of President Lincoln. The pair sought medical attention for Booth's broken leg as well as food and shelter. Dr. Mudd tended Booth's injury and had a crude pair of crutches made for him by a local carpenter. The pair went on their way the next day after Mudd failed in his effort to secure a carriage for them.

Controversy still surrounds how much Dr. Mudd was involved in the Lincoln Conspiracy and how well he knew Booth. Mudd was convicted for involvement in the conspiracy and sentenced to life imprisonment at the federal prison in the Dry Tortugas in Florida. Dr. Mudd became the prison doctor there in 1867 during a yellow fever epidemic and was credited with saving the lives of many fellow inmates and guards. For his heroic efforts, President Andrew Johnson pardoned him in 1869. After receiving his pardon, Dr. Mudd returned to this residence and lived there until his death in 1883.

The well-preserved house has remained in the Mudd family and contains period pieces and the original red settee that Booth rested on while Dr. Mudd examined him. Visitors can also see the bedroom and original bed where Booth and Herold slept. Interestingly, some descendants of Dr. Mudd work at the museum. On the grounds, there are also original outbuildings and a Farm Museum with historical farm tools. The Dr. Samuel A. Mudd House museum is open late March to late November on Wednesdays and Saturdays from 11 AM-4 PM and Sundays from 12 PM-4 PM. Admission is $6 for adults and $2 for children ages 6-16. On the first weekend in December they also are open for a Victorian Christmas celebration from 11 AM-8 PM.

Rose Hill Manor Park and Children's Museum

1611 North Market Street
Frederick, MD 21701
301-600-1650
www.rosehillmuseum.com

Built in 1792, this grand Greek Revival manor served as the retirement home of Maryland's first Governor, Thomas Johnson. It now serves as a hands-on history museum for children of all ages to learn about colonial life and the history of agriculture and transportation in Maryland. The grounds feature the manor house, a blacksmith shop, icehouse, log cabin and other outbuildings as well as a Carriage Museum and Farm Museum. The Children's Museum provides children with the opportunity to learn about colonial life by carding wool, grating spices and playing with period toys. The museum also holds special seasonal events including "Rose Hill Day" at the end of August. This event features crafts, old-fashioned games, antique cars and trucks, ice cream and refreshments. They also have special school programs and "Tots Time" programs offered for toddlers.

The park is open April-October from 8 AM-8 PM, but the manor hours are from Monday-Saturday from 10 AM-4 PM and Sundays 1 PM-4 PM. In November the manor is open Saturdays from 10 AM-4 PM and Sundays from 1 PM-4 PM. The last tour begins at 3 PM. Groups of 10 or more visiting in April-November should make an advance reservation either online or by calling. From December-March only groups of 10 or more can visit with an advance reservation. Tickets cost $5 for adults and $4 for seniors 55+ and for children ages 3-17.

Additional Attractions in Virginia

Woodlawn Plantation
9000 Richmond Highway (Rte. 1)
Alexandria, VA 22309
703-780-4000
http://woodlawn1805.org

Woodlawn is a 126-acre estate with a Federal-style mansion designed by Dr. William Thornton, who was the Architect of the U.S. Capitol. The mansion was built between 1800 and 1805. The land was given as a wedding gift by George Washington to his nephew Major Lawrence Lewis and his bride, Eleanor "Nelly" Custis Lewis. The original plantation was more than 2,000 acres and was worked by more than 90 slaves and other laborers. In 1846 the Lewis's son sold the property to two Quaker families who established a "free labor colony" with lots available for free black and white farmers. In the 20th century, private owners restored the site until it was purchased in 1952 by the National Trust for Historic Preservation, which maintains it today.

The manor is now presented as an early 19th century plantation residence with original and period furnishings and artwork. Woodlawn is open Thursday-Monday from 10 AM-5 PM with the last guided tour of the mansion beginning at 4 PM.

Frank Lloyd Wright's Pope-Leighey House

Located on the grounds of Woodlawn Plantation, the Pope-Leighey House is a fine example of Frank Lloyd Wright's Usonian House. The famed architect developed this type of house for modern life, blended into its surrounding environment at a relatively affordable price. Innovations included a flat roof, windows being a main part of walls, and heated concrete floors. Wright used four natural materials (wood, brick, glass and concrete) to skillfully create a sense of greater space in a house consisting of only 1,200 square feet. The house was originally located in nearby Falls Church and was donated and moved by its owner to its present site in 1964 to escape demolition. Tours are available every half hour from 10 AM-5 PM with the last guided tour beginning at 4 PM.

Tickets for Woodlawn Plantation or the Pope-Leighey House cost $8.50 for adults and $4 for ages 18 and under. Combination tickets for both sites cost $15 and $5, respectively. There are discounts for groups of 15 or more. All military personnel and their immediate family receive free admission from Memorial Day to Labor Day.

The Tucker Collection
Alleyway near 100 North Payne Street
Alexandria, VA 22314
703-836-4520
Metro: King Street (Blue/Yellow Lines). Take free King Street Trolley to North Payne Street.

This unique private museum featuring three original 1948 Tucker automobiles is located in an unmarked warehouse building in Old Town. Visitors need to venture into the first alley on the right off the 100 block of North Payne Street and walk to the white warehouse building at the end.

Preston Tucker was a legendary innovator in automotive design and well ahead of his time. His designs enhanced safety and overall performance and contrasted greatly with the staid designs of the major car companies, which had been stalled during World War II. Tucker faced fierce opposition from established car companies and, ultimately, his dreams of mass producing his new line of automobiles never materialized. Tucker only made 51 cars in 1948 and only 47 remain intact.

The Tucker Collection founder David Cammack is the only person in the world who owns three Tucker automobiles, including the first prototype vehicle off the assembly line. Cammack also has an amazing collection of Tucker parts, engines, blueprints, photos, and historic newspaper and magazine articles. To get a video preview of the museum go to: www.youtube.com/watch?v=HeCgFeadUY4.

Admission to the Tucker Collection is free, but visitors must arrange an appointment by calling in advance.

The Torpedo Factory Art Center
105 North Union Street
Alexandria, VA 22314
703-838-4565
www.torpedofactory.org

Metro: King Street (Blue/Yellow Lines). Take free King Street Trolley to end station at waterfront and walk 1/2 block to the left to Union Street entrance.

This three-floor building was once a torpedo factory making these deadly weapons for use in World War II. This art center features 82 artist studios, 6 galleries, the Art League School and the

Alexandria Archaeology Museum. The center hosts many workshops and presentations for artists of all ages and skill levels. The information booth on the first floor can give you an updated list of current activities at the Torpedo Factory and around Alexandria.

On the second Saturday of October **the Arts Safari** takes place at the Torpedo Factory in the Alexandria Archaeology Museum. This festival features a host of hands-on arts and crafts and archaeology activities for children.

Fort Ward Museum and Historic Site
4301 West Braddock Road
Alexandria, VA 22302
703-838-4848
http://alexandriava.gov/FortWard
Metro: King Street (Blue/Yellow Lines). Take DASH AT5 Bus toward Landmark, which stops in front of Fort Ward.

Fort Ward is the area's best preserved U.S. Civil War fort with 90% of its earthwork walls still standing. It was part of an extensive system of Union forts and batteries, known as the Defenses of Washington, which were built around Washington, D.C., to protect it from Confederate attack.

Visitors can get a feel for what a Union soldier's everyday life was like by touring the fort and museum. The site and museum feature original fortifications, cannons, weapons and artifacts as well as exhibits and interactive devices that provide information on life within a Civil War fort. Adjacent Fort Ward Park provides a relaxing wooded area for picnics and recreational activities. The museum is open Tuesday-Saturday from 9 AM-5 PM and Sunday from 12 PM-5 PM. The park is open daily from 9 AM to sunset. Admission is free, but donations are welcome.

Gunston Hall
10709 Gunston Road
Lorton, VA 22079
703-550-9220
www.gunstonhall.org

Gunston Hall was the home of one of America's founding fathers, George Mason, author of the Virginia Declaration of Rights. This famous document called for freedom of the press and religious liberties and profoundly influenced the writings of Thomas Jefferson. Mason never sought public office and refused to sign the U.S. Constitution because it didn't abolish slavery and because he felt it lacked enough protection for civil liberties. Because of this, he is not as well-known as some of his peers, but his intellectual influence was vital to the founding of our nation.

Gunston Hall, an excellent example of Georgian architecture, once sat at the center of a 5,500-acre corn and tobacco plantation. The mansion was constructed between 1755 and 1759 and features detailed interior carvings done by an indentured servant, William Buckland. Another English craftsman, William Bernard Sears, worked with Buckland to design impressive rooms of different architectural styles and produced unique furniture for the "Chinese" room. Mason's regular garden features the original gravel pathways, a 250-year-old boxwood allee tree, and wonderful views of Deer Park as it leads to the Potomac River.

The visitor center has an interesting introductory film called *George Mason and the Bill of Rights*, and artifacts and exhibits that demonstrate the important influence Mason had in founding the nation. Other exhibits focus on the tasks of everyday life on a colonial plantation. There are also outbuildings, gardens, and wooded grounds to explore. Visitors can also view the Mason family graveyard, which lies near the mansion.

Guided house tours are available year round every half hour from 9:30 AM-4:30 PM. These tours focus on the architectural features of the house and the daily life of the Mason family and their slaves and servants. The grounds close at 6 PM. Admission is $9 for adults, $8 for visitors 60+, $5 for ages 18 and under, and free to children ages 6 and under. A wide range of school and group tours are available at discounted rates. Please call or email in advance to plan and reserve school and group tours.

Claude Moore Colonial Farm

6310 Georgetown Pike
McLean, VA 22101
703-442-7557
www.1771.org

This site offers visitors a chance to experience life on a 1771 working class colonial farm. Reenactors in period costumes work the farm as a colonial family with reproductions of period tools and structures. Visitors can ask the family questions and help them with their chores. The farm also has a variety of livestock.

Groups can spend a weekend in the summer experiencing 18th century farm life. Register for this weekend program in advance online. Call or go online for more information. The site also hosts a Market Fair with food, crafts, gifts and entertainment on one weekend in May, July, and October. The farm is open Wednesday-Sunday from April-mid December from 10 AM-4:30 PM. Tickets cost $3 for adults and $2 for children 3-12 and seniors 60+.

Sully Historic Site

3650 Historic Sully Way
Chantilly, VA 20151
703-437-1794
www.fairfaxcounty.gov/parks/sully

The main house at Sully Historic Site was built in 1799 for Richard Bland Lee, who was Northern Virginia's first U.S. Representative to Congress and Robert E. Lee's uncle. The house ingeniously combines aspects of Georgian and Federal architecture. The grounds also include original out-buildings, including slave quarters, and relaxing woods and gardens.

Guided tours of the house are offered on the hour from 11 AM-4 PM with the last tour begin-ning at 4 PM. The last tour in January and February begins at 3 PM. An outside walking tour of the slave quarters and original outbuildings is offered daily at 2 PM and from mid-November to February by reservation only. The cost for a combined house and outside walking tour is $9 for adults, $8 for students ages 16 and up, and $7 for seniors 65+ and youths ages 5-15. The tickets for one tour cost $7, $6, and $5 respectively. The museum offers special school programs to learn about and participate in the daily activities on a large gentry farm in the early Federal period. Call to reserve spots in this program.

Colvin Run Mill Historic Site

10017 Colvin Run Road
Great Falls, VA 22066
703-759-2771
www.fairfaxcounty.gov/parks/crm

This site features a working mill built around 1811. There is also a historic general store selling fresh ground cornmeal, wheat flour and grits and historic candy and souvenirs. The grounds offer scenic trails and locations for hiking and picnicking. From February to December there are also special programs onsite including craft demonstrations, live music, and ice-cream making. Go online or call for an updated schedule.

The site is open daily except Tuesdays from 11 AM-4 PM. Guided tours are offered on the hour with the last tour at 3 PM. Mill grinding demonstrations featuring massive millstones and wooden gears are offered the first and third Sundays of the month from April-October from 12 PM-3 PM. Tickets for tours cost $7 for adults, $6 for students 16 and up, and $5 for seniors 65+ and kids ages 5-15. Call or go online to schedule school group tours and programs. Downloadable walking tour brochures are available online.

Manassas National Battlefield Park

12521 Lee Highway
Manassas, VA 20109
703-361-1339
www.nps.gov/mana

This now peaceful site located about 25 miles west of Washington, D.C., was the location of the first major battle of the U.S. Civil War between the newly formed Confederate States of America troops and the United States or Union forces on July 21, 1861. This battle was known as the Battle of Manassas in the South and the Battle of Bull Run in the North. The Union forces were sent to seize the key railroad junction at Manassas and were accompanied by politicians and civilians in carriages eager to witness the drama of warfare. The mostly inexperienced 90-day volunteer troops of the Union expected a quick fight as did the new enthusiastic recruits of the Confederate forces opposing them.

The back and forth battle turned at one pivotal moment when General Thomas Jackson of Virginia received his "Stonewall" nickname. Jackson and his troops had just arrived as reinforcements and showed a steely resolve in the face of the advancing Union troops. General Barnard Bee of South Carolina rallied his discouraged troops by pointing out Jackson "standing like a stone wall" and the Confederates regrouped to win the battle. The Union troops first retreated orderly but then got tangled up with the line of civilian carriages heading back to Washington, D.C., which slowed their progress. Confusion and panic soon turned the retreat into a rout with many disorganized troops running wildly back to the safety of fortified Washington, D.C.

This location was also the site of the bigger engagement known as the Battle of Second Manassas (Second Bull Run) at the end of August 1862. In this battle, Robert E. Lee was in command supported by the famed General James Longstreet and General Stonewall Jackson. This battle displayed the superiority of these Confederate generals and their veteran troops over Union General John Pope as the result was another decisive Confederate victory. This important victory opened up the opportunity for Lee to invade the North at Antietam, MD, and later at Gettysburg, PA, in an attempt to win foreign involvement and force the Union to sue for peace.

Begin your visit at the **Henry Hill Visitor Center** where you can pick up a brochure, maps, trail guides and a schedule of interpretive programs. Watch the 45-minute orientation film *Manassas: End of Innocence*, which provides information about both battles. The center also has a bookstore and a museum with Civil War artifacts, audio-visual displays and a fiber-optic battle map presentation that describes the various troop movements during the battles. Use the maps and trail guides to take interesting walking and driving tours around the battlefield and see a variety of original buildings, cannons, memorials and monuments.

The visitor center is open daily from 8:30 AM-5 PM with a $3 fee for adults 16 and older. Tickets are good for 3 days and free for kids 15 and under. The introductory movie is played on the hour with the last showing at 4 PM. Park rangers give daily guided walking tours at 11 AM and 2 PM starting from the visitor center. Daily tours are also given at 10 AM at Matthews Hill-Tour Stop #4 and at the Brawner Farm Center at 11 AM, 1 PM and 3 PM. There are also weekend only tours at Deep Cut-Tour Stop #7 at 1 PM and at Chinn Ridge-Tour Stop # 10 at 3 PM.

National Museum of the Marine Corps

18900 Jefferson Davis Highway (Rte.1)
Triangle, VA 22172
703-221-8430
www.usmcmuseum.org

This relatively new museum, near the U.S. Marine Corps Base at Quantico, pays tribute to the courage and sacrifice of U.S. Marines. The building is topped by a soaring roof symbolizing the flag raising at Iwo Jima during World War II. The 120,000 square foot museum is filled with historic vehicles, weapons and other artifacts as well as educational exhibits detailing the many battles and wars fought by U.S. Marines. The museum also features interactive and immersive exhibits that give visitors a feel for what it was like to be a Marine in dangerous and inhospitable environments. The museum is located about 30 miles south of Washington, D.C., and is open daily from 9 AM-5 PM. Admission is free.

PART FOUR:
Parks, Recreation And Entertainment

I n this part of the guidebook, I have provided recommendations for areas and venues where families can relax, participate in recreational and sports activities and amuse themselves in a variety of ways. I have also included a list of annual festivals, theater and performing arts locations, family oriented stores and games the family can play to overcome sightseeing overload.

My recommendation is for families to take advantage of some of these worthwhile opportunities outside of sightseeing, which will enhance the overall experience of visiting the Washington, D.C., area.

Parks

These areas provide visitors tranquil, beautiful green oases in and around the capital city. All these sites offer the relaxation benefits of parks, but they all also have unique attractions that provide entertainment as well.

Rock Creek Park

Nature Center and Planetarium located at:
5200 Glover Road NW
Washington, D.C. 20015
202-895-6070
www.nps.gov/rocr

This huge 1,754-acre park bisects the northeast and northwest quadrants of the District and provides relaxing green space and a wide variety of recreational activities. The park offers miles of scenic hiking and biking trails, horseback riding, a golf course, a tennis stadium with an annual USTA tournament, an outdoor concert and theater venue (see Carter Barron Amphitheatre in Theater section) and a Planetarium.

The **Rock Creek Park Nature Center** offers ranger-led hikes and other nature programs. The **Planetarium** provides displays on Saturday and Sunday at 1 PM for children 5 and older and at 4 PM for children 7 and older. There is also an after school show at 4 PM on Wednesday. Arrive 30-45 minutes early to get a ticket.

For those interested in renting a canoe, kayak or bicycle, visit **Thompson's Boat House** at 2900 Virginia Avenue, NW, off of the Rock Creek Parkway. For more information see entry in the "More Fun Things to do in the Washington, D.C., Area" section.

The **Peirce Mill**, an intact, well-preserved mill from the 1820s that operated until 1897, is located in Rock Creek Park at 2375 Tilden Street, NW. Visitors can tour the site Wednesday-Sunday from 9 AM-5 PM and see massive grinding millstones and old wooden gears in the historic structure.

Rock Creek Park also contains a number of Civil War forts and fortifications built to defend Washington. Visitors can obtain podcasts for walking tours of some of these forts at www.nps.gov/rocr/photosmultimedia.

East Potomac Park
1100 Ohio Drive SW
Washington, D.C. 20024
202-619-7222

This park is located on a 1.5 mile stretch of land between the Washington Channel and the Potomac River. This area has the highest concentration of cherry trees in the District and is especially beautiful during the peak bloom time in early spring. Attractions include biking paths, playgrounds, two 18-hole golf courses, a miniature golf course, a year round driving range, indoor and outdoor tennis courts, and an outdoor swimming pool.

Wheaton Regional Park
2000 Shorefield Road
Wheaton, MD 20902
301-905-3045
www.montgomeryparks.org/facilities/regional_parks/wheaton

This large park offers beautiful gardens, a hands-on nature center, a dog park, hiking and biking trails, horseback riding, fishing, playgrounds, athletic fields, picnic areas and year round ice skating. There is also a miniature train ride and a historic carousel for children to enjoy. Don't miss **Brookside Gardens**, the award-winning 50-acre public display garden, which includes a Children's Garden and Butterfly Garden and many other types of beautiful gardens.

Woodend Nature Sanctuary
Audubon Naturalist Society
8940 Jones Mill Road
Chevy Chase, MD 20815
301-652-9188
www.audubonnaturalist.org

This relaxing nature sanctuary is found on the 40-acre grounds of a Georgian Revival mansion known as Woodend. Famous architect John Russell Pope designed this mansion for the Wells family in the 1920s. The sanctuary is a must see for nature lovers young and old. Visitors can walk on wooded trails, explore the aquatic life at a pond, relax in a wildflower meadow and marvel at a variety of plants in the Blair Native Plant Garden.

The mansion serves as the headquarters of the Audubon Naturalist Society. It contains a naturalist library and hundreds of examples of preserved birds. The society features free beginner Bird Walks at Woodend starting at 8 AM on Saturdays, guided by experienced birders. They also offer a huge variety of nature classes, camps and programs for families and children; some free and others for a fee. Some recent examples include programs learning about: insects, snakes, pond life, flying squirrels, birds, tree leaves, and studying animal tracks in the snow.

Great Falls Park
9200 Old Dominion Drive
McLean, VA 22102
703-285-2965
www.nps.gov/grfa

This park offers visitors a chance to view spectacular waterfalls and river rapids in a peaceful wooded setting. The park features multiple overlooks of the falls, hiking trails and picnic areas. There is also a visitor center with an orientation film on the history of Great Falls and a children's table with games, coloring and drawing activities and a "please touch" table of items they might encounter in the park.

This park also offers the National Park Service Junior Ranger Program booklet of activities and a Junior Ranger Camp for two days in the summer time. Sign up on their website well in advance for this fun and educational camp. **Never enter the water as the water is too hazardous for swimming. Don't leave the marked trail areas when viewing the falls as the rocks can be slippery and dangerous**. The park is open year round 7 AM-dusk, and the visitor center is open 10 AM-5 PM through the spring and fall seasons.

Chesapeake and Ohio (C & O) Canal National Historic Park

The C & O Canal was a 184.5 mile canal stretching from Washington, D.C., to Cumberland, Maryland, which operated from 1831 until 1924. This park starts in Georgetown and stretches 13 miles along the C & O Canal until reaching the Great Falls Tavern Visitor Center area on the Maryland side. From here, the park continues along its long route through western Maryland with an additional four visitor centers.

The **Great Falls Tavern Visitor Center** at 11710 MacArthur Blvd. on the Maryland side offers boat rides on mule-drawn barges on the C & O Canal. Visitors can also tour the historic tavern site and look at a pictorial history of the canal. Please call 301-767-3714 or go to www.nps.gov/choh for more information. There are similar mule-drawn barge rides available at the Georgetown Visitor Center for the C & O canal.

Attractions within the park area include **Fletcher's Boat House**, where you can rent boating and fishing equipment, bike, jog or walk along the canal. You can also visit **Glen Echo Park**, a former amusement park and now a center for artwork, theater and dancing, and see the **Clara Barton National Historic Site**. I have described the latter two attractions in more detail in the "Additional Attractions in Maryland" section.

Patuxent River Park
16000 Croom Airport Road
Upper Marlboro, MD 20772
301-627-6074
www.pgparks.com

This enormous state park occupies more than 7,000 acres around the scenic Patuxent River. The park offers a variety of recreational opportunities including camping, hiking, bicycling, horseback riding, fishing, and boating as well as archaeology and nature study. The park is also the home of the **Patuxent Rural Life Museums**, which features a collection of late 19th century and early 20th century buildings and historic structures, which educate visitors on the rural heritage of the area. The park offers canoe and kayak rentals, special programs and events and a wide variety of educational and nature programs for all ages. The park is open daily 8 AM-dusk.

National Wildlife Visitor Center, Patuxent Research Refuge
10901 Scarlet Tanager Loop
Laurel, MD 20708
301-497-5760
www.fws.gov/northeast/patuxent/vcdefault.html

Operated by the U.S. Department of the Interior, this $18 million state of the art visitor center offers visitors a unique look at the work scientists do to preserve and protect nature and the environment. The center uses museum type displays, interactive exhibits and outdoor classes to educate visitors on global environmental issues and the preservation of wildlife habitats. The center also offers hiking trails, fishing, wildlife observation programs, films and lectures in their auditorium and narrated tram tours through the park grounds.

The center is open daily year round from 9 AM-4:30 PM except federal holidays. Admission is free except for tram tickets which cost $3 for adults, $2 for seniors 55+, and $1 for children ages 12 and under. Public tram tours are available weekends mid-March through mid-November and weekdays late-June through mid-August. The trams operate between 11 AM-3 PM. Reserved school and group tours and specialty tram tours are also available throughout the year at different times by appointment. The cost is normally about $60 for the 40-seat tram. Call 301-497-5766 or reserve spots online.

Huntley Meadows Park
3701 Lockheed Blvd.
Alexandria, VA 22306
703-768-2525
www.fairfaxcounty.gov/parks/huntley

This 1,425-acre park offers a visitor center with interesting exhibits on local wildlife and short hiking and bicycle trails through scenic woods, meadows with wildflowers, and wetlands. Children will especially enjoy climbing up an observation deck to view wildlife and walking on a wooden boardwalk trail through the wetlands area. This park is rich with waterfowl and other birds, deer, muskrats, frogs and turtles-including snapping turtles. The park is open daily from dawn to dusk. Admission is free, but donations are appreciated.

Fort Hunt Park

Fort Hunt exit off George Washington Memorial Parkway (2 miles north of Mount Vernon)
Alexandria, VA 22308
703-289-2553
www.nps.gov/gwmp/fort-hunt.htm

This former Spanish-American War fort was turned into a top secret World War II intelligence camp and also had a Prisoner-of-War camp on the grounds. This camp was used for the imprisonment and interrogation of captured German U-Boat crews and other enemy prisoners.

Fort Hunt is now a popular place for picnics and outdoor recreation. There is also a summer concert series on Sundays at 7 PM. Kids enjoy exploring the remnants of the fort's huge gun batteries and the commander's station and visiting the stables housing U.S. Park Police horses. Park rangers occasionally give talks on the interesting history of Fort Hunt.

Burke Lake Park

7315 Ox Road
Fairfax Station, VA 22039
703-323-6600
www.fairfaxcounty.gov/parks/burkelake

This 888-acre park features a 218-acre lake with boat rentals and fishing. The park has miles of walking trails, campsites, an old-fashioned carousel, miniature train rides, and an ice cream parlor. The park also offers an18-hole par 3 golf course and an 18-hole disc golf (Frisbee) course.

Natural Gardens

These breathtaking gardens provide families with relaxing locations where they can enjoy beautiful trees, plants and flowers and learn about the importance of protecting these important resources.

The United States Botanic Gardens

100 Maryland Avenue SW
Washington, D.C. 20001
202-225-8333
www.usbg.gov
Metro: Federal Center Southwest (Blue/Orange Lines)

Located on the grounds of the U.S. Capitol, this is one of the oldest botanic gardens in North America. Its mission is to inform visitors about the importance of plants to the welfare of mankind and to the planet's ecosystem. The Conservatory features indoor informational galleries and regional gardens displaying plants from around the world. Outside there is a National Garden displaying Mid-Atlantic plants. Across Independence Avenue is Bartholdi Park, which highlights different forms of home landscape.

Cell phone tours are available onsite by calling 202-730-9303. The Conservatory is open 10 AM-5 PM daily, including all weekends & holidays. The National Garden is open from late May to early September from 10 AM-7 PM daily. Bartholdi Park is open daily from dawn to dusk. Admission is free to all areas.

The Tulip Library

North side of Tidal Basin at the intersection of Independence and Maine Avenues SW
Washington, D.C. 20024
www.washingtongardener.com/index_files/TulipLibrary2007.pdf
Metro: Smithsonian (Blue/Orange Lines)

Created in 1969 by the National Park Service, this small but impressive garden displays 93 varieties of tulips with each type displayed in their own bed. More than 10,000 tulip bulbs are flown in from the Netherlands each year and hand planted in this garden by the National Park Service. After they have finished blooming from April into early May, the bulbs are removed and the beds are prepared for the planting of a display of annuals.

Many visitors are delighted to find this colorful garden treasure, especially those who have missed the peak blooming of the nearby cherry trees. For more information and an online map detailing the varieties of tulips found in the garden, go to the website listed above.

National Arboretum

3501 New York Avenue NE
Washington, D.C. 20002
202-245-2726
www.usna.usda.gov

This 446-acre site features plants and trees from around the world, which you can experience on foot, bicycle and car or via guided tram tour (on weekends and holidays from mid April-mid October). Stop at the Administration Building, which houses a visitor information center and pick up a comprehensive map of the sprawling grounds. There are 9.5 miles of winding roads through this scenic, wooded area. Highlights of the National Arboretum include: a variety of gardens and tree collections from around the world including the National Herb Garden, a Koi pond where you can feed pellets to the colorful fish, and the National Bonsai and Penjing Museum. At this museum, you can see an outstanding collection of carefully manicured trees, which have been lovingly taken care of for years and are extremely valuable.

The National Capitol Columns area features 22 sandstone Corinthian columns, which once stood on the East Portico of the U.S. Capitol Building starting in 1828. These beautiful columns now serenely sit on a knoll in the Ellipse Meadow with a reflecting pool below.

The National Arboretum has been operating the Washington Youth Garden for 40 years, which provides a unique food education program for local families. They also offer the SPROUT program (Science Program Reaching Out), an interactive and educational experience in the youth garden for school groups. In addition, they offer a special Saturday morning family program called "Growing Food…Growing Together." Call or go online to reserve spaces on these programs.

The National Arboretum grounds are open year round 8 AM-5 PM. The Administration Building is open November-February 8 AM-4:30 PM. From March-October this building is open 8 AM-4:30 PM on weekdays and until 5 PM on weekends. The National Bonsai and Penjing Museum is open 10 AM-4 PM year round. Admission is free.

Kenilworth Aquatic Gardens

1550 Anacostia Avenue NE
Washington, D.C. 20019
202-426-6905
www.nps.gov/keaq

This pleasant location covers about 700 acres in northeast Washington, D.C. The area has lily covered ponds full of turtles, fish and waterfowl to enjoy. Visitors hike along scenic trails and boardwalks across marshland, woods and water and sit at benches to admire the natural beauty. Some visitors paddle canoes to the gardens and it is a favorite spot for birders, too. This tranquil setting quickly makes visitors forget that they are still in a bustling city. The site is open in summer from 7 AM-6:30 PM and after Labor Day until 4:30 PM. Admission is free.

Amusement Areas

The main purpose of these areas is to entertain visitors. These locations offer diverse, fun-filled attractions, which appeal to families. These sites are great destinations to visit when the kids need a break from sightseeing.

Six Flags America
13710 Central Avenue
Bowie/ Mitchellville, MD 20721
301-249-1500
www.sixflags.com

This large theme park features more than 100 thrill and family rides, live shows, costumed characters, a full-scale water park, restaurants and shopping. It is located only 30 minutes from downtown Washington, D.C., and is open mid-April through October. Six Flags also offers special Halloween-themed events in October.

Regular admission to the park is $56.99 for adults and $36.99 for juniors under 48 inches tall and free for ages two and under. Online tickets and coupons found at stores and restaurants are available with discounts up to 50% off normal admission-between $28.50-$36.99.Tickets for groups of 15 or more cost $25.99 each. Season passes are on sale for $59.99 each with one free pass for every three purchased. Parking normally costs $15 with season's pass parking costing $50.

Kings Dominion
16000 Theme Park Way
Doswell, VA 23047
804-876-5000
www.kingsdominion.com

This large 400-acre theme park offers thrill and family rides including many intimidating roller coasters, live musical and theater performances, a huge water park, costumed characters, restaurants and shopping. There is also a special new park area that kids enjoy called Planet Snoopy. The park is located 75 miles south from Washington, D.C., on U.S. Interstate 95 and is open late March through the last Sunday in October. They also offer special Halloween-themed events in October.

Regular admission to the park is $58.99 for adults and $36.99 for juniors under 48 inches tall and seniors 62+ and free for ages two and under. Two Day Admission is $61.99 for ages 3 and older. Discounts are available online and coupons are found in various restaurants and stores. They also offer discounts for groups of 15 or more. They offer a variety of season passes costing between $69.99 and $159. Normal parking costs $12 with preferred parking costing $20.

National Capital Trolley Museum

1313 Bonifant Road
Silver Spring, MD 20905
301-384-6088
www.dctrolley.org

This private museum preserves and celebrates the history of electric and city railways in Washington, D.C., by displaying trolleys and related artifacts used in the area and from around the world. The museum also offers visitors a chance to ride in an authentic trolley or street car on a nearly two-mile track through scenic woods.

The museum is open year round on Saturdays and Sundays and on Memorial Day, the Fourth of July and Labor Day from 12 PM-5 PM. From March 15-May 15, June 15-August 15 and October 15-November 15 the museum is also open on Thursdays and Fridays from 10 AM-2 PM. The last trolley ride of the day departs 30 minutes before closing. Museum and trolley ride admission is $7 for adults 18-64 and $5 for children and seniors. Group rates, tours, and special charters are available by contacting 301-384-6352 or by emailing educator@dctrolley.org.

Flying Circus Air Show

5114 Ritchie Road (Rte. 644)
Bealeton, VA 22712
540-439-8661
www.flyingcircusairshow.com

This spectacular air show features vintage biplanes performing aerial acrobatics, wing walkers, parachute jumpers, and biplane rides for the adventurous. The amazing 90-minute air show takes place from May-October on Sundays at 2:30 PM. Tickets for adults ages 13 and up cost $10 and for kids ages 3-12 cost $3. For groups of 20 or more there are discounted tickets available at $7. They also host an annual **Hot Air Balloon Annual Festival** held on a weekend in late August.

Medieval Times Dinner and Tournament

7000 Arundel Mills Circle
Hanover, MD 21076
866-731-9313
www.medievaltimes.com/baltimore

Visitors are taken back to the 11th Century to watch a tournament of knights jousting and fighting with an assortment of weapons. Each section of the crowd is assigned a champion and encouraged to cheer him on during this exciting competition. The indoor show features a unique combination of theater, horse riding and fighting skills, and a hearty medieval meal.

Tickets cost $56.95 for adults and $35.95 for children ages 12 and under. VIP and other upgraded packages are available for additional fees. Group packages are also available with discounted tickets.

Enchanted Kingdom and Family Museum
Good Knight Magic Castle
11001 Rhode Island Avenue
Beltsville, MD 20705
301-595-8989
www.goodknight.org

This offbeat destination features a recreated magic castle and three acres of fantasy-themed grounds designed to appeal to fans of *Harry Potter* and *The Lord of the Rings*. The owners of the attraction and organization are ex-law enforcement officers with a mission to entertain and empower families and children groups and educate them on child safety. **This private facility does not offer general admission and is only open for group parties or programs organized in advance.**

Kids of all ages can participate in a variety of indoor and outdoor games, jump on a dragon moon bounce, experience interactive magical shows and sword and feather dueling competitions, and examine armor and weapons. There is also an optional video on child safety awareness. They offer additional programs including a summer camp for kids of all ages and can provide a pizza lunch for an extra $5 per person. Basic admission costs $15 per person for a 90-minute program. Contact them to organize a group visit.

Bohrer Park at Summit Hill Park
506 South Frederick Avenue
Gaithersburg, MD 20877
301-258-6350
www.gaithersburgmd.gov/poi/default.asp?POI_ID=6&TOC=2;6;

This 58-acre park has playground areas, open fields for recreational activities, picnic pavilions and volleyball nets. They also have a skate park for skateboarders, a miniature golf course and a water park with giant water slides, water cannons and a splash pool for young children. These outdoor activities are open seasonally. In addition, they offer a year round indoor activity center with basketball courts, fitness room and a multipurpose gymnasium. These activities are available for a fee or through annual passes.

Dave and Buster's
White Flint Mall
11301 Rockville Pike
Bethesda, MD 20895
301-230-5151
www.daveandbusters.com
Metro: White Flint (Red Line) Shuttle bus available to mall about a quarter of a mile away.

This noisy and bustling location offers arcade style video games of all kinds as well as carnival style midway games, billiards and shuffleboard. Kids can redeem coupons from some of the games for prizes at their gift shop. Every Wednesday is half-price games night. There is also a full service restaurant serving American food favorites with sporting events broadcast on big screen TVs. This is a great place to go when the kids have hit museum overload.

Madame Tussauds Washington, D.C.

1001 F Street NW
Washington, D.C. 20004
866-823-9565
www.madametussauds.com/Washington
Metro: Metro Center (Blue/Orange Lines and Red Line) and Gallery Place (Yellow/Green Lines and Red Line)

This popular attraction displays amazingly realistic wax figures of celebrities from politics, sports and entertainment. This location also features wax figures of all 44 U.S. Presidents in its Presidents Gallery. Get your camera ready to take some shots to fool your friends and family! They are open daily 10 AM-6 PM and until 8 PM on Saturdays. Tickets cost $21 for adults, $16 for kids ages 11 and under, and $19 for seniors 60+. Kids ages three and under enter free. There are discounts available for group tickets and online purchases.

Cameron Run Regional Park

4001 Eisenhower Avenue
Alexandria, VA 22304
703-960-0767
www.nvrpa.org/cameron_run

This park features the Great Waves Water Park with speed slides and a giant wave pool. There are also batting cages, a miniature golf course, a snack bar, a cafe and large pavilions for picnics. Great Waves Water Park is open Memorial Day to Labor Day 11 AM-7 PM. The miniature golf course and batting cages are open later in the summer than the water park with reduced operating hours in the early spring and fall. There are fees required for each activity.

Upton Hill Regional Park

6060 Wilson Boulevard
Arlington, VA 22205
703-534-3437
www.nvrpa.org/park/upton_hill

This wooded park features the Ocean Dunes Water Park with water slides, water dumping buckets and a huge swimming pool. There are also baseball and softball batting cages, hiking trails, a snack bar, a cafe and large pavilions for picnics. They also feature a beautifully landscaped miniature golf course complete with waterfalls and aquatic gardens. Ocean Dunes Water Park is open Memorial Day to Labor Day 11 AM-7 PM. The batting cages and miniature golf course are normally open later in the summer than the water park with reduced operating hours in the early spring and fall. There are fees required for each activity.

Shadowland Laser Adventures

5508 Franconia Road
Springfield, VA 22310
703-921-1004
www.shadowlandadventures.com

This company offers state-of-the art laser tag games at five locations in Maryland and Virginia. They offer packages for youth groups and families including special birthday party events. They also have an arcade and karaoke studio.

Their hours of operation are Monday from 11 AM-6 PM, Tuesday-Thursday from 11 AM-10 PM, Friday from 11 AM-Midnight, Saturday from 10 AM-Midnight, and Sunday from 10 AM-10 PM. Tickets are available for $7.75 per each "adventure," with discounts available for multiple adventures. There are also packages available for groups.

Laser Quest

14517 Potomac Mills Road
Woodbridge, VA 22193
703-490-4180
www.laserquest.com

This facility offers all varieties of live action laser tag games. They also offer a host of youth programs including an overnight option for youth groups allowing players to compete until the next morning. They are open Tuesday-Thursday from 6 PM-9 PM, Friday 5 PM-11 PM, Saturday 11 AM-11 PM, and Sunday 12 PM-6 PM. Mondays are available for private groups. General admission costs $8.50 with group packages available.

Go Ape!

Rock Creek Regional Park
6129 Needwood Lake Drive
Rockville, MD 20855
888-520-7322
www.goape.com

This unique treetop recreation center features ziplines, rope bridges, Tarzan swings and obstacle courses. The center provides a training briefing and all equipment for the various activities. The center's opening times vary depending on daylight hours. They are open in March and December on weekends, April to mid-June and Labor Day to mid-November from Thursday to Monday and every day in the summer. At least one adult must supervise and participate in the activities with children under 18. Spectators can watch from the ground at no charge. Call or go online to reserve a session. The 2-3 hour adventure session costs $55 for adults and $35 for children ages 10-17.

Sportrock Alexandria Climbing Center

5308 Eisenhower Avenue
Alexandria, VA 22304
703-212-7625
www.sportrock.com
Metro: Van Dorn (Blue Line)

This indoor facility offers a wide variety of climbing opportunities for beginners and experts alike. The center features: top roping, lead climbing, bouldering, movement and climbing classes, outdoor programs, a fitness area with cardio and weight equipment, and Crossfit classes. They also offer starter climbing programs for kids and the Kid's Nite program for children ages 6-14, which offers instruction-guided climbing and games. They are open Monday-Friday from 12 PM-11 PM and on weekends from 10 AM-6 PM.

Daily rates for adults cost $18 and $10 for children ages 12 and under. There are also multiple visit tickets available. The all gear rental package costs $11.

Theater/Performing Arts

The John F. Kennedy Center for the Performing Arts. Courtesy of Destination DC.

The Washington, D.C., area boasts an amazing variety of theaters and performing arts venues for families to enjoy. I have listed some of the most popular venues for families below. For more venues and performances and to purchase discounted tickets I recommend you visit www.Ticketplace.org. You can also visit their ticket office to get more information or purchase tickets in person at 407 7th Street NW, in Washington, D.C., close to the Gallery Place Metro station. This office is open Wednesday-Friday from 11 AM-6 PM and Saturday from 10 AM-5 PM.

A useful website for information on current theatrical productions in the area is www.dctheatrescene.com. They have a special section for children's shows that summarizes the area's current family friendly productions. Another useful reference for family friendly performances is www.artsfordckids.org.

It is also possible to take advantage of group and other ticket discounts for performances found on venue websites and at online subscriber sites.

The John F. Kennedy Center for the Performing Arts

2700 F Street NW
Washington, D.C. 20566
800-444-1324, 202-467-4600
www.kennedy-center.org
Metro: Foggy Bottom (Blue/Orange Lines)-Regular complimentary shuttle available from the Foggy Bottom Metro station to the Kennedy Center.

This striking, large landmark building on the bank of the Potomac River is the center of theater and the performing arts in Washington, D.C. The building was dedicated in 1971 as a tribute to President John F. Kennedy and his strong support for the arts. The Kennedy Center offers world-class theater, dance, and opera performances and hosts the National Symphony Orchestra. The **Millennium Stage** offers a free daily musical or theatrical performance at 6 PM with no tickets or reservations required.

The Kennedy Center Education Center offers specific musical, dance, and theatrical performances including puppet shows to entertain children of all ages. Check on the Kennedy Center website under Theater for Young Audiences for a schedule of performances and their specific venues. The Kennedy Center Theater Lab offers a daily performance of *Shear Madness*, a comedy/mystery play where audiences participate in solving a wacky murder case involving suspects at a hair salon in Georgetown. Tweens, teenagers and adults alike enjoy this amusing and zany play, which has been running for more than 20 years at the Kennedy Center.

Whether or not you are attending a performance, a visit to the Kennedy Center is a rewarding experience. Visitors enjoy exploring the interior of the building including the Hall of Nations, in which hang the flags of countries with diplomatic relations with the U.S. and the Hall of States, in which hang all U.S. state and territory flags. In the Grand Foyer, the 8-foot bronze bust of John F. Kennedy by sculptor Robert Berks is a popular and moving work of art paying tribute to the president. The view from the rooftop terrace stretching around the building is spectacular and worth a leisurely stroll. Dinner with a view is available at the Roof Terrace Restaurant and Bar and at the KC Café.

Discovery Theater

S. Dillon Ripley Center
1100 Jefferson Drive SW
Washington, D.C. 20024
202-633-3030
http://discoverytheater.org
Open daily 10 AM-5:30 PM
Metro: Smithsonian (Blue/Orange Lines)

For more than 30 years the Smithsonian Institution's Discovery Theater has offered a variety of live, educational performances for children with themes involving heritage, science and culture. The theater's usual venue is an underground theater in the S. Dillon Ripley Center located next to the Smithsonian Castle Building. There are also special presentations offered at some of the museum locations and frequent touring shows. View their website to find a schedule of upcoming presentations and to reserve tickets. Call 202-633-3030 for individual tickets or 202-633-8700 for group sales. Ticket prices range from $4 to $10 depending upon the performance and group size.

Marine Barracks Evening Parade

Marine Barracks Washington
8th and I Streets SE
Washington, D.C. 20390
202-433-4073
www.marines.mil/unit/barracks/Pages/GenInfo.aspx
Metro: Eastern Market (Blue/Orange Lines)

This unique performance takes place during the summer on Fridays at 8:45 PM at this "Oldest Post in the Corps." The U.S. Marine Band plays a concert followed by a host of drilling and marching marines in full dress uniforms performing with amazing skill and precision. Online or faxed reservations for the parade are required well in advance for individuals and groups. All guests should arrive no later than 8 PM for seating as standby tickets will be made available for guests without reservations at 8:15 PM. The Marine Barracks also offers free tours of the grounds on Wednesdays at 10 AM beginning at the front gate with no reservations required.

Sylvan Theater

15th Street and Independence Avenue SW
Washington, D.C. 20001
202-619-7222
Metro: Smithsonian (Blue/Yellow Lines)
www.artsfordckids.org

This outdoor theater is located in the northwest corner of the grounds of the Washington Monument and features concerts, musicals, plays, ballet, and puppet shows from the spring until the fall. They have special performances honoring veterans and the country on Memorial Day and on the Fourth of July. This theater is also one of the venues of the annual **Military Band Summer Concert Series** from June to August on various Tuesday, Thursday, Friday and Sunday nights starting at 8 PM. Bands representing the different military service branches perform free concerts featuring military marches, classical music and patriotic favorites. Call or check online for an updated schedule. All performances are free.

Military Band Summer Concert Series-West Steps of the U.S. Capitol
West Steps of U.S. Capitol
First Street and East Capitol Street NE
Washington, D.C. 20001
Metro: Union Station (Red Line), South Capitol (Blue/Orange Lines)
www.artsfordckids.org

The military service branch bands perform public concerts during the summer at the Sylvan Theater on the grounds of the Washington Monument and at the West Steps of the U.S. Capitol. Generally the free concerts run on weeknights at 8 PM alternating at these locations, but please check the website or call for an updated schedule.

Carter Barron Amphitheatre at Rock Creek Park
4850 Colorado Avenue NW (Intersection with 16th Street, NW)
Washington, D.C. 20011
202-426-0486
www.nps.gov/rocr/planyourvisit/cbarronschedule.htm

This 4,200 seat outdoor amphitheatre is located in the heart of wooded and tranquil Rock Creek Park and features theater pieces, plays, concerts, and outdoor film nights. Performances run Friday and Saturday nights at 7:30 PM from June into September. Events sponsored by the *Washington Post* and some other events are free, while admission is required for most performances. Tickets are required for most events even without admission because of demand.

Reserve tickets for paid shows at www.ticketmaster.com or purchase them at the Carter Barron Box Office on the performance day from 12 PM-8 PM. Tickets are available for free *Washington Post* shows on the day of the performance at the Carter Barron Box Office from 12PM-8 PM and from the *Washington Post* headquarters at 1150 15th Street, NW, starting at 8:30 AM. There is a limit of four tickets per adult.

The amphitheatre also hosts the annual **DC Blues Festival** starting on Labor Day Saturday at 12:15 PM. This festival is free to the public with no tickets required.

Arena Stage at the Mead Center for American Theater
1101 Sixth Street SW
Washington, D.C. 20024
202-554-9066
www.arena-stage.com
Metro: Waterfront-SEU (Green Line)

This theater offers first-rate productions of American classics including musicals. They also perform contemporary pieces. The Arena Stage offers regular workshops and classes for children and adults and a 2-4 week summer camp called Camp Arena Stage just for kids.

Dance Place

3225 8th Street NE
Washington, D.C. 20017
202-269-1600
www.danceplace.org
Metro: Brookland/CUA (Red Line)

The Dance Place presents year round weekend performances of a wide variety of dance styles including: contemporary modern, ballet, tap, hip hop and African dance. The venue features local, regional and internationally acclaimed dance companies. They also offer regular classes in many dance styles for kids and adults and the Energizers Summer Camp for children ages 7-14.

Imagination Stage in Bethesda, MD

4908 Auburn Avenue
Bethesda, MD 20814
301-280-1660
www.imaginationstage.org
Metro: Bethesda (Red Line)

The Imagination Stage presents entertaining and educational productions of modern and classic plays year round specifically designed for families. They also offer performances targeted for children ages 2-4. In addition, they offer after school and weekend classes in acting, dance and filmmaking for children of all ages. Contact the box office for group discounts for 10 or more attendees.

Strathmore
The Music Center

5301 Tuckerman Lane

The Mansion at Strathmore

10701 Rockville Pike
North Bethesda, MD 20852
301-581-5100
www.strathmore.org
Metro: Grosvenor-Strathmore (Red Line)

The Music Center offers world class performances by major international acts in a wide variety of musical genre in a modern theater setting. The Mansion features musical performances in the more intimate setting of the historic mansion and at its outdoor gardens and concert pavilions. In addition to musical performances and classes in the arts, families are also invited to attend regular "Children's Talks and Tours" where children are given specially guided tours of the facilities and artworks at Strathmore. Children also enjoy storytelling sessions and hands-on opportunities to create their own art.

Olney Theatre Center

2001 Olney-Sandy Spring Road
Olney, MD 20832
301-924-3400
www.olneytheatre.org

This award-winning regional theater company produces American classics as well as new works, reinterpretations of classics and musical theater. Their Family Entertainment Series focuses on enjoyable performances suited for the entire family. They also offer a free summer Shakespeare Festival and intensive summer training sessions for high school students.

Wolf Trap Foundation for the Performing Arts

1645 Trap Road
Vienna, VA 22182
703-255-1900
www.wolftrap.org
Metro: West Falls Church (Orange Line), Take Wolf Trap Express Bus, operated by Fairfax Connector, to Filene Center. **This shuttle bus begins service two hours before performances at the Filene Center only.**

This huge venue features the Filene Center, a large outdoor performing arts amphitheater with covered seating and a lawn area. They host top flight theater and musical acts from May through September at this location. Wolf Trap also offers a "Children's Theatre in the Woods" from the end of June through August. This program features a small stage in the woods with daily (except Monday) family friendly performances at 10 AM and 11:15 AM. Each summer they offer about 70 shows in theater, puppetry, storytelling, dance and music targeted at children between Kindergarten and 6th grade.

The Capitol Steps

Ronald Reagan Building and International Trade Center
Amphitheater on Concourse Level
1300 Pennsylvania Avenue NW
Washington, D.C. 20004
202-312-1427
www.capsteps.com
Metro: Federal Triangle (Blue/Orange Lines)

The Capitol Steps is a musical theater group that began 30 years ago as a group of U.S. Senate staff members looking to satirize their bosses and other politicians. The group has developed into a professional troupe with multiple casts performing in the District and around the country. They have recorded more than 30 albums and have been featured on National Public Radio and the major television networks.

The Capitol Steps mock all parties and public figures equally and are quick to make fun of the latest political scandals. Their performances are especially entertaining for adults and older children who follow political figures, events and controversies. They perform Fridays and Saturdays at 7:30 PM. Tickets cost around $40 and can be purchased at www.ticketmaster.com or by phone at 202-397-SEAT. Discounted tickets for groups of 10 or more are available by calling 202-312-1427.

Now This!

Riot Act Comedy Theater
801 E Street NW
Washington, D.C. 20004
202-364-8292
www.nowthisimprov.com
Metro: Gallery Place (Green/Yellow Lines and Red Line)

This improvisational comedy group performs regularly at the Riot Act Comedy Theater and also offers specially designed performances and workshops for school groups. At these performances the audience participates in acting, singing and creating scenes along with the professionals. They also offer improv lessons for children and adults. Call or go to their website to find out about upcoming performances.

Synetic Family Theater

4041 Campbell Avenue
Arlington, VA 22206
703-824-8061
www.synetictheater.org

This intimate 100-seat theater offers family friendly theater staging classic productions, comedies and dramas. The theater is unique in the area as it offers colorful staging and stylized acting found in the Russian dramatic tradition. They also offer regular acting classes for children and adults and an Arts and Drama summer camp specially designed for kids ages 16 and under.

Blair Mansion Restaurant Mystery Dinner Theater

7711 Eastern Avenue
Silver Spring, MD 20912
301-588-1688
www.blairmansion.com
Metro: Silver Spring and Takoma (Red Line)-.8 and .7 miles walking distance.

This late 19th century historic mansion features fine dining and popular mystery dinner theater productions on weekends. Visitors begin the evening with a delicious all-you-can-eat buffet and then are entertained by skilled improvisational actors challenging them to solve a funny whodunit. The show works best when the audience members enthusiastically participate, so be prepared to get involved. The shows take place on Friday and Saturday evenings with an occasional Sunday afternoon event.

Mystery Dinner Playhouse

Doubletree Hotel-Crystal City
300 Army Navy Drive
Arlington, VA 22302
888-471-4802
www.mysterydinner.com
Metro: Pentagon City (Blue/Yellow Lines)

This dinner theater takes place in a relatively small room where the cast members serve you a full course meal as well as various clues to solve the comic murder mystery. The performance is not on a stage, but instead takes place around you as you dine. Bribing the actors with play money and asking enthusiastic questions makes the experience even more enjoyable.

Lazy Susan Dinner Theater
10712 Richmond Highway (Rte.1)
Lorton, VA 22079
703-550-7384
www.lazysusan.com

The Lazy Susan Dinner Theater offers a Pennsylvania Dutch style all-you-can-eat buffet with beverages served by the cast members before the performance. They differ from the other dinner theaters in the area by performing classic dramas and musicals as well as comedies in a more traditional theater setting.

Medieval Madness
1121 King Street
Alexandria, VA 22314
703-329-3075
www.medievalmadness.com
Metro: King Street (Blue/Yellow lines)

This interesting show combines a Renaissance Fair atmosphere with a dinner theater performance in an intimate setting. The show, which changes every few months, takes place in 15th Century England with performers and servers authentically recreating the time period. Adults like the silly atmosphere of the play and enjoy the bonding experience of sharing a full course meal with neighbors at the table. There are also bottomless drinks poured by faithful serving "wenches." Older children enjoy the overall fun experience, especially being knighted by the cast in a special ceremony. A positive, fun-loving attitude and willingness to join in the festivities enhance the experience. Shows run on most Friday and Saturday nights from 7 PM-9:30 PM.

Annual Festivals and Celebrations

The Washington, D.C., area has a wide selection of annual festivals and celebrations appealing to a variety of interests. In this section I have included the most popular festivals of interest to families. In addition to these events, parades and celebrations occur throughout the area on St. Patrick's Day, Chinese New Year and other national and ethnic holidays. Check for additional events and festivals occurring during your stay on the events calendar section at http://washington.org.

Spring

National Cherry Blossom Festival-Centennial Celebration in 2012

Washington, D.C.'s most famous festival occurs every year for 16 days at the end of March into April. The festival honors the springtime blooming of thousands of cherry trees on the Tidal Basin and throughout the city. The first 3,000 cherry trees were originally given to the U.S. in 1912 by the Mayor of Tokyo. In 1954, the Japanese Ambassador presented a 300-year-old Japanese stone lantern to commemorate the 100th anniversary of the first Treaty of Peace, Amity, and Commerce between the two countries. The lighting of this lantern traditionally begins the annual festival.

The festival features a parade, fireworks, theater and concert events, a kite flying contest, and lantern tours led by national park rangers. The blooming trees are spectacular and the festival is enjoyable, but you will also have plenty of company from around the world. Plan well in advance if you want to get the most out of a visit during this busy time. Visit www.nationalcherryblossomfestival.org for more information.

In 2012 there will be a special centennial celebration of the cherry blossom trees, which will feature more events in an extended festival lasting five weeks from March 20-April 27, 2012.

White House Easter Egg Roll

The Easter Egg Roll has been taking place on the South Lawn of the White House on Easter Monday since 1878. The U.S. Congress had passed a law in 1877 to forbid the activity on the U.S. Capitol grounds after enthusiastic crowds had torn up their lawn during previous years. President Rutherford B. Hayes saved the day by allowing relieved families to use the South Lawn of the White House for the fun event on Easter Monday 1878 and it has taken place at this location ever since.

The event has evolved to include a variety of egg-related games with famous celebrities and politicians as well as normal families participating. The main event of the day is the rolling of colored hard boiled Easter eggs across the lawn using long spoons. The official White House Easter Bunny and the president and first lady take part in the festivities. Every child receives a special presidential wooden egg with the signatures of the president and first lady.

To participate in the event, families must have at least one child age 12 or under. About 30,000 people take part in the Easter Egg Roll. Tickets are only available about a month in advance through an online lottery. Visit www.whitehouse.gov/eastereggroll for more information.

National Cathedral Flower Mart

The volunteer organization, All Hallows Guild, has been organizing this event on the grounds of the Washington National Cathedral for garden enthusiasts and families since 1939. The cathedral is located at 3101 Wisconsin Avenue, NW.

The Flower Mart takes place over the first Friday and Saturday in May and features plants, herbs, puppet shows, antique carousel rides and entertainment for the whole family. The Flower Mart also features floral displays, vendors selling garden items, food and beverages, arts and crafts objects, and one featured foreign embassy honoree. Visit www.allhallowsguild.org/fm for a full schedule of events.

St. Sophia's Spring Greek Festival

This three-day event occurs in May on the grounds of the beautiful St. Sophia Greek Orthodox Cathedral. Visitors can sample delicious Greek cuisine and drinks, browse stalls selling arts and crafts and enjoy Greek music and dancing. The ornate cathedral itself is worth a visit at any time of the year. The festival takes place at 36th Street and Massachusetts Avenue, NW. For more information call 202-333-4730 or visit www.saintsophiawashington.org.

Passport D.C.

The organization Cultural Tourism D.C. presents Passport D.C. on three weekends in May. This event celebrates international culture by showcasing Washington, D.C.'s embassies and cultural organizations with open houses, and a variety of performances, films, lectures and exhibits. Visit their website at www.culturaltourismdc.org for a full schedule of events.

Memorial Day Weekend

Memorial Day weekend in Washington, D.C., features events honoring the memory of servicemen and women who have died serving their country. Special ceremonies take place on Memorial Day at all the monuments and memorials to our armed forces and at Arlington National Cemetery.

One main event of the weekend is the **Rolling Thunder Motorcycle Rally,** which involves thousands of veterans on motorcycles honoring their brothers-in-arms by riding into the District in one large group. The veterans seek to improve veteran benefits and they also advocate for POWs and MIAs. The veterans ride from the Pentagon to the Lincoln Memorial on Sunday at noon and then take part in a speaker program with musical performances at the Lincoln Memorial.

On Sunday there is a free National Memorial Day Concert on the West Lawn of the U.S. Capitol at 8 PM with gates opening at 5 PM. The concert features famous performers and the National Symphony Orchestra. Memorial Day festivities culminate on Monday with the National Memorial Day Parade, which includes veterans units and marching bands from around the country. The parade normally begins around 2 PM and stretches from 7th Street and Constitution Avenue, NW, past the White House to 17th Street, NW.

Summer

Imagination Bethesda- A Children's Street Festival in Bethesda, MD
Metro: Bethesda (Red Line)

This street festival designed for kids ages 12 and under occurs normally on the first Saturday in June along Woodmont Avenue and Elm Street in Bethesda, MD. The festival features musical performances, dance groups, jugglers, costumed characters, face painters, and arts and crafts activities. For more information, go to www.bethesda.org.

National Capital Barbecue Battle
Metro: Federal Triangle (Blue/Orange Lines)

This event features the nation's best grilling specialists fighting it out to be crowned national barbecue champion and win a $40,000 prize. Visitors enjoy sampling delicious barbecue entrees from around the country while also being entertained by musicians, magicians and other performers. Celebrities and local sports stars also make frequent appearances. The event takes place on a weekend in late June on Pennsylvania Avenue in D.C. between 9th and 14th Streets, NW. Tickets cost $10 for adults and $5 for kids ages 6-12. All proceeds go to charity. Visit the official website at www.bbqdc.com for more information.

Fourth of July

The nation's capital celebrates the Fourth of July in great style starting with the National Independence Day Parade along Constitution Avenue from 7th to 17th Streets, NW. The parade begins at 11:45 AM, but arrive early to get a good vantage point. The National Symphony Orchestra and popular artists perform patriotic music on the West Lawn of the U.S. Capitol Building from 8 PM until the fireworks. Admittance begins at 3 PM for this event called "A Capitol Fourth Concert."

At 6 PM there is another concert on the southwest corner of the grounds of the Washington Monument that is open to the public. The U.S. Navy Band provides the featured entertainment lasting until 9:10 PM when a dazzling fireworks display is launched from near the Lincoln Memorial Reflecting Pool. Great views of the fireworks display can be seen from the National Mall and across the Potomac River from the Marine Corps War Memorial or the Air Force Memorial in Arlington.

Smithsonian Folklife Festival
Metro: Smithsonian (Blue/Orange Lines)

The Smithsonian Folklife Festival takes place on the National Mall between 7th and 14th Streets, NW, at the end of June into early July. This free festival is organized by the Smithsonian Institution and celebrates cultural traditions from around the world. The fair-like atmosphere features exhibits on several highlighted countries or regions with musical and dance performances, arts and crafts, cooking demonstrations, traditional storytelling and discussions of cultural issues. The festival runs from late June to mid-July from 11 AM to 5:30 PM with evening events starting at 5:30 PM. Call 202-633-7484 or visit www.folklife.si.edu for an updated schedule of events.

Fall

Maryland Renaissance Festival

This festival recreates life in the fictional 16th century English village of Revel Grove. The festival features authentic period food and drink, costumed re-enactors, musical and theatrical performances on 8 stages, a children's play area, and a huge variety of shops offering Renaissance arts and crafts. Children also can take free pony rides, practice archery, enjoy strolling musicians and magicians and try to find their way through a maze. Visitors are encouraged to get in character (costume rentals available) and participate in everyday life and festival time in Renaissance England. One highlight is a realistic jousting competition in an arena with armored knights battling each other while riding on horseback at amazing speeds. The festival is open on weekends in late August through October and is located in Crownsville, Maryland-about 30 miles from Washington, D.C. Single and multi-day tickets are available online or at the gate. Call 1-800-296-7304 or visit their website at www.rennfest.com for more information.

Adams Morgan Day Festival
Metro: Woodley Park-Zoo/Adams Morgan (Red Line)

This lively neighborhood celebrates its cultural diversity with a festival of music, arts and dance activities and plenty of mouthwatering delicacies from around the world. There is also a new Green Pavilion for environmentally friendly products and a special Kids Area with fun activities. The festival normally takes place the second Sunday in September at the intersection of 18th Street and Florida Avenue, NW.

WalkingTown D.C. and BikingTown D.C.

The organization Cultural Tourism DC offers visitors and residents a 10-day festival of free biking and walking tours and special events. This event is designed to showcase the city's cultural heritage through healthy educational activities in all eight wards of the city. The event takes place from late September to early October. Visit www.culturaltourismdc.org for an updated schedule of events.

Fort Belvoir Oktoberfest

This event celebrates the traditions of the German Oktoberfest in a carnival-like setting complete with a huge tent featuring German bands and performers and authentic food and beverages. There are also carnival rides and midway games, food and souvenir booths and special games for kids at the Kinder Korner. The event takes place the last Thursday of September to the first Sunday of October on the grounds of the U.S. Army base at Fort Belvoir, on Route 1 just south of Alexandria, VA. This is an active military base, so visitors must show identification and go through a security check to enter the grounds. Go to www.belvoirmwr.com/features/Oktoberfest for more information.

Taste of DC
Metro: Federal Triangle (Blue/Orange Lines)

This festival of food, wine, beer and culture takes place on Pennsylvania Avenue between 12th and 15th Streets, NW, over Columbus Day weekend. Pavilions feature food and beverages from more than 80 popular area restaurants along with musical performances and interactive family activities. Visit www.thetasteofdc.org or call 202-618-3663 for an updated schedule of events.

Kids Euro Festival

This month-long festival, organized by the French-American Cultural Foundation, takes place from mid-October to mid-November and features family friendly performers from European Union countries at venues throughout the area. The program includes entertainers such as jugglers, clowns, magicians, puppeteers, musicians and singers. There are also special events featuring films, storytelling, concerts, plays and dance performances. The festival also offers special workshops for families and kids. Some events require reservations. Go to www.kidseurofestival.org or call 202-944-6558 for a complete schedule of events and more information.

Butler's Orchard Pumpkin Festival
22200 Davis Mill Road
Germantown, MD 20876
301-972-3299
www.butlersorchard.com

This family farm has been organizing this popular Halloween-themed event for more than 30 years. The festival features tractor-driven hay rides, jumps from the hayloft, a Cinderella pumpkin coach, giant slides, barnyard animals, live music, a straw maze, arts and crafts, refreshments and sweets such as caramel apples. This festival takes place on weekends and Columbus Day in October from 10 AM-5 PM. In addition, throughout the year Butler's Orchard offers a farmers market, pick your own opportunities, blossom and foliage tours, and evening hay rides.

Winter

National Christmas Tree and the Pageant of Peace
Metro: McPherson Square and Federal Triangle (Blue/Orange Lines)

President Calvin Coolidge started the tradition of lighting a National Christmas Tree on the Ellipse in 1923. The Ellipse, part of the President's Park, is the oval shaped grassy area located between the White House and the Washington Monument. The Christmas Pageant of Peace started in 1954 with a beautifully illuminated National Community Christmas Tree surrounded by 56 decorated smaller trees representing the states and territories of the United States. Organizers also included a nativity scene, a children's corner, a stage for musical and dancing events and other exhibits. In 1973 a Colorado Blue Spruce tree was planted to serve as the permanent National Christmas Tree, but it became diseased and was replaced by a similar tree in 1978. This tree stood more than 40 feet tall, but was damaged in a wind storm in 2011 and replaced by another Colorado Blue Spruce tree. The current planted tree measures 27 feet tall and will continue to grow.

The annual **National Christmas Tree Lighting Ceremony**, led by the president, takes place in early December. The Pathway of Peace area is open to the public daily until 11 PM through January 1. The organizers have expanded the celebration to include a Yule Log, Santa's Workshop, model trains, additional decorations and frequent performances on the Ellipse Stage. Performances on the Ellipse Stage occur from 6 PM-8:30 PM on weekdays and from 4 PM-8:30 PM on weekends. Tickets are only required for the lighting ceremony at the start of the festival. For more information on the festival go to www.thenationaltree.org or call 202-208-1631. An online lottery for tickets to the opening ceremony takes place annually in early November at www.recreation.gov with a link available on the festival website. There are 3,000 seats and 10,000 standing room tickets available through the online lottery and they are all quickly distributed. Visitors can enter the Ellipse at 15th and E Streets, 17th and E Streets, and 15th Street and Constitution Avenue, NW.

Also located on the Ellipse is the **National Hanukkah Menorah**, honoring the eight-day Jewish holiday. The menorah is lit each night of Hanukkah with a celebration featuring musical performances, hot latkes and donuts. The ceremonies begin at 4 PM the first day of Hanukkah. Free tickets are available online for reserved seating. No tickets are needed for standing room. Please visit www.nationalmenorah.com or call 202-332-5600 for more information.

The U.S. Capitol sets up a tree every year on their West Lawn in early December and holds the Capitol Christmas Tree Lighting Ceremony. This event offers musical entertainment and culminates with the tree lighting by the Speaker of the House. Visitors enter through security gates at First Street and Maryland Ave., SW and First Street and Pennsylvania Ave., NW. For more information visit www.aoc.gov.

The Campagna Center's Scottish Christmas Walk Weekend and Parade

This popular family event in Old Town, Alexandria, VA, occurs over the first weekend in December and features a Scottish clansmen parade with bagpipes and drums, Scottish dancers, and Scottie dogs. The activities-packed weekend also offers tours of historic homes, Scotch whisky tasting, a children's tea party, a Celtic Concert, and a Christmas Marketplace and café. On Saturday there is also the **Annual Holiday Boat Parade of Lights** with a variety of pleasure boats lit up to celebrate the season. This colorful boat parade repeats in Georgetown on Sunday. For detailed festival information go to www.scottishchristmaswalk.com.

Discover Strathmore Festival
Music Center at Strathmore
5301 Tuckerman Lane
N. Bethesda, MD 20852
301-581-5200
www.strathmore.org
Metro: Grosvenor-Strathmore (Red Line)

This free all day family event celebrating music and the visual arts occurs normally in mid-February at the Music Center at Strathmore. This performing arts center features year round world-class musical, dramatic and dance performances. The festival features live performances, demonstrations and hands-on activities that entertain and educate children. Each year's festival focuses on a theme and provides a range of entertaining classes and workshops for children and adults.

ZooLights at the National Zoo
3001 Connecticut Avenue NW
Washington, D.C. 20008
202-633-4800
http://nationalzoo.si.edu
Metro: Woodley Park-Zoo/Adams Morgan and Cleveland Park (Red Line)

The National Zoo stays open from 5:30 PM-8:30 PM from early December until January 1 with a dazzling display of lights in creative arrangements. This free festival features light displays with animal ice sculptures, winter-themed arts and crafts, ice sculpting demonstrations, musical entertainment and storytelling. The regular animal exhibits stay open late as well.

Sports and Recreational Activities

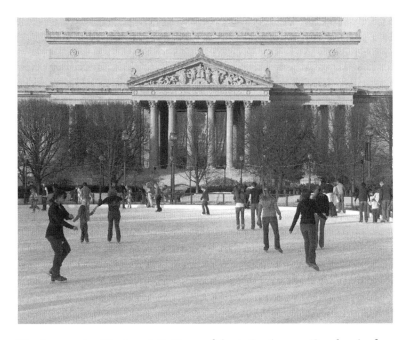

Ice Skating at the National Gallery of Art's Sculpture Garden in front of the
National Archives. Courtesy of Destination DC.

The Washington, D.C., area offers a multitude of sports and recreational activities appealing to many interests. These indoor and outdoor activities will keep families active and entertained throughout the year.

Ice Skating

In the winter months, outdoor skating complete with lessons and rentals is available at the following locations:

Sculpture Garden of the National Gallery of Art
National Mall
7th Street and Constitution Avenue NW
Washington, D.C. 20004
202-216-9397
www.nga.gov/ginfo/skating.shtm
Metro: Archives-Navy Memorial (Green/Yellow Lines)

Pentagon Row
1101 South Joyce Street
Arlington, VA 22202
703-418-6666
www.pentagonrowskating.com
Metro: Pentagon City (Blue/Yellow Lines)

Silver Spring Ice Skating at Veterans Plaza
8523 Fenton Street
Silver Spring, MD 20910
301-588-1221
www.silverspringiceskating.com
Metro: Silver Spring (Red Line)

In addition, some area indoor ice rinks are listed below:

Mount Vernon Recreation Center
2017 Belle View Boulevard
Alexandria, VA 22307
703-768-3224
www.fairfaxcounty.gov

Fairfax Ice Arena
3779 Pickett Road
Fairfax, VA 22031
703-323-1131
www.fairfaxicearena.com

Rockville Ice Arena
50 Southlawn Court
Rockville, MD 20850
301-294-8101
http://rockvilleice.pointstreaksites.com/view/rockvilleice

Cabin John Ice Rink
10610 Westlake Drive
Rockville, MD 20852
301-765-8620
www.montgomeryparks.org/enterprise/ice/cabin_john

Roller Skating

The Skate N Fun Zone has a roller skating rink and also offers laser tag and a rock climbing wall.

Skate N Fun Zone
7878 Sudley Drive
Manassas, VA 20109
703-361-7465
www.skatenfunzone.com

Skateboarding

These area skate parks will challenge skateboarders of all skill levels.

Powhatan Springs Skate Park
6020 Wilson Boulevard
Arlington, VA 22205
703-533-2362
www.arlingtonva.us/departments/ParksRecreation/scripts/planning/powhatan/
ParksRecreationScriptsPowhatanMain.aspx

Alexandria Skate Park
3300 Duke Street
Alexandria, VA 22304

Rockville Skate Park
355 Martins Lane
Rockville, MD 20850
301-545-5656
www.rockvillemd.gov/skatepark

Gaithersburg Skate Park
Bohrer Park
506 South Frederick Avenue
Gaithersburg, MD 20877
301-258-6350
www.gaithersburgmd.gov/poi/default.asp?POI_ID=343&TOC=1;343

Horseback Riding

These locations offer lessons as well as riding excursions for all levels.

Rock Creek Park Horse Center
5100 Glover Road NW
Washington, D.C. 20015
202-362-0117
www.rockcreekhorsecenter.org

Reddemeade Equestrian Center
1701 Ednor Road
Silver Spring, MD 20905
301-421-4481
www.reddemeade.com

Meadowbrook Stables
8200 Meadowbrook Lane
Chevy Chase, MD 20815
301-589-9026
www.meadowbrookstables.com

Wheaton Park Stables
1101 Glenallan Avenue
Wheaton, MD 20902
301-622-2424
www.wheatonparkstables.com

Camp Olympia
5511 Muncaster Mill Road
Rockville, MD 20855
301-926-9281
www.camp-olympia.com

Golf

The National Park Service operates three historic golf courses in Washington, D.C. These courses are scenic, affordable and excellent for all levels of play. The locations offer pro shops, clinics, private and group lessons, food and drink, and short game areas. The East Potomac Park site also offers a year round driving range and a miniature golf course. The courses are listed below:

East Potomac (Hains Point) Golf Course
972 Ohio Drive SW
Washington, D.C. 20024
202-554-7660
http://golfdc.com

Rock Creek Golf Course
6100 16th Street NW
Washington, D.C. 20011
202-882-7332
http://golfdc.com

Langston Golf Course
2600 Benning Road NE
Washington, D.C. 20002
202-397-8638
http://golfdc.com

Indoor Tennis

There are many public outdoor tennis facilities available to the public throughout the Washington, D.C., area offering first-come, first-served playing opportunities. Listed below are some excellent public indoor tennis facilities. These areas offer courts for public use, tennis leagues, clinics, private and group lessons, locker rooms and pro shop services. There is also a snack bar at the Rock Creek Park Tennis Center.

East Potomac (Hains Point) Tennis Center
1090 Ohio Drive SW
Washington, D.C. 20024
202-554-5962
www.eastpotomactennis.com

Rock Creek Park Tennis Center
16th and Kennedy Streets NW
Washington, D.C. 20011
202-722-5949
www.rockcreektennis.com

Sailing

The following locations offer sailing lessons for all ages and boat rentals. For different types of boat rentals (canoes, rowboats, kayaks) and fishing, please see the entry on boathouses in the "More Fun Things to do in the Washington, D.C., Area" section.

Washington Sailing Marina
1 Marina Drive
Alexandria, VA 22314
703-548-9027
www.washingtonsailingmarina.com

Mariner Sailing School
Belle Haven Marina
6401 George Washington Memorial Parkway
Alexandria, VA 22314
703-768-0018
www.saildc.com

Chess

The U.S. Chess Center is a private organization whose mission is to teach chess to children to help improve their academic and social skills. The center offers lessons, tournaments, leagues and other youth activities throughout the year.

U.S. Chess Center
1501 M Street NW
Washington, D.C. 20005
202-857-4922
www.chessctr.org
Metro: Farragut North (Red Line)

Bowling

Bowl America
6450 Edsall Road
Alexandria, VA 22312
703-354-3300
www.bowl-america.com

Additional locations:

140 South Maple Avenue
Falls Church, VA 22046
703-534-1370

9699 Lee Highway
Fairfax, VA 22031
703-273-7700

AMF Bowling Alley
6228A N. Kings Highway
Alexandria, VA 22303
703-765-633
www.amf.com

Additional locations:

9021 Baltimore Blvd.
College Park, MD 20740
301-474-8282

4245 Markham Street
Annandale, VA 22003
703-256-2211

The following two listings are upscale bowling locations, which are more adult-oriented. These locations have lounges and are open only for ages 21 and up after 8 PM and 9 PM, respectively. They offer daily bowling hours for all ages and will organize kids parties and events:

Lucky Strike Lanes
701 7th Street NW
Second Floor
Washington, D.C. 20001
202-347-1021
www.bowlluckystrike.com
Metro: Gallery Place-Chinatown (Green/Yellow Lines and Red Lines)

Bowlmor Lanes
5353 Westbard Avenue
Bethesda, MD 20816
301-652-0955
www.bowlmor.com

Swimming

In addition to the water parks and other parks with swimming areas already listed, I am including some popular public indoor and outdoor swimming areas in the region. Most of these facilities are free to residents and charge small fees for non-residents.

Outdoor Pools

Volta Park
Georgetown
3400 Volta Place NW
Washington, D.C. 20007
202-282-0381
http://dpr.dc.gov/DC/DPR

Francis D.C. Public Pool
2500 N Street NW
Washington, D.C. 20037
202-727-3285
http://dpr.dc.gov/DC/DPR
Metro: Foggy Bottom (Blue/Orange Lines)

Rockville Swim and Fitness Center
355 Martins Lane
Rockville, MD 20850
240-314-8750
www.rockvillemd.gov/swimcenter
Metro: Rockville (Red Line)

Indoor Pools

Woodrow Wilson Aquatic Center
4551 Fort Drive NW
Washington, D.C. 20016
202-730-0583
http://app.dpr.dc.gov/dprmap/details.asp?cid=3
Metro: Tenleytown (Red Line)

Marie Reed Recreation Center
2200 Champlain Street NW
Washington, D.C. 20050
202-673-7771
http://app.dpr.dc.gov/dprmap/details.asp?cid=68

Chinquapin Park Recreation Center
3210 King Street
Alexandria, VA 22302
703-746-5553
http://alexandriava.gov/recreation/info/default.aspx?id=12352#rixse

Martin Luther King, Jr. Swim Center
1201 Jackson Road
Silver Spring, MD 20904
240-777-8060
www.montgomerycountymd.gov/rectmpl.asp?url=/content/rec/Recipix/Martin_cen.asp

Playground Areas

Indoor Play Areas

The Family Room
411 8th Street NW
Washington, D.C. 20003
202-640-1865
www.thefamilyroomdc.com
Metro: Eastern Market (Blue/Orange Lines)

This indoor play area is designed to entertain kids 7 and under and their parents as well. They offer regularly scheduled activities including arts and crafts, music and story time. In addition, kids can entertain themselves using an indoor climbing area and a variety of toys, books and art supplies. There is also a quiet area for adults to relax, use their free Wi-Fi, and read magazines or books from their lending library. They also offer movie nights, special events and parties for groups. Parents can drop in and pay $10 per child and $5 for additional siblings for the day or become members by paying a monthly membership fee.

Jonah's Treehouse
2121 Wisconsin Avenue, C1 Level NW
Washington, D.C. 20007
202-298-6805
www.jonahstreehouse.com

This indoor play area is designed for children 5 and under. The children participate in play and movement classes and climb their way through safe tunnels and cylinders and over bridges. Jonah's Treehouse integrates bright colors, music and textures into their soft obstacle courses for entertainment and to strengthen motor, cognitive and social skills. They also organize birthday parties and other group events.

JW Tumbles Playzone
2499 Harrison Street
Arlington, VA 22207
703-531-1470
http://arlington.jwtumbles.com

The JW Tumbles Playzone is an indoor play area next to the JW Tumbles Gym in Arlington. This area features a host of tunnels, slides and structures to climb in and around. This soft-play area offers fun and exercise for young children in a safe environment. JW Tumbles calls itself a learning playground and features growth development classes that develop physical and social skills for kids ages 4 months to 9 years old. They also offer summer camp programs and private playzone programs for groups.

Outdoor Playground Areas

These popular locations offer a variety of outdoor playground equipment and recreational activities. Parents should always supervise their children when playing in these public playground areas.

East Potomac Park
Hains Point & Ohio Drive SW
Washington, D.C. 20002
202-554-7660

Kalorama Park
19th Street and Kalorama Road NW
Washington, D.C. 20009

Turtle Park
4500 Van Ness Street NW
Washington, D.C. 20016
202-282-2198

Lafayette Park
5701 Broad Branch Run NW
Washington, D.C. 20015

Woodmont Park
2422 N. Fillmore Street
Arlington, VA 22207
703-228-6525

Great Falls Grange Playground
9818 Georgetown Pike
Great Falls, VA 22066
703-938-8835

Clemyjontri Park
6317 Georgetown Pike
McLean, VA 22101
703-388-2807

Candy Cane Park
Beach Drive & Rollingwood Drive
Chevy Chase, MD 20815

Cabin John Regional Park
7400 Tuckerman Lane
Rockville, MD 20852
301-495-2525

Pick Your Own

These locations offer a seasonal variety of pick your own fruits and vegetables. This is a great opportunity for families to have fun working together to find and pick the best fruit and vegetables, which they can enjoy later. These sites also offer additional fun activities such as hay rides, corn and straw mazes and barnyard animals.

Butler's Orchard
22200 Davis Mill Road
Germantown, MD 20876
301-972-3299
www.butlersorchard.com

Becraft's Farm
14722 New Hampshire Avenue
Silver Spring, MD 20905
301-236-4545

Larriland Farm
2415 Woodbine Road
Woodbine, MD 21797
301-854-6110
www.pickyourown.com

Hollin Farms
1524 Snowden Road
Delaplane, VA 20144
540-592-3574
www.hollinfarms.com

Professional Spectator Sports

The nation's capital has professional teams in football, baseball, basketball, ice hockey, soccer and tennis. Venue/ticketing information is listed below:

Football: Washington Redskins, play at FedEx Field, 1600 FedEx Way, Landover, MD, www.redskins.com, **301-276-6800**

Baseball: Washington Nationals, play at Nationals Park, 1500 South Capitol Street, SE, Washington, D.C., www.washington.nationals.mlb.com, 202-675-6287

Basketball: Washington Wizards, play at Verizon Center, 601 F Street, NW, Washington, D.C., www.nba.com/wizards, 202-661-5050

Women's Basketball: Washington Mystics, play at Verizon Center, 601 F Street, NW, Washington, D.C., www.wnba.com/mystics, 877-D.C.-HOOP1

Ice Hockey: Washington Capitals, play at Verizon Center, 601 F Street, NW, Washington, D.C., http://capitals.nhl.com, 202-397-SEAT

Soccer: D.C. United, play at RFK Stadium, 2400 East Capitol Street, SE, Washington, D.C., www.dcunited.com, 202-587-5000

World Team Tennis: Washington Kastles, play at Kastles Stadium at the Wharf, 800 Water Street, SW, Washington, D.C., www.washingtonkastles.com, 202-4-TENNIS

Legg Mason Tennis Classic: The ATP (Association of Tennis Professionals) Tour stops in D.C. at the end of July/beginning of August featuring some of the top men and women professional players. Matches are played at the William H.G. FitzGerald Tennis Center in Rock Creek Park, 16th and Kennedy Streets, NW, Washington, D.C. www.leggmasontennisclassic.com, 202-721-9500.

Professional Golf: Congressional Country Club, 8500 River Road, Bethesda, MD. This famous club hosts a PGA tour event every year normally in June or July. In June 2011 they hosted their third U.S. Open. www.ccclub.org, www.pgatour.com, 301-469-2032.

More Fun Things to Do in the Washington, D.C., Area

The Washington, D.C., area has something of interest for everyone. Outside of the areas already covered in this guide, there are other fun activities for families to experience. Here are some of my favorite miscellaneous fun things to do for families:

Watch planes take off and land from Washington Reagan National Airport at Gravelly Point Park

This location is accessible by car on the George Washington Parkway adjacent to the airport in Arlington, VA. People of all ages marvel at how low the planes fly when they pass overhead.

Fly a kite on or near the National Mall

Buy a kite at the Smithsonian gift shops or bring your own. Good spots are found anywhere on the National Mall or in the open grassy area near the FDR Memorial.

Visit a farmers market or a flea market

Some of the most popular weekend or Sunday outdoor farmers and flea markets are found at Eastern Market on Capitol Hill, Union Station, Georgetown, and at Market Square in Old Town Alexandria. The Eastern Market indoor market is open every day except Monday. The

U.S. Department of Agriculture also organizes a farmers market on Fridays from June to Mid-November from 10 AM-2 PM located at 12th Street and Independence Avenue, SW.

Stroll through Georgetown

The Georgetown neighborhood boasts a wide variety of excellent restaurants, interesting shops and quiet streets filled with beautiful historic homes to enjoy. The hilltop Georgetown University campus also offers beautiful architecture and facilities and an impressive view of the area.

Visit Theodore Roosevelt Island

This wooded island in the Potomac River across from Georgetown serves as a national memorial to our 26th president. The tranquil island has walking trails and a monument to the president. President Theodore Roosevelt was dedicated to the conservation of the country's natural resources and created the U.S. National Park Service. The island is located across from Georgetown and can be reached via a walking bridge from the George Washington Parkway near Rosslyn in Arlington. There is limited parking available. The closest Metrorail station is Rosslyn. Another alternative is to walk or bike to the island using the nearby Key Bridge in Georgetown. For more information go to www.nps.gov/this.

Take a cruise on the Potomac River

A wide variety of sightseeing, dinner, and Mount Vernon cruises depart from Washington Harbour in Georgetown, the Washington Marina in Southwest D.C., National Harbor in MD, and from Old Town Alexandria's historic waterfront. Some popular companies are the Potomac Riverboat Company in Alexandria and Odyssey Cruises and Spirit Cruises in Washington, D.C. Their websites are www.potomacriverboatco.com, www.odysseycruises.com and www.spiritof-washington.com.

Visit a private art gallery in the Dupont Circle area

The Dupont Circle neighborhood has many foreign embassies, fine restaurants and trendy shops. It also has many private art galleries located primarily on R Street and along Connecticut Avenue. These galleries feature contemporary and traditional art, paintings, prints, photography, glass, and sculpture. On the first Friday of every month, many of the galleries host free receptions (some with refreshments) between 6-8 PM.

Take a drive or walk along Embassy Row

As a capital city, Washington, D.C., is the site of many foreign embassies. A majority of these embassies are located on Massachusetts Avenue, NW, along a long stretch of road nicknamed "Embassy Row." The embassies start roughly with the Australian Embassy in the Scott Circle area and line either side of Massachusetts Avenue as it runs past Dupont Circle up toward the National Cathedral at the main cross street of Wisconsin Avenue.

One of the highlights of this tour is seeing the 1966 statue of famed British leader **Winston Churchill** in front of the British Embassy at 3100 Massachusetts Avenue, NW. William McVey's sculpture features Churchill holding up his right hand in a V for Victory salute popular during World War II. Churchill's other hand firmly clutches a walking stick along with his trademark cigar. One foot is standing on the British soil of the British Embassy while the other is on American soil, symbolizing Churchill's Anglo-American (his mother was American) roots.

The best way to view Embassy Row is by using a bicycle, car or taxicab before or after rush hour.

Watch a movie in a classic theater

If you want to see a movie in style at a restored classic theater, visit these theaters:

Uptown Theater in D.C. at 3426 Connecticut Avenue, NW, 202-966-8805, Cleveland Park Metro station

AFI Silver Theater in Silver Spring, MD at 8633 Colesville Rd., 301-495-6700, Silver Spring Metro station.

Watch a movie on the National Mall

The Screen on the Green program presents free classic movies on Monday nights in July and August on the National Mall between 4th and 7th Streets, NW. The films begin sometime between 8:30 PM and 9 PM, but arrive at least two hours earlier to get a good location for watching the movie. Be sure to bring a blanket and refreshments, but note that folding chairs are prohibited in the main area. A special part of each presentation is the "HBO Dance" that people do just before the main feature-stand up and join in the fun! Call the Screen on the Green hotline at 877-262-5866 for more information.

Rent a paddle boat on the Tidal Basin

These fun foot-powered boats (also called pedal boats) are available for rent on the Tidal Basin near the Jefferson Memorial. Two and four passenger boats are available for rent at $12 and $19 per hour, respectively. These boats provide fun, exercise and a close up look at the Jefferson Memorial and the entire Tidal Basin area. Make sure you bring bottled water and sunscreen as it gets hot on the water when your legs are working hard. The boats are located at 1501 Maine Avenue, SW. Call 202-249-2426 or make online reservations at: www.tidalbasinpaddleboats. com. You can rent boats every day from March 15 to Labor Day from 10 AM-6 PM with the last boat rented at 5 PM. Boats are also available Wednesday-Sunday after Labor Day through Columbus Day weekend.

Rent a canoe, kayak or rowboat on the Potomac River

Washington, D.C., has some excellent boathouses that will outfit you for your self-powered cruises along the river. Rates are by the hour or day. This is a great way to get some exercise and enjoy viewing the city, monuments, and Roosevelt Island from the water.

D.C. boathouses include: the **Thompson Boat Center** at 2900 Virginia Avenue, NW, off of Rock Creek Parkway-www.thompsonboatcenter.com-202-333-9543, **Jack's Boat House** at 3500 K Street, NW, under the Key Bridge in Georgetown-www.jacksboathouse.com-202-337-9642, and **Fletcher's Boat House** at 4940 Canal Road, NW, between Key Bridge and Chain Bridge-www.fletchersboathouse.com-202-244-0461.

The boathouses sell food, beverages and other supplies and also rent out bicycles. Fletcher's Boat House also sells fishing gear and licenses. The Thompson Boat Center also rents out rowing shells and Sunfish sailboats.

Explore the area's Civil War forts and battlefields

The area around the District is dotted with the ruins of 68 Civil War era forts built or reinforced to defend the capital from the threat of land and water attack from the nearby Confederacy. These fortifications are known as the Civil War Defenses of Washington.

In 1864, Fort Stevens in Rock Creek Park within the city limits actually withstood and repelled a sustained Confederate attack from General Jubal Early and 20,000 troops. President Abraham Lincoln dangerously viewed the battle on the ramparts and became the only serving president to ever come under enemy fire. Remnants of the partially restored fort and Civil War era cannons are found at the site maintained by the National Park Service at 13th and Quackenbos Street, NW.

Fort Ward in Alexandria is one of the best preserved of these Civil War forts and has an interesting museum on the grounds. Information on Fort Ward is found in the "Additional Attractions in Virginia" section.

Famous battles in the area include the first major battle of the Civil War, which was fought at nearby Manassas, VA, and known as the Battle of Bull Run in the North. Detailed information on this site is found in the "Additional Attractions in Virginia" section. In addition, the most famous battle of the war was fought in Gettysburg, PA, only about 90 minutes away. Important battles were also fought at Fredericksburg, VA, and Antietam, MD. Go to www.civilwartraveler. com for a good overview of Civil War-related sites in the area. Another useful site is www.virginia.org/CivilWarTrails.

Visit or drive by the monuments, memorials, and federal buildings at night

A nighttime drive or walk in Washington, D.C., is an unforgettable experience as the illuminated monuments, memorials, and federal buildings are breathtaking. Visiting the monuments and memorials at night when the crowds have thinned is a special experience.

Visit the Verizon Center

The Verizon Center in the Penn Quarter area is the home indoor arena for the local professional basketball and ice hockey teams. It also hosts a wide variety of concerts, performances and events. Check their website to see their schedule during your visit at www.verizoncenter.com.

Visit National Harbor in Maryland

This complex of shops, restaurants, bars, a marina, and hotels (including the massive Gaylord National) lies across the river from Old Town Alexandria, VA and is connected to that location and Georgetown by water taxis. These boats leave from the marina near the Chart House restaurant in Old Town Alexandria and from Washington Harbour in Georgetown. National Harbor hosts many special events and festivals and provides frequent entertaining fireworks displays.

A popular statue called "**The Awakening**" was moved to National Harbor from Hains Point in Washington, D.C. This 70-foot-long aluminum statue was made in 5 separate pieces and portrays a giant man struggling to rise out of the earth. Kids love to climb and pose on this fascinating statue. Visit www.nationalharbor.com for more information.

Family Oriented Stores

I have listed below some popular family oriented stores including: arts and crafts stores, toy stores, bookstores, and clothing/supplies stores.

Arts and Crafts

These galleries are designed for people of all ages to create their own artwork on different types of pottery. The stores then glaze and fire the piece for later customer pick-up.

All Fired Up
3413 Connecticut Avenue NW
Washington, D.C. 20008
202-363-9590
www.allfiredupdc.com
Metro: Cleveland Park (Red Line)

and

4923 Elm Street
Bethesda, MD 20814
301-654-3206
Metro: Bethesda (Red Line)

Clay Café Studios
101 North Maple Avenue
Falls Church, VA 22046
703-534-7600
www.claywire.com

Paint This!
1013 King Street
Alexandria, VA 22314
703-519-7499
Metro: King Street (Blue/Yellow Lines)
www.paintthis.com

Build- A-Bear Stores
www.buildabear.com

Children design and decorate their own stuffed bears and other stuffed animals at these stores. Some area stores are listed below:

National Harbor
173 Waterfront Street
National Harbor, MD 20745
301-567-2641

Tysons Corner Center
8026 Tysons Corner Center, Suite H3U
McLean, VA 22102
703-448-2327

Build-A-Bear Workshop
Make your own Screech (Washington Nationals mascot)
On game days at Nationals Park
1500 South Capitol Street SE
Washington, D.C. 20003
202-863-1163
Metro: Navy Yard (Green Line)

Toys

Sullivan's Toy Store and Art Supplies
4200 Wisconsin Avenue NW
Washington, D.C. 20016
202-362-1343
www.facebook.com/sullivanstoys
Metro: Tenleytown (Red Line)

Tugooh Toys
1319 Wisconsin Avenue NW
Washington, D.C. 20007
202-333-9476
www.yirostores.com

Why Not
200 King Street
Alexandria, VA 22314
703-548-2080
Metro: King Street (Blue/Yellow Lines), use complimentary King Street Shuttle.

Kinderhaus Toys
1220 North Fillmore Street
Arlington, VA 22201
703-527-5929
www.kinderhaus.com
Metro: Clarendon (Orange Line)

Toy Kingdom
Rockville Town Center
36 Maryland Avenue, Unit C
Rockville, MD 20850
301-251-0220
www.toykingdomllc.com
Metro: Rockville (Red Line)

Barston's Child's Play
www.barstonschildsplay.com

This toy store specializes in educational and specialty toys and has 4 locations in the D.C. metro area:

Washington, D.C.
5536 Connecticut Avenue NW
Washington, D.C. 20015
202-244-3602
Metro: Friendship Heights (Red Line)

Rockville, MD
Congressional Plaza
1661 Rockville Pike
Rockville, MD 20852
301-230-9040
Metro: Twinbrook (Red Line)

Arlington, VA

4510 Lee Highway
Arlington, VA 22207
703-522-1022

Mclean, VA

Langley Shopping Center
1382 Chain Bridge Road
Mclean, VA 22101
703-448-3444

The Toy Soldier Shop of Washington, D.C.

503 11th Street SE
Washington, D.C. 20003
202-546-2201
http://toysoldiershop.com
Metro: Eastern Market (Blue/Orange Lines)
Open on Saturday and by appointment only.

Bookstores

Politics and Prose

5015 Connecticut Avenue NW
Washington, D.C. 20008
202-364-1919
www.politics-prose.com

Hooray for Books!

1555 King Street
Alexandria, VA 22314
703-548-4092
www.hooray4books.com
Metro: King Street (Blue/Yellow Lines)

Fairy Godmother-Children's Books and Toys

319 Seventh Street SE
Washington, D.C. 20003
202-547-5474
Metro: Eastern Market (Blue/Orange Lines)

Clothing/Supplies

Dawn Price Baby
325 7th Street SE
Washington, D.C. 20003
202-543-2920
www.dawnpricebaby.com
Metro: Eastern Market (Blue/Orange Lines)

Kid's Closet
1226 Connecticut Avenue NW
Washington, D.C. 20003
202-429-9247
www.kidsclosetdc.com
Metro: Dupont Circle (Red Line)

The Children's Place
Fashion Center at Pentagon City Mall
1100 South Hayes Street
Arlington, VA 22202
703-413-4875
www.childrensplace.com
Metro: Pentagon City (Blue/Yellow lines)

Twixt-A Tween Boutique
The Shops at Georgetown Park
3222 M Street NW
Washington, D.C. 20007
202-333-3274
www.shoptwixt.com

Yiro
1419 Wisconsin Avenue NW
Washington, D.C. 20007
202-333-0032
www.yirostores.com

Yiro and Tugooh Toys
4823 Bethesda Avenue
Bethesda, MD 20814
301-654-2412
www.yirostores.com
Metro: Bethesda (Red Line)

Piccolo Piggies of Georgetown
1533 Wisconsin Avenue NW
Washington, D.C. 20007
202-333-0123
www.piccolo-piggies.com

Full of Beans
5502 Connecticut Avenue NW
Washington, D.C. 20015
202-362-8566
Metro: Friendship Heights (Red Line)

Games for the Family

At some point during your tour it is likely your family or group will be waiting in a long line to get into an attraction. Also, museum/sightseeing overload can occur at any time. When this happens some of your party will inevitably be bored and irritable. I have listed a few games below that can provide a temporary diversion.

Ask 10 or more fellow visitors where they are from

How many people are international? How many are from your home state?

Find this in line or at the site

Find three people wearing hats, someone wearing orange, someone older than you, someone younger than you, someone holding something other than a cell phone or camera in their hand, someone wearing glasses, and someone wearing a tie. After you've completed these tasks, make up other things to find.

Count Pigeons, Ducks or Squirrels

Assign one person to count pigeons, one to count ducks and other waterfowl and one to count squirrels during an hour or so as you walk to memorials and museums. Bonus points for anyone who sees an elusive black squirrel!

I'm thinking of a famous person

One person thinks of someone famous living or dead and the others can ask up to 10 yes or no questions to guess their identity. The first one who guesses the person wins and then takes a turn thinking of a famous person for others to guess.

Draw your favorite attraction(s) of the day

It's always good to keep paper and pens, pencils, and crayons handy. Challenge your young family member to draw something they have seen that day.

Closing Word

I have worked hard to include many interesting sites and a lot of relevant and useful information about the Washington, D.C., area to make your visit an educational and enjoyable one. However, this guidebook is not the final word on information or advice about the Washington, D.C., area as all visitors and local residents will have their own valuable experiences and insights. If you have tips on attractions, businesses, restaurants, or lodging that you would like to share, I will try to include them in the next edition of this guidebook. Any suggestions for the Scavenger Hunt section are also welcome! Please send any feedback on this book and any recommendations and tips to info@dccapitalkids.com.

I hope you have enjoyed this guide and your visit to the capital city of the United States!

Index

Accommodations Index and Restaurant Index are located at the end.
Bold numbers represent the main description of items when there are multiple occurrences.

H

I

J

K

L

O

P

T

U

Y

Z

Accommodations Index A-Z

Restaurants Index A-Z

About the Author

Chris Sylvester is the owner of the tour company, DC Capital Kids, which specializes in private customized tours for families and groups visiting the Washington, D.C., area. Chris is a licensed tour guide who has been leading tours and introducing visitors to the wonders of the Washington, D.C., area since 2006. He lives in the Old Town area of Alexandria, VA.

For more information on DC Capital Kids visit
www.dccapitalkids.com.

Sarah Bixler

10449199R00242